URBAN DEVELOPMENT IN INDIA

About the author

B. Bhattacharya, Educated at Calcutta University and (as Commonwealth Scholar) at the London School of Economics and Political Science. B. Bhattacharya has consistently pursued a career of teaching and research, having taught in many institutes, including Gauhati University (Assam), Indian Institute of Technology (Kharagpur, W. Bengal), Presidency College (Calcutta), and the University of North Bengal (W. Bengal), at the last of which he has been a senior Professor as well as the Dean of the Faculty of Science. His research in geography spans a large area with publications in academic journals and a number of books including 'Samaj Bijnaniya Bhugol' ('Social Geography' in Bengali) jointly with A. Bhattacharya, published by the West Bengal Govt. 'Urban Development in India Since Pre-historic Times' (New Delhi), 'Sikkim—Land and People' (New Delhi).

URBAN DEVELOPMENT IN INDIA

(SINCE PRE-HISTORIC TIMES)

Second Revised Edition

Prof. B. Bhattacharya
Formerly Professor and Head of the Department of Geography
& Applied Geography and the Dean, Faculty of Science,
University of North Bengal

CONCEPT PUBLISHING COMPANY, NEW DELHI-110 059

Cataloging in Publication Data—DK
Courtesy: D.K. Agencies (P) Ltd. <docinfo@dkagencies.com>

Bhattacharya, B. (Bimalendu), 1931-
Urban development in India : since pre-historic times / B. Bhattacharya. — 2nd rev. ed.
p. cm.
Includes bibliographical references.
Includes index.
ISBN 818069240X

1. Urbanization—India—History. I. Title.

307.760 954 22

ISBN 81-8069-263-9 (PB)

First Published 1979

Second Revised Edition 2006

Published and Printed by
Ashok Kumar Mittal
Concept Publishing Company
A/15-16, Commercial Block, Mohan Garden
NEW DELHI-110 059 (India)
Phones : 25351460, 25351794
Fax : +91-11-25357103
Email : publishing@conceptpub.com

Preface to the Second (Revised) Edition

The appreciation of this book by readers, specially interested in the historical aspect of urban development in India, has exceeded the expectation of the author which is the *raison d'etre* for bringing out the second edition of this book.

There have been three censal enumerations in the country since first publication, indicating changes in the urban position and this have been incorporated in the last chapter, thoroughly updated to ascertain India's comparative status in the world perspective.

The bibliography has also been revised for this edition.

The author is deeply indebted to Prof. (Mrs.) A. Bhattacharya (wife) and Dr. Bashabi Fraser (daughter) and Mr. Neil Fraser (son-in-law) for constant encouragement for this work.

Lastly, it is indeed a great pleasure to work with the Concept Publishing Company, New Delhi of taking on the publication of the Second (Revised) Edition of the book and thus making it available again for people interested in the subject.

1 August, 2004 **B. Bhattacharya**

Preface to the First Edition

Not many countries of this world have seen urban development for a longer period than India, which maintains an almost uninterrupted record for over four-and-a-half millennia. It is really puzzling to find that the first city to appear in India has also been the first planned city of the world, built on a grandiose scale and the planning principles were scrupulously followed for nearly a millennium. The height of urban prosperity that was reached during the first phase of development, the vast territorial expansion of this cultural movement, the far-flung commercial links that were established during this phase baffle all imagination.

The higher civilisation, if we may call it so, sprouting into full form, free of any foreign influence, generates curiosity about its indegenousness. No doubt however remains about the role of this first phase in laying the foundation for urban development in the following phase when a fresh beginning was possible after the towns and cities of the earlier phase permanently disappeared. Those coming to life during the second phase were not the progeny of the first phase; nor were they imitations in any form; yet they followed the same course as far as their activities are concerned, and thus revived the commercial contacts in no time, giving India an unchallenged position in world trade. That all important commercial routes led to India over centuries long before the arrival of Alexander the Great, the position remaining unchanged till the beginning of the eighteenth century, or even some time after that, the roads leading to the country from the west and the north constantly throbbing for centuries under the pounding hooves of the marauding forces, directly point to the highly prosperous state of the country. All this could not happen without a strong urban base and this is amply proved by cities and towns functioning for millennia without any break in their career. Many of them have outlived their former glory of being busy metropolises and have already degenerated into a much lower position now, but still many more have flowered into a greater life, revealing the inherent strength of the urban base set a few thousand years ago.

The source of this basic strength, making for the very foundation of urban development in this country and sustaining it, in spite of crushing misfortunes, for tens of centuries, has to be carefully looked into. Once the foundation weakened, the entire structure sagged visibly, making contrasting results. This becomes very much evident in the changing economic situation of the country which, beginning in the eighteenth century, worsened further in the following decades. All these had their desired effects on the course and development of urbanisation, slowing down the pace and prosperity of individual centres.

It is, however, highly important to note that, the urban pattern that originally emerged through the economic as well as political performaces of the country, did not change even during this disturbed period. New centres appeared here and there, no doubt, and some of them presented an altogether different character in particular cases. Yet, the overall urban scene did not alter greatly for a long time till the middle of the present century when positive signs of the impact of industrialisation came to be felt for the first time in the settlement history of this country. Nevertheless, the base has not undergone any drastic change to instil lasting change in the urban character of India. This is largely because the life-force of urban centres is in a large measure derived from its rich soils, worked under different physical conditions.

It may appear surprising to see that the majority of the Indian masses are still ruralites when the country forges a head in urbanisation with multiple cities including nearly a dozen super-cities in existence and a few more in the making. The progress of urbanisation assessed on the basis of adopted principles may conceal the real achievement in this direction where a large number of settlements are left out of consideration as they fail to fulfil certain predetermined conditions. A more flexible principle, following some other advanced countries of the world, may yield different results, bringing the real progress in its true perspective.

There are five chapters in this book, each dealing with the urban development of a specific period. In doing so, special care has been taken to identify the factors that have made urbanisation a natural rather than an accidental phenomenon.

University of North Bengal (1979) **B. Bhattacharya**

Acknowledgements

In writing this book I have been constantly helped by Mrs. Bhattacharya who has taken great pains in going through the manuscript, suggesting additions and alterations, without which the book would not have attained its present form.

I am also indebted to Shri Chitrabhanu Sen, Librarian of the University of North Bengal, for his unstinted help.

The maps have been drawn by Shri Nirmal Chanda, the departmental artist, and the manuscript has been typed by Shri Jayanta Ghosh, the departmental Junior Assistant. I am thankful for their kind assistance.

A word of greatful thanks is also due to my publisher Shri Ashok Kumar Mittal of Concept Publishing Company, New Delhi, who greatly encouraged me to undertake this arduous work of living through the dark passages of history.

Lastly, my debt to scholars, both dead and alive, who have enlightened me through their works in various fields, is quite large. I have no way of reaching them, but my deep gratitude remains all the same.

B. Bhattacharya

CONTENTS

List of Tables

List of Figures

Abbreviations

ESA	:	Early Stone Age
MSA	:	Middle Stone Age
LSA	:	Late Stone Age
KGM	:	Kili Ghul Mohammed
Company	:	East India Company
EIC	:	East India Company
Mds.	:	Maunds.

1

The Cultural Setting Prior to Urban Development

In the quest of ancestry as well as the developmental stages, the beginning of urban life in India remains a great puzzle. The seeds of urbanisation germinated first in the Indus plains around 2500 B.C., but the sequence of events leading to this great happening is obscured in complete mystery. The time-gap between the first appearance of tool-making man about 600,000 years ago[1], as dated by the solar radiation method, and the formation of the earliest agricultural settlements sometimes at the end of the fifth millennium B.C.[2], or, in the first quarter of the fourth millennium B.C.[3] is far too wide for assuming any essential cultural link between them; rather, one could not have any bearing on the other. In other words, the agricultural communities need not necessarily evolve out of the primitive hunting communities; the former could be migrants from elsewhere, settling down permanently on favoured spots in the course of their search for new lands. Such migration had constantly been taking place over a long period of the pre-historic times when pressure of population mainly triggered long marches for unknown destinations. The assumption made above that the formation of settled life may be an isolated phenomenon at some selected places, quite independent of any evolutional process, is largely strengthened by ample evidences of existence of tool-making man in different parts of India living almost side by side with the urban civilisation over a space of centuries.

The explanation being inadequate in this direction, one may turn to the early village settlements for a more positive clue to the understanding of the successive urban development.

The regions, where the earliest village settlements appeared, were the arid mountainous tracts of north and central Baluchistan and the date was between the end of the fifth and the first quarter of the fourth millennium B.C. Traces of settled life are not available from any other region prior to this date. In the subcontinent, as a whole, man was still at the primitive level, using stone-implements and leading a nomadic life based on hunting and gathering. However, no skeletal remains of the Palaeolithic man has so far been found in India. But evidence of stone-implements indicates that the earliest tool-making man first appeared in Northern India in the Potwar (Rawalpindi) Region and also probably in Central India—in the upper Narmada valley, sometimes between the last phase of the Second Glaciation and the beginning of the Second Interglacial period. This Neolithic culture has three distinct phases—the Early Stone Age, the Middle Stone Age and the Late Stone Age, all of them together representing a sequential development[4]. Tools of these early men, belonging to the three major groups, discovered from various sites show the wide distribution of these in the country. The scarcity of information, however, make it extremely difficult to form any clear idea about the mode of their life, except that of Late Stone Age people. But there is little doubt that the society during the entire period of the Early and the Middle Stone Age consisted of nothing more than extended family groups[5], living in the open within the bounds of their loosely defined territories.

No settlements of these two earlier periods have so far been traced anywhere in the subcontinent and there is no indication that they ever lived in permanent dwellings[6]. It was during the Late Stone Age that people left the open air and started living regularly in selected caves and rock-shelters. The sites for such settlements were invariably chosen on the summits of hills or ridges. The first radio-carbon date available for such rock-shelters excavated at Adamgarh hill in the Narmada valley representing settlements of the Late Stone Age culture is 5500 B.C.[7] Along with the living habits the economy of the Late Stone Age people had similarly undergone substantial change. The economy of the Early Stone Age is characterised by the simplest type of hunting and gathering, without much fore-thought for making provisions for the future, which means that they lived on daily hunting and had no storing habit. Improvement in tools and their variety during the MSA indicate a greater degree of fore-thought. Hunting and gathering made the primary basis of life for the LSA people as well, but marked improvement in tools suggest that hunting methods had become more efficient than in the earlier two periods. Besides, in the areas of moderate and low rainfall, hunting took a much greater role than gathering, while in the high rainfall areas, or, in the coastal regions fishing made an important basis of economy.

The life-style, as depicted, above, did not change much during the succeeding melliennias and it was the close of the fifth or the opening of the fourth millennium B.C. that for the first time the cultural scene adopts a new character: agriculture replaces hunting and gathering, villages appear in the place of rock, or cave-dwellings. This sensational change first took place in the north-western parts of India and remained confined for another thousand years within the mountainous tracts of Baluchistan and Afghanistan and the lower Sind plains. Beyond this region life in the rest of the Indian subcontinent followed its old pattern of hunting and gathering, using sharpened stones as basic implements.

The flowering of this earliest village culture, in many ways forming the primary steps towards later urban development, does not appear to be a direct result of the process of transition from food-gathering to food-production. Although it happened on Indian soil, its Indian parenthood is doubtful. Almost at all the sites the beginning of settled life as agricultural communities has an abruptness which cannot conceal the truth that the people, who pioneered living in permanent settlements, were used to such life. The excavations at these sites reveal no data about the existence of any pre-agricultural stage with hunting and gathering as the primary basis of living. In these settlements production of crops had taken time to begin, but domestication of animals was already in practice. In other words, the emergence of the first agricultural village was directly associated with the beginning of the economy of production. There is no evidence, so far, to suggest that this economic change, ushering in a new era in the human life of the Indian subcontinent had been foreshadowed in whatever shape or form at anyone of the sites discovered over the entire region. On the contrary, evidences of cultural affinity in certain fields between these settlements and those of Western Asia speak of non-Indian influence working at the base of their origin.

Such a possibility cannot be ruled out. A minute examination of the data available on the economic and cultural behaviour of the people living between the close of the fifth millennium B.C. and the following centuries in the North-Western region of India bring them much closer to Western Asia than any other part of the country. The most simple but extremely important basis for this is the identification of cultural items common between then as well as their contemporaneity. The first of them to be considered is agriculture which, having been practised in Western Asia since the sixth millennium B.C., took the same role in giving rise to the earliest settlements in India. The similarity further extends to the nature of principal crops produced in the regions lying widely distant from each other: they were wheat and barley, suited to a drier climate. The cultivation of rice, a wet crop, and perhaps truly Indian in origin, did not begin till around 2000 B.C. *i.e.*, after more than a thousand years of the introduction of wheat and barley in North-Western India. The practice of irrigation by impounding river-water artificially, was nearly similar to the practice prevalent in Western Asia. The domestic animals—the sheep and goat—were the same as in the latter. The second most important similarity is found in the art of pottery. The pottery is not only wheel-thrown—a device needing long experience, but also in shape, colour and motifs they sometimes strangely resembled the West Asiatic types. In the third place, in the selection of sites the earliest Indian settlements closely followed the example of Western Asia. All of them developed on the river valleys, in a semi-desertic climate with extremes of summer and winter temperatures as prevalent in the river valleys of Western Asia. The fourth important factor is the use of copper instead of stone for making working implements which seems to have had started not very long after the settlements in North-West India were established. The use of copper is highly significant in view of the fact that, apart from the knowledge about the quality of the metal, the requirement of very high temperature for smelting and casting — about 700° to 800°C for the former[8] and about 1085°C for the latter[9] — needed special type of kilns, which indicates an advanced level of technology. The techniques involved in both smelting and casting were discovered earlier in Western Asia. Lastly, the West Asiatic culture, though much older, was alive and functioning in full vigour when the settlements were taking shape one after another in North-West India. The latter, thus, could easily draw on the, former's experience perfected through at least three thousand years' trials and errors.

From all appearances, such a possibility cannot be ignored. Indians, living at the stone-age level at that date, cannot be imagined to have had the faculty of changing their mode of life almost overnight. It was not possible through imitation; the entire process of such acculturation depended largely on some degree of acquaintance with the mechanism of that system. No evidence has so far been traced indicating any feeble sign of changes in the existing pattern of hunting and food-gathering economy. The techniques of hunting had improved, no doubt, as suggested by increasing variety of stone implements; the communities had started living in caves or rock shelters; but agriculture was still far from sight; so also was permanent living which could not develop in the absence of any dependable, renewable source of food. On the other hand, the appearance of the agricultural settlements in the North-Western parts of India, carrying no sign of any transitional phase preceding the agricultural phase, indicate the only possibility; that they originated through the efforts of people who had immigrated from Western Asia. Such migrants were always the deserters, pressed out of the homeland by various circumstances, and thus having no bond with their country of origin. The place where they came and settled down ultimately turned out to be their new home; the culture they carried lost its old flavour in course of time, adopting newer traits in the new environment. As a result, the settlements they founded in the narrow confines of the mountainous tracts of North-West India, the question of security in all probability having been a primary factor in the selection of sites, gradually became Indianized. This seems to be the only possible explanation for their abrupt beginning, the absence of the transitional phase and above all the great cultural akinness with Western Asia.

An idea about the mode of living and the cultural traits of these earliest settlements in India may be obtained from the scraps of evidences unearthed through excavation at the sites.

The Pioneer Village Settlement of North-West India

The first village settlement to appear on Indian soil was Kili Ghul Mohammad, situated in the central part of the Quetta valley, about two miles away from the modern city of Quetta (Fig. 1.1). Excavations have revealed four cultural phases of which Period I represents the lowest. A radio-carbon date places it at the end of the fifth millennium B.C.[10] The data available for this period indicate that the inhabitants lived in small huts made of mud-brick or hard packed earth and had domestic sheep, goats and oxen. Agriculture had not yet started and it was a pastoral society, depending largely on the abundant forage and the permanent source of water.[11] Ceramics were not known and neither was copper. Stone and bone implements were in use.

This pre-pottery phase of pastoral life changes during Period II when mat-marked, hand-made pottery appears for the first time, soon to be followed by fine wheel-thrown decorated pottery. According to the findings of Fairservis in 1950, the displacement of the original hand-made pottery by wheel-turned decorated varieties in the Quetta valley indicates the arrival of the Iranian immigrants from the Helmand area of Sistan[12] in Eastern Iran. This, along with the introduction of copper metallurgy during the succeeding phase, Period III, is a definite indication of a cultural diffusion coursing eastward from its ancestral place of discoveries.[13]

Further instances of settlement development are available from the north-eastern part of Baluchistan. The river valleys of Lorlai and Zhob came to be settled by these early agricultural colonizers. Rana Ghundai in the Lorlai valley (Fig. 1.1) produces nine occupation levels[14] of which the lowest one, Period I, began some time in the end of the fourth millennium B.C.[15] on the virgin soil. The absence of any structural remains indicate that the inhabitants were probably semi-nomadic, living in temporary huts or tents. The pottery was unpainted and hand-made; the domestic animals included the humped ox, sheep, ass and, for the first time, the horse; implements made of bone, including an eyed needle, and of stone, were in use. The succeeding period shows signs of the arrival of newcomers who constructed houses on boulder plinths and made extremely fine painted pottery on wheels. The wares were of various shapes and decorated with animal designs. The drawings of humped bulls and black buck, being both typically of Indian origin,[16] point to the direct contacts with the Indian plains while the shapes of the wares closely parallel the styles then prevalent in Northern Persia.[17] Period Ill, much longer in duration than the previous one, contains three phases of buildings identified

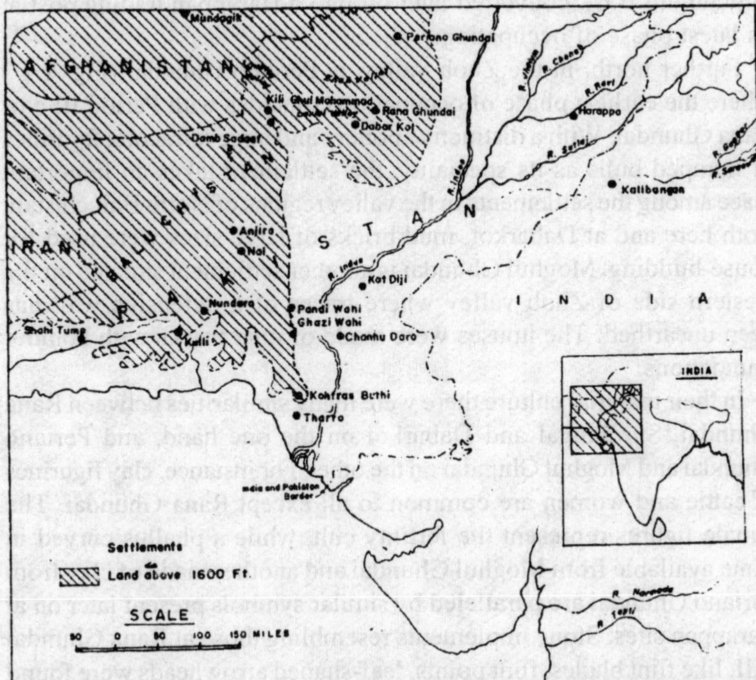

Fig. 1.1 : Pre-Harappan Early Village Settlements

by a stylistic evolution of the pottery.[18] The end of the period came in a great fire in about 2000 B.C.[19]

The neighbouring site of Rana Ghundai is Sur Jangal where the earliest phase of occupation began sometimes about the closing part of Rana Ghundai I[20]. Evidences of beautiful painted pottery, resembling Quetta and Sistan wares[21] have been traced. The size of the settlement seems to be small, the mound measuring 40 yards across. In comparison Dabarkot, situated further south, was a very large settlement. The size of the mound, 500 yards in diameter, implies that it grew into an important place during the middle of the third millennium B.C., converted later on into a Harappan trading post at its latest phase of occupation.

Further north, in the Zhob valley, is Periano Ghundai (Fig. 1.1) where the earliest phase of occupation coincides with Period III c of Rana Ghundai. With a distinctive pottery and large terracotta figurines of humped bulls as its speciality, the settlement takes an important place among the settlements in the valley regions of North Baluchistan. Both here and at Dabarkot, mud bricks of large sizes were used for house-building. Moghul Ghundai is another settlement situated on the western side of Zhob valley where traces of a defensive wall has been unearthed. The houses were made of mud bricks with boulder foundations.

In their material culture there were many similarities between Rana Ghundai, Sur Jangal and Dabarkot on the one hand, and Periano Ghundai and Moghul Ghundai on the other. For instance, clay figurines of cattle and women are common to all except Rana Ghundai. The female figures represent the fertility cult, while a phallus curved in stone available from Moghul Ghundai and another made of clay from Periano Ghundai are paralleled by similar symbols present later on at Harappan sites. Stone implements resembling those at Rana Ghundai I-III, like flint blades, flint points, leaf-shaped arrowheads were found at Sur Jangal, Periano Ghundai and Dabarkot. Alabaster cups, lapis lazuli, jade and beads, bangles and needles made of bone were reported from Periano Ghundai of which the bone-needles strongly resembled Rana Ghundai I specimens. Beads of stone were found is Dabarkot and Moghul Ghundai and bone beads occurred at Dabarkot. Till Period III, Rana Ghundai shows no metal object, but a copper rod and a ring have been dug up at Periano Ghundai and broken pieces of a copper cup come from Dabarkot, the latter also producing a gold pin and sheet metal which probably date to the Harappan times.

In the Quetta valley another group of settlements has been discovered round the city of Quetta. They are known as Kechi Beg. Here the earlier hand-made, mat-marked pottery is replaced by a wheel-thrown painted pottery brought in by immigrants from Iran who most likely came from Sistan.[22]

Anjira Siah-damb provide other instances of the earliest settlements developed in the Surab valley of Central Baluchistan sometimes in the first third of the fourth millennium B.C.[23] At Anjira, the first phase of occupation, Period I, contemporary with KGM II; developed upon natural gravel, produces stone and bone implements, fine wheel-thrown pottery consisting of buffware with motifs similar to those of KGM II, but no structures of houses were traced. Life during the first phase at Anjira was, most likely, nomadic.[24] The next phase yields evidences of house walls made of river boulders and pottery comparable with that of KGM II and III. Besides, a large number of hand-made pottery have also been found.

The dry tributary of the Arghandab river, in South-East Afghanistan, provides instance of another settlement, known as Mundagik (Fig.1.1) Structures are absent in the first two occupation levels ℓ_1 and ℓ_2, but begin in the third occupation levels ℓ_3, producing houses made of pressed earth, the latter being soon replaced by mud bricks. The first settlers here too appear to be semi-nomadic. Pottery, mostly wheel-turned, with painted varieties and motifs, similar to that of KGM II and Anjira I, is present from the beginning of the settlement. The presence of a great variety of cultural objects, like alabastar vases, beads of steatite, lapis lazuli, copper needles and blades, etc., in Period I reveals a closer contact with Iranian sites. All these evidences, along with those yielded by Rana Ghundai II, and also IV and V, are suggestive of an influence which, following the ancient trade routes across Southern Afghanistan, had started infiltrating into the mountain-confines of North and Central Baluchistan in the closing centuries of the fourth millennium B.C. and continued thereafter for a long time, introducing important cultural changes in the village settlement of the regions. Though sufficient data are still lacking on the total effect of this cultural intrusion, it cannot be denied that the most significant contribution made by these new arrivals was the extension of settled life farther south and east.

Prior to that, however, the immediate result of the new arrivals was the increase in the number of settlements in all parts of Baluchistan as well as the incidence of cultural improvements. For instance, in Period II the settlement at Mundagik became more compact, the houses were well-built with hearths inside the rooms, including a well having a brick-head in one house, and the first stone seal made its appearance. But the pottery, being hand-made and undecorated unlike those of Period I, suggests cultural stagnation[25]. The following Period (III), with six phases of construction, saw a great development in all fields. The pottery became mostly wheel-made, with a great range of painted decoration; the number and variety of copper and bronze objects increased; among other objects numerous terracotta figurines, including those of humped bull and female forms, square and circular stone seals were traced. The cultural objects exhibiting "many features reminiscent of Sialk and Hissar"[26] provide another instances of direct contacts with Iran. The last phase of this Period III has been dated to 2360 B.C. In Period IV the settlement developed into a town massive defensive walls and square bastions made of sun-dried bricks. A place and a temple complex have been identified in the ruins. The town was, however, destroyed and built twice during same period.

In the history of the development of the earliest settlements Togau, situated further south of KGM, takes an extremely important place. It produced a typical pottery with distinctive designs developed some time in the middle of the fourth millennium B.C.[27] and onwards which has been traced at different sites spread over a large region extending from Kej valley in the west near the Iranian border, to Amri in Sind valley in the east, and from Quetta valley in the north to Bala Kot in the south. Such a wide distribution of this single ware in the far gone days provides one more irrefutable instance of cultural diffusion and of the growing human contact between the isolated valley cultures.

In about late 3700 B.C.[28], the settlement at KGM came to an end and it took nearly two hundred years for another settlement to emerge in the Quetta valley at Damb Sadaat (Fig.1.1), ten miles south of KGM. Here three phases of occupation, producing a homogeneous culture of improved variety, have been traced. The presence of mud-brick houses, hearths, bread ovens, painted pottery, grinding slabs—probably used for crushing cereals, terracotta figurines, clay seals, copper objects and large structures with brick walls in the last phase tell also about the life of the inhabitants who had not still then abandoned stone implements. The styles and motifs in the ware of Damb Sadaat I—III paralleling those at Mundagik II and III indicate cultural contact between them.

It is rather difficult to establish the development of agricultural settlements in Southern Baluchistan, though the available evidences indicate that it started quite some time later than in the central and northern parts. The history of settled life in the last two regions, in all probability, goes back to the end of the fifth millennium B.C., while the date for that in South Baluchistan cannot be pushed back beyond the closing part of the fourth millennium B.C. Here, again, settled life chose the narrow river valleys of the Nal, the Mashkai, the Hab, isolated from each other by the projected ridges of the high mountains.

The Nal River Valley gave rise to a flourishing settlement at the site of Nal, which came to life in around 3300 B.C.[29] The excavations revealed at least three occupation levels of which the lowest, developed on virgin soil, yielded nothing of interest except, perhaps, clay figurines. In the second level of occupation remains of house-walls made of large mud-bricks were revealed. The houses with two floors, containing rooms varying in size from 11×13 feet to thick-walled chambers measuring 5 square feet in area or less, and with wooden beams and rafters have been found. Most important of the discoveries, however, is a series of mud-brick graves built into the ruined walls of the earliest settlement[30], producing a vast store of highly interesting cultural objects present in the burials as offerings to the dead. The most noteworthy among the materials is the wheel-made painted pottery of a great variety in colours and designs. The geometric motifs, the principal identifying features of the ware, are comparable to the type of pottery found at Amri on Sind plain, thus suggesting possible association between the two cultures at least at the late Amri phase. Other objects of great cultural significance are listed as follows: beads of agate, carnelia and lapis lazuli for which an artificial paste with glass frit called faience had been used; bead necklaces; two hoards of copper implements containing flat axes, parallel-sided chisel, a straight-sided saw and knives; a steatite seal with a vulture engraved on it and a copper stamp seal; a perforated stone weight, strikingly similar in shape to the Harappan weights; besides, the graves yield bones of sheep or goat, pointing to their domestic character. The top-most level of occupation reveals a number of small rooms, probably with thatched roof, occupied by the people of Periano Ghundai III, who migrated here under pressure of increasing population in their original settlements in the Zhob valley[31]. The settlement ended in a great fire in around 1800 B.C.

South of Nal, explorations have revealed identical pottery at the site of Nundara which appears to be contemporary with Nal. Here stone slabs had been used for house-walls upto window-height; but instances of mud-brick walls and masonry structures have also been discovered, showing the traces of white plaster on the inner faces of the stone and brick walls. The most striking feature about the Nundara is its blocks of buildings systematically divided into large and small rooms or courtyards, pointing to a planned, construction. The streets between the blocks of houses are 6 to 8 feet wide. Another notable aspect of this settlement is the painting on the pottery, including the pipal leaf which is rather symbolic of the Harappan culture. Among the objects of art found here is a copper bangle.

Siah Damb, a neighbouring settlement of Nundara, has produced ruins of several houses with stone-walls rising to a height of ten feet, and pottery of the Nundara style suggesting contemporaneity.

In contrast, however, a distinctive culture developed in the Kolwa district and the Valley of Mashkai in Southern Baluchistan with its outliers on the Dasht valley. The distinguishing character of the pottery style designate it after its site as Kulli Culture. The occupation at Kulli began some time in about 2500 B.C.[32] or some time earlier, thus establishing its contemporaneity with Harappan settlements beyond doubt. The pottery discovered at Kulli provides another unmistakable instance of cultural fusion where both Iranian and Harappan influences are closely manifest respectively in its early and late periods of development. At Kulli, again, the culture is preceded by a phase of pottery-making, bearing identity in style with that of Nal[33] which antidates the Kulli phase. Information is scanty about the houses at Kulli but evidences of stone stairways indicate more than one storey. The walls were made of stone with white plaster inside, and rooms, varying in size from 12×8 feet to 8×6 feet, have been found. Apart from the decorative schemes of the Kulli ceramics the female figurines appearing at all the sites of this culture—made of baked clay—are of great interest in view of their hairdressing and ornamentation, both closely resembling the style of the Harappan down to the modern days. The finds of a copper pin, stone saddle-querns and riders, suggesting corn cultivation, beads of agate and lapis lazuli, and lastly a fragment of sheet gold bear witness to a high level of cultural achievement.

Two more sites, Shahi Tump and Mehi, yield a great number of evidences in support of the developmental aspect and the wider contact of Kulli settlements with both Harappan cities and the regions beyond India. Excavations at Shahi Tump, on the Kej River in Baluch Makran, revealed two phases of occupation, with a possible third. Stone was the common building material though mud-bricks, used for making walls, have been traced in the latest level. Besides wheel-turned pottery of intricate shapes and decorations, the most important find is a model of a clay cart similar to Harappan types. Cultural objects discovered at Mehi are far more varied in type and interesting than those of Shahi Tump. Here the ceramics exhibit two distinct influences, the earlier being local and the later Harappan, superimposed on the former. The occurrence of toy clay carts point to connections with Harappan culture, but the presence of a type of vessels, carved out of soft stones, indicate close relations with Mesopotamia[34]. The cemetery as Mehi produces some rare articles, such as a copper mirror with a handle—undoubtedly of local origin, the like of which is absent in the Ancient East, and another ordinary mirror, copper pins, copper bracelets and a small copper bowl, bone stud and clay bangles. In all likelihood, Kulli Culture terminated in about 2150 B.C.[35]

The settlements discussed above do not exhaust the list of the places where settled life flourished. Many others discovered have not been fully studied, while many more yet remain to be unearthed and explored. In spite of the wide gap in our knowledge about those known and unknown settlements still hidden by thick blankets of soil, a general picture emerges out of the piecing-together of the fragmental evidences already made available by the archaeologists through their excavations at different sites. What we gather may be summarised as follows:

In the closing centuries of the fifth millennium B.C. settled life made its first appearance in the sheltered river valleys of Baluchistan and Afghanistan highlands. The natural setting for making permanent settlements could not be better for the earliest settlers. The valleys, offering partial protection, against interference from outsiders, guaranteed uninterrupted continuation of constructive activities. The climate at comparatively higher elevations was less exacting than on the desertic plains; small amount of summer and winter precipitation was especially suited for the production of major crops, like wheat and barley. The rich pastures on the mountain slopes provided food for the domestic animals. The abundant supply of water never dried up to make the settlement unstable. But, above all, two factors played a more important role than any other in the emergence of permanent settlements. First, the area under consideration was the nearest to Western Asia from where the major, if not the primary, impetus came when the area itself lay across the routes followed by the ancient migrants. Second, the valley floors, poor in natural game, were avoided by the primitive food-gatherers and presumably offered an undisturbed atmosphere for experimentation made by the earliest settlers.

The settlements grew in isolation in a number of river valleys and in many cases the formation of small clusters can be traced. The Zhob, the Lorlai, the areas around modern Quetta and Kulli provide such examples. The village cultures, growing independent of each other, gave rise to the great diversity in their cultural manifestations, though there was contact between them in the exchange of ideas, products and, perhaps, even of people. The most surprising fact about these rural cultural complexes is that, concrete evidences are completely lacking on the existence of any conflict or warfare between these divergent cultures, living not far from each other. Life led by them was peaceful and constructive, as profusely displayed by their beautifully decorated; multicoloured ceramics, the great variety of art objects of clay and metal, and the high level of structural development. Life, in all certainty, remained undisturbed for over at least five hundred years at KGM, for nearly nine hundred years at Anjira, and for over seven hundred years at Mundagik. The signs of violence .are absent throughout the period, except the great fires destroying the settlements of Rana Ghundai, Nal, Dabarkot, etc. Such fires need not necessarily be caused by the invaders as life renewed at the same site after the destruction.

As most of the settlements started on virgin soil, one may call the inhabitants colonizers. In the beginning, the colonizers, at many instances, were semi-nomadic, possibly unacquainted with agricultural practices. Yet, they had, undoubtedly, crossed the stage of food gathering when they came to settle, and it, did not, take them long to start agriculture.

The size of the settlements, in general, was small; they were compact in built. The size, at best, can be measured today from the mounds where they remain untouched or from the ruins revealed through excavations. The largest of the five mounds around Quetta measures 600 feet in diameter[36]. The ruins of Kulli give an impression that the settlement was about 200 yards square[37] and that at Mehi 360×330 yards[38]. The settlement as Nundara was about 220×180 yards[39] and that of Shahi Tump 80 to 90 yards across, covering an area of nearly two acres[40]. The mound at Nal, partly excavated, is 600 feet across at its greatest length[41]. In contrast, Suir Jangal is only about 40 yards in diameter and Dabarkot 500 yards in diameter.[42]

The principal building materials were stone, both cut and uncut, used mainly for the foundation of the houses, and sunbaked bricks for the walls. Wood was used for making beams; in one case the upper floor of a house was made of wood while in another case a wooden lintel of a door has been discovered. Except the frames, the remains of doors and windows have not been reported from any site. It can, however, be guessed that wood, having entered into use for cross-beams, rafters, etc., may possibly have been used for making doors and windows. The houses were both large and small with more than one storey. Rooms ranging in size from 15 ft. × 15 ft. (Nundara) to 5 ft. × 5 ft. (Nal) have been found. The roofs of the houses were probably flat in a country of scanty rainfall, though materials used for their construction are not known. The interior side of the walls had been plastered white in some places. The size of the bricks varied widely between different sites, but it had been standarized. For instance, at Nal bricks of two standard sizes were used: (*a*) 12 × 12×7½ inches, and (b) 23×9×3¾ inches[43], at Rana Ghundai they were 13×6 - 8 × 2½ inches[44]; at Periano Ghundai 14×9×2 inches[45]; at Shahi Tump 19×10×3 inches[46] at Nundara 21×10×4 inches[47]; and at Dabarkot 24×16×4 inches[48].

Turning to the different products of these divergent cultures, we notice that stone implements were still largely in use although copper had made its appearance in the manufacture of the knives, spearheads, stamps and seals, mirrors, bowls and ornaments. Among other metals, gold has been reported only from one Site. Semi-precious stones, like, lapis lazuli, agate, carnelian, alabastor, etc., were in use for making ornaments at most of the sites. The most exciting among the list of articles are, however, the ceramics where the industry attained an exceedingly high degree of perfection. Lastly, the clay figurines, representing both animal and human figures, carry great significance in view of the impression made by some of them about the religiosity of the people and repetition of the similar forms later in the Harappan cities.

The settled life, which flowered in the mountainous terrains of Baluchistan for over a millennium and a half between the end of the fifth to the middle of the third millennium B.C. or thereabout, naturally increased the population at a much faster rate than hitherto experienced under the food-gathering economy, and this gradually started putting pressure on the limited resources of the narrow valley-regions. It is, therefore, not unlikely that the energetic ones were in the look for fresh grounds in newer surroundings. The arrival of the Zhob people at Nal in about 2000 B.C. provides an example of such intercultural movements taking place during the long period of this cultural evolution. On the other hand, fresh arrivals from Western Asia, continuing almost from the beginning of this cultural phase, further heightened the search for new lands. The Sind plains, though with a very different natural environment, offered such an opportunity to these upland villagers who, to all appearance, extended the settled life on to the plains in the east[49]. It is curious to note that the appearance of settled life on the plains, beginning later than on the Baluch hills and mountains, coincided with its major phase of development and, as it will be seen in the following paragraphs, repeats almost identical features and records of intimate cultural contact. The colonizers of the upland settlements equipped with improved knowledge in farming, irrigation and food control, early evidences of which have been traced by Sir Aural Stein in his explorations of Baluchistan, found the situation alluring. It is true that the Indus, with its dangerous annual floods, threw a big challenge to the new-comers; but, once the immense agricultural potentialities of the new alluvium were realised, it appeared as a tempting situation calling for all-out efforts at overcoming the major handicaps.

The most important point here is the urge for expansion. This led the earliest settlers to leave their homeland in Western Asia time and again for the tiny river valleys of Baluchistan. Available evidences establish it beyond any doubt that the immigrants contributed greatly to the development of settled life in the upland valleys. Taking this as a fact we can now turn our attention to the other most important aspect of the situation. This concerns not only the cultural achievements and aspirations of the people, but also the dire need of living space. It is not difficult to understand that prolonged existence, backed by a developed economic system, based on permanent sources of food, decreased death rate, resulting in more mouths to be fed, more hands to be employed and more families to be housed. The proliferation of settlements, spreading from Northern and Central to Southern Baluchistan, could not possibly accommodate this growing population. The settlements, in all likelihood, came to bursting points; the limited resources of the tiny river valleys could no longer support the mounting pressure. Under such circumstances people naturally wanted to expand. Improved life made this urge all the more powerful. Instances of the end of the settlement at some period without being caused by natural disasters strongly point to massive desertion by the inhabitants for newer locations.

It is this urge for expansion which ultimately led to the extension of settled life on to the Indus Plains. At the same time, this, draining away the capable ones from their original haunts, indirectly put a seal on the further development of the upland villages which slowly pined away into a dusty death. One is not thus surprised to note that, in spite of the existence of a large number of developed societies in the Baluch valleys, it was the Indus Plains that saw the first emergence of towns. However materially developed they were, the resources of the diminutive, sequestered societies were too limited for giving rise to any massive settlement.

The Village Cultures on the Plains

Physically, Indus Valley, with its unending stretch of uninterrupted plains, presented a superior situation to that of the small river valleys of the Baluch hills. The vast plains of the Indus, with its rich alluvial soils, revitalised every year by floods coming in clock-like precision, held out immense prospect of a rich harvest without going into the troubles of irrigation and terracing. On the other hand, the rivers themselves offered a vast store of food in their innumerable types to fish; besides, being navigable round the year, they made communication easier in different directions for the collection and distribution of man and commodity. And above all, the wide expanse of the plains, giving unbound scope for expansion in case of necessity or emergency, created a feeling of having something to look forward to instead of keeping his vision squeezed between the towering walls of the mountains closing in on the ribbons of the valley-floors. The climate in the Indus plains too had possibly come to the aid of the pioneers in colonization. The region was comparatively wetter, with warmer summers and winters than in the Baluch uplands. According to the data provided by pollen-analysis of the salt lake deposits of Rajasthan, the climate took a turn to wetter condition from circa 3000 B.C. and this lasted till about 1000 B.C. after which the climate became drier[50]. Rao is of the opinion that, Indus valley receiving an average of 15 cms of rainfall today had more than 50 cms in the third millennium B.C.[51], which means that it was wetter than today. The chronicler of Alexander's expedition found Sind a fertile country in the fourth century B.C.[52] The research conducted by Dr. Bryson in collaboration with Indian scientists during the last seven years in Rajasthan corroborates this view. In his estimation, Rajasthan received about 100 cms, or 40 inches of rain 3000 years ago[53].

The natural advantages, briefly outlined above, did not go unnoticed by the early adventurers, but it is not yet known who first utilised the situation. Success in the colonization of the lower part of the Indus plains, at a minor scale though, was achieved in about the middle of the fourth millennium B.C. when, for the first time, a village culture took shape at Amri (Fig. 1.1), situated about 100 miles south of Mohen-jo-daro, the first Harappan city. The date mentioned here is suggested by meadow who made his conclusions on the basis of two radio-carbon determinations. But Gordon places the beginning of Amri at about 2800 B.C., thus pushing the date by about seven centuries. Meadow's dating of Amri ID, that is the last phase of Amri Period I, to the end of the fourth millennium B.C.[54] appears rather confusing in the light of the discovery of Harappan pot-shreds found associated with Amri ID-level, the time being at least four to five centuries earlier than the Harappan culture.

Contemporary with the Baluch Valley Cultures, Amri presents an extremely interesting case where we find the existence of two cultural sequences sharply divided by cultural ancestry — the pre-Harappan village culture and the Harappan urban culture, representing a case of transformation where the antecedent culture is practically superimposed by a superior subsequent culture. The difference in the cultural make-up is profoundly manifest in the two distinctive phases of development, as represented by Period I and II of pre-Harappan succeeded by Harappan Period (Ill). Period I is sub-divided into four sub-periods of which the earliest (lA) does not reveal any occupational structure; it produces, however, a number of ditches, buried storage jars, pottery — mostly hand-made, fragments of copper, bronze as well as chert blades. The second sub-period (IB) shows definite signs of cultural improvement with two phases of mud-brick buildings, a greater variety of ceramics with different painted designs, but chert blades and bone tools still continue. The succeeding period (IC), containing not less than four structural phases, definitely marks the culminating point of overall development. Mud bricks and stone were used for building houses; the ceramics, mostly wheel-made show a greater range of shapes and decorations. The closing phase of the first period (ID) is represented by only one building level and beautifully painted pottery. The most significant aspect of this phase is the presence of some broken pottery belonging to Harappan Culture[55]. The culture continues uninterrupted in the following Period II, divided into two phases, A and B, with signs of levelling and reconstruction. During this period the presence of Harappan pottery increases, and appearing side by side with Amrian pottery makes it transitional between the earlier Amrian and later Harappan culture of Period III. The site got burnt at the end of the Period II, after which it became a Harappan settlement.

The Amrian Culture did not remain in isolation in its earlier, pre-Harappan stage of development. It had cultural links with its contemporary cultures thriving in the Baluch uplands. For instance, the earliest the two sub-Periods, IA and IB, maintained contacts with Anjira III, KGM III and IV, and Mundagik III, while sub-Period ID bears many similarities with the late phase of Mundagik III, and Anjira III and IV, Amrian II compares with Mundagik IV, and Damb Sadaat II. Similar cultural contacts are found to have had been established with the other pre-Harappan cultures on the Lower Indus plains[56].

The Amrian culture had brought into existence a number of settlements occurring behind the present delta of the Indus of which the fortified Settlements of Tharro and Kohtras Buthi and those, namely, Pandi Wahi and Ghazi Shah deserve to be mentioned. The settlement of Tharro, built on a flat-topped hill and surrounded by two massive walls set at 250 ft. interval, probably served the purpose of a fort[57]. The site at Kohtras Buthi, on a hill-spur South-West of Amri, provides the most important example of a fortified settlement. Two defensive walls, separated by about 100 ft. open space between them, run around the settlement having four exterior bastions on the inner wall. Within these walls traces of innumerable large and small rooms, grouped into separate blocks joined by narrow alleys—3 to 2½ ft. wide—have been found. A bath in one of the rooms and the remains of a stairway leading to upper floor have also been discovered[58]. Evidences of fortifications similarly have been traced at another Amrian site, Dhillanijo-kot, in Sind. Among the other Amrian settlements, Pandi Wahi and Ghazi Shah are small in size, measuring about 150 × 115 yards and 170 × 160 yards[59] respectively. They do not show any traces of buildings, though it is most likely that mud-bricks were used here for the constructions. Damb Buthi and Othmanjo Buthi, developed on Sind plains, belong to the same cultural group.

North of the Amrian group of settlements traces of a somewhat identical culture have come to light from below the levels of Harappan occupations at Kot Diji and Harappa. The wheel-made painted pottery of the pre-Harappan period found at these sites differs from that of the Amrian type, and suggests Baluch ancestry[60]. About 25 miles east of Mohen-jo-daro, Kot Diji developed on the opposite side of the Indus, now twenty miles away from the river-bed. Here excavations have revealed sixteen occupation levels, of which the earlier twelve represent an antecedent culture, the thirteenth is a mixed one of Kot Dijian and Harappan elements, and the last three belong to the mature

Harappan phase[61]. The pre-Harappan settlement at Kot Diji was fortified by a mud-brick wall[62], with stone foundations and the houses were made of both stone and mud-brick. Stone implements in use include chert blades, leaf-shaped arrows, querns and pestles. The pottery is wheel-turned, with painted decorations. Apart from the fragment of a bronze bangle, no other copper objects have been reported from the pre-Harappan levels. At the end of this period the settlement got completely burnt by two fires, the last taking place in about 2100 B.C.[63]

Wheeler takes 2750-2100 B.C. as the time-span for Kot Diji Period I[64]. Rao also suggests nearly a similar time-bracket, 2700-2100 B.C. for this period[65], but gives a different date for the beginning of Period I which, in his opinion, is contemporary with Amri ID, belonging to the end of the fourth millennium B.C.[66]

Similar instances of cultural replacement are reported from the site at Harappa and Kalibangan (Fig. 1.1). At Harappa Wheeler came upon some ceramics and the relics of a mud-brick wall, probably a defensive measure, in the intervening layer between the levels of Harappan occupation and the natural soil[67]. The pot-shred resembles the style prevalent at Rana Ghundai III[68] in North Baluchistan. The second site yielding important evidences of this type is Kalibangan, situated nearly 100 miles south-east of Harappa, on the left bank of the Ghaggar river in the Ganganagar district of Rajasthan. Here, beneath the citadel of the Harappan period—Kalibangan II—a settlement of an antecedent culture occur, with five building phases—Kalibangan I—, overlying the natural alluvium. The earlier settlement, measuring about 273 yards × 197 yards[69], was fortified by a mud-brick wall and within this mud-bricks of the same standard size were used for the houses. The pottery, made on wheels, is of great variety in forms and painted decorations, some of which actually anticipate the Harappan styles, while others parallel Kot Dijian and Amrian types. The material culture of this early period is further represented by such finds as stone blades with serrated sides resembling sickles, shell bangles, beads made of steatite and other materials[70], stone querns and mullers, copper celt, bangle[71] and flat axes. The presence of toy cart-wheels prove the acquaintance of the inhabitants with ox-drawn wheeled vehicles. Besides, the discovery of furrowed fields in earlier level indicates the use of ploughs[72]. According to radio-carbon date the early pre-Harappan phase, continued from 2370 to 2100 B.C. and the beginning of the next phase, the Harappan, is placed between 2100 to 2000 B.C.[73] This is further corroborated by the explorations made lately by Suraj Bhan in the lost river valleys of Saraswati, Drisadvati, the Yamuna (westerly course) and the Ghaggar. He places the earlier phase of Kalibangan, Period I, between circa 2300-2000 B.C. and the later, the Harappan phase, between circa 2000-1700 B.C.[74], thus throwing light on the expansion of Kalibangan I culture colonizing in its late phase the whole of the upper Saraswati basin.

Apart from these conclusive evidences, the finding of a particular type of ware, with roughened surface, by Mackay in the lowest levels of Mohenjo-daro, and the discovery of occupation deposits to a depth of 39 ft. below the modern level of the plain by Dales and Raikes at the same site lend support to the possible existence of a pre-Harappan culture here as well. Further, the occupation levels below the water table at Chanhu-daro, reported by Mackay, might similarly contain the traces of a pre-Harappan culture. Pottery found at sites in Bhawalpur—such as, those at Bhoot, south of Khairpur, and at Jalilpur in Multan district suggest the possibility of a cultural antecedence.

Possible Link Between the Rural and the Urban Phases

The emergence of settled life, whether in the Baluch-Afghan uplands or in the Indus plains, throw a flood of light on the cultural background of the country in the middle of the third millennium B.C. Making its first appearance some time between the end of the fifth millennium and the middle of the third millennium B.C., settled life continued uninterrupted for more than a thousand years with progressive changes in various fields of activities, as profoundly manifest in the improved techniques employed in house building, in the manufacture of ceramics and household implements, in the use of semi-precious stones for making various types of ornaments, and in the slow replacement of stone by copper and bronze.

The sequence of events leading to the earliest cultural upheaval seem to have had given rise to a number of cultural complexes, maintaining a higher level than a mere village culture. The wide range of pottery, the various types of motifs and their colourful decorations the quality sometimes being finer than that of the Harappan products, prove a great degree of sophistication than normally expected of ordinary village communities. This is revealed much more in the highly skilled craftsmanship exhibited by the great variety of ornamental articles and the terracotta figurines, besides directly pointing to the high level of prosperity. The use of standardized bricks, the evidence of block structures — a sign of planned construction, the existence of fort settlements and the presence of cultural contacts between the far-flung societies mark the degree of development that had taken place among the pre-urban cultures. Aural Stein's discovery of a large number of stone-built dams and associated terraces for irrigational purposes, locally known as gabarbunds in Jhalawan of Baluchistan and a large barrage near Lakorian Pass, north of Jhalawan, built by these ancient people bear testimony to the high level of technology[75].

It can now safely be assumed that, although the actual impetus came from Western Asia, a process of Indianization had set in from the very beginning, and the upland villages grew as a local product, a product of cultural evolution utilising the local environment. The same process achieved a still greater success in giving rise to more cultural complexes on the Indus plains which, in turn, influenced the Baluch settlements at a later date, as clearly reflected in the motifs and shapes of pottery as well as other objects therein. The culmination of antecedent cultural evolution is lastly witnessed in the succeeding urban phase in the plains[76]. The presence of hand-made pottery in the earlier phases of many of these settlements, the differences in the shapes, types, and decorations on the wheel-turned pottery, the survival of the flat axes, the use of mud-bricks and, above all, the virtual absence of transformation from village to urban life during the whole length of a millennium reject any possibility of a direct and useful contact with the advanced urban civilisation of Western Asia. The influence which came, no doubt, was carried by the peasant population—the ejected surplus in all likelihood—who appeared at long intervals and possibly in small numbers and therefore eventually were swallowed up by the stream of culture which by then had evolved into a pattern in newer situations. Even if the violent end of settlements at certain places were associated with the arrival of the new comers, there is no proof that they ever beloged to urban stock. This particular fact is of supreme importance, since it establishes once for all that no time foreign influence had any direct hand in triggering the urban revolution that took place immediately after this.

The cultural evolution is the North-Western part of India, however, did have no effect whatsoever for a long time on the life-pattern of the inhabitants of the subcontinent where life continued uninterrupted at the base level of food-gathering economy. The question thus naturally follows is — whether these primary cultures had anything to do in starting the next most important phase of settlement development, the Urban.

Archaeological evidences derived so far do not provide any direct link between the pre-urban and the urban cultures though such a possibility cannot be rejected outright. The slowly accumulating evidences give a contrary idea to this date. They focus on the fundamental differences between these two incompatible phases of cultural development which took place sometimes in almost analogous situations. To cite examples, the earlier village cultures did not know writing; they were not acquainted with the systematic planning methods and the elaborate systems of sanitary arrangements, all these being the major identifying features of the urban civilisation of the Harappan period; besides, the village cultures were not accustomed with the various mechanisms of trade as symbolised by the wide range of weights and the characteristic seals of the Harappan culture[77].

The ancestry of the succeeding urban culture viewed form this angle remains undetected, though a possible connection between the two, at some stage, in some form, cannot altogether be ruled out. It is important to note that, for the first time in the history of settlement making in North-West India, those in the newest surroundings improved in size and function, where both Amri and Kot Diji developed into "small-town agricultural societies"[78], and thus becoming at least attitudinally different from their Baluch predecessors or contemporaries. Besides, considerable uniformity of culture among the pre-Harappan settlements, distributed over to wide an area on the Indus plains, indirectly suggests the existence of some sort of central control which, later on, proved to be one of the guiding principles of the Harappan city-builders. Forgetting for the moment the major weakness of the village cultures, one may find a number of elements providing common grounds between the two for which one might have been indebted to the other. As a matter of fact, the pottery techniques, the methods of agriculture, including perhaps the types of crops, the domesticated animals, the use of standardized bricks, the fashions in ornaments made of stone and metals, the custom of making terracotta figurines—especially those of females bearing symbolic significance, and the use of stone implements, etc., have a lot of sameness between them to suggest some sort of kinship. It is true that Harappan ceramics were not the exact imitation of those of the village cultures. They need not necessarily be so, as difference in styles was a common feature everywhere. But the occurrence of such motifs like the pipal leaf and the humped bull on both pre-urban and urban potteries, is very significant. The major point is that, the technology, perfected through centuries of trials and errors, was ready at hand when the urban civilisation was taking form. Similarly, the knowledge in engineering technology for food-control and irrigation practices had been acquired by the same people long before the urban phase came into existence. It will not sound absurd therefore to think that, the knowledge was borrowed by the city-builders later on. Agriculture forming the basic economy of the two periods made no difference in the farming techniques and the use of the plough as well as the practice of flood-irrigation among the Harappans strongly suggest a continuation of the same process. Borrowings of ideas possibly also took place in the field of construction and the most tempting examples are offered by the universal use of bricks, standardisation of its size and, in certain cases, blocks of buildings constructed according to plan. It may, however, be argued that the Harappans used fired bricks instead of sun-dried bricks; the size of the bricks was different; and the planning was much more elaborate, applying to the entire settlement rather than to particular blocks of buildings. Such differences do not alter the fact that the idea of brick-technology originated with the pre-urban cultures and, perhaps, the technique of firing bricks was not unknown to them either. A closer study reveals further that, the artistic aptitude of the people, belonging to the two cultural phases, was not greatly different either. The tastes for stone ornaments, first developed with the pre-urban people and its repetition in the urban society later on, make another case where the question of cultural debt arises. This equally applies to the manufacture of art objects, like human and animal figures and toys. The striking similarity of some forms, especially those of the female figurines, representing the mother goddess, and that of the phallus representing the male organ, mark the continuity of the religious faith. The survival of the stone implements and the flat axes may equally raise the issue of indebtedness. The characteristic absence of any religious structure like temples, monuments, etc., and the general poverty in battle arms in both the pre-urban and urban societies bring them attitudinally closer to each other.

On all these counts, however, urban society may not be a direct descendent of the earlier cultures. The pottery differed in many ways; perhaps the variety of crops increased; the mud-bricks were rarely used; the settlements were built according to plan and an elaborate system of sanitation had been introduced; the range of ornamental articles, made of semi-precious stones, became wider; the objects of art spread from clay modelling to the casting and carving of metal and stone figures; the use of metal was more frequent; over and above these, the art of writing, the measuring systems, the preponderance of engraved seals and the presence of land and water communication give this later culture an entirely separate identity.

Nevertheless, the question of succession cannot be ignored altogether. The underlying unity is far too strong and relevant to be denied on the basis of dissimilar ware or the presence of literacy. The difference in the styles of ceramics, not having been imported, could result locally from the sustained efforts of the people who gave rise to a superior culture. The beginning of urban life took place after more than a thousand years of agricultural life in the uplands and plains. The knowledge and experience gathered through this long period of time came useful when the superior culture was taking form. Most of the basic elements of the later culture show a large measure of resemblance with those of the earlier culture, and presenting a sort of parallelism which could not have been achieved had the later culture been completely uninfluenced by the former. Cultural objects like seals and weights also had appeared in the earlier cultures, making the Harappans so distinctive. Apart from the art of writing and the methods of planning, the differences in other fields were more superficial to make a substantial disunity between the two. Such differences were more likely the results of further development, or rather, improvement of the original ideas obtained from the antecedent cultures. Improvements changed their original character so much so that they looked different in a changed atmosphere. Further, the two fundamental elements of writing and planning, on which the subsequent culture differed substantially from the antecedent culture, could have evolved in the same process of development. The fact should not be lost sight of that when we know the urban culture, we come to know it at its mature stage. Its earlier stages of development, which most likely took place at the site of Mohenjo-daro, have so far remained closed to us. We do not know what happened and how it happened during the earlier stages. But we can fairly conjecture that — the urban culture could not grow in isolation. In the absence of any foreign influence, it quite possibly had to lean on the local resources which was rich enough to meet the various needs at the initial stages of this higher culture. The village cultures provided this resourceful background and, in all likelihood, set the stage for succeeding phase of urban development. This does not appear to be unusual or at all impossible in view of the fact that, the situation that led to the emergence of the earliest settled life had improved a great deal after a thousand years or so, and the vast store of accumulated knowledge and experience sought a new avenue for their fuller expression. The advanced economy and the higher technology set the stage for the fulfilment of higher desires of the ancient people. The recent work of Rafique Moghul (1970), referred to by Dales, strongly points to the development of an Early Harappan phase in the region stretching from the plains of Rajasthan and Sind to the highlands of Northern Baluchistan, and Afghanistan and extending as far as to Turkestan. The entire region, as demostrated by Moghul, presents the scene of a striking cultural consistency which, beginning in about 3000 B.C., finally, gave rise to the dazzling urban phase[79]. City-building gave that opportunity.

Thus, the initial momentum, in all appearance, came from the earliest village cultures, and once the momentum was gathered, the cultural hiatus went on increasing between the two, as it happens where progress is the watch-word for urban culture with a greater degree of innovations, while the village generally keeps to old, established form. No evidence has so far come to light showing the gradual transformation of any of the earliest villages into urban centres. In the cases of the double phase of rural and urban life — Amri, Kot Diji, Kalibangan, etc., — this is marked by a break in the cultural sequences, the urban phase having been imposed directly upon the rural settlement. Hence, it may be said that the urban culture did not directly evolve out of these rural environments, but its ancestry, probably, lies in this direction.

The Beginning of Urban Phase

It was not till the middle of the third millennium B.C. that true urban life found its full expression in India and it began first in the valley of the Indus—now in Pakistan — with its mature phase at the principal site of Mohenjo-daro dated to 2500 B.C.[80] Wheeler suggests a time-bracket of 2500-1500 B.C. for this urban culture[81], making it at the same time clear that the absence of data from the untapped lower depths of Mohenjo-daro make the dating difficult. In fact, borings carried out in 1965 by Dales below the present level of the flood-plain at Mohenjo-daro showed that the earliest occupation begins not less than 39 ft. below the present surface. Adding the height of 30 ft. of the adjacent mound to that depth, a total accumulation of about 70 ft. must be accepted. But, till now, the excavation has not penetrated the 25 ft. of water drowning the lowest strata[82] which might conceal the developments of another thousand years or so[83]. The presence of copper and bronze articles from the lowest levels of occupation opened by excavation so far, and the absence of any neolithic implements at that level make it imperative that the people were well-advanced in the use of metals. Gordon has dated the founding of the city of Mohenjo-daro to 2600 B.C.[84]

The urban development, designated by the archaeologists as the 'Harappan Culture', found its full expression in the two metropolitan cities of Mohenjo-daro and Harappa. The two cities, nearly 400 miles apart, acted as the twin capitals of the Indus Empire[85] which turned out to be the most extensive civilisation of the pre-classical world[86]. The vast empire in its heyday extended beyond Sind and Punjab.

From Sutkagen Dor (Fig.1.2), near the shores of the Arabian Sea, 300 miles west of modern Karachi, the empire stretched up to the Jamuna Basin, covering a distance of over 1000 miles from west to east, and southward it reached as far as the coasts of Gujarat and the mouths of Narmada and Tapti rivers. Excavations carried on since the time of Sir John Marshall (1921) to this date have revealed a rich crop of sites where urban culture bloomed at the patronage of the Harappan leaders. The total area of the empire amounted to about half a million square miles and within this nearly a hundred sites developed as urban centres[87]. Not all of them are fully known. Apart from Mohenjo-daro, and Harappa, some of the most brilliant examples of urban development are provided by the sites at Chanhu-daro, Kalibangan, Lothal on the Gulf of Cambay, Bhagatrav at the mouth of the Narmada, Megham and Telod at the mouth of Tapti river, Rupar in the Punjab, and Alamgirpur near Meerut in Jamuna basin. Among sites of lesser significance are Desalpur in Cutch, Rangpur, Somnath and Rojdi, Halar, Amara and Kinnarkheda in Gujarat. Besided, Harappan or Late Harappan settlements discovered south of Mohenjo-daro, on the western bank of the Indus, include Lohunjo-daro, Pandi Wahi, Ali Murad, Gazi Shah, Damb Buthi, Dhal, Amri, Shahjo-Kotiro and Thano Bula Khan; to the north and north-east of Mohenjo-daro Judeirjo-daro and Kotasur; near the city of Harappa are Chak Purbane Syal and Kotla Nihang Khan. Late Harappan sites traced near Rupar are Bara, Mandiala Khan, Deheru in Ludhiana district, and Kat Palon in Jullundur district, etc. The unfolding of these lost settlements made during the recent years throw light on the development as well as the areal extent of the urban culture. The civilisation, extending over this vast territory, possessed an unmistakable identity which is, no doubt, an indigenous, individual and independent growth[88]. (Fig. 1.2)

The cultural conquest of the Harappans, beginning, in all likelihood, some time in the middle of the third millennium B.C., was not completed over this vast tract of land in a single movement. If Gordon's dates are taken, the city of Mohenjo-daro was founded in around 2600 B.C., Chanhu-daro between 2500–2400 B.C., and Harappa in about 2300 B.C. Rao, however, accepts Wheeler's view and places the beginning of the mature urban phase of Mohenjo-daro and Harappa at 2500 B.C.[89]; he further suggests 2450 B.C. for Lothal[90], 2300 B.C. for the Harappan phase at Kalibangan[91], and 2100 B.C. at Kot Diji[92],

1900 B.C. for Rojdi and Prabhas in Gujarat[93]. At Dabar Kot in Baluchistan Harappan occupation began in about 2200 B.C. and the colonization of the Saraswati valley was set in motion some time in 2100 B.C.[94]

The different dates are suggestive of a slow progress of the civilisation and this particular fact alone supports the view that it had not been implanted over-night by any foreign agent. The slow process of development is further brought to light by Gordon, giving different radio-carbon dates for the building of the Citadel, the Granary and the Great Bath of Mohenjo-daro. It is not difficult to imagine that all the new experiments started first at the principal site and after being perfected were copied in toto elsewhere at later dates so that in physical details the urbanscape looked strangely alike throughout the empire. In all certainty, therefore, Mohenjo-daro became the mother city for spreading the seeds of urban culture during the succeeding centuries.

Both Mohenjo-daro and Harappa developed into the two Metropolitan Cities in the urban system of the Indus Civilisation. Being more than three miles in circuit, both have remarkable uniformity in their physical setting, internat layout, basic architecture, sanitary arrangements, street planning, cultural products and also, perhaps, in the social stratification as displayed by the houses of different categories. The two cities have almost similar situation, each by the side of a large navigable river. Mohenjo-daro stands on a narrow strip of land between the main bed of the Indus and the western Nara loop, and Harappa grew up beside an old confluence of the two branches of the river Ravi, itself a tributary of the Indus. In the matter of actual plan and basic lay-out, they are strikingly similar and "both seem to have conformed with certain distinctive and evolved principles of urban planning"[95], providing the first example of planned cities in the world. That some sort of central control was fully operative in building the other cities and towns of the empire according to the scheme of planning devised and implemented in the twin capitals is clearly discernible in the physical configuration of all the urban settlements which show a "regular orientation"[96]. As for instance, both at Mohenjo-daro and Harappa, the city consists of two principal elements: on the west is the Citadel, built on a high platform of mud-brick, with its long axis from north to south, and on the east lies the

Fig. 1.2 : Harappan Settlements

'Lower City' or the city proper. The Citadel is fortified by a massive baked-brick wall, supplemented by solid towers, and contains the public buildings, including pillared halls of assembly, a large building (230 × 78 ft.) used probably as the residence of the high priest, or as a College, the Great Bath and the State Granary. The Citadel was, thus, the religious and the secular headquarters of the empire. Below the Citadel, sprawling over a large area, the Lower City was built on a grid-iron plan which remained unaltered through centuries of occupation, as typified by Mohenjo-daro, where traces of at least nine phases of rebuilding in the city's history have so far been unveiled. The two cities had, perhaps, been encircled by walls though they have not been fully traced.

Strict enforcement of building regulations is observed in all the earlier phases of construction when buildings were never allowed to encroach upon the public thoroughfares. It is only at the latest levels that the rigidity slackened, converting streets and lanes into built-up areas[97]. In town-planning, however, the first thing that strikes the eye is the street-planning. A principle of coordinated measurement used to be stubbornly followed in the construction of the streets so that the largest—about 45 ft. wide was twice the width of the smaller, and three or four times that of the side lanes. The alignment of the streets from east to west and from north to south at Mohenjo-daro is thought to have been purposely made for keeping the urban area properly ventilated under the prevailing north-south winds[98]. The cities are furnished with an elaborate underground drainage system. House drains are connected with the street-drains by earthenware pipes and the latter used to be cleared through manholes. The city's sewage finally found its way into soak-pits which ultimately emptied into the river. All these signify the existence of a strict municipal vigilance[99]. The excellence of the masonry is testified by the brick-linings where the joints even today are hardly visible. Large brick culverts with corbelled roofs built in the outskirts of the cities for carrying away the storm water is another important feature of this drainage system.

The architecture and the size of the private houses give an idea about the social status of the citizens. Houses, ranging from barrack like blocks of workmen's quarters and small buildings with two living rooms to palatial structure, having a frontage of 88 ft. and a depth of 97 ft. with outer walls, have been traced. The diverse characters positively indicate the different status of the occupants, comprising the wealthy administrative and the merchant class, large group of the artisans, and the labour class. Some of the big houses have two or more floors. Fired brick makes the principal building material for all types of constructions. The supply of drinking water came from brick-wells, 2 ft. 6 inch in diameter, constructed in most of the large buildings and dwelling houses, accessible to all. Besides, the houses are equipped with drains, bathrooms and a privy on the groundfloor.

Metallurgy had a significant place in the industrial activities of the people. From the beginning of city life, about 2000 B.C., copper and bronze have been in plentiful use for the manufacture of utensils, blade axes, bronze saw, knives, spear-heads, fish-hooks, chisels and eyed-needles. Figurines made of bronze exhibit great workmanship and that of dancing girl is of superb beauty. Mace-heads made from limestone and alabaster, saddle-quern made from a hard gritty stone, used for grinding cereals like wheat and barley, stones with large holes, probably used for making curry-powders[100], a large number of weights made mainly from highly polished chert or alabaster, limestone, quartzite, slate and jasper, and the beautifully carved stone figures are some of the most important examples of stone implements found to have been in use among the city population. The presence of pottery candle-stick directly points to internal lighting practices. But one of the most remarkable evidences is provided by the wide range of ceramics made on wheels and colourfully decorated with innumerable designs. The artificially glazed surfaces of the ceramics make them unparalleled in the ancient world.[101] The excellence of clay modelling is further noticed in the terracotta figures of deities, like the Mother Goddess, animals, birds, snakes, fish, drain pipes, spindle-whorls and toys. Besides, toys and various types of games made of shell and ivory have survived to show the varied interests of the inhabitants taken in indoor and outdoor life.

The extraordinary skill is also demonstrated in the manufacture of seals, a very symbolic constituent of this culture, usually made of steatite and of agate, chert, faience, terracotta and copper[102], with different motifs carved on them. Another craft developed to perfection is represented by shell products, with inlay works and the ivory products. Among the various types of industries, cotton textile occupied a prominent place. The discovery of copper and bronze needles, innumerable baked clay spindle-whorls, and two gold needles suggests the development of embroidery in those days.

The remains of charred wheat, barley[103], peas, sesamum[104] place them among the principal crops of the Indus valley. Rice, cotton and bajra—a type so millet, have been more popular in the south, Melonseeds and dates, identified in the remains, occupied an important place among the agricultural products. The domesticated animals include sheep, both humped and humpless cattle, buffalo, pigs as sources of food, dog as a pet, onager and camel as beasts of burden, including the ox, and most likely horse in the south probably for drawing chariots. The construction of boats and sea-worthy vessels is likely to have featured in the industrial pursuits of the people as without them the water-traffic on such a wide scale could not have developed and continued for centuries.

At the head of the Gulf of Cambay, on the low-lying ground near a tributary of the Sabarmati river, Lothal represents another large city and the greatest port built by the Harappans when the sea lay not more than 3 miles away from the site[105]. Prior to the arrival of the Harappans, the site had developed into a village, belonging to an antecedent culture where, according to Rao, in about 2450 B.C. a small colony was established by the sea-faring traders of the Harappan Empire, and it did not take long for the local village culture to lose its identity under the over-powering influence of this greater, more developed culture. As a consequence, the overseas trade proliferated and so also the industries producing shell and ivory objects, cotton goods and beads of gemstone"[106] along with barbed fish-hooks, flat celt, arrow-head, leaf-shaped dagger and spear-head made of copper, the latter imported from outside. Thus, in no time Lothal became the most important commercial and industrial centre of the Harappan Empire, though the physical conditions of the urbanscape did not improve till the catastrophic food of 2350 B.C.[107] swept away the entire habitation. The city was built anew and enlarged soon after this but was revisited by floods on two more occasions in quick succession, one in 2050 B.C. and the other, more devastating than the former, in 2000 B. C. after which, in spite of re-building, the city could not regain its former self either in commerce or in industry. The widescale destruction wrought on the buildings, the factories and the warehouses, the complete disruption of the sanitary system due to choked up underground drains, and change in the course of the silted up channel, leaving the inland dock dry, cut at the very base of its prosperity. The buildings were rebuilt, the dock was repaired, connecting it with a newly dug two-mile long canal, the industries were revived and a new factory was established for the largescale production of luxury and essential goods having high demands in the market, but all these efforts failed to instill the vitality of the past. The decline had set in, and the pace was quickened by another flood in 1900 B.C. which left the city in a veritable ruin, compelling total desertion of it by its residents. The destruction was so complete that the city turned into an "ill-planned village"[108] after its reconstruction, having low-type reed houses, with its dock, overlain by a thick mantle of debris, closed for good and a deterioration in the pottery style. The degraded culture continued for three more centuries, and then was replaced by a non-urban culture.

The most important aspect of the Harappan phase of occupation during its mature phase between 2450 and 1900 B.C. is revealed in the same pattern of urban planning, as found in Mohenjo-daro and Harappa, strictly maintained all through the centuries of rebuilding. The city of Lothal had been surrounded by a mud-brick wall, the latter serving as a protection against recurring floods. The city, about 1.3 miles in circuit, repeats all the features typical of Harappan planned cities: the city is divided into two parts: (*a*) the Acropolis, built on a raised platform, containing the administrative and residential headquarters of the ruling class, represents the Citadel elsewhere, and (*b*) the Lower Town, containing the market centre, occupying the northern, the industrial sector the western, and the residential quarters the north-western part. The physical build of the city, with its numerous baths in the Acropolis and the Lower Town, the straight streets, the sanitary arrangements, the warehouse or the Granary, etc., give the same look as those of Mohenjo-daro and Harappa except that the eastern part of Lothal is dominated by a large dockyard — 702 × 118 feet[109] — connected by an artificial channel to the river. A massive brick wharf runs along the entire length of the dock.

The excavated ruins at Kalibangan (Fig.1.2), in Rajasthan, present similar spatial arrangements through its nine structural layers of occupation[110], though on a smaller scale, with a fortified Citadel on the west and the Lower Town on the east built on a street-plan of grid type. The houses in the Citadel were built on mud-brick platforms. This well-planned town, however, lacked the elaborate system of sanitation which indicates a fall of urban standard maintained so meticulously all through the mature phase of this culture. In fact Harappan culture started degenerating since 2000 B.C. and this is very much evident from further deterioration of civic amenities in the late levels of occupation.

The town of Chanhu-daro shows five successive levels of occupation of which the first three represent the Harappan culture. Platforms absent during the first phase appear in the next two phases on which houses were built. The town lacks the Citadel, but in other details, such as the street-planning, the underground and surface drains made of bricks, the use of fired bricks, the Granary, etc., it was a real prototype of the larger cities. The industrial character of this town is profoundly manifest in the major occupation of the people who were mostly engaged in the works of bead, shell and copper.[111]

The prevalence of a central control pervading the entire building process in producing towns and cities did not slacken even when urban centres were founded in the far corners of this vast empire. Sutkagen-dor provides one of such outstanding examples. Lying on the Dasht River near the Makran coast in South-West Baluchistan, Sutkagen-dor developed into an entrepot[112] of fairly large size. The three building phases reveal here a fortified settlement divided into two parts — the Citadel and the Lower Town of which the former was built on artificial mud-brick platforms. The houses and street were constructed according to plan and a dockyard, made of brick, connected the town with the adjoining sea[113].

Evidence of this central control is further available from Rupar, a frontier town, situated in the far corner of the empire, on the left bank of the Sutlej in Ambala district of Punjab where limited excavation has already revealed the existence of drains and artificially built platforms[114].

The Harappan phase at Rangpur, in Kathiawar, produces similar results. Here also the houses were built on platforms with provisions of baths and drains.

The Progress of the Harappan Culture

The limited nature of excavations is still the major handicap in building up a complete picture of this greatest cultural revolution. We do not know yet when it actually began; we have yet to surmise how and where it began. The intermediate stage between the pre-urban and the post-rural cultures of the Indus plains remains untraced. The sites discussed above have not been completely explored. Many other sites already discovered a wait investigation, while many more may yet come to light. Before entering into this intriguing issue we may tread on more solid ground for getting a clearer view of the growth of this Urban Culture and its special identifying features.

The evidences already available from numerous sites give us a strong impression that the urban development, at its mature phase, had a simultaneous start at both Mohenjo-daro and Harappa. This does in no way contradict the notion, stated earlier, that the formative stage of development might have taken place at Mohenjo-daro and definitely not at Harappa as the lower levels at the former site remaining unexplored very likely keep important clues concealed, while the occupation at the latter site, Harappa, from the beginning belong to the mature phase of development. It is, therefore, quite likely that in 2500 B.C. the urban development, attaining its major phase at Mohenjo-daro, inspired the city-fathers for building the second capital at Harappa in the urge for keeping hold on the slowly growing empire from its farthest end. Between Mohenjo-daro and the head of the delta of the Indus a number of settlements grew, though none of them came to be a large city. In the stride of urban development some of the old sites, with records of antecedent culture, also got a new lease of life. Most noteworthy among them are Amri, Kot Diji, Pandi Wahi, Gazi Shah and Tharro. North of Mohenjo-daro, however, the entire course of the Indus and its immediate tributaries, like the Jhelum and the Chenab, are completely devoid of any urban centre, the farthest one—Harappa—appearing on the bank of another tributary, the Ravi.

At the time when Harappan culture penetrated into Gujarat, small communities practising agriculture and producing well-turned pottery, had already appeared at sites like, Lothal, Prabhas (Somnath), Rojdi and Desalpur. The arrival of the Harappans, therefore, did not greatly interfere with the local traditions and the slow ingress gradually replaced the antecedent cultures. The urge for this southward expansion was motivated by the need of getting access to the raw materials and the markets for the industrial products of the empire. According to the opinion of archaeologists, Kathiawar provided chank shells for the production of shell objects having a high demand at Ur, Kish and Susa[115] in those days; besides, agates, carnelian, onyx and chalcedony were available at Katiawar[116] for the fabrication of beads. The same region was also, perhaps, the source of ivory where elephants had been traced down to the fourth century B.C.[117] Among the other important raw materials probably lead used to come from Ajmer[118], steatite, slate, jasper, blood-stone, and green chalcedony from different parts of Rajasthan. In all likelihood, South India provided many of the important raw materials needed by the metropolitan and the other cities. As for instance, Kolar and Hatti mines in Mysore were the source of gold. The presence of artifacts of Harappan origin in the gold-bearing region here dating back to 2300 to 1700 B.C.[119] positively indicate cultural contact between them; the Malabar coast used to supply wood and probably Mysore provided the grey and yellow steatite while Kashmir and the Himalayan forests in the north were the main sources for wood, perhaps, floated down the rivers. Countries beyond India are believed to have taken considerable part in this trade. Baluchistan might have sent steatite, silver, bitumen and alabaster; Afghanistan most likely supplied lapis lazuli, silver and turquoise[120]; Persia quite possibly sent gold, silver, lead and tin.[121]

Without making the list long, it can be said that the collection of so many types of raw materials from such a large number of sources made it obligatory on the part of the Indus Valley Civilisation to establish settlements around its frontiers, *i.e.* in the peripheral regions. Thus, settlements pushed forward in all directions and the primary push in all certainty, was made southward into Gujarat and Kathiawar from where both land and water routes could be equally utilised. Stray evidences make it sufficiently clear that the colonization, in the earlier period, followed coastal or near-coastal locations. Such early settlements were Lothal, Bhagatrav in the Kim estuary; Navinal on the South-Eastern coast of the Kathiawar peninsula; Lakhapar Pabumath and Desalpur near the southern margin of the Great Rann which, in the opinion of Rao, was much wider and deeper in those days than at present. It is interesting to observe that, all of them developed as ports for handling the great traffic originating from the Harappan empire and the overseas lands. The development towards the interior of the peninsula took place much later during the Late Harappan phase, between 1900 and 1700 B.C., when settlements spread out, further giving rise to three important ports of Kinnarkheda, Prabhas or Somnath and Kanjetar on the west coast of the peninsula, important settlements, like Adkot, Akru, Alau, Rojdi, Gop, Babarkot and Vanivadar in the interior, and Amara and Lakhabawal on the North-Western coast of the peninsula. Near the mouth of River Narmada, Megham and Telod developed as Late Harappan ports. Most of these settlements developed in the interior of the peninsula were nothing but ill-planned villages, inhabited by the people, who had deserted Lothal after the great flood of 1900 B.C., and were joined by refugees from the Indus plains where also the flood havoc seems to have had been equally serious. The decline of the urban prosperity, as it appears, had finally set in some time around 1900 B.C., but this time the colonization of the Southern region, comprising Cutch, Kathiawar and part of Gujarat lying west of the Sabarmati River had been completed.

Westward, the march of the Indus Civilisation is not less spectacular either. Beginning through cultural contacts in the earlier period, the Harappans gradually established their colonies at many of these older sites among which Dabarkot makes an outstanding example of a large trading-post, built up by the Harappans in 2200 B.C.[122] Traces of Harappan influence are found to have been introduced to Damb Sadaat some time in the same period[123]. Kulli and Mehi also produce evidences originating, perhaps, from similar influence. The discovery of ceramics resembling Harappan style in the mounds of Edith Shahr in the Las Bela district of Baluchistan provides another convincing instance of the westward extension of this culture. The most important of all the urban centres founded by the Harappans was Sutkagen-dor, acting as the principal frontier port of the empire. Further east, at Sotka-koh, near modern Pasni, another fortified port-town has been traced.

The extension of the Harappan culture eastward, beyond the Indus, make some interesting revelations. The movement took a north-easterly direction, producing perhaps the largest concentration of settlements in the region between the river basins of the upper Sutlej and the Saraswati, or the modern Ghaggar. South of this traces of Harappan settlements become almost scarce, indicating an easterly limit set by the now-extinct bed of the Saraswati. Taking its rise in the sub-Himalayan ranges of the Punjab and joining the Ghaggar near Shatrana, Saraswati once used to flow in a South-Westerly direction. The presence of another ancient river-bed, west of this, suggests Sutlej joining Saraswati instead of the Beas in those days. River Chautang in the Punjab, anciently known as the Drishadvati, coming out of the hills further south of the Saraswati joins the latter near Suratgarh in the Ganganagar district of Rajasthan. This is represented today by the dry beds. It is highly curious to note that the tongue of the land lying between the Sutlej on the west and the Drishadvati on the east represent a later colonization which, according to Gordan, started around 2100 B.C. The Harappan phase at Kalibangan has been dated to 2300 B.C., but the absence of certain characteristic types of ceramics and the occurrence of a particular type of seal suggests a much later date for Rupar[124]. Bara, another site excavated near Rupar, similarly represents a Late Harappan settlement[125]. Kotla Nihang, Mandiala Khan, Deheru in the Ludhiana district, and Kat Palon in Jullundur district, and most of the other sites discovered here offer instances of a degenerate culture, belonging to the Late Harappan. It is generally believed that, the great flood in 1900 B.C. causing irreparable damages to Lothal and Mohenjo-daro hurled the final blow to the urban prosperity and the cities never could recover their previous position. The degraded cities could no longer support a large population and created bands of displaced persons who from time to time migrated to new areas. It is quite likely that the new-dried-up beds of the Sutlej and the Saraswati provided the two most important routes for these trans-valley migrations. The settlements they established within the Sutlej-Saraswati fork and further east in the Jamuna-Ganga doab were not only later in time, but also inferior in standard. As a matter of fact, east of Harappa, none of the settlements had ever reached the high urban level witnessed in any of the cities like. Mohenjo-daro, Harappa or Lothal.

A large number of sites, mostly representing small settlements of the decadent phase occur in the Lower Saraswati-Drishadvati course. Here, stretching from the Bhawalpur State in Pakistan to the Ganganagar district in India, the presence of more than two dozens of such settlements, including Sandhanawala, Derawar and Fort Abbas, indicate the early agricultural prosperity of the region. The cultural decadence is more pronounced with the Harappans who moved further eastward. Degenerate Harappan settlements appear at Singoli, 20 miles west of Delhi which is more eloquent of this cultural degradation. Settlements developed during this phase at sites like Alamgirpur, about 30 miles North-East of Delhi, Bargaon and Ambkheri in the Saharanpur district make it abundantly clear that the colonizers at this stage were hard-pressed toilers of the soil, bereft of the imagination and ability that once inspired their predecessors for creating the greatest civilisation on of the ancient East.

The areal extension of this urban culture having been considered makes it amply clear that the southward as well as the westward expansion was made with a particular view to build up trade relations with, the outside world, whereas that towards the east was caused by compelling circumstances completely different in nature. The former contributed to the prosperity of the empire while in the latter one distinctly notices the gasping attempts of this culture for survival at a time when its prosperity had already finally vanished. It is quite obvious that, in extending its cultural domain southward and westward, the Harappans directly proved their intimate knowledge of a higher economic system. They knew that urban prosperity depends largely on well-developed industry and trade which again depend on the abundant sources of raw materials and a large, wealthy market. The movement towards the south into the Kathiawar Peninsula was farsighted and deliberate for getting access to the raw material sources of Peninsular India as well as the market of Western Asia and Egypt; the westward movement into the Baluch hills was motivated by the same intention. In the former, water routes got a greater prominence; in the latter, the land routes were more important.

The possible sources of raw materials, mentioned earlier, give some idea doubt the wide connections built up by the empire in those days. More positive evidences are available indicating the existence of an extensive trade between the Harappans and the countries lying further west. According to Gordon, Sumer and the Harappans had trade relations continuing from 2400 to 2150 B.C.[126] which, as Piggot says, did exist between 2300 and 2000 B.C.[127] Indian traders had established traders colonies in such urban centres as Ur, Kish, Brak, Asmar and Lagash in the Tigris-Euphrates valley and Failaka Island in the western end of the Persian Gulf where they used local seals engraved with Indian like ivory rods, have been traced in the Syrian coast; weights and beads in South Mesopotamia. The cylindrical seal discovered by Frankfort at Tell Asmar, dated to 2400 B.C. and the fragment of a pottery found by him at the same site have been claimed to be of Indian origin[129]. On the other hand, a vessel fragment made of light green steatite with peculiar mat-marks on it unearthed at Mohenjo-daro bear strange familiarity with Sumerian vessels found at Tell Asmar, Kish and in the east at Susa suggest it to have been imported from either Sumer or Susa in Persia some time in the third millennium B.C.[130] Clay tablets discovered in Sumer and Akkad (Northern Babylon) mention ships bringing timber from Dilmun to Lagash in 2450 B.C. and from Dilmun, Magan and Melulah to the capital of Akkad in 2300 B.C.[131] Dilmun has been identified with Kuda, near Hathab in Kathiawar, the former being still known locally by that name, Magan with the Muscat Cast and Melulah with the land of the Harappans[132]. The Sumerian ships, sailing from Dilmun in about 1950 B.C., carried various goods like gold, copper, silver ivory-combs and inlays, lapis lazuli, gemstone beads, pearls and some types of wood[133]. Similar contacts had also been maintained with Persia, the Nile valley and East Africa. The pottery candlestick found at Mohenjo-daro closely resembles those recovered from Egyptian sites having same shape and belonging to almost same date. The practice of using imitation mussel-shells, though made of different substances, was the same between Egypt and the Indus Valley[134]. In all possibility, therefore, it must have been a two-way trade. But barring the cases of metals and such other objects used primarily as raw materials, clear, tangible evidences are yet lacking on the nature of imported finished stuff. (Fig. 1.3)

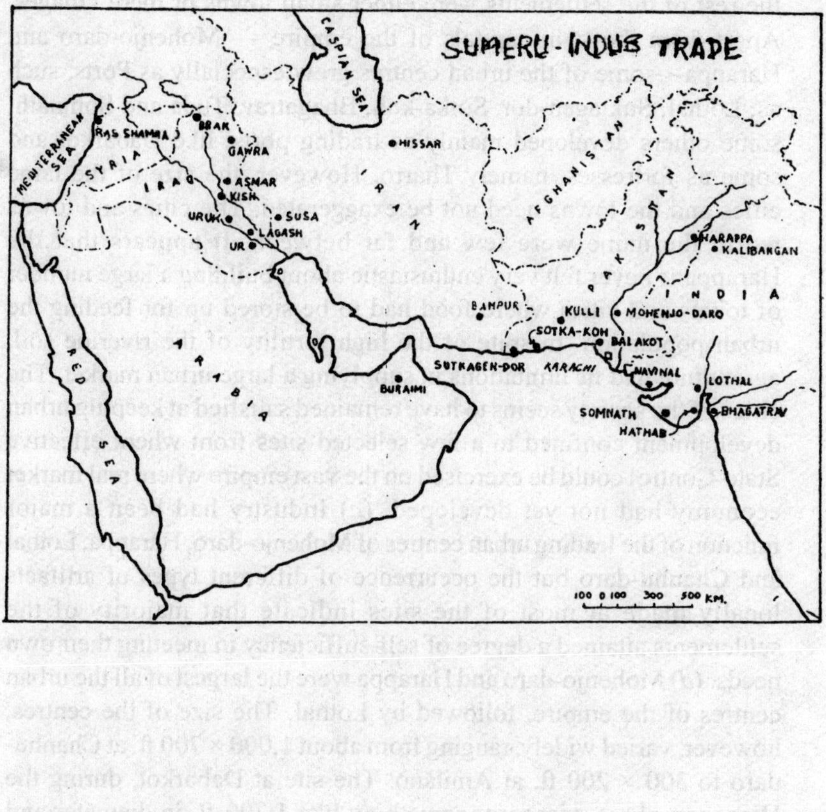

Fig. 1.3 : Indus-Sumerian Trade

An assessment of the urban development of this period leads to some major conclusions: (*a*) the majority of the towns and cities were built during the mature phase lasting between 2500 and 1900 B.C. Settlements developed after this, belonging to the decadent phase — 1900 to 1700 B.C. — were nothing more than villages, with visible lowering of civic and economic standards. (*b*) Among the explored sites only three, namely Mohenjo-daro, Harappa and Lothal, reached the status of a city. Large towns were equally few in number, while the rest of the settlements were either small towns or mere villages. Apart from the twin capitals of the empire — Mohenjo-daro and Harappa—some of the urban centres grew especially as Ports, such as, Lothal, Suktagen-dor, Sotka-koh, Bhagatrav, Tuda and Somnath; some others developed mainly as trading ports, like Dabarkot and some as fortresses, namely Tharro. However, the size of the large cities and the towns need not be exaggerated. The cities and towns worth the name were few and far between. It appears that the Harappans never felt very enthusiastic about building a large number of towns and cities where food had to be stored up for feeding the urban population. In spite of the high fertility of the riverine soil, agriculture had its limitations in supplying a large urban market. The elites of the society seems to have remained satisfied at keeping urban development confined to a few selected sites from where effective State-Control could be exercised on the vast empire where real market economy had not yet developed. (*c*) Industry had been a major function of the leading urban centres of Mohenjo-daro, Harappa, Lothal and Chanhu-daro but the occurrence of different types of artifacts locally made at most of the sites indicate that majority of the settlements attained a degree of self-sufficiency in meeting their own needs. (*d*) Mohenjo-daro and Harappa were the largest of all the urban centres of the empire, followed by Lothal. The size of the centres, however, varied widely, ranging from about 1,000 × 700 ft. at Chanhu-daro to 300 × 200 ft. at Amilano. The site at Dabarkot, during the Harappan phase, measures something like 1,200 ft. in diameter and that at Sandhanawalla, on the dry bed of the Ghaggar, is about 750 × 500 ft. The different size of these settlements, whether urban or rural, does convey the impression that the population similarly varied accordingly though there is no way of knowing the number of their inhabitants. It is generally surmised that Lothal contained between

10,000 and 15,000 heads during its height of prosperity; in both Mohenjo-daro and Harappa the number was slightly more than double of that[135].

The Originality of the Harappan Culture

The individuality of this culture is clearly manifest in its uniqueness in many fields of cultural achievements.

(i) The Indus City-Builders were the first to introduce the method of strict discipline in the form of town-planning and saw to the principle being meticulously observed in the cities built at different dates so much so that the street-plan did not undergo any material change over a period of about eleven to twelve centuries. In fact, the twin capitals seem to have sprung up fully planned[136]. It is rather fascinating to observe that, even the bricks used all through the period were of standard size — measuring 9.2 × 4.5 × 2.2 inches in the early period and 11 × 5.5 × 3 inches in the later period[137]. Baked bricks of standard Harappan proportions occur as far a field as Rupar on the Upper Sutlej. Derawar in Bikaner, Rangpur in Gujarat and Chanhu-daro on the Indus bank[138]. Again, for the first time in the history of the world the cities become fully equipped with permanent underground sewers maintained effectively by a civic body, that is, a municipality. Besides, nowhere in the ancient world social stratification was so marked and the dwelling houses belonging to each class were built in such an ordered fashion as in the Indus cities. The existence of public amenities, such as wells, bathrooms and privies in private houses stand for a high culture not attained till then in any other urban-quarters of the ancient world. The presence of the Great Bath, the State Granary, the Collegiate Building and the Hall of Assembly were the other unique features of the urbanscape. Thus, the fundamental differences in the physical structures of the Indus cities make them characteristically different from their counterparts elsewhere in the world, whether contemporary or not, and this alone brings out their distinctiveness and independent origin.

(ii) This distinctiveness is further magnified by the complete lack of any public monuments displaying the vainglory of military conquests, or temples make the urban aspect very different from those of the West where monuments, namely the Pyramids of Egypt,

temples such as Ziggurats in the Mesopotamian cities of Babylon[139], Eridu[140], Ur[141], etc., were so characteristic features of the urban landscape.

(iii) The independent character of this culture is very strongly revealed by its wheel-turned pottery[142] which, with its black-on-red ware and designs painted on a deep red lustre slip-bearing some similarity with Kulli style — attained characteristically independent form[143]. The originality was in the scripts as well which, with about 250 signs or characters[144], remained unchanged throughout the period. Besides, its famous seals, generally of steatite, are "distinctive and unique in quality"[145]. The Harappan seals are usually square and the fact that cylinder seals — an entirely Sumerian invention and typical of the West Asiatic Cultures — are rare among the Harappans stresses further the independence of the latter culture[146]. Another example of the uniqueness of this culture is found in its weights, uninscribed but falling into a well-defined system unlike any other in the ancient world[147] and their constant accuracy prove the high rate of civil discipline rare in the contemporary civilisations. In the lower weights the system was binary : 1, 2, $^{1}/_{3} \times 8$, 4, 8, 16, 32, 64 etc., with traditional Indian ratio of 16; in the higher weights the system was decimal with fractional weights in the third. Measurements of length used to follow a decimal system[148]. The originality of the culture is also brought out by its characteristic religious symbols. Figures inscribed on some of the seals represent deities that were later on adopted by the Aryans and are still worshipped by the Hindus. Chief among them is the Siva with its Bull. The idea of phallus-worship in the form of 'Linga' and 'Yoni', prevalent among the Hindus today in all likelihood has got the same ancestry[149]. The existence of numerous terracotta figurines of almost nude females, representing the Mother Goddess, the semi-human, semi-bovine monster attacking a horned tiger, the astral trefoil, the image of 'unicorn' carried in procession, etc., and their ubiquitous association with the Sumerian and the Egyptian cultures might indicate a cultural link between the Indus and the West Asiatic cultures. But, from all appearance, the worship of Siva along with the Bull and that of Linga attained a greater statewide recognition among the Harappans than any other God. And both Siva and Linga retaining this position in the hierarchy of Hindu gods later

on strongly justify the individuality of Indus religion. Many of the terracotta figurines, exhibiting logic postures, convey the idea that yoga science was highly developed among the Harappans.

(iv) Similarly, the metal industry too developed by the Harappans and remaining strangely uniform in style through the entire length of time and space had its own speciality. The fools and the weapons were generally made of copper—either crude or refined—and of copper-arsenic alloy as well as of bronze though the best tools were usually of bronze, but not of copper[150], while silver bowls, cups, vases and other vessels generally without subtlety of form were less in use. The most interesting and characteristic aspect of the techniques is that, they did not change whatsoever all through the period of over a thousand years. A standard range of tools and other objects occurring at all levels of occupation at site after site[151] reveal an extraordinary degree of standardization, called by Piggott as "competent dullness"[152]. There is, however, no doubt that the metal-smiths attained a high degree of workmanship and this is clearly exhibited by their products, like chisels, knives, razors, spears, fish-hooks, flat axes and handled mirrors. The independent character of the industry is further accentuated by the fact that closed-mould casting process—discovered by the Sumerians in very early times and adopted by the urban civilisations of the West—was never used by the Harappans. In the same context, the type of axes deem consideration. To illustrate, the axes used by the Harappans were of the simplest flat type, discovered as early as the fourth or the fifth millennium B.C. in Mesopotamia and mostly replaced by metal shaft-hole axes there, but the latter never appeared in the Indus Valley. It seems probable that the idea of flat axes was inherited from the older civilisation and the existence of this singular type from the date of urban beginning to its end suggests that the inheritance belonged to a much earlier period and the city-builders carried that with them into their newly built settlements.

(v). In the realm of arts, apart from the seals forming a class by themselves, the stone and bronze sculptures are the monumental products of this culture, and very much authentic expressions of the pre-historic Indian art in the third millennium B.C. According to Piggott, the naturalistic human sculpture produced by the Harappans, foreshadowing the later Indian artistic modes, were already essentially

Indian[153]. Even in terracottas, representing figures of both males and females, as well as a large variety of toys, the whistles made in the form of a hollow bird, were typically characteristic of this culture.

(vi). This individuality finds expression in its trading articles as well. The most exciting example is provided by cotton-textiles exported to Western Asia from here[154] and the earliest traces of cotton known anywhere in the world is obtained from the Harappan cities. The objects mentioned earlier, like ivory products, such as combs—made to same pattern even today in India, pearls, peacocks, apes were special items of export. Documents referring to the export of gold, silver, lumps of lapis lazuli, stone beads, ornaments and inlays, eye-paint and wood of the city of Ur in the 20th century B.C. make it sufficiently convincing that an organized trade did exist between Sumer and the Indus valley before and after 2000 B.C.

(vii) Another important feature making Harappan culture different from that of Mesopotamia and Egypt was the virtual absence of any elaborate system of irrigation typical of the latter two cultures as mentioned by Woolley[155]. The Indus agriculture instead was generally dependent on flood-irrigation a natural phenomenon, occurring every year with the onset of monsoon, adding fertility to the soil; even if irrigation had been practised at all, it was far more modest in style than in either of the two other countries where the State had been directly involved in the construction and maintenance of the irrigation works. This part, differences between the Indus valley and Western Asia also arise in the use of agricultural implements. The absence of the plough-symbol and the occurrence of the harrow as a common Indus ideograph symbol indicates that harrow was, perhaps, the only tilling equipment among the Harappans in contrast to Mesopotamian and Egyptian plough[156]. Similarly, the Harappans had their own speciality in the crops grown. Both cotton and rice, grown by these people, were completely unknown to other civilisations till then.

(viii) On the defensive side differences were not lacking either. It is noteworthy to mention that unlike the Sumerian and the Egyptian States, the vast Indus Empire had a very weak defence organisation. No supportive evidence having been found so far about the existence of body armour, helmets or shields, swords or bronze arrow-heads, describe the profound weakness in the art of warfare and thus making the race far from martial. In sharp contrast, the States in Mesopotamia,

thriving in this period, had been in constant wars with each other. Further, the political set-up was widely different between these civilisations. The Indus had given rise to a vast empire—the first of its kind in the world—unified by two capitals under a rigid system of political and economic control. In contrast, the Sumerian cities had developed into independent City-States.

(ix) Lastly, the impressive uniformity of its products, ranging from architecture to toys and ornaments undergoing no change over a space of nearly thousand years, gives it a special character, unparalleled anywhere in the world. The expression, whether in ordinary or in the cultural chores of life, remained the same all through this period, focusing particularly on the iron discipline of the society so different from others elsewhere.

All these characteristic features underline the fundamental differences that lay in almost every aspect of material to aesthetic life of the people living in the Indus valley on the one hand, and those in the twin river valleys of the Tigris and Euphrates as well as of the Nile on the other. The principal aim here being the identification of the individuality of Indus culture, it is necessary to stress upon the fact that the distinctive character is positively of local origin, unaffected by foreign influence whatsoever. Contacts between the Indus and Mesopotamian cities did exist, but it was purely of commercial nature and that too were established around 2400 B.C. or before 2300 B.C., ceasing soon after 2000 B.C.[157] Further, it was not very impressive and powerful enough to change the character of the Harappan culture which, so to say, remained impervious to any influence from outside. The best impression they make is that the Harappans were out and out strong traditionalists, keeping the homogeneity of their culture unraptured for more than a millennium. The extent as well as nature of individuality of this culture having been considered, it can now be accepted for certain that such an individuality and the unprecedented scale of success attained in empire building could not be achieved had the people not been associated with the environment for a long time. The challenge of the environment, as mentioned earlier, was, in fact, successfully faced by them and their genius got fully expressed in the cities they built. The slow ingress of the Harappan influence traceable on the potteries of the pre-Harappan-settlements does not imply a sudden change in the cultural sphere. On the contrary, indication of a cultural continuity is very strong between the two periods of pre-Harappan and Harappan cultures at Amri, Kot Diji and Kalibangan[158]. However, the dramatic suddenness in the appearance of a full-fledged city at Mohenjo-daro, giving no trace of its formative stage of development, need consideration. Regarding the growth of the other cities of the Harappan Empire it can safely be assumed that they derived the experience and initiative from the parent city Mohenjo-daro. The question therefore remains to be answered on the origin of the city-builders of Mohenjo-daro itself. But, as long as the unsounded depths of Mohenjo-daro are not known, it is neither possible to throw light on this problem, nor is it possible to gauge how the process was. Having no knowledge of the lower depths of occupation, it will be rather a long guess to say that the traces of an evolutional process do not lie buried in those unopened layers.

Origin of the City-Builders

In general, however, opinion widely differs on the origin of the makers of this civilisation. According to Kosambi, the sudden completion of the cities within a century or so and having no predecessors points to a stimulus that came from outside and in his opinion, they came from some "restricted but developed locality"[159], though that does not refer to Sumer. Mishra, on the other hand postulates Central Asia, or, the Caspian-Aral region — extending from the valley of Syr Daria upto the Plateau of Pamir — as the original homeland of the founders of the Indus Civilisation[160]. He contends that the migration of these people was a forced one who, after colonizing the upland valleys of eastern Iran, Afghanistan and Baluchistan, gradually came down upon the plains of the Indus and in course of time built up the earliest Urban Civilisation of India[161]. In support of his contention, Mishra draws extensively from different authors : the strong similarity of skulls found at Mohenjo-daro and different sites of Caspian-Aral region as well as Baluchistan, as shown by Mackay[162]; the production of bread-wheat by the Harappans in the third millennium B.C. which, according to Piggott, emerged first in Turkestan[163] but unknown till then elsewhere; the similarity of domestic animals, such as one-humped camel of Mohenjo-daro and Harappa being contemporary with that of Anau in Turkestan and horse known to the earliest inhabitants of

Rana Ghundai in North Baluchistan appearing in the same period at Turkestan, establishes the cultural affinity between the two distant lands. Mishra further shows that about a dozen sites excavated recently at the initiative of the Soviet Government at Altin Depe "have produced the largest amount of material comparable to the Harappan antiquities"[164] ranging from almost identical pottery, using the same process of manufacture, to such objects as straight handed copper frying pan, different types of beads, segmented faience head, ivory sticks used as dices, terracottas with solid wheels and nude female figurines, compartmented toilet containers of soap-stone and terracotta, etc., showing a striking parallelism in shape, material as well as manufacturing process. Many of these are not confined to Altin Depe alone, but occur widely at other sites in South Turkmenia. Besides, the use of a common seal—motif between the two regions appear to be highly suggestive of a close cultural contact[165].

On the basis of these evidences Mishra develops the hypothesis that a group of the Central Asiatic people, called the Asuras, expelled by other tribes inhabiting the same region, finally, took shelter in the Indus Plains and on their way to this region gave rise to the Iranian-Afghan-Baluch upland village settlements.

Nevertheless the extent of cultural identity still leaves gaps that cannot be filled in with all evidences put forward by Mishra. The extraordinary character of the physical layout of the cities, taking full form at the very beginning of urban life along with all its sophistications as vividly manifest in their civic amenities, had no near parallel at any site of Central-Asia. In the absence of any precise data available from a more thorough archaeological exploration revealing the evolutional stages of the urban culture and in the absence of any precise knowledge of their script any conclusion on the origin of the architects of the Indus Civilisation seems to be hazardous. Besides, the aim of this study being the evolution of Indian Urbanisation, any attempt at tracing the lost pieces of the jigsaw puzzle is simply beyond its scope. The pattern that emerges is, however, quite distinct at least in two respects: first, the culture was the outcome of a process developed through centuries of occupation in the Indus valley itself and, second, that it was more indigenous than being the product of transplantation by foreign agents. It can further be said that the people, initiating the

Harappan culture, made a final break-through on the basis of their earlier experiences gathered and experimentations carried on through trials and errors in the same environment, perhaps at the same sites sometimes, during all through the pre-Harappan period. Instances of overlapping cultural sequences at many of the sites are strongly indicative of such a peaceful transition, or rather, an evolutional process in existence, and as long as the lower depths of Mohenjo-daro—the first site to develop into a typical Indus city — are not opened, it is not possible to ascertain the intensity of this 'break through'. The mystery of the untraced levels of Mohenjo-daro may hold the key to the actual secrets of its real beginning. If the accumulation of 30 ft. of the present mound can contain a history of about eight centuries—taking the span of Mohenjo-daro's city-life running from 2500 to 1700 B.C.—the accumulation of the lower 39 ft. deposits, still lying unexposed, may have resulted from a much longer period of occupation. On the other hand, if the space of about a century or so is accepted as the time-gap between the end of the pre-Harappan and the emergence of the Harappan culture it may be taken as the period of experimentation, allowing sufficient merging for these highly talented people to make phenomenons progress in creating the first planned city of the world, examples of which were later on emulated at other sites. This is amply substantiated by the fact that Mohenjo-daro emerged much earlier than other cities, namely Lothal, Kalibangan, Kot Diji, etc., where the same planning principles were pursued in all rigidity.

This stubborn attitude in planning—symbolising Harappan Culture in the best possible manner—remaining unaltered through centuries may be explained from two different angles: (1) That, since it evolved out as the most effective one in response to the typical environmental conditions and needs, no drastic change was deemed necessary for incorporation at any later stage. As a result an element of indigenousness pervades the entire cultural process from its very beginning, revealing further that the people were extremely conscious of their surroundings putting innumerable obstacles at every effort for progress. (2) In contrary to this, another view may be taken which refers to the sloth and indolence that crept slowly into the society, signs of that being discernible in the upper layers of occupation at Mohenjo-daro, making innovations a far-cry. But it does not rule out the element of indigenousness of the culture. An analysis of the skeletal remains give an interesting idea about the ethnic composition pertaining to this early civilisation. The existence of four different races have been identified to this date in the population of the Indus cities. They are Proto-Australoid, Mediterranean, Mongolian and Alpine[166] of which the Mediterranean seem to have predominated during the mature phase at Mohenjo-daro, Harappa and Chanhu-daro[167]. The presence of so many races definitely gives a cosmopolitan character to urban population, making them distinct among their contemporaries elsewhere.

Evaluating all these various aspects it can be conjectured that the architects of this urban civilisations came from distant lands, no doubt, but that at a distant past and their stay in the plains of the Indus preceding the birth of the cities was long enough to Indisanize them so fully that what they produced became "essentially Indian"[168], having no legacy whatsoever. The civilisation was thus the creation of the ingenuity and tireless efforts of a people, with a leadership more determined, farsighted, imaginative and fortunate than the rest of the colonizers.

The Collapse of the First Urban Civilisation

From about 2500 B.C. onwards, that is, since the foundation of the City of Mohenjo-daro, the dual pattern of the settled life, consisting of the small, sequestered, peasant communities of Baluch uplands and those of the cities, towns and villages in the Indus plains, continued simultaneously, unaltered for nearly another thousand years or so. Once the Harappan culture was established, communities—both rural and urban—maintained an absolutely peaceful life in the vast empire for centuries. Then something catastrophic happened and in the turmoil the great cities crashed down like house of cards. The dazzling examples of human labour and genius, brilliantly conveyed through architecture, art and various other achievements developed through peaceful centuries vanished as suddenly as they had made their first appearance on the banks of the Indus and elsewhere.

But however sudden it may appear on the surface, the fall of such a widely developed structure could not be so consistent and attributable to a single cause, like violence, unless something more powerful, more damaging had shaken the very foundation of this vast empire. It cannot be doubted that a general decline was definitely in progress for a long time, constantly eroding the base and ultimately weakening it sufficiently for the final collapse even without any challenge from exterior agent. As a matter of fact, Mohenjo-daro, Lothal and Chanhu-daro provide glaring signs of such a progressive decadence[169] where an increasing degree of deterioration is marked in the standards of buildings and living at laterday levels of occupation. The street-frontages were less strictly observed, brick-work became shoddy with re-use of brickbats, the large houses were divided up into smaller rooms, housing poorer sections of people—thereby increasing congestion, and even the domestic courtyards were partitioned in untidy fashion. Pottery kilns, invariably located beyond the city-boundaries at earlier stages, made serious inroads into the city boundaries at earlier stages, made serious inroads into the city precincts. Slackening of civic services, general decline of residential areas into industrial slums, insecurity and, perhaps, the threat of raids are the convincing signs of a general degradation and of a poorer economy fated for the impending breakdown.

The causes leading to such a physical as well as economic decline of the city seem to have originated from two different grounds:

(*a*) one is the menace of incessant floods occurring every year and taking violent form, putting on occasions unusual strain on the available resources of engineering skill and labour for the adoption of constant protective measures. According to Wheeler, deep static floods due to recurring tectonic uplifts pounding back the normal outflow aggravated the situation further, needing houses to be raised from time-to-time to safer heights on artificially built platforms. Three such main phases of deep flooding have been traced by the archaeologists at Mohenjo-daro and similar phases at lower depths cannot be ruled out, each of which needed massive re-building to be city on an increasingly higher level of deposition. Hazards of this nature, finally, eclipsed the fate of Harappan settlements at Lothal and in its surrounding area where they could not survive the last flood havoc in about 1900 B.C. when the invading water bulldozed the city to the ground. According to Rao, constant deposition at river-mouths gave rise to sheet-floods in circa 2000 B.C., submerging the low-lying areas and destroying the city of Lothal and other towns in the region. The destruction was more severe in 1900 B.C. when the floods virtually demolished all the towns, including Rangpur, Desalpur and Bhagatrav left to ruins.[170]

This proved to be too much of a burden for the city-builders even with technological knowledge in the field.

(*b*) The other reason leading to the decline and precipitating the crisis greatly, though not supported by any tangible evidence, yet quite evident from what happened all through the centuries for cultural build-up and construction, is the general impoverishment of the surrounding farmlands through over-cultivation, inadequate maintenance of the bunds and over-grazing. Over and above this, continuous destruction of the major vegetation for baking billions of bricks that went to the building and re-building of the city through the centuries and thus constantly baring the soil had a direct effect on the moisture content of the air as well as in reducing the rainfall where it was much higher than today. The land yielded gradually less and less, and the slow encroachment of desert on the sown shattered the economy so arduously built-up by the architects of the earlier periods. This steady 'wearing out of the landscape'—as Wheeler calls it, made conditions more and more unsuitable for a flourishing life. The lowering economy had its effect on the trade as well which ceased altogether with Mesopotamia after 1900 B.C., or thereabout[171]. It is therefore not difficult to imagine that both physical and economic degradation of the capital city loosened the control of the central authority which so long had successfully maintained its surveillance on the vast empire in following a uniform rule of action. At the same time, the capital itself became less and less hospitable and inviting, giving rise to slew desertion.

According to both Childe[172] and Wheeler[173], the deepening internal crisis weakened the entire system so much so that it could not withstand the invasion when it took place some time in the middle of the second millennium B.C. and completely destroyed the city in about 1500 B.C.[174] Very strangely though this has got relevance to the events of similar nature taking place for some time in Mesopotamia as well. The whole of Western Asia and its bordering countries faced a period of complete unrest and disorder between 2100 and 1800 B.C.[175] when the spread of superior weapons among the neighbouring tribesmen turned them into invaders of the superior valley cultures. The emergence of these warrior peoples, including the earliest known Indo-Europeans, or, the Aryans, between 2000-1550 B.C. is of great concern since they made headway gradually eastward. The earliest evidence relating to the movement of the Aryans in Baluchistan is available at Shahi Tump in South Bahuchistan, showing copper stamp seals, a copper shaft hole axe, footed and legged bowls of West Asian type and unknown till then in India, dating back to 1800 B.C. In contrast, the arrival of these new-comers at this time in North Baluchistan are indicated by violent destruction of the entire settlements at Rana Ghundai and Dabar Kot[176]. All the small settlements in the Zhob valley were burnt down by the invaders. The remains of the culture of these invaders are scarce, but evidences are quite plenty on what they did in the whole region. Throughout Baluchistan, for example, the painted pottery cultures at Kulli, Nal and Periano III came to an abrupt end.

The original home of these new-comers, in the opinion of Piggott, lay stretched between South Russia and Turkestan[177] where a loose confederacy of tribes speaking a closely related dialects within the Indo-European framework. It is quite axiomatic that the invaders, failing to settle down either in Sumer or on the high plateaus of Western Asia in the face of stronger opposition from other marauding tribes of same origin, ultimately turned eastward in search of new lands and thus arrived first in the mountain-girt valleys of Baluchistan. The latter, however, failed to satisfy their hunger and led their war path towards the extensive fertile plains of the Indus where the declining Harappan culture offered them little resistance.

Once arrived in the plains they settled down and developed a culture known as 'Jhukar', evidences of which are available at the town site of Jhukar (Fig.1.2). Amri, Chanhu-daro and Lohumjo-daro, wherefrom the Harappans were evidently driven out by the these new adventurers. The continuity of occupation at these places without any apparent break strengthens the view. It is likely that the city of Harappa, taking the Metropolitan leadership of the Civilisation in its last days, had its citadel-wall re-built at the at time[178], and fell first to the onslaught of the usurping culture, while Mohenjo-daro continued to resist the invaders still for some time when all the small towns had already been overrun and occupied by the latter. That this was the period of great unrest and trouble in the plains is signified by the discovery of buried hoards of jewellery and copper objects, plainly suggesting a deep sense of prevailing insecurity. On the other hand some sort of contact seem to have had developed between the citizens of Mohenjo daro and the invaders settled in the nearby towns. The discovery of a fine copper shaft-hole axe-adze superior to Harappan type, swords and daggers unlike Harappan types lend support to this idea. However, unlike other towns and cities, Mohenjo-daro never came to be occupied again after it fell to the attack to the invaders where the evidence of Jhukar occupation is entirely absent.

Wheeler cites Rigveda as the most authentic source, constantly referring to such invasions made on the Indian soil. According to Rigveda, the Aryans destroyed many walled cities which they called 'pur' meaning 'rampart', 'fort' or 'stronghold'. The situation prevailing at that time conforms closely to the idea of fortified Citadels of Mohenjo-daro, Harappa, Suktagendor, Ali Murad and Kalibangan, representing the 'pur' of Rigveda. Wheeler even goes as far as to suggest that 'Hari-Yupa' in Rigveda is nothing but the Harappan city where the non-Aryans were defeated by the Aryans[179].

Here again Mishra strongly disagrees with Wheeler on the date of arrival of the Aryans. According to the former, Wheeler's theory, supported also by Piggot, on the destruction of Harappan Civilisation by the Aryans in or about 1500 B.C. is not valid since pottery discovered at Navdatoli on Narmada River in Madhya Pradesh and at Eran in Madhya Pradesh closely resembling each other were of Aryan origin, dating back to about 1800 B.C., and the painted Grey Ware of Rupar and other sites and the copper-hoards traced in the Ganga valley having possible associations with the Aryans "dated in or about 2000 B.C."[180] suggest that the Aryans entered India "in more waves than one and impliedly, even before 1500 B.C."[181] Lacking more evidence carrying convincing proof along with radio-carbon datings of Aryan origin, it is yet premature to conclude that there had been a large scale invasion of the Aryans prior to the date of the downfall of the Harappan Civilisation. On the other hand, even if intermittent flow of new arrivals is accepted, starting as early as 2000 B.C., it does in no way dispute the main contention of Wheeler's theory that the urban structure ultimately succumbed to the attack of the Aryans and this particular action could have its beginning as early as 1800 B.C., or even earlier, when the arrival of the invaders is authenticated ay substantial evidences available from the settlements of Baluchistan.

But this particular part of the hypothesis built-up by Wheeler, Gordon Childe and supported by Piggott and D.H. Gordon is strongly refuted by Rao on the basis of observations made by Dales and Raikes. Rao puts more emphasis on the recurring floods, a consequence of tectonic upliftment of the coastal areas, as the root-cause of the final dissolution of this culture. The ancient inland beaches of the Makran coast, traced by Dales and his identification of Sutkagen-dor and Sotka-koh as coastal ports situated today far inland are taken as evidences for coastal upliftments. Further, Raikes refers to the alluvial and marine deposits in the pre-Harappan layers at Amri as an instance on encroachment of the Arabian Sea due to tectonic disturbances. The great flood of 2000 B.C. is attributed to rise of the coast when the raised river-mouths, getting heavily choked with silt, upset the normal flow, the dammed up water ultimately drowning the entire region[182]. This also is presumed to be the reason for the later great flood of 1900 B.C. Flood deposits found at Chanhu-daro in its last layer of Harappan occupation after which the site was abandoned by the Harappans is taken as another convincing proof of flood devastation. In Rao's estimation, the occasional floods, destroying the settlements now and then, gradually weakened the entire system. The continuous re-building naturally disrupted the normal activities and the last Great Flood in 1900 B.C. put the final seal on its age-long prosperity.

Its survival during the succeeding four centuries or so was much subdued in form and appearance with virtual absence of real urban development. The history of that period is of dislodged persons, seeking safer sites in naturally more secure surroundings. It was thus a period not of actual revival and reconstruction with renewed energy, out one of settlements at new sites in newer environments without any hope for a bright future. It is not that sloth and indolence had crept into the society out of easier and opulent life over centuries of peace and prosperity. The deterioration of civic standards is first observed after the great flood devastations of 2000 B.C. at Lothal and in the later levels of Mohenjo-daro and Chanhu-daro presumably after their destruction by flood in the same period. Prior to that, signs of decline or sluggishness are not reported from any sphere of urban activity although indiscriminate use of the land over centuries had already, in all probability, enfeebled the system enough to absorb any great shock. The last flood, destroying the industrial plants, dismantling the agricultural system and disrupting the communication network completely loosened the already weak grip of the society; the economic as well as the political system was shattered to pieces; the towns and cities stripped of their major activities, gradually shrank in size and went into utter neglect. The light of urban civilisation went out once for all sometime between 1500 and 1600 B.C.

There is general agreement between Rao and others on the point of gradual disintegration of this culture the pace of which having been quickened by natural calamities. But the difference of opinion arises on the ultimate disappearance of the towns and cities. Rao takes it as a consequential happening, while Wheeler, Childe and Piggott find the end accidental, violence drawing the final curtain. Rao's contention does not fully explain the reasons for the sudden abandonment of sites at Mohenjo-daro and Harappa when the two cities were still maintaining their precarious existence. It is evident that the deserters did not leave for a better situation; nor did they expect so. It was not unknown to them that migrations during the preceding periods had produced nothing comparable to their earlier successes in the Indus plains or elsewhere in the south and west. Thus, the mass exodus from these cities indicate a great urgency, a threat the people, possibly, did not dare to fight. Such a threat could come from another flood, but available evidences rule out that possibility, except in the case of Chanhu-daro where the Harappan episode closed earlier than at Mohenjo-daro or Harappa. In the absence of any imminent danger of this nature one is led to the conclusion that something more perilous and extraordinarily grave than natural calamities threatened the very existence of this dying culture. People at every earlier instance had fought nature's attack; this time they relented, as if, rather, gracefully, to the onslaught coming from an unknown quarter and bowed out on to the declivity of unpromising destiny.

REFERENCES

1. Piggott, Stuart, *Prehistoric India to 1000 B.C.*, Penguin Press, 1961, p. 22.
2. Meadow, R.H., *A Chronology for the Indo-Iranian Borderlands and Southern Baluchistan 4000-2000 B.C., in 'Radio-carbon and Indian Archaeology'*, Ed. by Agrawal, D.P. and Ghosh., A., Tata Institute of Fundamental Research, Bombay, 1973, pp. 190-191.
3. Bridget and Allchin, Raymond, *The Birth of Indian Civilization; India and Pakistan before 500 B.C.*, Penguin Books, 1968, p. 101 and Basham, A.L., *The Wonder that was India*, Orient Longmans, 1953, p. 11.
4. Bridget and Allchin, Raymond, *op.cit.*, p. 52.

5. *Ibid.*, p. 233.
6. *Ibid.*, p. 234.
7. *Ibid.*, p. 83.
8. Piggott, Stuart, *Prehistoric India to 1000 B.C.*, p. 51.
9. *Ibid.*, p. 52.
10. Meadow, R.H., *op.cit.*, pp. 190-191.
11. Sankalia, H.D., *Prehistory and Protohistory in India and Pakistan*, University of Bombay, 1962, p. 177.
12. Gordon, D.H., *The Pre-Historic Background of Indian Culture*, Bhulabhai Memorial Institute, Bombay, 1960, pp. 37-38.
13. Childe, Gordon, *What Happened in History*, Penguin Books, 1965, p. 83.
14. Piggott, Stuart, *Prehistoric India to 1000 B.C.*, p. 120.
15. *Ibid.*, p. 214.
16. Gordon, D.H., *The Pre-Historic Background of Indian Culture*, p. 42.
17. Piggott, Stuart, *Prehistoric India*, p. 122.
18. Bridget and Allchin, Raymond, *op.cit.*, p. 111.
19. Piggott, *op.cit.*, p. 214.
20. Bridget and Allchin, *op.cit.*, p. 104.
21. Piggott, *op.cit.*, p. 126.
22. Gordon, *op.cit.*, p. 38.
23. Meadow, *op.cit.*, p. 191.
24. Bridget and Allchin, *op.cit.*, p. 104.
25. *Ibid.*, p. 106.
26. *Ibid.*
27. Meadows, R.H., *op.cit.*, p. 191.
28. *Ibid.*, p. 201.
29. *Ibid.*
30. Gordon, *op.cit.*, p. 39.
31. *Ibid.*, p. 41.
32. *Ibid.*
33. Meadow, *op.cit.*, p. 200.
34. Piggott, *op.cit.*, p. 110.
35. Gordon, *op.cit.*, p. 41.
36. Piggott, *op.cit.*, p. 73.
37. *Ibid.*, p. 97.
38. *Ibid.*
39. *Ibid.*, p. 77.
40. *Ibid.*, p. 97.
41. Gordon., *op.cit.*, p. 39.
42. Piggott, *op.cit.*, p. 124.
43. *Ibid.*, p. 125.
44. *Ibid.*
45. *Ibid.*
46. *Ibid.*, p. 98.
47. *Ibid.*, p. 78.
48. *Ibid.*, p. 125.
49. Bridget, *op.cit.*, p. 106.
50. Thaper, B.K., *Synthesis of the Multiple Data as Obtained from Kalibangan, in 'Radio Carbon and Indian Archaeology'*, Ed. by D.P. Agrawal and Ghosh, A., p. 265.
51. Rao, S.R., *Lothal and the Indus Civilization*, Asia Publishing House, London,

1972, p. 8.

52. McCrindle, J.W., *The Invasion of India by Alexander the Great etc.*, Today and Tomorrow's Printers and Publishers, New Delhi (New Edition), pp. 202-203.
53. *Statesman*, October 9, 1976 (Calcutta Edition).
54. Meadow, *op.cit.*, p. 193.
55. Bridget, *op.cit.*, p. 117.
56. *Ibid.*
57. Piggott, *op.cit.*, p. 77.
58. *Ibid.*, p. 79.
59. *Ibid.*, p. 77.
60. Bridget, *op.cit.*, p. 123.
61. Wheeler, Mortimer, *Civilizations of the Indus Valley and Beyond*, Thames and Hudson, London, 1966, p. 21.
62. Rao, S.R., *op.cit.*, p. 25.
63. Bridget, *op.cit.*, p. 118.
64. Wheeler, Mortimer, *Early India and Pakistan to Ashoka*, Thames and Hudson, London, 1968, p. 106.
65. Rao, S.R., *op.cit.*, p. 25.
66. *Ibid.*, 193.
67. Wheeler, Mortimer, *The Indus Civilization*, etc., Third Edition, Cambridge University Press, 1968, p. 20.
68. Rao, S.R. *op.cit.*, p. 168.
69. Thaper, B.K., *op.cit.*, p. 269.
70. Bridget, *op.cit.*, p. 120.
71. Rao, S.R., *op.cit.*, p. 15.
72. Thaper, *op.cit.*, p. 267.
73. Bridget, *op.cit.*, p. 122.
74. Bhan, Suraj. *The Sequence and Spread of Prehistoric Cultures in the Upper Sarasvati Basin, in 'Radio Carbon and Indian Archaeology'*, pp. 252-257.
75. Piggott, *op.cit.*, p. 69.
76. Sankalia, *op.cit.*, p. 180.
77. Rao, *op.cit.*, p. 172.
78. Wheeler, Mortimer, *The Indus Civilization* etc., p. 24.
79. Dates, G.F., *Pre and Protohistoric Researches in Pakistan and Afghanistan,* in *'Radio Carbon and Indian Archaeology'*, p. 120.
80. Rao, *op.cit.*, p. 207.
81. Wheeler, Mortimer, *Civilizations of the Indus Valley and Beyond*, p. 72.
82. Wheeler, Mortimer *op.cit*, p. 70.
83. Mackay, Ernest, *Early Indus Civilization*, (Revised and Enlarged by Dorothy Mackay), Indological Book Corporation, Delhi, 1976, p. 9.
84. Gordon, *op.cit.*, p. 63.
85. Bridget, *op.cit.*, p. 129 and Piggott, p. 158.
86. Wheeler, *Civilizations of the Indus Valley and Beyond*, p. 94.
87. Wheeler, *The Indus Civilizations etc.*, Table.
88. Clarke, Grahame, *World Prehistory : A New Outline*, Cambridge University Press, 1969, p. 210; and, Mookerjee Radhakumud, *Glimpses of Ancient India*, Bharatiya Vidya Bhavan, 1961, p.15.
89. Rao, *op.cit.*, p. 163.
90. *Ibid.*, p. 55.
91. *Ibid.*, p. 6.

92. *Ibid.*, pp. 25 and 162.
93. *Ibid.*, p. 166.
94. Gordon, *op.cit.*, p. 63.
95. Wheeler, *Civilizations of the Indus Valley etc.*, p. 14.
96. Bridget, *op.cit.*, p. 131.
97. Mackay, *op.cit.*, p. 18.
98. *Ibid.*, p. 19.
99. Wheeler, *Civilizations of the Indus Valley, etc.*, p. 24.
100. Mackay, *op.cit.*, p. 101:
101. *Ibid.*, p.129.
102. Rao, *op.cit.*, p. 90.
103. Mackay, *op.cit.*, 101.
104. Rao, *op.cit.*, p. 79.
105. *Ibid.*, p. 50.
106. *Ibid.*, p. 55.
107. *Ibid.*
108. *Ibid.*, p. 60.
109. *Ibid.*, p. 109.
110. Bridget, *op.cit.*, p. 143.
111. Rao, *op.cit.*, p. 24.
112. Gordon, *op.cit.*, p. 75.
113. Bridget, *op.cit.*, p. 131.
114. Rao, *op.cit.*; p. 26.
115. Rao, *op.cit.*, p.115.
116. Piggott, *op.cit.*, p. 175.
117. Rao, *op.cit.*, p. 115.
118. Piggott, *op.cit.*, p. 175.
119. Rao, *op.cit.*, p. 116.
120. *Ibid.*, p. 115.
121. Piggott,. *op.cit.*, p. 174.
122. Gordon, *op.cit.*, p. 52.
123. Rao, *op.cit.*, p. 162.
124. *Ibid.*, p. 26.
125. *Ibid.*
126. Gordon, *op.cit.*, p. 73.
127. Piggott, *op.cit.*, p. 208.
128. *Ibid.*, p. 210.
129. Mackay, *op.cit.*, p. 148.
130. *Ibid.*
131. Rao, *op.cit.*, p. 117.
132. *Ibid.*, p. 118.
133. *Ibid.*, p. 117.
134. Mackay, *op.cit.*, p. 150.
135. Rao, *op.cit.*, p.152.
136. Kosambi, D.D., *The Culture and Civilisation of Ancient India in Historical Outline*, Routledge and Kegan Paul, London, 1965, p. 63.
137. Gordon, *op.cit.*, p. 61.
138. Piggott, *op.cit.*, p. 172.
139. Hawkes, Jacquetta and Woolley Leonard, *History of Mankind : Cultural and Scientific Development*, Vol. I, George Allen and Unwin, London, 1963, p. 706.
140. Hawkes, Jacquetta and Woolley Leonard, *op.cit.*, p., 539.

141. *Ibid.*, p. 422.
142. Childe, *op.cit.*, p. 181.
143. Piggott, *op.cit.*, p. 192.
144. Rao, *op.cit.*, p. 127.
145. Wheeler, *Civilizations of the Indus Valley, etc.*, p. 37.
146. Piggott, *op.cit.*, p. 184.
147. Wheeler, *The Indus Civilization, etc.*, p. 83.
148. Wheeler, *Civilization of the Indus Valley, etc.*, p. 83, and Piggott, p. 181.
149. Wheeler, *The Indus Civilization, etc.*, p. 109, and Bridget, *op.cit.*, p. 138.
150. Kosambi, *op.cit.*, p. 59.
151. Bridget, *op.cit.*, p. 133.
152. Piggott, *op.cit.*, p. 200.
153. Piggott, pp. 186-187, and Wheeler, *The Indus Civilization, etc.*, pp. 86-90.
154. Kosambi, *op.cit.*, p. 59.
155. Hawkes & Woolley, *op.cit.* pp. 416, 418-419.
156. Kosambi, *op.cit.*, pp. 61-62.
157. Piggott, *op.cit.*, p. 208.
158. Bridget, *op.cit.*, p. 142.
159. Kosambi, *op.cit.*, p. 65.
160. Mishra, D.P., *Studies in the Proto-History of India*, Orient Longmans, 1971, p. 66.
161. Mishra, *op.cit.*, p. 70.
162. Mackay, *op.cit.* p. 76.
163. Piggott, *op.cit.* pp. 153-154.
164. Mishra, *op.cit.*, p. 79.
165. *Ibid.*, pp. 79-81.
166. Mackay, *op.cit.*, p. 153.
167. Rao, *op.cit.*, p. 157.
168. Hawkes and Woolley, *op.cit.*, p. 396.
169. Rao, *op.cit.*, p. 180.
170. *Ibid.*, p. 177.
171. Wheeler, *The Indus Civilization, etc.*, p. 129.
172. Childe, *op.cit.*, p. 136.
173. Wheeler, *The Indus Civilization, etc.*, pp. 131-133.
174. Hawkes & Woolley, *op.cit.*, p. 397.
175. Gordon, *op.cit.*, p. 77.
176. Bridget, *op.cit.*, p. 145.
177. Piggott, *op.cit.*, p. 249.
178. *Ibid.*, p. 239.
179. Wheeler, *Civilizations of the Indus Valley and Beyond*, p. 78.
180. Mishra, *op.cit.*, p. 104.
181. *Ibid.*, p. 105.
182. Rao, *op.cit.*, pp. 179-180.

2

The Period of Transition

The wave of Aryan invasion, starting as early as 2000 B.C.[1], or before 1500 B.C., as suggested by Piggott[2], did not abate till 1300 B. C.[3] With the light of civilisation extinguished, the whole of Sind and Punjab plunged into complete darkness and nothing about the cultural evolution is known for certain till the Aryans are firmly established, heralding a new civilisation. At Harappa the remains left by successive occupation prove that the post-Harappan culture is much poorer in quality — termed as squatter-culture by Wheeler[4]—nothing comparable with the past grandeur of this old capital. The settlements in the south—from Kathiawar to Narmada Valley—were not, however, directly hit by the mass exodus. Most of them had come into existence after the Great Floods of 2000 B.C. and 1900 B.C. as creations of the people pressed out of the large cities of Mohenjo-daro and Lothal and from the settlements in their adjoining regions damaged by the floods. Almost all of them were village settlements and none of them ever became a town of any significance. But the most interesting fact presented by many of these settlements is the gradual change of culture—the Harappan phase being succeeded by a post-Harappan phase—without any dramatic break in between[5]. This is found at Rangpur, Rojdi, Somnath, Megham, Telod, Bhagatrav and also in the city of Lothal. The cases of such cultural fusion, where debased Harappan strains ultimately got lost in the succeeding indigenous culture, are designated as the 'Lustrous Red Ware Culture.'

However explained, the question on the complete disappearance of urban culture is not fully answered. It is true that even before the twin capitals had presumably fallen to the attacks of the invaders, signs of general deterioration in all the spheres of life had become very much pronounced. The cities were far from welcome sites and the inhabitants suffered from a high degree of inertia, palpably demonstrated by their inaction in the face of inevitable doom. They took to mass flight. It is expected that the dislodged people, with a rich urban-heritage, would build towns and cities again in different localities where they came to settle and where the arms of the invaders could not directly reach. But, strangely enough, this did not happen; on the contrary, urbanisation went into total eclipse over the vast territories of the empire and when it reappeared after a pretty long gap, the leadership came from a different people, the Aryans.

Perhaps, the answer to this apparently puzzling question may be found from a critical analysis of the whole situation. The Indus people did no longer remain masters of their own once the twin capitals were lost for good. Deprived of the political and economic backing of the capitals, they turned into fugitives without leadership and control; the drive, the indomitable courage and the genius that led to the emergence of the first fully-fledged urban culture of India were completely lacking in those rootless people representing the surviving Harappans. Even at such provincial urban centres as Lothal, Rangpur, etc., Harappan culture did not continue for more than a generation or two after the fall of Mohenjo-daro and Harappa[6]. The eastward push gradually brought them more and more into uninviting environments, especially in the Ganga-Jamuna plains where densely forested lands made colonization a difficult task. This, coupled with the hostility of the indigenous people[7], never allowed the stragglers to settle permanently in any place. The two oppressive factors very likely kept them on a constant move—in divided bands rather than in large groups—and thus giving them no scope for concerted action in building large, permanent settlements. The strikingly short span of occupation at the sites so far dug up in the region stretching from the Upper Sutlej plains to the Ganga-Jamuna plains, the rural character as well as the small size of the settlements, and the absence of cultural contacts between them from their isolated positions, bear indisputable testimony to the melting stage of this culture. The presence of new elements in the artifacts manufactured by them followed by the disappearance of some of the characteristic Harappan objects strongly suggest the termination of the over-powering influence which slowly giving way to sub-graded cultures, ultimately lost its identity. It is not difficult to imagine that the village settlements, established by the Harappans during this period, could not hold back all the artisans, smiths or craftsmen who sought more profitable situations. Many of them, quite possibly, strayed away carrying their trade to distant places instances of which are available from Central and South India. The constant mingling with the indigenous population and the gradual depopulation of the late settlements removed the last traces of their existence, and by 1500 B.C. the Harappans had become completely merged with the rest of the Indian population.

What is really curious to note is that—such a high-grade civilisation utterly failed to transmit the rich ideas concerning planning, architecture, civic amenity services or even sculpture to their successors. The only field reflecting the continuity of this culture to a little degree is religion. The reasons are, perhaps, too obvious to be ignored. Since the fall of the Indus cities the overall situation of the country was not at all favourable for a long time for the emergence of urban culture. Apart from being 'city-destroyers' — a term happily and frequently used by the Aryans for themselves in the texts of Rigveda, they were no lovers of urban life of which they had no practical experience when they came to India. It is to be noted that, the word '*nagara*' (city) does not occur in the early hymns of Rigveda nor there is any mention of individual cities as is found in the later texts[8]. So far as it can be gathered, the Aryans were copper- , or, bronze-using people with stock-raising and farming as their principal occupation. Their houses were made of either timber or thatch, and they used horse-drawn chariots for sport as well as for war, while wagons were drawn by oxen[9]. But they were not indifferent to trade and industry. Tanning, weaving, metalwork and pottery were the most important branches of their industries. Among the chief articles of trade were clothes, coverlets and skins which used to be bartered against cow or necklets of gold. The settlements established by them in the earlier period were but villages, a number of them "being generally federated for purposes of mutual protection under the rule of a 'raja' or King"[10]. It can therefore be assumed that, at least for some centuries the Aryans did not build towns or cities as that ran contrary to the way of life they were used to. As conquerors they established new settlements—essentially villages—following a rigid planning principle. Unlike the Harappan towns and cities, these were more democratic in their layout. The typical form of such villages was a "rectangular enclosure with four sides facing four quarters, and divided into four wards by the two main streets which crossed each other in the centre and were terminated at each end by the four principal gates"[11]. A broad belt of land surrounding the villages used to be the communal property of villages for cultivation or for grazing and it was the duty of the Village Council—a body elected every year—to see to the security of that right. The choice of an area for establishing a village was a careful one, taking consideration of soil and availability of water so that cultivation and animal rearing—the two principal occupations—went on undisturbed.

Naturally, urban-economy did not fit in well with the mode of life led by those wandering people. Not that it was entirely beyond their comprehension, but quite for some time the internal conflicts among the various groups of the contending Aryans on the one hand, and their struggles with the non-Aryans on the other[12] gave them little respite for any sustained creative action. In the same context it is to be remembered that the Aryan invasion of India was not a single concerted action; it went on for centuries, involving many tribes of whom some were not Aryans at all. This tribal warfare, in fact, compelled the Aryans ultimately to move eastward from the area of their earlier occupation which lay mostly in Sind and in Western Punjab.

The area eventually occupied by the early Rigvedic people can be identified from the names of the rivers, the most important among them being Kubha (Kabul), the Suvastu (Swat), the Krumu (Kurram), the Gomati (Gumal), the Sindhu (Indus), the Sushoma (Sohan), the Vitasta (Jhelum), the Asikui (Chenab), the Marudvridha (Maruwardhan), the Parushni (Ravi), the Vipas (Beas), the Sutudru (Sutlej), the Saraswati, the Drishadvati (the Rakshi or Chantang), the Jamuna, the Ganga and the Saraju. It can thus be derived that the country stretching from Afghanistan to the Upper Ganga Valley was in their occupation. The major part of this area was called by them as 'Sapta Saindhava' or the Land of the Seven Rivers, though the exact identification of the principal seven rivers is not clearly made anywhere in Rigveda[13]. It does not, however, mean that the entire area was under the active control of the Aryans, wherein some other non-Aryan clans had also established their claims[14]. Within the vast area, the actual region of

Aryan concentration was the 'Firm Middle Country', mentioned by them as the 'Dhruva Madhyama Disa' comprising the land lying between the Saraswati River and the Ganga Doab, and occupied by the most distinguished among the tribes, namely the Kurus and the Panchalas. The tongue of the land between the Saraswati and the Drishadvati—known as the Kurukshetra—along with the districts of Delhi and Meerut were under the control of the Kurus while the districts of Bareilly, Badaun and Farrukkabad, along with some adjoining tracts formed the domain of the Panchalas[15].

The colonization, or better to call it the land-grab policy of the Aryans, vastly extending their domain gradually made village-federations which, in the long run, became quite inefficient in keeping effective control over their possessions. This, supplemented further by community-feuds, resulted in the rise of kingdoms, defining the territorial limits of different groups or dynasties. Such consolidation of the Aryan tribal system into large or small kingdoms made the most important contribution to the urban history of India as it was only then that some of the village settlements, serving the purpose of royal capitals of kingdoms, ultimately developed into towns and cities.

In many ways this may be called the real beginning of urbanistion in the country for two reasons : first, from this period onwards there had been no break in the history of urban development though, at times, the progress had been extremely tardy or faltering; second, quite a number of towns and cities born at this time, in spite of many vicissitudes, have maintained their existence down to this day which, as it will be found time and again, is also equally true about many of the later ones born at different periods of the succeeding centuries. The fact of this continuity—the urban momentum—is of super significance in the context of later urban development in the country.

The Fresh Beginning of Urbanisation

Indus Civilisation, ending in around 1500 B.C. or thereabout, left a vacuum of about five centuries during which urbanisation appears to have completely halted in the entire country. According to available archaeological evidences, a fresh beginning did not take place till the opening centuries of the first millennium B.C., the initiative this time having come from the Aryans.

This generally accepted view, however, finds an indirect challenge offered by the evidences uncovered by the most recent excavations at Bhagwanpura. The site occurs on the bank of the dried-up course of River Saraswati, situated some 25 miles from Kurukshetra, produces unmistakable evidences of an important settlement which with a 13-room building complex, might have served as a capital, of the Kuru Dynasty. Equally exciting is the presence of Late Harappan pottery—red ware in the lowest levels of occupation, overlain by painted Grey wares of the, Aryans occupying the upper one-third of the occupation levels in combination with red wares suggest co-existence of these two different cultures. According to the propounder of this theory, S.B. Roy, the Kuru king, after whom Kurukshetra is named, established the Kuru Dynasty in about 1800 B.C. and the Mahabharata War and the composition of the great epic took place in 1400 B.C.[16] Both Basham and Kosambi place the date of the war at the beginning of the 9th century B.C.[17]

The first mention of the Aryan cities is found in the two great epics of the Mahabharata and the Ramayana. By this time the Aryans had pressed further eastward, establishing the kingdoms of Kosala and Kasi, the former situated to the west of the Ganga-Jamuna Doab, and the latter comprising the region of present Varanashi. The cities that grew here as the capitals of different kingdoms were as follows : Hastinapura, the capital of the Kauruva Kingdom of the Puru-Kuru branches of the tribe; Indraprastha, established at the site of the present Old Fort of Delhi (Purana Quila), was the capital of the Pandavas[18]; Ahichhatra, near modern Ramnagar in Uttar Pradesh, was the capital of North Panchala Kingdom which the Kurus wrested from the King of Panchala; Mathura and Kanyakubja or present Kanauj were the twin capitals of the Kingdom of the Panchalas; Ajodhya, situated on the bank of river Saraju near present Fyzabad, was the capital of the Kosala Kingdom; Kasi was the capital of the kingdom of its namesake; Kausambi, on river Jamuna, became the capital of the Puru-Kuru Kingdom when they were driven out of Hastinapura by a severe flood[19].

Apart from the literary evidence provided by Mahabharata and Ramayana, the most important evidence identifying the Aryan cities, mentioned above, is the wheel-made pottery—painted Grey wares—that marked the beginning of the earliest mature Aryan Civilisation of the Ganga Plains[20]. However, besides identification it is also necessary to make an appraisal of the urban development that took place under the leadership of the Aryans which may throw some light on the evolving pattern emerging slowly in the early part of the first millennium B.C.

At Hastinapura the excavations have revealed five main phases of occupation of which Period II shows the signs of a developed township. This period, beginning as early as 1000 or 800 B.C. and continuing upto 500 B.C., is associated with distinctive Grey painted pottery, mud or mud-brick walls, copper objects, an antimony rod, terracotta figurines, lumps of iron ore and, most important of all, two glass bangles in its upper layer, the last one providing the earliest evidence of that in India. At the end of this period a devastating flood occurred after which occupation ceased for a while. With the renewal of the settlement during Period III — between 500 and 200 B.C. — the pottery changed into Northern Black Polished Ware and the use of baked bricks started which went to the construction of buildings and drains. Soak-pits of superimposed jars with perforated bases and ring-wells made of burnt clay also made their appearance in 500 B.C., similar types of which are found in some of the towns even today. For the first time iron came into use for the production of both weapons and tools, but copper was still in use. Over and above this the introduction of silver and copper money at this time indicates the existence of a developed trade. In around 200 B.C. Period III ended in a devastating fire following which the Northern Black Pottery Ware also ceased to exist. The succeeding Period IV, characterised by Red ware pottery, continued uninterrupted down to the 3rd century B.C.[21]

Ahichhatra, the renowned capital of the North Panchala Kingdom, was rebuilt eight or nine times and continued its existence till 1100 A.D. On each occasion of rebuilding the plan changed, the alignment of the buildings differing from that of the earlier phase. However, the excavations being far from complete do not provide much information on the different phases of construction. No structural remains could be traced for the earliest period of occupation. The most important feature is the remains of an earthen rampart, 3½ miles in circuit, built on two successive periods and crowned by a baked-brick wall, dating back to 500 B.C. or even earlier. Painted Grey pottery was found both in and below the first phase of its construction and this is succeeded by Northern Black polished pottery belonging to some time between 500 and 200 B.C. when coins came into use[22].

The site of Kausambi, situated on river Jamuna, 28 miles south-east of Allahabad, reveals the remains of one of the great cities of ancient India, with twenty structural phases of occupation broadly grouped into four periods. Literary and archaeological evidences trace its antiquity to about 1200 B.C.[23] and the first period of occupation continued till the end of the 9th century B. C. The most imposing remains of the earlier period are the ramparts—about 4 miles in circuit and over 40 ft. in height—consisting of mud bank faced externally with a baked-brick wall. In the opinion of Puri, the earthen rampart was built in the earliest period and lasted till the end of the 9th century B.C.[24] after which it was supplemented by another in the second period with such provisions as guard rooms, bastions and stone paved corbelled drain. Wheeler, however, puts the construction of the earliest defences to some time earlier than 500 B.C.[25] Remains of well-built brick houses have been traced within the defences. An uninscribed cast copper coin— the earliest to be found anywhere in the world—derived from Kausambi has been dated by Sharma to 945 B.C.[26] and in his estimation, full-fledged urban development had firmly become established in the Ganga-Jamuna Valley by 1000 B.C. But Sinha contradicts the view of taking the antiquity of Kausambi to a date much earlier than 600 B.C.[27] The date for the last structural phase at Kausambi has been fixed at 515 A.D.[28] though the city continued its life well into the middle of 1100 A.D.

Recent excavations have further revealed the antiquity of some of the other cities, such as Kasi, part of which was built before 500 B.C., and that of Vaisali, in the Muzaffarpur district of Bihar, built in 600 B.C. or even earlier[29]. Similarly, Indraprastha, the first Delhi, built by the Pandavas as their capital after firing the forest, belong to the early part of the first millennium B. C. In the case of Mathura and Kanyakubja — the twin capitals of the Panchala Kingdom—supportive archaeological evidences are yet lacking. But their constant references in Mahabharata as well as their development into two of the most important Metropolises of ancient India immediately afterwards make their early origin almost an undisputed fact.

All these cities provide definite instances of an urban civilisation which, making its beginning in about 1000 B.C. or some time earlier, became firmly established within the following few centuries and extended its influence eastward upto the middle-Ganga basin. Unlike the Harappan Civilisation, developed along the north-south axis of the Indus river, the Aryan Civilisation followed the east-west axis of the river Ganga and this, maintaining its supremacy down to the modern time, proved to be one of the most important turning points in the urban history of India. Besides, it is highly interesting to note that the whole of Sind and Punjab, where the Aryans settled first, were completely ignored by them when they were set on building cities. This was, perhaps, largely due to the disturbed condition that prevailed there during the early part of their stay in the region, having a difficult time in fighting among themselves as well as in facing stiff resistance from the indigenous tribes called by the Aryans as 'Dasa' or 'Dasyu', and also from the new invaders who came from time to time from the West. In fact from the time-of-the Mahabharata War, the centre of Aryan Culture and political power had shifted permanently to the Ganga-Jamuna Doab from where they gradually pressed eastward following the course of the Great River Ganga. By this time quite evidently the first home, lying west of the Indo-Genetic Divide was practically forgotten. But this forgetfulness appears to be more calculated than a result of long dissociation. The Indo-Gangetic Divide, commanding a higher elevation from the adjoining plains on both east and west, had definitely a thick forest cover in those days; east of that the physical conditions were equally uninviting as the gradually increasing rainfall obviously kept the whole of the Ganga Plain densely forested. The Aryan colonizers had to clear these forests during their eastward migration. The main idea that guided this migration was the security of the uninhabited lands as well as the fertility of the soils since the later Vedic people depended more and more on agriculture than stock raising. The quest for this new land was therefore politically motivated. The land lying at increasing distance from the disturbed areas of Sind and Punjab offered the real breathing ground. The hard reality of this compelling situation can further be gauged from the fact that the land, offering the first home to these invaders, is scarcely mentioned in the later Vedic literature and that too also with much abhorrence, calling it as an 'impure land'[30]. Once settled in a comparatively peaceful surrounding, they could divert all their energy to building the capital—as a first step towards the effective consolidation of their power which eventually led to the emergence of the first set of Aryan cities in India.

Doubts might arise about the capability of the Aryans as city-builders although one cannot refute the fact that even the earliest cities built by them were in no way imitations of the Harappan examples.

Though the Aryans, probably, had not built any city during the preceding centuries of the first millennium B.C., it does not mean that they were less equipped for that. True, their original mode of life was never urban and in the early period of their settlement in India they did not feel the urge for that. But, apart from being agriculturists and stock-breeders, they were well-advanced in industrial and commercial activities using wheeled transport for movement which made them sufficiently equipped as city-builders when necessity arose. There is, however, no supporting evidence for adopting a view that they were experienced in the art of city-building. Yet it cannot be said that they were completely ignorant of the city-culture and especially the importance of cities in both the political and the economic, life of the communities. It is perhaps too much to say that "they had never known a city"[31]. Hailing from the region-stretching from South Russia to Turkestan or according to another author, from the region extending between the Rhine and the Central and Southern Russia[32] they were well acquainted with the urban way of life which lay across their path during their movements through Western Asia. This earlier acquaintance, often through direct encounters, with urban civilisations of the twin-river valleys of the Tigris and the Euphrates was not lost altogether through the centuries of their stormy passage into India. The impression went deeper with time as experience taught them both in the twin-river valleys and in the Indus Valley that cities were the real seats of power, protecting the authority as well as the life of the society against the marauding raids of outsiders. That no attempt at city-building was made by them in the earlier centuries of their settlement in India was because the extremely disturbed condition prevailing in the land neither allowed them any respite needed for such constructive action, nor did the area appeared safe enough for making such painstaking endeavours.

What made them successful in the attempt of heralding the second urban revolution of India is directly related to their unequalled mobility made possible by a movable food-supply in cattle, the horse-chariot for war and the ox-cart for heavy transport, making migrations eastward into the Ganga Valley easier than in the case of other warring tribes inhabiting the lands of Sind and Punjab. That they were well-equipped as well as competent for ushering in a new age in the history of urban development is sufficiently proved by the works of the bronze-smiths and the carpenters who were technically superior to their Harappan counterparts[33]. The use of iron, introduced from the beginning of the first millennium B.C.[34] opened up new horizons of construction and progress as iron tools, gradually replacing copper-tools, were far more suitable for clearing the forested areas of the Ganga Valley. Latest evidences conclusively prove that the Aryans brought iron technology to India, which reached its frontiers in about 1000 B.C. and its introduction in the country was complete by 800 B.C.[35] According to Kosambi[36], the early Aryan settlements developed close to the Himalayan foothills extending into southern Nepal in a narrow band from where, later on, they swang southward, reaching the banks of the River Ganga which, until then, were thickly forested. This later development was intimately associated with the introduction of iron axes and heavy ploughs made of iron. Besides, the practice of navigation, referring to sailing ships with hundred oars[37] being "indubitable testimony to a very early intercourse between Vedic India and distant lands beyond the seas"[38] was definitely the product of a society well-advanced in both industry and commerce for which an urban background seems to be the essential prerequisite.

Opinions, however, differ on the origin of the first Aryan cities, which is partly attributed to the efforts of a mercantile class referred to in Rigveda as the 'Panis', and also called '*Dasas*'(slaves) or '*Dasyus*'(robbers) by the same source. They were non-Aryans and formed a class of wealthy traders or craftsmen with a rich traditional background. It is presumed that they represented the late Harappans or the aboriginal tribes of India, ultimately subjugated by the Aryan victors. For some time their craftsmanship went unutilised, but in course of time the various crafts revived again under Aryan leadership, contributing directly to the rise of markets and cities. Rai, advocating this view, draws further instances from Mahabharata to show that even in architecture the Aryans are largely indebted to the aboriginals for their unequal excellence as in crafts and industries[39]. He is strongly of the opinion that, Aryan cities were never a creation of the Aryans alone; the Late Harappans as well as the aborigines of India had taken a significant role in bringing them into existence.

The apparent truth behind the origin of Aryan cities as the product of a joint endeavour cannot be denied. But Rai views it from a wrong angle. He admits that it was the employed, or, rather, the forced labour who gave rise to different arts and crafts of the society. It is nowhere mentioned that the *Dasas* or slaves did enjoy equal rights of the citizens. Hence, the revival of the crafts and industries was possible at the behest of the conquerors who, by that time, had permanently settled down to consolidate their position. It is nothing surprising that they will utilise all the resources—land as well as labour—for improving the conditions of life. Too much emphasis need not be laid on the pastoral economy of the Aryans. They were equally agriculturists as much as they were animal herders; at the same time long association with industrial pursuits and trading activities made them fully aware of the vital importance of them in the society. It is quite unlikely that the vanquished people had offered their services, or made a living by selling their products to the ruling community; on the contrary, the services were compelled out of them as forced labour. In that case, the idea of utilising their services for the production of useful and marketable products sprang from the minds of the employers, the Aryans. Thus, if the idea is not a borrowed one, we cannot say that the Aryans lacked the imagination for building cities and markets. They appear to have been more capable in that respect then the Late Harappans or the aboriginal Indians. This becomes more evident from the absence of any urban development that may be claimed by either the Late Harappans or the aboriginal people of India as their own creation. No town or city has so far been reported as founded by either of them after the fall of the Indus Civilisation. The Late Harappans were still there when the Aryans were infiltrating into the Punjab Plains, but the settlements established by the former nowhere had the pretensions of an urban settlement even before 1500 B.C. All of them were nothing more than villages representing an impoverished culture, completely depleted of its urban characteristics. The poverty had gone far, the people had become more despirited and disillusioned in the following two to three centuries—by the time when the Aryans had set about building their own cities. The long tradition of urban life could not be more than a misty past to them heard as oft-repeated stories told by the older generations. It is, therefore, very difficult to imagine that the Late Harappans did really posses that faculty to guide or to contribute to the urban development during the Aryan period. In this context, one may refer to the absence of urban development in the whole of Peninsular India which did not begin till the arrival of the Aryans on the scene in about 500 B.C. But here the Harappan influence had penetrated as early as 1800 B.C., and the Neolithic communities adopted many of the Harappan traits in the manufacture of implements, including the use of copper. The influx of Late Harappan refugees, composed mainly of skilled craftsmen, is evidenced by many of the South Indian sites, but here too they failed to introduce the urban way of life. Similarly, the aboriginal peoples of India do not show any instance of their resourcefulness in making towns or cities. Nothing has yet come to light indicating a high cultural level of the indigenous population.

Taking all these into account, it becomes needless to stress on the role of the non-Aryans in building Aryan cities in which the former could have no interest whatsoever. The Aryans, firmly established in the country and building Kingdoms, needed more and more land to be cleared of forests, agriculture to be extended, settlements to be enlarged, house to be constructed and roads to be laid. The introduction of iron replacing copper for making axes, saws and agricultural implements made felling of trees, sawing of wood, tilling of soil and harvesting of crops greatly easier and speedier than before. The virgin soil turned out greater returns and settlements proliferated at a much more rapid scale than even before. Agricultural prosperity offered the necessary stimulus for industrial activities which naturally became concentrated in the larger settlements and such places acting as market centres, with perhaps individual branches of specialisation, made an important position among all the other settlements and gradually developed into towns and cities. The seats of the rulers enjoyed a priority over the other settlements in attracting those functions giving urban-status. Thus, the capital cities of the Aryan Kingdoms emerged one after another followed by transformation of some villages into market centres or trading posts. All these achievements were not possible if, on the one hand, the Aryans had no mind at building cities, and, on the other, they had to depend on the experience and genius of the people whom they had subdued. Cities, built on the plan originally followed in making their villages in India, were different in every other respect—ranging from building material to the internal spatial arrangement of the cities—which made them truly Aryan in character. The economic prosperity heralding urban development was a result of the advanced knowledge, at least in the use of iron, which placed the Aryans much ahead of the non-Aryans, whom not only they employed as slaves but taught the secrets of iron technology.

As has been mentioned above, the process of urban development at the initial stage was however simple enough. Each of the earliest cities mentioned above had its origin as the seat of capital and those, course of time, became also the principal industrial and trading entries.[40] The patronage of the royal court used to be the dominant factor in attracting and thus localising the craftsmen and the business communities to and at the Capital City as a result of which cities independent of capital function did not develop as long as the city building remained the sole objective of protecting the rights and the powers of the king. The Aryans built walled cities; the imposing ramparts, already traced in the ruins of Ahichhatra, Kausambi and Hastinapura, bear witness to the adoption of elaborate defensive measures. In their planning also the cities followed the same principles in which the original Aryan village units were grouped round the royal palace and the citadel[41].

In many aspects though, the Aryan cities differed greatly from their predecessor Harappan cities, the physical layout lacking meticulous planning, the city centring round the royal palace and developed into a compact whole instead of having distinctive parts of the Citadel and the Lower Town. The width of the streets of different orders were never maintained as scrupulously as in the Harrapan cities; public amenity services, coupled with municipal vigilance, were completely lacking in them. Neither had they the State Granary nor the Stately Hall of Assembly. Over and above this, the absence of seals, sculptures, jewellery, beads as well as any type of cosmetic objects—such as faience, strongly suggests that it was a far less opulent society much lower in culture than what Indus Valley possessed.

Perhaps, one needs to be cautioned before making such a sweeping conclusion about the economic and cultural status of the Ganga Civilisation. But it does not escape the notice that, while the Harappans had been using baked-brick for a long period, which, besides being a sign of material progress, became an absolute necessity in a rainy climate and an environment constantly threatened by floods—the Aryans started with mud-brick and quite a few centuries elapsed before they turned to baked-brick even though their cities were located in a rainier climate. The copper and iron axes being in use and the forests being abundant and near at hand offered greater scope than the Harappan environment for firing the bricks. The only possible explanation may be that the art of making fired bricks was not known to the Aryans in the beginning, and the compelling circumstances forced them to learn that eventually. Again, there is no way of knowing the architectural style of buildings as no remains conveying a concrete idea could be traced through excavations. It is true that the comparatively drier climate of the Indus Valley had been greatly helpful in preserving much of the relics therein, while a moister climate and the capricious courses of the rivers in the Ganga Valley were equally responsible for obliterating the signs of urban development made by the Aryans. Yet, the idea of such a complete obliteration appears to be an undue exaggeration in view of the fact that where massive bastions remained almost uninterrupted at places—as at Kausambi, for instance—it can be expected that at least the structural outlines of the buildings made of solid and lasting material like fired bricks, if at all built, would have survived the violence of natural forces. The absence suggests that either the large buildings were not made of fired-brick, or they were never built. Both of these premises seem to be reasonable enough considered against what is gathered about the mode of life of the Aryans as well as about the construction of some of the most important cities built at even a much later date. The original Aryan buildings were made of wood, rectangular in size with a thatched roof divided into more that one compartment[42]. This old tradition of using wood as the principal building material seems to have had been carried down to the days of city-building, at least in the earlier period of construction. Instances are provided by both Hastinapura and Pataliputra, the latter as the capital of Magadha Kingdom, built at a much later date[43]. Presumably, the habit was not given up by the Aryans while building the first cities in a region rich in forests. Such structures were definitely flimsy to withstand either the moist climate or the fury of the floods, thus leaving no trace whatsoever for the future inquisitors. On the other hand, the physical layout of the excavated ruins do not suggest that there were too many large buildings in contrast to Mohenjo-daro where even in the Lower Town there were palatial buildings.

What can be gleaned from the material evidences traced so far in the ruins at the sites of these forgotten cities give a definite impression about their poverty in the cultural standard and the material achievements in sharp contrast to the dazzling examples of the Harappan cities. In the same context, however, it has to be admitted that archaeological excavations being far from complete make a thorough probe into the actual life of the cities impossible. This leads us to the next most pertinent question, that is, how many cities there were in the first half of the first millennium B.C.? In fact, it is not possible to know how many cities and towns had been lost permanently under the depositions of the innumerable rivers since that time. But it would be rather wrong to conclude that there were only two large cities as late as the seventh century B.C.[44] Even if the date of the Mahabharata War is taken as late as 900 B.C., the existence of at least those cities, namely Indraprashta, Hastinapura, Ahichhatra, Mathura, Kanyakubja, Kausambi, Kasi and Ajodhya cannot be doubted. Similarly, it is yet too early to say that only two cities were really large and the others were mere towns. Pre-industrial cities were never very large owing to the limitations put by the availability of food and a high death rate. In the absence of any clear idea about the total population of these cities, the only consideration of largeness may be based upon the areal size of the cities and in that respect as well the vastly incomplete data do not provide a definite idea. But, from what little we know, it can be established without any prejudice that at least two of these earliest Aryan cities—Ahichhatra, 3½ miles and Kausambi, 4 miles in circuit—were either equal or little larger in size than the Metropolitan cities of Mohenjo-daro and Harappa, both being upwards of 3 miles in circuit[45]. The gap in our knowledge about the other Aryan cities does not justify that they were smaller than either Ahichhatra or Kausambi. Rhys Davids, for example, mentions following as the principal cities of India in the seventh century B.C.: Ajodhya; Varanasi or Kasi, including its suburbs extending for 12 leagues or about 36 miles[46]; Champa; Kampilla; Kausambi—which, apart from being the capital of the Kingdom of the Vatsas, acted also as the chief entrepot for both land and water traffic passing between Kosala and Magadha Kingdoms situated in the west and south respectively[47]; Mathura, on the River Jamuna, the capital of the Surasena Kingdom; Mithila with its urbanised area having a circumference of 7 leagues[48] probably included the suburbs; Rajagriha, or modern Rajgir, the capital of Magadha Kingdom; Rourka, the capital of Sovira, or modem Surat which was an important centre of coastal trade, receiving caravans carrying merchandise from as far east as Magadha[48]; Sagala or modern Sialkot in Punjab; Saketa; Sravasti, the capital of Northern Kosala; Ujjain, the capital of Avanti; and Vaisali, the capital of the Lichhavi Kingdom, which was a great city[49].

The list includes the names of fourteen cities flourishing before the time of Buddha, some of them teaching a high stage of prosperity and an unbelievable size in areal expansion. Varanasi offers one so such cases where urban growth, giving rise to suburban development— a surprising phenomenon for such an early period — had extended the city-area for twelve leagues or nearly thirty-six miles. Mithila, another great city of this time, had a circumference of about twenty-one miles. The credibility of such enormous size cannot be challenged as pointed out by Rhys Davids who cites the example of Pataliputra, with a circuit of its walls running for 220 stadia or about 22 miles (l 0 stadia = about 1 mile[50]) around the city which is given by Megasthenes from his personal experience. The size of this order is a direct evidence of the stage of urban prosperity attained by some of the ancient cities when they turned out as the most important centres of trade, commerce and industry. In fact, Varanasi's fame in its textiles and other branches of industry by this time was an accomplished fact. Kausambi and Souvira are mentioned as maintaining a high degree of economic development and this may equally be attributed to other principal urban place like Varanasi, Champa, Rajagriha, etc., enjoying advantageous location on the principal highways of trade and commerce. This is largely borne out by the trade routes and the major trading points of the period discussed elsewhere in this chapter. Another very interesting point emerging from the observation of Rhys Davids made in the case of Ajodhya and Saketa where he compares them with London and Westminster[51]. In the latter case, the two cities were actually one, representing respectively the commercial and the, administrative headquarters of the City of London whereas both Ajodhya and Saketa—located very close to each other—maintained completely separate existence, and thrived as two of the principal cities of India in the seventh century B.C. though about a century later, during Buddha's time, only Saketa, and not Ajodhya, was considered to be one of the six Great Cities of India. What seems plausible is that, Saketa and Ajodhya were twin cities, enjoying similar prosperity in the seventh century B.C., but a century later Ajodhya slided down from its earlier position while Saketa still continued the prosperous role of a great city.

All these direct as well as indirect information, when pieced together, give us more or less a general picture, conveying the idea that with the Aryans urbanisation came to stay, and supplying the basic needs of civilisation, gradually acquired the required momentum. Thus, by the middle of the first millennium B.C. the amenities of city life were no longer unknown to the people of the Ganga Valley. Introduction of heavy iron ploughs and new kinds of grain and fruit crops largely improved the agricultural scene, considerably widening the scope of urbanisation. Industries became, more specialised, producing objects of wood, leather, fur, and such prized articles as embroidered garments and dyed materials. Merchants, forming a distinct caste-group among the Aryans, made flourishing trade. The intimate knowledge of the sea and the introduction of alphabetic writing, convenient units of value and weights greatly facilitated the inland as well as the foreign trade.

Urbanisation daring the Early Historical Period

From 600 B.C. onwards, urbanisation made remarkable headway not only in the number of flourishing cities but also in their wider spatial distribution. Hitherto urban activities were mostly confined to the Ganga-Jamuna Doab, although Aryan influence had, by then, already extended to a far greater domain—from the banks of the Upper Jamuna to beyond the Himalayas in the north, from the basin of Chambal in the south to Magadha in the west[52]. By 600 B.C., the political situation underwent a tremendous change and the focus of civilisation shifted eastward where four great Kingdoms emerged, totally eclipsing the cld Kingdoms developed earlier by the Aryans in the Upper Ganga-Jamuna plains. Further, the period witnessed the birth of two new religions—Buddhism, preached by Buddha (566-486 B.C.[53]) and Jainism, preached by Mahavir (540-468 B.C.[54]), both greatly undermining the religious supremacy of the Aryans. This had a profound effect on the political situation of India which ultimately came to define the progress of urbanisation in the country. From this period onwards our knowledge about the urban development becomes more accurate and systematic as it can be based on the Buddhist and Jain literature written at this time, illuminated further by the more authentic accounts of Megasthenes who came to India inabout 300 B.C. and the chroniclers of Alexander.

The sources mentioned above, making direct reference to some of the most important cities, do not, however, give any concrete idea about the scale as well as nature of urban development obtaining in the periods of early and late Aryan rule in India. But there is at least one source yielding information on the progress of urbanisation and this is represented by the 'Janapada States' of ancient India existing before the days of the Mauryas.

The first mention of 'Janapada' is found in the later Vedic literature, composed earlier than the Buddhist literary records, namely the 'Rigvedic Brahmana', the 'Aitareya', the 'Yajurveda' and its 'Brahmana', and the 'Tattiriya'.[55] Repeated reference to such States occur in the literary records of the later periods, such as in the 'Puranic' literature, namely the 'Matsya', the 'Vayu', the 'Markandeya', Brahmana', 'Vamana', etc., in the great epics of the 'Mahabharata' and the 'Ramayana', in the earlier Buddhists literatures like the 'Anguttara Nikaya' and in the Jain literature like the 'Bhagavati Sutra'[56], in Panini's Astadhyaya'[57], in Kautilya's 'Arthasastra', and further in the writings of the Greek Ambassador to the Court of Pataliputra.

The great significance of the word 'Janapada' lies in its association with the independent states, having taken shape as early as 1000 B.C. or thereabout[58], and disappearing finally by the end of the fifth century A.C.[59] when the Gupta Empire had come into existence. Misra, however, gives different dates for the rise and the decay of the Janapadas or the Hindu Republics. He places them between the bracket of 1500 B.C. to 500 B.C.[60], the end coming with the rise of the Magadhan Empire though he admits elsewhere that the complete extinction of the system did not take place till the time of Gupta Emperors. What appears really interesting about the 'Janapadas' is that each of them was a distinct political unit, defined by territorial boundaries and possessing two distinct administrative units—the

'Pura' or the capital and the 'Janapada', or the remaining territory of the State[61], the latter divided into a number of villages and townships[62]. Misra, referring to Ramayana, observes that — the 'Pura', or the capital developed, in each case, into the most prominent city of the State, provided with wide and spacious roads, regularly sprinkled with water. The city had a large market-complex offering all sorts of commodities. Besides, the city contained the residences of the elected King, the dignitaries of the ruling class, the scholars, the warriors and the rich merchants. Residential arrangements also used to be made for the foreigners visiting the Capital City[63].

Before looking into the economic life of the Janapadas, it becomes imperative to assess the popularity of this system prevalent in the earlier period of Aryan rule in India. The word 'Jana' refers to different tribes of the Aryans, such as the Kurus, the Kosalas, etc., who were mobile communities in the beginning but later on settled permanently in different areas and the defined territories gradually gave rise to individual Janapadas —the word 'pada' referring to the territory occupied by the tribe. Each Janapada came to be identified by the original name of the tribe, as for example, the Kuru, the Panchala, the Kosala, etc. In course of time, however, the tribal significance was lost and the name defined only the territorial units[64]. There is no mention of Janapadas in the Rigveda and in the Atharvaveda, the earliest of the Vedic Literature; they refer only to the 'Janas', which means that Janapadas had not taken form till then. The Aryans were, still then, composed of a great number of communities moving from place to place, without any fixed territory of their own. The first mention of Janapada occurs in Aitareya Brahmana and the names of eight Janapada States appear in later Vedic Literature[65]. The number increases to about 170 in Puranic Literature, while Mahabharata provides a list of 230 Janapada[66] States when the Aryan rule had become firmly established in the country. If the location of the Janapadas, as defined by Misra, is to be accepted, the influence of Aryan culture had, by that time, extended over a vast tract—from the southern tip of India to the Sino-Tibetan borderland in the north, from the Eastern Hills bordering Burma in the east to the central plains of River Amudaria and Eastern Persia in the west. Not that all the land belonged to the Aryan tribes, but, as it appears, the Janapadas belonged to the non-Aryan tribes maintained cultural links with the more superior Aryan tribes settled mostly on the Ganga-Jamuna plains from whom they had, very likely, derived the idea of the Janapadas.

The form of the Government of the Janapada States thriving during the Vedic period was mostly monarchy though the very conception of a republic seems to have already developed in the later Vedic period, and this is further corroborated by the evidence of 'Ganas', meaning 'Republic'[67] which had taken form during the epic era of Mahabharata.[68] The changes in the forms of government from a monarchical to a republican system became more prevalent in the succeeding centuries so that by 600 B.C. sixteen Mahajanapadas or Great Republican States had emerged on the scene. The popularity of people's rule and the success achieved did not wane for another three centuries or more. Panini, writing his monumental work 'Ashtadhyaya' in the middle of the fifth century B.C.[69], refers to a great number of Republican States though the system of monarchy was still alive Megasthenes, visiting India between 302 and 288 B.C., found democratic form of government as a universal case adopted by most of the cities.[70] Similar references to Janapadas, having republican governments, are also found in Kautilya's 'Arthasastra', composed some time in the end of the fourth century B.C.[71], with cases of transformation from monarchy to republics, such as the Kuru and the Panchala mentioned as monarchies in Mahabharata had turned into republics in the days of Kautilya[72]. Patanjali, writing still later, in about the middle of the second century B.C., gives an exhaustive list of Janapadas in his 'Mahabhashya'. In his time the whole of India and the land continuing upto the pamir region in the north were divided into a very large number of Janapadas[73], being either monarchy or republic, but each representing a defined geographical unit with cultural and political homogeneity[74]. The origin of some of these Janapadas may be traced back to the Vedic period.

The study of the Janapadas brings us to something very much relevant to the urban development in the country. Agrawala finds "unmistakable parallels"[75] between the Janapada States of India and the Greek City-States, both in their orgin and evolution. The Greek Acropolis or the fortified city grew out of an evolutional process, with four succeeding stages of development and this has a strange similarity with the rise of Janapada or capital-based political territory in India. In Greece, the Genos or the patriarchal clan making the primary societal unit formed the first stage of this developmental process, followed by the Phratries or the formation of families and these, viewing the necessity of defence and security, gave rise to the Phulai or the military groupings in the society, which ultimately brought the Polis or the fortified capital into existence with its jurisdiction clearly laid down by defined boundaries. All these stages are faithfully mirrored by four stages of the Jana (the clan), the Kula (the family), the Janapadin (the tribe), and the Janapada taking part in the growth of the 'Pura' or the walled city which provided the basis for the rise of Janapada States in India. Misra presents the same view as Agrawala about the identical character of origin of the States[76] in the two widely distant countries, but thriving more or less in about the same period[77].

The most important connection between the Janapada States and the urban development in India is borne out by the fact that, as a City-State, each had developed around a capital-city from where the political, economic as well as the cultural functions of the State were carried out and thereby making the very existence of the State entirely dependent on it. It will, therefore, be no exaggeration of the fact that the Janapada States developed all over the country had brought into life a great number of centres in the form of capital-cities. The two distinct constituent elements of a Janapada — 'the Pura' or the capital-city and the remaining territory of the State — make urban development inevitable for the functioning of the City-States.

What little we gather from the early records gives us a sufficient ground to believe that the political and economic stability of the different Aryan tribes in India had gradually paved way for urban development in India on a much larger scale with a greater spatial distribution, and in more contrasting physical environments than even before. Urban culture had, in fact, spread almost all over the country irrespective of geographic barriers. It is quite axiomatic that with the emergence of so many greater and lesser kingdoms, the seeds of urbanisation were spread over far larger a field than it had happened at any other period. The Aryans pushing eastward and southward carried the light of civilisation far beyond the original cradle of 'Sapta-Saindhava' and 'Madhyamadisa'. For the first time urbanisation made significant advance into the plains of north-east India and into the far reaches of the South Indian plateau regions. Much of it has vanished through the aeons, but stray evidences occurring from different sources leave no ground for doubt the flourishing stage of urbanisation.

An authentic clue to the presence of a number of prosperous cities is provided by the Mahajanapadas thriving in about 600 B.C. There were sixteen of them at that time superior in rank and power to other Janapada States and hence called by the Buddhist and Jain writers as the 'Maha' or the Great Janapadas. They were as follows :

1. *Kasi* : Of the sixteen Mahajanapadas, Kasi, comprising the district of Varanasi, was, perhaps, the most powerful in the beginning. Its capital, Varariasi, was the chief city in India.

2. *Kosala* : Comprising present Oudh the kingdom had three great cities, namely Sravasti, Ajodhya and Saketa of which Sravasti, situated on River Rapti, was the capital, known today as Sahet-Mahet. In Buddha's time Ajodhya declined to an unimportant position and Sravasti became one of the six great cities of India. There were a number of minor towns in this kingdom of which Setavya and Ukkattha are worth mentioning[78].

3. *Anga* : Comprising the modern districts of Bhagalpur and Monghyr and the western part of Purnea the kingdom had its capital at Champa, near present Bhagalpur. Considered as one of the six great cities of Buddha's time, Champa was famous for its wealth and commerce[79]. Other important cities of the kingdom were Assapura and Bhaddiya, the latter represented today by Bhadariya, situated eight miles south of Bhagalpur.

4. *Magadha* : It corresponds roughly to the present districts of Patna and Gaya in Bihar. The Kingdom's earliest capital was Giribraja or 'Mountain-Stronghold'.[80] It was a hill-fortress, surrounded by five hills and built on a plan of the architect, Maha Govinda[81]. It was, however, abandoned and the capital was shifted to it new site at the foot of the hills by King Bimbisara who came to the throne in about 545 B.C.[82] The new capital came to be known as Rajagriha. Dating back from the early Vedic period, the Kingdom acquired more power later on and the capital was again shifted by Ajatsatru, the successor of Bimbisara, to a new site at the village of Pataligrama, situated at the confluence of the Ganga and Son rivers, which gradually developed into the great city of Pataliputra.

5. *Vajji (Vriji)* : Comprising a part of Muzaffarpur district of North

Bihar, it included eight confederate clans of whom the Videhas, the Lichhavis, the Jnatrikas and the Vrijis were the most important. The Videhas had their capital at Mithila or modern Janakpur lying within Nepal border; the Lichhavi capital was at Vaisali or modern Basrah and Bakhira. The city of Vaisali also did serve as the Metropolis of the entire Confederacy[83]. The Jnatrikas had their capital at Kundapura or Kundagrama and Kollaga, forming the suburb of Vaisali.

6. *The Malla* : Comprising the Gorakhpur district of Uttar Pradesh, it was divided into two parts by a river and having two capitals, namely Kusavati or Kusinara or modern Kusinagara, and Pava or modern Fazilpur. Kusavati or Kusinagara was a great city in those days. Other important cities were Anupiya and Uruvelakappa[84].

7. *Chedi* : Corresponding roughly to the Bundelkhand and its surrounding region, its capital was at the ancient Metropolis of Suktimati, near present Banda. Other important towns were Sahajati and Tripuri.

8. *Vatsa or Vamsa* : Comprising the region lying south of the River Ganga, its capital was at Kausambi or modern Kosam on the River Jamuna near Allahabad.

9. *Kuru* : Covering Thaneswar, Delhi and Meerut districts, the Kingdom had its capital at Indraprashta or the Purana Quila area of Old Delhi. Another important city was Hastinapura.

10. *Panchala* : Comprising Bareilly, Badaun and Farrukhabad district of Uttar Pradesh, the Kingdom was divided by the River Ganga into two parts, namely Uttara or Northern Panchala and Dakshina or Southern Panchala. The Northern Panchala's capital was at Ahichhatra or modern Ramnagar, and that of the Southern Panchala was at Kampilya or modern Kampil in Farrukhabad district[85].

11 *Matsya* : The Kingdom, corresponding to the present Jaipur district of Rajasthan, had its capital at Bairat or Viratanagara, near the City of Jaipur today.

12. *Surasena* : Comprising the surrounding region of Mathura, its capital was at Mathura, on the River Jamuna.

13. *Assaka or Asmaka* : Lying in the upper reaches of the Godavari Valley, the Kingdom had its capital at Potal or Podana, identified with Bodhan[86].

14. *Avanti* : Comprising Malwa and its surrounding region in Madhya

Pradesh, the Kingdom was divided into two parts, the northern part having its capital at Ujjain, and the southern part at Mahishmati. Several other cities mentioned by the Buddhist and Jain authors like, Kuraraghara, Makkarata and Sudarsanapura are not identifiable today.

15. *Gandhara* : Comprising Peshawar and the Rawalpindi districts and the Vale of Kashmir, it had its capital it Takshasila which, as an educational centre of Brahminical School of Spiritualism, was greater in reputation than Varansi, to which even the King of Kasi sent his son for higher learning[87].

16. *Kamboja* : The Kingdom comprised the south-western part of Kashmir and parts of Kafiristan. During the period of Mahabharata, the capital was probably at Rajapura,[88] identified by Cunningham with Rajaori. Nandi-nagara was another city of this Kingdom.

Cultural Background of Eastern and Southern India on the Eve of Urban Expansion

The slow encroachment of urban culture into the eastern coastal plains and the southern plateau regions makes it necessary to take a stock of the situation prevailing therein. It is imperative that, urbanisation in those days could not proceed against a cultural vacuum; some sort of cultural background provided by the permanent settlements on the one hand, and an affluent agricultural economy on the other were the essential pre-conditions required for any type of urban ingress.

The progress of urban culture as well as its geographical distribution during the Vedic and the early historic periods cannot be understood unless one makes an assessment of the course of cultural evolution setting the stage for the emergence of the cities.

Before studying the condition of the eastern regions and South India it is necessary to evaluate the case of Western India since it was here that the first synthesis of the Harappan with the exotic cultures took place in the lands of Saurashtra, Rajputana and Malwa from where waves of post-Harappan expansion developed. As has been mentioned earlier, it is here at the urban sites of Lothal, Rangpur, Somnath, Rajodi, etc., that the end of the Harappan Culture did not mean a break in occupation, but was succeeded by an inferior culture, the latter showing distinct traces of Iranian influence. In the light of available evidences it is not difficult to imagine that a group of the early Aryans—the Yadavas, to a considerable degree Iranian in blood and even in speech — not finding favour with the orthodox Vedic Aryans, settled in the Ganga-Jamuna plains, made their way into the seemingly inhospitable lands of the south and west and ultimately dominated the indigenous peasant communities as well as the Late Harappans. And it is through these Yadava Aryans that the developed urbanity of the Ganga-Jamuna Doab arrived here some time around 500 B.C.[89] Cities like Mahishmati, Ujjain, Tripuri (Tiwar), Vidisha, Dwaraka have intimate associations with the Yadava Aryans who gradually spread into the region stretching from Kathiawar to the banks of the river Narmada and from there subsequently moved on to Vidarbha (Berar) and the Godavari region. A branch of these Yadavas, namely the Andhaka, gave rise to the Andhras in the lower valley of the river Godavari.[90]

On the eve of the arrival of Aryan Culture into these lands, the local conditions had reached a stage where cultural fusion was not very difficult. For instance, in Saurashtra, Malwa and the adjoining regions a village-culture had already taken shape by that time. Their houses were built of timber-posts and bamboo-screens and the floors were made of clay and cow-dung with a thin coating of lime. Apart from a rich stone-blade industry, the village also produced copper flat-axes, fish-hooks, pins and rings. In the Narmada valley rice-culture seems to have had started in around 1700 B.C.[91] These busy village communities, beginning their career some time in 2000 B.C., maintained this cultural continuity uninterrupted, except with minor changes now and then, down to 600 B.C., and it is not until 500 B.C. or thereabout that the urban phase began. The change in the cultural sequence—from rural to urban—had been rather sudden, the higher culture having been directly imposed upon the lower without any period of transition between them. This is amply evidenced at the sites of both Ujjain and Mahishmati[92] in the Narmada valley where it arrived first from the Ganga-Jamuna Doab utilising, in all probability, the natural traffic lines through the Vindhya Ranges.

A geographical reason for the selection of the region of Saurashtra, Rajputana and Malwa as one of the primary recluse of a branch of the dissident Aryans was perhaps the climate which, with low rainfall and a drier aspect, was nearly identical with the land of their origin. This determining factor possibly defined one of the later movements of these Aryans. Since, from here they spread through the low rainfall areas of the Deccan where they came in contact with the local peasant communities and, mixing with them, gradually moved eastward into the east coast, stretching from Bengal to Andhra. Besides this, another movement took place from the Narmada Valley region to the hills of Central India, while from north Rajputana a branch of the Aryans moved into the Upper Ganga valley where the orthodox Vedic Aryans were already busy in expanding their newly established urban culture[93].

Apart from stray beginnings here and there, the real extension of civilisation, that is the urban culture, southwards into the heart of the Deccan and Peninsular India did not take place before the opening of the third century B.C. and then also it was intimately associated with the southward expansion of the Maurya Empire built by Asoka's father Bindusara. Townsites at Maski in Raichur district of Andhra Pradesh and Brahmangiri in Mysore yield evidences in support of this view. In the east—in Bengal and Orissa—the wave arrived almost in the same period for which the city of Pundranagar, in the Bogra district of modern Bangladesh, and the city of Sishupalgarh, near Bhubaneswar in Orissa, provide irrefutable evidences. The results of these diverse movements were not same though, the eastward movement being much less fruitful than the southward movement[94].

All these movements of colonisation naturally raise again the question about the condition of life that prevailed in the regions prior to the arrival of the Aryans. Excavations at many sites in the plateau region of South India throw some light on the life of the earliest settlements. There is at least one radiocarbon date testifying to the origin of the earliest settlements in around 2300 to 1800 B.C., although the origin of the people is still obscure. The settlements were generally made on the tops of the granite hills or on levelled terraces on hillsides, or on saddles and plateaus in between the hills. From the beginning, they domesticated animals like, cattle, sheep and goats, and probably produced grains. Hand-made pottery was in use and they developed a ground stone-axe industry. Metals were completely absent, but terracotta figurines and rock paintings indicate an artistic bent of mind. The next phase, continuing from about 1800 to 1500 B.C., is marked by important developments. Circular hutments were made of wattle and daub on a wooden frame with mud-floors; the stone-blade industry developed further and the original pottery was replaced by another type with new elements, suggesting contact with North India. Metal objects of copper and bronze made their first appearance during this period with increasing frequency during the later part. The third or the last phase of this agrarian culture, extending from about 1400 to 1050 B.C., was characterised by an increasing number of copper and bronze tools, although the use of stone-axes and blades were not altogether given up. The pottery became wheel-turned and the first indication of horse-raising is available from rock-paintings.

These three phases indicate a remarkable continuity of these settlements which, once established, kept to the same site for a period of over a thousand years. Such a continuity is also observed in their stone-blade industry as well as in the economy which primarily developed throughout on stock raising, supplemented by the production of such crops as grams and millets[95]. Discovery of large stores of stone-axes of similar nature from different sites occurring as far south as the southern extremity of the Peninsula and also from Mysore Plateau eastward down to the coastal plains of Tamil Nadu, suggests that the prevailing mode of life of the village communities was, perhaps, not very different from those discussed above.

In contrast to the cultural background provided by Western and Southern India in general, that of Eastern India however hazy, is not very promising. The surface collections of stone-axes, etc., coming from the hill areas of Assam, whether produced *in situ* or redeposited, and the cord-impressed hand-made pottery are entirely different from either that of the North or the South Indian types, but identical with the types prevalent in China and South-East Asia. Besides, no metal objects were found anywhere in the region. Similarly, the surface collections from eastern Bihar, the western part of West Bengal and parts of Orissa—mostly coming from the hilly areas—do not give a very clear picture. The deposits of stone-axes gritty pottery from a site in the Mayurbhanj district of Orissa show some affinity with the South Indian types, while the surface collections of stone-axes from the Santhal Paraganas of Bihar resemble those of Assam types and beyond. So far no dates are available for these early tools. But the appearance of stone-axes and ill-fired pottery just below the early historic levels at Tamluk in West Bengal and in the late copper-bronze or early Iron Age levels in Pandu Rajar Dhibi in the Ajay River Valley of Burdwan district in West Bengal and from the area lying north of this, near the Ganga Plains[96], do not give a very definite idea about the level of culture. However, the evidences yielded by Pandu Rajar Dhibi and Mahishadal of West Bengal provide sufficient ground to believe that the cultural level of the settlements developed in the western part of West Bengal was in no way less advanced than those in South India. At Pandu Rajar Dhibi, the two pre-iron periods are characterised by a stone-blade industry, a number of copper objects including fish-hooks and two types of painted pottery with a radio-carbon date of 1012+B.C. This cultural sequence is corroborated at Mahishadal where the finds, including charred rice, date between 1380 and 855 B.C.

Apart from the instances of settled life developed in both the southern and the eastern India by the agricultural communities long before the emergence of urban culture at the initiative of the Aryans, another important development cannot be ignored. This concerns the discovery of copper objects, occurring in large piles, at some thirty four sites, distributed over 800 miles of forested lands strewn over Uttar Pradesh, Madhya Pradesh, Bihar, West Bengal, Orissa and Andhra Pradesh. The archaeologists call them 'copper hoards' which include eight main types of implements, such as, flat axes, shouldered axes, bar celts or chisels, rings, harpoon-heads, spear-heads, swords and a strange man-like object. Their origin has still remained obscure; but the specialised character and skilful manufacture of these different types of implements undoubtedly suggest them to be the work of whole time experts who depended on the local mines for their raw materials and produced them under conditions of a developed agricultural economy. The implements roughly date back to circa 1700 to 1000 B.C.[97] and in spite of their doubtful parentage, they give a further indication of the cultural advancement already made on the eve of urbanisation.

The most important facts emerging out of all these evidences may be summarised in the following manner : (*a*) in both Western and Southern India the community life based on an agricultural economy was sufficiently advanced to respond favourably to the urban culture imposed upon it while the condition in eastern India, particularly beyond Bengal Plains, were different; (*b*) the primary impetus of urbanisation in Western and Central India came from the Yadava-Aryans but the real urban-beginning in South India did not take place till the opening of the third century B.C. and that was at the behest of the city builders of the Ganga valley.

Cities in the Early Historic Period

It will now be worthwhile to make an inventory of the cities that had already made their appearance in the opening centuries of the historic period, that is in 600 B.C. and thereabout. They are as follows:

Varanasi; Sravasti; Ajodhya; Saketa; Champa; Assapura; Bhaddiya; Rajagriha; Pataliputra; Mithila; Vaisali; Kundapura; Kusavati; Pava; Anupiya; Urubelakappa; Suktimati; Sahajati; Tripuri; Kausambi; Indraprastha; Hastinapura; Ahichhatra; Kampilya; Bairat; Mathura; Podana; Ujjain; Mahismati; Kuraraghara; Makkarata; Sudarsanapura; Takshila; Rajapura; Nandinagara.

It has to be admitted that the scrappy nature of information makes our inventory far from complete. Yet it is not difficult to trace the existence of some other cities and important towns maintaining a flourishing life at that time though none had the pretensions of being the capital of a great kingdom like most of the cities mentioned above. Instances are provided by cities like, Gaya, Kanyakubja, Prayaga, Sakala, Vidisa, Dwaraka, Broach, Nalanda, Tamralipti, Pragjyotishpur, Sisupalgarh or Kalinganagara, Rupar and Nasik. Further, it is not unlikely that within the next few centuries urbanisation had spread further south and a number of new cities arose, *viz.* Arikamedu, Nagarjunikond, Kanchipura and Madurai.

Turning to them again it cannot be said for certain how many of them were really great cities. Old Buddhist texts refer to six great cities at the time of Buddha's death—486 B.C. They were—Sravasti, Champa, Rajagriha, Saketa, Kausambi and Kasi[98]. At least in one case the greatness of the city has been revealed by archaeologists. The stone-walls of the fortified city of Rajagriha, accredited to be the first of its kind in India[99], had a perimeter of twenty-five miles. The entire area within the walls was, perhaps, not entirely built up, but it was a garden city with a central core[108]. Greatness in its real sense was also achieved by Pataliputra, as the capital of the Mauryan Empire, the latter being the largest that India ever had produced earlier. Recent excavations at the site—covered largely today by the urban sprawl of Patna City—have thrown much light on this old Metropolis and the facts agree very much with what is gathered from the accounts of the city written by the Greek envoy, Megasthenes, who visited the court of Emperor Chandragupta some time in 302 B.C. Megasthenes found Pataliputra straddled along the bank of the river Ganga for nine miles in length and over a mile and a half in width, defended by a timber-wall pierced by sixty-four gates, which was crowned by some five hundred and seventy towers, fortified further by a broad moat two hundred yards wide. Kangle has strong reservations against the wooden wall which, in his opinion based on archaeological investigations, might have been made of brick[101]. According to the Greek writer, the royal palace excited admiration and even those of Susa or Ekbatana in Persia, with all their splendour and magificence, were no match to it[102]. The size of Varanasi and Mithila has already been discussed. Not much is known about the ground plan of the early cities, neither we know anything about the condition of urban life. The houses in urban areas were possibly made of wood or brick with a plaster of lime on both the inside and the outer side of the walls, having brilliant fresco paintings on them[103]. Buildings made of seven stories are mentioned and there were arrangements for hot baths in the houses[104], which also had drains[105]. The prevalence of wood in architecture has disappeared in the third century B.C.[106] and was probably replaced by brick and stone. As a matter of fact, stone had come into use much earlier, at least for the construction of walls and staircases. The stone-wall around Giribraja was built before the sixth century B.C.

It is curious to note that most of the cities mentioned so far were the capital-cities. Such a list does not convey a definite idea about the scale of urbanisation in the country at that time, nor does it mean that towns or cities independent of capital-function failed to attain any importance. A number of cities listed above were quite important urban centres during that period although they had no distinctive function as capitals. It cannot, however, be denied that the city-building process was largely confined to capitals. But the idea of one-city for each State is incompatible with the existing practices where building of the capital did in no way forbade building of the other towns and cities. On the other hand, consolidation of power meant economic progress and this was not possible where the entire economy of any particular kingdom remained focused on a single city—that is, the capital alone—which, in the fitness of things, was more engrossed in defensive rather than economic activities. It is true that, as the seats of power, the capital cities, enjoying royal patronage, became the premier industrial and commercial centres, but, for reaching that stage they needed the cooperation of lesser places serving as transmitting points for raw materials and also — in the long run—acting as the distributing points for the finished products. It is, therefore, not unlikely that commercial activities gradually transformed some of the lesser centres into urban places, while a more advantageous location or such other factors turned at least a few of them into important towns and cities.

Listing of great or small towns and cities alone does not take us far as many names cannot be identified today, nor we can expect to find all the names from the literary records composed mostly on philosophical or religious matters. It will rather be more prudent on our part to look into the writings of the contemporary writers for getting a better glimpse of the overall urban situation of the country.

Panini writing about his time—the middle of the fifth century B.C.—divides settlements into four categories: (1) Nagara or town, (2) Grama or village, (3) Ghosha or the abode of the herdsmen, and (4) Kheta or hamlet. For settlements lying east of the river Saraswati, Panini made distinctions between a village and a town, but for those lying west of the river the distinction is not properly maintained. The reason for this different treatment, as given by Agarwala, is the large size of the villages occurring west of the river Saraswati which often looked like prosperous towns. In support of this one might turn to the accounts of Alexander's chroniclers stating at one place about the existence of thirty-seven cities in the region lying between the upper courses of the Jhelum and the Chenab and the Ravi, the smallest of them having not less than 5,000 inhabitants and many others containing more than 10,000[107]. On the other hand, in Strabo's opinion, there were 500 cities at that time in the land between the rivers Jhelum and the Beas occupied by nine nations[108]. It is further mentioned that, the country beyond the Beas was extremely fertile, giving rise to prosperous villages[109]. According to Arrian, the land subjugated by Alexander in India had 2,000 cities at that time[110], while Plutarch places the number of cities at 5,000, all of them of considerable size, developed in the region encompassed by the Jhelum and the Beas[111].

One need not be cautioned about the great degree of exaggeration in the last two statements. The Greek writers were apparently guided by hearsay. But what should not escape our notice is that such an exaggeration could not be made without some solid basis for credulousness. This was provided by the presence of a large number of towns and cities, posperous and peaceful villages, and the abundant resources of the land traversed by the Greek army. Panini gives the number of towns as 500[112] existing at his time in the north-western part of India, which has a strange similarity with the number of cities mentioned by some of the Greek historians.

Among the most important cities of his time, Panini makes special reference to Kapisi or modern Begram, about fifty miles north of Kabul, Takshasila, Saketa, Hastinapura, Samkasya or modern Sankissa, on the northern bank of the Ikshumati river in Furrukkabad district, Varanasi and Pataliputra, the latter being a vast metropolis in his time having two divisions, the eastern on the Ganga and the western on the Son. Important also were the cities like, Gaudapada or Gaur in Bengal, Sravasti, Kausambi, Pava, Mahanagar or Mahasthana, Navanagara or modern Nabadwip in West Bengal, Sairishaka or Sirsa in the Hissar district, etc. Panini also mentions the prevalent practice of employing noted architects for the preparation of an elaborate plan which used to precede construction of any city. The tasks of the City-Planner included the testing of the site for the city, the moat, the palace[113], the alignment of the roads, etc. The walled cities were built on rectangular plans, generally square in size, with four gates in the middle of each side of the four walls—a pattern set by the Aryans earlier for the construction of their villages. The physical structure of the city—surrounded by a moat, parapet, wall and gateways in successive order—gave a well-planned appearance with a large number of buildings inside used for defence, residential and business purposes. The city contained the King's palace, including the Council Hall (Raja-Shava), the royal store-house (Koshthagara), a number of buildings used for the purposes of dramatic performances (Preksha), Dancing, Music, Concerts and Sports (Prahama-Krida), the business quarters and the residential buildings (Geha, Griha) intersected by streets. In the big cities there were also Hostels for Women (Chhatrisala), Rest Houses for travellers (Nishadya)[114], market places (Aparna) where commodities (panya) imported from different places were displayed for sales[115]. As a matter of fact, Panini has different names for buildings for respective purpose, as shown within the brackets. It is highly interesting to observe that the city, as described by Panini, has a strong resemblance with the Pura or the Capital described in the Ramayana, composed by the Aryans much earlier.

The picture of urban affluence as obtained from Panini's Ashtadhyaya did not dim one and a half century later when Megasthenes came to visit India. According to him the number of cities was so great that it was difficult to state that with precision[116]. Unlike Panini, he does not give any direct information about the urban development in the country. He describes Pataliputra, the greatest city of his time in India, and casually mentions a few more cities like, Kanauj or Kanyakubja, Mathura, Dantapura, Patala, Takshasila, etc.

Kautilya's Arthasastra, composed some time by the end of the fourth century B.C.[117], provides us with a mine of information about the economic life of India in his time, but there is no direct reference to the actual urban development in the country. From his writings we gather that capital-cities did exist and so, probably, the towns of lower order. To take, for instance, the plan he suggests that for an ideal Janapada or Kingdom the Capital-City or the 'Sthaniya' should be a fortified city located in the centre of the Janapada serving eight hundred villages, while 'Dronamukha', centrally situated, serves four hundred villages, the 'Karvatika' with similar situation serves two hundred villages and 'Samgrahara', the lowest in the ladder, serves only ten villages[118]. The rigidly fixed administrative jurisdiction of these four grades of urban centres points to their orgin political headquarters of the State.

The graded order of urban centres, as offered by Kautilya reveals very important facts about the nature of urban development and its spatial pattern. Taking eight hundred villages as the limiting size of a state, the latter, on the principle of Kautilya, would give rise to one Major or Central City, two Major Towns or Minor Cities having central locations, four Towns with central locations and eighty sub-towns each centrally placed within a group of the villages. The distance between the centres of same order is likely to be uniform, increasing progressively with each successive higher order. There would be, altogether, eithty-seven towns and cities of this type in the Janapada, spaced uniformly so that the higher order places are nearer to the capital-city and each urban centre, being centrally placed, had its tributary region clearly defined. It is not possible to know whether Kautilya's principle had actually been followed in practice. The pattern of urban development in that case, would, in someway, resemble the distribution pattern shown by Christaller in his study of Southern Germany[119]. But the main difference between them lies in two aspects: (*a*) the functional zones of Kautitya's urban centres are defined once for all by administrative boundaries, whereas distance becomes the primary factor in carving out the functional zones of Christaller's Central Places; (*b*) the entire hypothesis of Kautilya is built up on administrative needs, while economic functions play a greater role in Christaller's theory.

Kautilya, however, does not rule out the possibility of urban centres having developed based purely on economic functions. In fact, such towns did exist in his time as we find reference to Ports[120], market towns[121], Harbour towns[122], and Forts[123] in his 'Arthasastra'. An elaborate plan is given by Kautilya for building the 'Sthaniya' or the Fortified Capital. The site, having a central location in the Janapada, should be selected by expert engineers, preferably at the confluence of rivers, or on the bank of a permanent lake, either natural or artificial, or at least by the side of a man-made tank. Six royal highways, three running from east to west and another three running north to south, were to divide the city into sixteen squares, each of the latter having different types of land-uses. The royal palace was to be built on an excellent ground in the ninth part lying north of the residential areas. The residences of the preceptor and the Chaplain, the Councillors to the King and the places for royal sacrifices were to be placed in the north-eastern sector of the city whereas the kitchen, the elephant stables, and the magazine were to be in the south-eastern part. The area beyond that was to be inhabited by the dealers in perfumes, flowers and liquids, besides the manufacturers of toilet articles in general, serving the needs of the royal house-hold. The warrior class was to occupy the eastern part of the city. The east-south sector was to accommodate the Warehouses for general goods, the Records and Audit Offices, and the labour colony; the west-south sector was to contain the warehouse for forest products and the royal armoury. Beyond that the extreme southern part of the city was to be occupied by the residences of the Factory and Army Officers, the Merchants, the general shopowners dealing in cooked food, wine and meat as well as the Courtesans and the Dancers, die latter probably the entertainers of the royal court. The workshops, and the stables for the donkeys and camels were to be in the south-western sector, while the stables for the carriages and chariots were to be in north-western sector. The western quarter was to be devoted to the use of the craftsmen in wool, yarn, bamboo, leather and war materials. The Sudras, or the lowest caste of the society, were to live in that sector. The west-northern sector was to have the stores for the wares and medicines and the east-northern sector was to house the Royal Treasury, the cattle and the horses. Beyond that the northern part of the city was to be occupied by the principal temple, the residences of the Brahmins and by the workers in metals and jewels. The quarters for the guilds and foreign merchants were to be in the non-residential enclosures. About seven hundred feet away from the city sanctuaries, the waterworks, etc., were to be built.

The picture of urban land-uses in Kautilya's fortified city displays the prominence of social stratification working at the base of spatial arrangements where hierarchy in social positions, as determined by four castes of the Aryan Hindu Society — namely, the Brahmins, the Kshatriyas, the Vaishyas and the Sudras — became clearly reflected in the appearance of particular activities and the people associated with them living in particular quarters of the city. This became very much pronounced at this time when even particular streets were fixed for the residence-cum-workplace belonging to different tradesmen. In Varanasi, for example, reference is made to ivory-carvers' street[124]. In general, the northern and the eastern quarters of city, representing the better parts, were reserved for the higher class of citizens and superior group of activities. Thus, the King, and his Councillors, the priests and the Brahmins, the Kshatriyas or the warrior class were to live in the northern and the eastern parts of the city. In contrast, the southern and the western parts were to be largely devoted to the economic functions, inhabited by people engaged in them. But there also the distinction is clearly visible in the distribution of castes as well as functions of higher and lower order. As for instance, the business community, represented by the Vaishyas, was to live in the southern part which, in all appearance, would become the principal, market area of the city.

Here, besides the Vaishyas, also would live the high ranking officers of the factories and the army, and people engaged in different professional activities, serving the interests of the Court and the citizens. The western part of the city, on the other hand, would be occupied by the lowest caste of the society, the Sudras, providing perhaps, forced labour to different types of productive activities concerning various crafts and industries. The western part, thus, would represent, by and large, the Industrial Sector of the city, and containing the royal stables, the armoury and the warehouse it would become the most socially and culturally backward area, kept purposefully segregated from the general flow of life in the remaining parts of the city.

We do not know how far Kautilya's plan for city-building materialised. There is no definite instance to show that cities had been built on the plan elaborated by him in Arthasastra. Even the grand Metropolis Pataliputra of his time does not appear to have conformed to the sector-wise distribution in its built. The city, sprawling for about nine miles on the banks of the Ganga and the Son, was less than two miles wide and the development of sixteen sectors seems to have been much less probable than in a city where the length and breadth were so disproportionate. In fact, Kautilya advocated for rectangular or square-shape cities[125], with twelve gates opening on each of the four sides of the city-walls[126] and the streets running parallel to each other would divide the city into sixteen squares. The principle of town-planning, as given by Kautilya, doesnot, however, fall through on the single premise that concrete instances of this nature do not appear from the layout of the ancient cities. The ancient cities so far discovered and explored do not lead us far in many other aspects as well. In spite of that, the existence of an order in the spatial arrangement of different economic functions in these cities is the most likely expression of a caste-bound society where functions were determined by castes. The idea of town-planning as presented by Kautilya, closely reflects the prevailing societal conditions, and cities existing in his days had naturally been divided into various sectors apportioned for different caste-groups with their traditional functions confined to respective quarters. Kautilya's theme, developed on the basis of this social segregation, produces something more correct and coherent about the urban society than hitherto known from any other source.

In giving his plans for the towns and the cities, Kautilya offers specifications for street-planning as well. Inside the State Capital the street-plan, with three royal highways running at right angles to three more royal highways, gave rise to a grid—iron pattern. These roads have standard width of twenty-four feet. But outside the towns and the cities, the roads become wider, being uniformly forty-eight feet wide[127], maintaining links between different places in the country. Those on the irrigation works and in the forests are, however, less wide, twenty-four feet, and these for the use of elephants and those along the agricultural fields are only twelve feet in width[128]. Besides, there is also some hint on the duties of the city-residents. Every house in the city had to arrange for the disposal of the rubbish and waste water, needed to have channels for letting out rain water and had to be provided with animal and carriage-sheds. The big houses, referred to in 'Arthasastra,' were to have a courtyard, pounding sheds, latrines etc., for the common use of the tenants. Over and above this, strong vigilance was required of the city-administrators were intended to keep complete records for each household in the city, had to check all arrivals and departures and to regulate movements at night[129].

Patanjali, writing his 'Mahabhasya' in about 150 B.C.[130]—almost two hundred years after Kautilya — gives an idea about the political divisions of India and refers to some of the important cities existing as the Capitals of the Janapada States or his time. Among the settlements, he distinguishes between the 'nagara' or large cities and the 'grama' or the village and the 'ghosha' or the places of animal-herders[131]. The most important among the cities mentioned by him are Hastinapura, Ahichhatra, Kanyabubja, Samkasya, Gavidhumata—identified with Kudarkot in the district of Etah, Uttar Pradesh, Saketa or Ajodhya, Varanasi, Pataliputra, Takashasila, Mathura, Kausambi, Ujjain, Mahishmati, Nasikaya or modern Nasik, and Kanchipura. Sakala or modern Sialkot, the capital of the Vahika Janapada lying between the Sutlej and the Indus, is mentioned by Patanjali as a 'Vahika-Grama', meaning a large village unit.

There are at least forty Janapada States directly named by Patanjali whose interest, though, was mainly confined to 'Aryavarta', that is, the part of the North Indian Plain lying between the Himalayas in the north and the Vindhyas in the south, stretching from near Saketa in the east to about the region of the Delhi Plains in the west.

The small number of cities mentioned by Patanjali does not rule out the existence of a still greater number when the number of the Janapadas or independent kingdoms were much larger than the names of cities cited by him. Aryavarta having been his principal concern, Patanjali is not very particular in giving the name of all the Janapadas functioning in the remaining parts of the country. As City-States, each of the Janapada developed around a city and accordingly there would be at least forty cities for the forty Janapadas finding reference in his writing. The cities figuring in Patanjali's list in all likelihood are the largest of his time while those, lesser in importance, have no place in the list. This appears to be a more possible explanation for such an omission, being neither deliberate nor careless, where cities like Prayaga or modern Allahabad, Champa, Vidisa, Kundina or modern Amraoti, Madurai, to name a few only, leading a prosperous life at this time are completely ignored by him. It is further interesting to observe that, the origin of most of the important cities of Patanjali may be traced back to the period of Mahabharata, that is, ten or twelve century B.C. and even earlier. The long continuity of urban life, leading the cities into prominent position among the urban places of the country gives a positive indication of the over-all urban development, remaining uninterrupted over a passage of nearly a millennium or more. This is really striking and could not have been possible had the cities remained confined with capital-function alone. The large size of the cities could not be the result of their function as only the capital where the individual Janapadas covered not more than a few districts of the modern period. On the contrary, they acquired their wealth, power and size from other functions, namely commerce trade and industry which were at a flourishing stage at that time as we find from the accounts left by Patanjali. The widespread nature of trade and commerce carried on throughout the country makes it imperative that a large number of urban places were really in existence, providing both means and market for such a huge transaction of goods of multifarious nature as discussed elsewhere in this chapter.

On the other hand, such urban places were not only the Capitals of the Janapadas or the Kingdoms; there were others too taking origin and functioning as market places, trading centres, ports and harbours. There is no direct way of knowing them till some time later, although it is not difficult to imagine that settlements performing urban functions had come into existence all over the country where rivers and long distance roads provided much easier communication for the movement of people and merchandise in all directions. Thus, urban places engaged in trade, commerce and industry on the one hand and those functioning as capitals as well as forts of the innumerable Kingdoms or Janapadas on the other gave rise to a considerable number of towns and cities making a fruitful existence in the middle of the second century B.C.

References to many of the cities mentioned above and names of many others occurring in the writings of the Roman and Greek authors of the early centuries of the Christian Era further reveal the extent of urbanisation in the country, lending strong support to the view that urban functions, other than administrative, did give rise to a large number of towns and cities some of which were really great, called by them as 'metropolis'. It may be worthwhile to mention the cities known to these foreign authors.

Strabo, born (60 B.C.-19 A.D.[132]) in Greece gives us his 'Geography' which, in the words of Humboldt "surpasses all the geographical writings of antiquity both in grandeur of plan, and in the abundance and variety of its materials"[133]. In it, he refers to Palibothra or Pataliputra, situated at the confluence of the Ganga and the Son, as a 'very large city'[134], 80 stadia (eight miles) in length and fifteen in breadth, having the shape of a parallelogram and encircled by a wooden wall[135]. Specific reference is also made to Patala, the Capital City of the country called Patalene, situated on the Indus, the 'great city'[136] of Taxila or Takshasila and the city of Puskalavati. In Strabo's opinion, there were about three hundred cities in the region lying between the River Jhelum and the Chenab[137].

Pliny, a Romon Geographer, living between circa 23 to 79 AD.[138] wrote his 'Natural History' in thirty-seven books of which the sixth is the 'Geography of India'. Though his principal source of information about India is the 'Indika' of Megasthenes, yet for the first time we come across certain names of towns, evidently very important centres which have not figured in the list of any of the early writers. Pliny states that, the nations as well as the cities in India at that time were. "numberless"[139]. He mentions Patala (Hyderabad?) as a celebrated port[140]; Seigerus or modern Jaigarth for Rajapur[141] as a seaport[142]; Muziris or modern Cranganore, Neacynodon or Melkynda of Ptolemy and Modur or modern Madurai of which the first two were obviously seaports and the last one an inland city. It is true that the accounts at Strabo, carrying a lot of information about India gives little on the geographical details of the country. While Pliny's accounts are more concerned with the position, boundaries, physical characteristics and races of India than its to towns and cities. Similarly, Arrian, a Greek Historian (circa 96-160 A.D.), writing about India, pays little attention to the urban development of the country. Basing actually on what is left by Megasthenes about the great munber of cities in India, their location on river-banks or on sea-coasts about the construction of the houses as being made of wood, brick and mud, and about the towns and cities being built on high grounds[144]. The only city of eminence, mentioned by Arian, is Palimbothra or Pataliputra, which was the greatest city of India[145], though both Patala and Killouta, the latter identified with modern Karachi, are named by him. Killouta is referred to as a "commodious and secure harbour"[146], which was renamed as the Port of Alexander by Nearkhos, the Admiral of the Expedition on Alexander's return journey from India[147].

The poverty of information about the urban-side is rather compensated to some extent by the anonymous writer of 'The Periplus of the Erythraean Sea', written shortly after the death of Pliny, some time between 80-89 A.D.[148] The Erythraean Sea meant in those days the entire expanse of water lying 'between' the coast of Africa and the coasts of India, or, perhaps, the East Indies and the accounts give accurate and useful information about the trade and commerce between India and other western countries in those days, referring at the same time to a large number of towns and cities, trading marts, etc., taking prominent role in the economic activities of the country. The urban places finding reference in the Periplus are follows.

Barugaza (Broach), a great emporium[149] on the river Narmada, the principal port as well as the collecting and the distributing centre of the Western India; Barbarikon, a city and a trading sea-port situated on the river Indus[150], Minnagar, a metropolis[151], situated little below Barbarikon; Ozene (Ujjain), a city and a great trading centre[152]; Paithana (Paithan or Pratisthana in Sanskrit) and Tagara (Ter), 'the greatest city in the country'[153]; both of which were very important trading centres; Akabarou (unidentified), lying south of Barugaza, was a mart; Soupara (Sopara, near Bombay), another large trading centre[154]; Kalliena

(Kalyan), a city and a trading centre[155]. Marts occurring further south in succession are Semulla (Chaul or Chimula on the Bombay Island), probably a large mart like Sopara and Kalyan[156]; Mandagora (probably Bankot) and Palaipatmai (Probably Dhabol); Melizeigara (Jaigarh or Rajapur[157]; Buzantion (Vijaydrug); Toparon (Togaron or Devagarh) and Turannosboas (Banda); Naoura (Havovar)[158]; Tundis (Tanur); Mouziris (Cranganore) and Nelkunda (near Kottayam) are both capital cities and great commercial centres, the former being at the height of its prosperity[159], and both visited by large ships carrying heavier cargo[160]. The Periplus also refers to the city of Kolkhoi (Kolkai)[161]; Komar (Cape Comorin)[162], Komara (Kaveripattam)[163]; Padouke (Pondicherry)[164], Sopatma (Markanam)[165] — all of them being famous trading centres involved in the transactions of Indian and foreign goods of a great variety[166]; Masalia (Machilipatnam), another port of fame producing "immense quantity of fine muslins"[167]; further cast the Periplus reports Gange, on the mouth of River Ganga, as an important trading mart handling a considerable amount of cargo, including the finest of all muslins, called the 'Gangetic'.[168]

The name of the urban centres appearing in the account may not lead us far about the general urban development in the country. But it opens a new window on the high pitch of commercial as well as industrial performances of the country with its chain of busy ports, more on the western than on the eastern coast, the position enjoyed in the number by the former remaining unrivalled till today. The account, for the first time, gives us an accurate knowledge about the extensive nature of maritime activities bringing such a large number of sea-ports into existence which, quite apparently, was the result of a long and remarkable tradition. At the same time, it should not be lost sight of that, as a marine guide-book, the records in the Periplus are mostly confined to the ports and those commercial centres situated near the coasts, having a direct role in the sea-bound traffic. Nevertheless, it is not difficult to understand that the development of such a large number of ports handling articles of innumerable varieties, collected from various centres of their manufacture, directly point to the existence of a large number of urban centres in the country, far too great than the port already reported by the Periplus. Such centres, in fact, were at the root of the rich heritage for the production of rare luxury goods, and having a high demand in lands beyond the seas, providing wide markets for the inland as well as goods imported from foreign countries in equally large volume as exports, and thus acting as the chief collecting and transporting points for all the outgoing and incoming transactions.

The picture conveyed by the Periplus, reflecting the economic prosperity of a very high order, itself being a concomitant result of widespread urbanisation in the country, is borne out by facts obtained from 'An Outline of Geography', written by Klaudios Ptolemaios, or popularly known as Ptolemy (90-168 A.D.) a few decades following the Periplus, some time in 145 A.D.[169] In spite of certain mistakes made by him, Ptolemy is acknowledged as the "first scientific geographer"[170] communicating to us more specific and direct information about the towns and cities of India than obtainable from any other earlier source. Considered thus, the source is invaluable in making any proper assessment of the urban development in India that had taken place already by the middle of the second century A.D. The following urban places find mention in Ptolemy's work :

Syrastra (Junagadh)[171]; Monoglosson (Mongrol)[172], a port; the city of Baryagaza (Broach)[173]; Ozene (Ujjain)[174]; Nausaripa (Nausari, eighteen miles south of Surat)[175]; Soupara (Sopara)[176]; Simyalla (Chaul), a mart and a cape[177]; Tyndis (Tanur)[178]; Mouziris (Cranganore), an emporium[179]; Melkynda or Nelkynda of the Periplus (Nelisuram); Elangkon (Quilon)[180]; Kottiara (Kataut or Cochin?), a metropolis[181]; Komaria (Cape Comorin) a cape and town[182]; Sosikouri (Tuticorin)[183]; Kolkhai (Korkai), an emporium[184]; Nikama (Negamapatam), a metropolis and a capital[185]; Thelkheir (Nagor); Kouroula (Karikol), a town[186]; Khaberis (Kaveripattam), an emporium[187]; Sabouras (probably Cuddalore), an emporium[188]; Padouke (Pondicherry), an emporium[189]; Melange (Krishnapatnam or Bandar on one of the Godavari mouths), an emporium[190]; Manarpha (Manara), a mart[191]. Koddolura (Gudur)[192]; Allosygne (Koringa), a port little beyond Godavari[193]; Paloura (Palura in Ganjam district), a town[194]; Nanigaina (Puri); Katikardama (Cuttack); Kannagara (Konarak)[195]; Minagara (Jajhpur)[196]; Kosamba (Balasor)[197]; Poloura (Jelasur near Subarnarekha river); Tilogrammon (Jessore)[198]; Proklais city (Pushkalavati)[199]; Naulibi City (Nilab)[200]; Taxila City (Takshasila)[201]; Labaka City (Lahore)[202]; Sagala (Sakala or Sialkot)[203]; Astrassos (Atrasa)[204]; Labakola (Lohore?)[205]; Batanagra (Bhatneer or

Kotanagara)[206]; Ostobalasara (Thaneswar); Kashpeira (Capital of Kashmir)[207]; Daidala (Probably Dudhal, east of Bhatneer); Indabara (Indraprastha)[208]; Modoura (Mathura), 'the city of the gods'[209]; Gugasmirs (Ajmer or Jhajhar near Delhi)[210]; Erarasa (Varanasi), a metropolis[211]; Kota Town (Kunda, south-east of Saharanpur on the left bank of the Jamuna)[212]; Margara (Marhara, north-east of Agra)[213]; Sambalaka (Sambhal in Rohilakhand)[214]; Adisadra (Ahichhatra)[215]; Kanagora (Kanyakubja or Kanauj)[216]; Kindia (Shahjahanpur)[217]; Sagala (Kushinagara)[218]; Andrapana (Dera Ismail Khan)[219]; Patala (Hydarabad)[220]; Naagramma (Naoshera)[221]; Kamigara (Aror)[222]; Binagara (Probably Minnagar of the Periplus)[223]; Arinagara (Agar, thirty miles north-east of Ujjain)[224]; Tiatoura (probably Chittur)[225]; Nasika (Nasik)[226]; Sageda (Tewar near Jabalpur)[227]; Sambalaka (Sambalpur in Orissa)[228]; Palimbothra (Pataliputra)[229]; Tamalites (Tamralipta)[230]; Kartinaga (probably Karnagarh near Bhagalpur)[231]; Kartasina Karra (Sonagarh near Berhampur)[232]; Gange[233]; Baithana (Paithan)[233]; Deopali (Devgadh or Daulatbad)[234]; Tabaso (Tabasoi)[235]; Sirimalaga (probably Malkhed in Hyderabad, Mysore)[236]; Kalligeris (probably Kanhagiri near Mudgal)[237]; Modogoulla (Mudgal in Hyderabad district)[238]; Banaousei (Banavasi, on the upper Varada, a tributary of the Tungabhadra)[239]; Mousopake (probably Miraj), a metropolis[240]; Olokhoria (Kheda in Ratangiri district)[241]; Kouba (Goa)[242]; Aloe (Yellapur in North Canara)[243]; Karoura (Karur in Coimbatore district), a capital[244]; Bideris (Erod or Yirodu)[245]; Peringkerei (Perungari on the River Vaigai)[246]; Tangala or Taga (Dindigul) [247]; Modoura (Madurai)[248]; Abour (Ambudurg in North Areot)[249]; Orthura (Uraiyur)[250]; Krounkala (Worankal in Telengana)[251]; Pityndra (probably Dharanikota, about twenty miles of Bejwada)[252]; Barake (Dwaraka)[253]; Aganagora (Agradwip, little below Katwa in West Bengal)[254]; Korygaza (Gorakhpur)[255]; Selampoura (Selempur, on a tributary of the river Sarayu)[256]; Kanogiza (Kanauj)[257]; Kassida (Kasi or Varanasi)[258]; Souanagoura, Suvarnagram or Sonargaon, (twelve miles from Dacca)[259]; Sagoda (Ajodhya)[260]; Rhadamarkotta (Rangamati on the western bank of the lower Brahmaputra, now called Udayapur)[261]; Tosalei (situated on the bank of a pool called Kosala-Ganga in Orissa was a capital during Asoka's reign), a metropolis[262]; Rhingiberi (Rangamati in the Chittagong Hill Tracts of Bangladesh)[263].

The above list, however, does not include the towns and cities mentioned by Ptolemy which have remained so far unidentified. Ptolemy mentions well over three hundred places of which seven are marts, one hundred and thirty-seven are towns, one hundred and nineteen are cities, six are emporiums, nine are metropolises. In spite of our failure in identifying many of them, their existence cannot be doubted as Ptolemy mentions the location of most of these places by latitude and longitude. One cannot ignore the fact that his list, however, exhaustive, is not complete; many of the important urban centres present at that time do not appear in his list. The Ganga-Jamuna Plains may be cited as the singular case in this respect to which Ptolemy has not done proper justice where more flourishing centres were extant in his days than mentioned by him. This will be revealed from later records. The omission is not tendentious, but rather coincidental, as his attention was primarily focused on the commercial role of the country. His 'Geography' like that of the Periplus, carries information about the economic activities and the places involved directly in handling them than about those having other roles, even when the latter were enjoying equal prosperity as the former. We do not have any glimpse of the rich cultural and political life of the urban centres from any of these two sources, though unmistakably, they provide the very basic foundation on which the economy prospered. Such a lacuna on the part of the Periplus and Ptolemy is not unlikely. For all that India mattered to the people inhabiting the shores of the Mediterranean, Red Sea and Persian Gulf was its inexhaustible variety of products and manufactures of unrivalled quality; at the same time, it provided an extremely rich market for the products of the trading countries of the West. The discovery of the monsoons by Hippalus paved the way for the maritime trade route which became more popular than the circuitous land routes and this alone brought the western, and later on the eastern coasts of India to the limelight, giving rise to a great number of ports in no time, though some of them have a long heredity going as far back as the heyday of the Harappans. Ptolemy's major aim was to make India known to his people and in doing so he has carefully calculated the mathematical position of all the places so that they can be easily reached. His 'Geography' largely ignores the character of the land, soil, rivers, climate, agriculture and the people which feature so prominently in the writings of Megasthenes and others.

But this does not lessen the importance of Ptolemy's 'Geography', as it gives us a more comprehensive idea about the urban development in the country than provided by any other source. We know for certain that urbanisation has coursed into different parts of the country, that the spatial distribution, showing tendency of concentration along the coastal regions and major water as well as land routes, have taken on a defined pattern, that economic activities—mainly trade and commerce—have taken a powerful role in the urban prosperity of the country, and lastly, that the supremacy of the Ganga Basin, hitherto providing the major axis of urban development in the country, came to be threatened in the wake of a newly emerging urban order.

Ptolemy is the first geographer to determine the latitudinal and longitudinal positions of the places he records, he was the first one to place India on the map of the globe drawn by him, showing its places, rivers and mountains. Whatever inaccuracy there is, the attempt is highly commendable, and the navigators could at least chart their ways for coming to India and visiting its different places with greater ease than ever before.

Besides, he is also the fist geographer to recognise the graded importance as well as the functional characteristics of the places mentioned by him, arranging them in different categories like, mart, town and port town, city, city of gods, that is, religious places, metropolis, emporium, capital and royal residence or royal city or royal seat. This has a significant place in our understanding the nature of urban process prevalent during that period in India. And it confirms our growing conviction, expressed earlier, that economic forces were already taking a greater lead than political in the emergence and subsequent growth of urban centres. Thus, dominance did no longer remain an absolute monopoly of the capital-cities when some of the economic centres had already emerged as Metropolises in different sectors of the country. It is of little consequence whether many of the minor or major cities of Ptolemy's time had their origin as Capitals; even if they had, the original trait was submerged in the tide of subsequent developments. This becomes quite evident from the writings of the author of the Periplus and Ptolemy. Barring a few instances, none refers to the political role of these centres although it cannot be denied that many of them owed their origin to such functions, pursuing the same till that period. Ptolemy's specific reference to certain centres as 'Royal Residences' or 'Royal City', etc., implies that their predominating functions were as Capitals in contrast to others where capital function had a subordinate role.

The nature of urbanisation, as revealed in the functional character of towns and cities, did not remain the same through the successive centuries. The fall of empires, the incursion of barbarian hordes from Central Asia and Persia leading to the establishment of foreign rules in North-West India and the mushrooming of new kingdom kept the political map of India constantly changing during this period. Such a political unrest naturally had its effects on the economic condition of the country, disrupting the commercial and the industrial activities of the existing towns and cities. Many of the previously flourishing cities, deprived of their political status, slowly declined while many others went into complete eclipse. Their places were taken up by new centres developed at different locations. This is very much clear from the travel accounts of Fa Hian (405-411 A.D.)[264] and especially of Hiuen Tsang who visited India in the seventh century A.D., travelling the country most extensively between 629 and 645 A.D. Of the two accounts, the latter is more revealing as it covers a large part of the country and carries more information about the urban places than the former. The following list shows the names of towns and cities visited by Fa Hian and Hiuen Tsang.

List A : Places Visited by Fa Hian

1. Takshashila; 2. Purushpura (Peshawar); 3. Hidda; 4. Mathura; 5. Kanauj; 6. "Sha-Chi", or Vaisali; 7. Sravasti, mentioned as the capital of Kosala Kingdom; 8. Na-pi-ka, a town near Kapilavastu; 9. Kusinagara; 10. City of Vaisali; 11. Pataliputra, in ruins; 12. Gaya; 13. The City of Varanasi; 14. Kausambi; 15. Champa; 16. Tamralipta; 17. The City of Charitrapura.[265]

List B : Places Visited by Hiuen Tsang

1. Takashasila Capital; 2. Prushpura; 3. Simhapura, capital or Khetas[266]; 4. Urasa, a capital in Hazara district[267]; 5. Adhishthana,

capital of Srinagar[268]; 6. Old Capital Puranadhishthana or Pandrethan in Kashmir[269]; 7. Punach, capital of the country lying between river Jhelum and the Pir Panjal Range[270]; 8. Rajapuri, capital of the country lying south of Kashmir[271]; 9. Takka, capital of the country lying near river Chenab[272]; 10. Sakala or modern Sialkot[273]; 11. Jayapura[274]; 12. Lahor or modern Lahore[275]; 13. Chinapati or probably modern Patti, formerly capital of the country between the Ravi and the Sutlej[276]; 14. Jalandhara[277]; 15. Nagara or modern Nagarkot, formerly capital of the Kulu Valley[278]; 16. Capital of Satadru, probably Sarhind[279]; 17. Capital of Paryatra, not named; 18. Mathura, capital[280]; 19. Sthaneswara or modern Thaneswar, capital[281]; 20. Srughna at or near Kalsi[282]; 21. Matipura, identified with Madawar or Mundore, a large town in Western Rohilakhand, near Bijnor[283]; 22. Gangadwara, Mayapura or Haridwar[284]; 23. The chief town or capital of Brahmapura, the latter identified with Garhwal and Kumaon[285]; 24. Govisana, represented by the modern village of Ujain[286]; 25. Ahichhatra, capital[287]; 26. Virasana, capital but not yet identified[288]; 27. Kapitha, identified with Sankisa, forty miles south-east of Atranji[289]; 28. Kanyakubja or Kanauj, capital[290]; 29. Karnasuvarna or Rangamati near Murshidabad, capital of a kingdom of Eastern India[291]; 30. Ajodhya, capital[292]; 31. Hayamukha, placed by Cunningham at Daundiakhera, about 104 miles north-west of Allahabad, a capital[293]; 32. Prayaga, capital[294]; 33. Kausambi, capital[295]; 34. Kasapura, a town identified with Sultanpur on the Gomati river, Hindu name of this old town being Kusabhanapura or Kusapur[296]; 35. Visakha, capital, probably Saketa or Ajodhya[297]; 36. Sravasti[298]; 37. Kapilavastu[299]; 38. South of Kapilavastu an old town, identified with Nagra[300]; 39. North-east of Nagra an old capital, identified with Kanakpura[301]; 40. Ramagrama, an old capital, not satisfactorily identified[302]; 41. Kusinagara, capital[303]; 42. Varanasi, capital[304]; 43. Gajapatipura, capital, or modern Ghajipur[305]; 44. Mahasara, a town, identified with Masur, a village little west of Arrah[306]; 45. Vaisali, capital, identified by Cunningham with the present village of Bearh, east of the Gandak[307]; 46. Janakapura, capital[308]; 47. An old city, not named by Hiuen Tsang; 48. Pataliputra[309]; 49. Gaya, a town[310]; 50. Kusagara-pura, called Rajagriha; capital[311]; 51. The capital of Hiranya Parvata, not named. Hiranya Parvata is identified by Cunningham with the hill of Monghyr in Bihar; 52. Champa, capital[312]; 53. Pundravardhana, identified with a place on river Karatoya, near Bogura in Bangladesh[313]; 54. The capital of Kamarupa, probably Pragjyotishpura, a village near Gauhati in Assam[314]; 55. The capital of Samatata or perhaps Jessore in Bangladesh[315]; 56. Tamralipti, capital or modern Tamluk[316]; 57. Karnasuvarna, capital, modern Rangamati, about eleven miles south of Murshidabad[317] (a repetition); 58. The capital of Udra or modern Orissa, generally identified with Jajipur on river Baitarani[318]; 59. Charitrapur, identified with modern Puri[319]; 60. The capital of Konyodha or probably modern Ganjam[320]; 61. The capital of Kalinga, not named, but it may be modern Rajahmundry or Koringa lying between River Godavari, and River Indravati[321]; 62. The capital of Kosala, not named lying to the south-west of Orissa. Cunningham identified Kosala with Berar, and places the capital at Chanda, with Nagpur, Amaravati or Ilichpur as alternatives of which Amaravati is more likely to be the old capital, while according to Fergusson, Wairagarh is a more probable place[322]; 63. Vingila, probably Vengi north-west of Elur Lake between the Godavari and the Krishna[323]; 64. The capital of Dhanakataka, identified with modern Vijaywada[324]; 65. The capital of Chola Kingdom, not named; 66. Kanchipura, capital[325]; 67. The capital of Malakuta, not clearly mentioned by Hiuen Tsang, which probably was Madurai[326]; 68. The capital of Konkanapura, probably near Golkunda[327]; 69. The capital of Maharashtra, identified by different authors with Devagiri or Daulatabad, Kalyan or Kalyani, Paithan respectively[328]; 70. Bhamkachha, capital, modern Broach[329]; 71. The capital of Malava, the kingdom identified with Dharanagara[330]; 72. The capital of Atali, appears to be situated far north of Cutch, not yet properly identified[331]; 73. The capital of Kachha (Cutch), probably Kheda[332]; 74. Valabhi, capital of the kingdom lying in modern Gujarat[333]; 75. Anandapura, not yet identified[334]; 76. The capital of Saurashtra, not named, the kingdom forming part of Gujarat[335]; 77. Balmer, capital of Gurjjara, the latter forming part of southern Rajasthan and Malwa[336]; 78. Ujjayini, capital[337]; 79. Another capital not yet identified; 80. Mahesvarapura, capital not properly identified[338]; 81. The capital of Sindh, suggested differently as Vichavapura, Vasamapura, or Balmapura or Minagara[339]; 82. Mulasthanapura, capital, or Multan[340]; 83. The capital of Parvata, not properly identified[341]; 84. Pitasila, capital[342]; 85. The capital of Avanda or probably Avanti, not named by Hiuen Tsang[343].

During his travels in India, Hiuen Tsang found many of the old towns and cities in complete ruins or almost deserted. This is attested by him in the case of many illustrious cities of the preceding centuries and for this we may turn to the actual report of the author:

(*a*) *Purushpura* : "The royal family is extinct... Inside the royal city, towards the north-east is an old foundation"[344] (or a ruinous foundation).

(*b*) *Takshasila* : "The royal family being extinct, the nobles contend for power by force;... Although there are many sangharamas, they have become ruinous and deserted, and there are very few priests"[345].

(*c*) *Alor* : "the ruins of which are still traceable"[346].

(*d*) *Kausambi* : Its sangharamas were "in ruins and deserted"[347].

(*e*) *Sravasti* : "is ruined and deserted. There is no record as to its exact limits. The ruins of the walls encompassing the royal precincts give a circuit of about 20 li"[348] (5 li = 1 mile).

(*f*) *Kapilavastu* : "There are some ten cities in this country, wholly desolate and ruined. The capital (Kapilavastu) is overthrown and in ruins. Its circuit cannot be accurately measured. The royal precincts within the city measure some 14 or 15 li round. They were all built of bricks. The foundation walls are still strong and high, it has long been deserted"[349].

(*g*) *Ramagrama* : 'The kingdom of Lan-mo (Ramagrama) has been desolate for many years. There is no account of its extent. The towns are decayed and the inhabitants few'[350].

(*h*) *Kusinagara* : "The capital of this country is in ruins, and its towns and villages waste and desolate. The brick foundation walls of the old capital (Kusinagara) are about 10 li in circuit. There are few inhabitants, and the avenues of the town are deserted and waste"[351].

(*i*) *Vaisali* : "The capital city of Vaisali is to a great extent in ruins. Its foundations are from 60 to 70 li in circuit... There are a few people living in it"[352].

(*j*) *Janakapura* : "It is mostly in ruins. In the old royal precinct (citadel or the inner city) there are yet some 3,000 houses; it may be called either a village or a town"[353].

(*k*) *The Country of Magadha* : "The walled cities have but few inhabitants"[354].

(*l*) *Pataliputra* : "Although it has been long deserted, its foundation walls still survive... There only remain the old foundation wall (of the city). The sangharamas, Deva temples, and stupas which lie in ruins may be counted by hundreds. There are only two or three remaining (entire). To the north of the old palace, and bordering on the Ganges river, there is a little town which contains about 1,000 houses"[355].

(*m*) *Kusagara-pur or Rajagriha* : "The outer walls of this city have been destroyed, and there are no remnants of them left; the inner city (walls), although in a ruined state, still have some elevation from the ground, and are about 20 li in circuit"[356].

(*n*) *Sakala* : "Although its walls are thrown down, the foundations are still firm and strong. It is about 20 li in circuit. In the midst of it they have built a little new town of about 6 or 7 li in circuit"[357].

In contrast, however, the Chinese pilgrim saw many of the old cities still maintaining their existence, though in many cases they did not represent their glorious past. They are Jalandhara, Multan or Mulasthanapura, mentioned by Ptolemy in the second century A.D. as Kasperia, Hyderabad or Patasila or the Pattala of the Greeks—though the identity between Hyderabad and Patisala has been disputed[358], Broach or Baryagaza of Ptolemy, Sthaneswara or Thaneswara, Bairat, Ahichhatra, Mathura or Modoura of Ptolemy, Pawa or Pabh, Kanoj or Kanyakubja, Prayaga, Nalanda, Modagiri or modern Monghyr, Champa, Mahishmati, Uttain, Tamralipta, Rajahmundry or perhaps Pityngra Metropolis of Ptolemy, Kanchipura, Madurai Cochin or Kottiara of Ptolemy, Paithan or Pratisthana or Baithana of Ptolemy. Among all the cities of India in Hiuen Tsang's time Kanoj, the Imperial capital of Harsha's Empire, was a very strongly defended city, extending along the east bank of the Ganga for about four miles, and adorned with lovely gardens and clear tanks[359] and with lofty structures everywhere it became the premier city of Northern India. The great assembly held at Kanauj in 643 A.D. and attended by Hiuen Tsang himself was joined by twenty kings and thousands of Buddhist, Brahminical and Jain theologians and priests. Another assembly held in the same year at Prayaga attracted 5,00,000 people to receive gifts from the Emperor who was accompanied by the Chinese pilgrim[360], the latter bearing witness not only to the religious sanctity but also perhaps the greatness of the city itself.

Apart from the cities of earlier origin, Hiuen Tsang mentions many others for which records are not sufficient to prove their antiquity. Principal among them are Adhisthana or Srinagar, Asarur, Kasur, Chinapati, and Shor-kot, all being in Punjab, Alor, the capital of Sindh, Brahmanabad, the chief city of Middle Sindh, Koteswar in Cutch, Balmer, Valabhi, Junagadh, the capital of Saurastra, Dharanagar or Dhar, the capital of Malwa, Gangadwara or Haridwar, Garjapatipur or Ghazipur, Khajuraho, Mahasara, Pundravardhan, Jessore, Charitrapura or Puri, though disputed by both Fergusson and Waddel[361], Jajatipura in Orissa, Ganjam, Chanda in Berar, Elgandel, as the capital of Andhra, Kheda or modern Khaira of Gujarat, Vadari or Eder in Malwa.

Hiuen Tsang's travel accounts, on the whole, carry a very significant place in the study of Indian urbanisation on the eve of the Medieval period. Other than offering a reliable basis, they help us to construct more or less a general picture of urban conditions in the country prevailing at that time. It is not that Hiuen Tsang dealt with all the urban centres since his travels did not cover each and every part of the country. As a matter of fact, the names too few as compared with the earlier accounts of either the Periplus or that of Ptolemy. In spite of this fundamental, drawback, we get a personal view of the author about urban life in general from his experience gathered through visits to the places mentioned in his accounts. The list of urban places complied by him is far from complete as Hiuen Tsang was extremely cautious about speaking of those only which he visited personally. Thus, however incomplete or inconclusive, the list is an authentic guide to, at least the contemporaneity of the urban centres of that period.

Hiuen Tsang's observations make important revelations about the urban situation in India. For the first time we get an accurate idea about the prevailing physical character and conditions of the towns and cities, come to know about their social life, the areal size of the individual centres, the respective distance between them and also about the size of the kingdoms. The veracity of statements on the actual distance as well as the size of the kingdoms in some cases may not go unchallenged, but that does not blurr the picture. In his words, "the towns have inner gates; the walls are wide and high, the streets and lanes are tortuous, and the roads winding. The thoroughfares are dirty and stalls are arranged on both sides of the road with appropriate signs. Butchers, fishers, dancers, executioners, and scavengers, and so on, have their abodes without the city... The walls of the towns are mostly built of bricks or tiles. The towers on the walls are constructed of wood or bamboo; the houses have balconies and belvederes, which are made of wood, with a casting of lime or mortar, and covered with tiles. The different buildings have the same form as those in China... The walls are covered with lime and mud, mixed with cow's dung for purity"[362]. It needs pointing our here that, barring a few cases, Hiuen Tsang mentions only the capitals which might indicate that his itinerary was mostly confined to the Capital Cities. Besides, his apparent silence about the industrial and commercial activities of the places he visited is in sharp contrast with the accounts left by other earlier authors. Although speaking about the character of soil, climate, density of population, produce of the country and the collection of rare and valuable products from distant regions and stored in great quantities in some of the cities, he is strangely indifferent about the individual role of these cities either in the industrial or in the commercial fields. Even while writing about Bharukachha (Broach) or Tamralipti—ports of international fame during the earlier centuries, he casually refers to former as making "sole profit... from the sea"[363], and the latter where "wonderful articles and gems are collected... in abundance"[364].

There are two possible explanations for his capital-bound tours and for his reticence about the secondary as well as tertiary activities. First, Hiuen Tsang was a traveller of a different set. As a Bhikshu or priest[365], his principal interest lay in getting acquainted with the original Buddhist Literature, visiting the places directly associated with Buddha at the latter's life-time and those where the disciples had established 'Sangharamas' or monasteries. This particular quest for the knowledge and the teachings of the Great Master (Buddha) neatly defined his course, taking him from place to place which could illuminate him on his singular mission. It is quite natural that during the Buddhist era Buddhism as the religion of the King made the capitals more important seats of Buddhist Culture than other places. It is interesting to observe in every case that Hiuen Tsang is more eloquent about the religious side of the city than its other aspects. This leads to the second explanation. Most of the towns and cities, visited by the Chinese pilgrim, are capitals, either of kingdoms existing then, or of those disappeared long ago. Towns or cities, without capital-functions, almost do not appear in his list. In all likelihood towns and cities thriving otherwise lay beyond his concern and he did not take any notice of them as they generated little interest and had nothing to offer to satisfy his religious curiosity. This is, perhaps, the only reason for ignoring to record the material progress of the country. But what really strikes is the sign of general deterioration recorded by him in the case of certain cities which seem to have had outlived their long active periods and contained little life-force to carry on further.

This does in no way mean that urbanisation was on a much lower key than in the earlier centuries of the Christian era. Facts available do not indicate any possibility of urban character having undergone a drastic change during the intervening centuries and the process reverting to its old position where the development becomes more centred on the capital—ensuring greater protection and security of economic pursuits —than the non-political centres. This becomes more imperative from a comparative study of urbanisation between the periods covered by Ptolemy and Hiuen Tsang.

A look at the two different lists of urban centres, available from their writings, will reveal that they agree on less than a score of names, while Ptolemy gives more than three hundred names against about a hundred given by Hiuen Tsang. The wide disagreement between them does not mean that the towns and cities alive and thriving during Ptolemy's time ceased to exist four centuries after when Hiuen Tsang was visiting the country. The fact is otherwise. Most of those mentioned by Ptolemy and also by the authors of the Periplus exist still today, thereby indicating that they have maintained their existence all through the last seventeen to eighteen centuried or so. Cities found in ruins by Hiuen Tsang have disappeared and many others found by him in a better position are extant till this date. Curiously enough, besides four, all the urban centres recorded by Fa Hieun in the early part of the fifth century A.D.[366] are extinct now, though cities not mentioned by him were still there making a fruitful existence before he appeared on the scene and continuing their chequered career two centuries later when Hiuen Tsang was around. All these facts lead us to the unavoidable conclusion that—authors, with their individual bias, were led to select cities and towns of their own choice to be included in their account Sometimes ignorance also was responsible for understatements.

Factors Contributing to Urbanisation since Early Historic Period

Urban development on such a widescale and in such a prosperous manner could not have taken place without material progress in other sectors. Agriculture, industry as well as communication systems provided the matrix in which the urban edifice had taken its roots. Hence, it will be worthwhile to review the situation.

A. The Village Settlements and Agriculture

In the rural sector, a sort of community life had developed even before Buddha was born, signs of which had already been observed in the villages established by the Aryans when they came to settle down on the Indian soil. Instances of isolated houses are not available. A group of houses separated by narrow passage-ways gave rise to village settlement, each surrounded by extensive stretch of agricultural lands and having a large patch of pasture of grazing and cattle of the community and another patch of jungle with common rights of waste and wood as fuel. The village life was based on a joint-enterprise, headed by the Village Headman and governed by general custom. Cultivation used to take place simultaneously on all, the fields and, water was supplied according to needs from the irrigation channels dug by the community. The owner of the field had no right to fence off his portion of land. As a matter of fact, the entire agricultural land belonging to a village used to be divided among the houses in proportion to the number of heads in each family and the actual share for a family changed in conformity with change in the size of the family. Thus, no property-right by inheritance could grow on the agricultural lands and also on both the pasture, and the jungle-land and these could not be sold by one family to another. The produce of the field was shared between the families in accordance with the decision of the village council. The Village Headman, on the other hand, had the responsibility of keeping contact with the Government and it was equally his duty to see to the construction of the roads and attend to the royal visitor. There is no mention of using forced labour for the construction works; on the contrary, the villagers united on their own accord for building Mote-Halls, Rest Houses, Reservoirs in their own villages, sometimes laying out parks and taking repair works of the roads leading to the adjacent villages. Even women used to offer free labour in such community projects.

The life in such villages was simple, without economic stratification where nobody had a way of acquiring more wealth, than his neighbour Needs were met for all and security was guaranteed, giving peace and happiness as long as famines did not occur due to drought. The situation seems to have had improved further a few centuries later when Megasthenes was visiting the country[367]. According to Rhys Davids, nearly 76 to 80 per cent of the total population of the country lived at that time in villages[368] when the entire territory had about fifteen to twenty million people[369]. Both the figures are highly speculative, without any definite ground to be relied upon. Yet, the strange similarity in the proportion of rural population between circa 600-700 B.C. and today is very much striking.

The scene of agricultural affluence becomes more vivid from the accounts of contemporary writers like Panini. Writing in the middle of the fifth century B.C., Panini finds three names for the rural settlements and, in order of importance, they are the *'Grama'* (village), the *'Ghosha'* (the settlement of cowherds) and the *'Kheta'* (hamlet). It appears that ranching by this time had made for itself a distinct place in the agricultural economy of the country.

The villages, specially marked out by natural boundaries like forests, thickets or jungles, rivulets, hills, etc., were surrounded by arable land (sitya), pasture (gochara), plantations of bamboo thickets or reeds (vamsa-kathina), fruit-orchards (phalegrahi), reserves of herbs and plants used for food preservation and for medicinal purposes (aushadi-vanaspati vana), forests of timber and waste land (ushara). In the, case of the Goshta, or ranches, the grazing land, the land for dumping manure, the agricultural land and the land for habitation within the settlement used to be clearly demarcated of which the first three types were correspondingly shifted in a twelve-year cycle.

The houses in the village were probably made of mud with reed and straw roofs. Every village consisted of a number of families and a group of villages formed a 'Gramata'[370]. The source of water for the village were wells, with attachment of water-troughs for the cattle. The wells used to be regularly cleaned by specially trained hands, known as 'Udagaha'[371].

Unlike the situation prevailing about a century ago, individual ownership had become a practice in these villages for agricultural land which used to be divided into private holdings on the basis of some sort of cadastral survey[372] made by special officers appointed by the government, though the term 'kaidarya' perhaps refers to the presence of some consolidated holdings as well[373]. In contrast, however, pastures became the community property. In the days of Panini, two crops a year were produced and the fields were classified according to the crops they grew. River irrigation was in practice, and important rivers like, the Indus, the Swat, the Beas, the Chenab and the Sarayu are mentioned as sources of irrigation. Irrigation from well also was practised, water being lifted in leather-buckets, drawn by bullocks[374]. A large variety of crops were grown, chief among them being five variety of crops were grown, chief among them being five varieties of rice[375], barley, wheat, sesamum, linseed, hemp, different types of pulses, sugarcane, and cotton. Plants like, 'manijistha' or madder and 'nili' or indigo were cultivated for supplying dye-stuff[376].

Megasthenes, speaking of India in the early part of the fourth century B.C., presents a very bright picture. According to him, the high fertility of the soil, greater part of which was under irrigation, gave two crops a year[377]. The double rains, summer and winter, supplemented by widescale irrigation, made it possible to produce a great variety of crops like, rice, wheat, millet, sesamum, different varieties of pulses and vegetables, fruits of all kinds known to agriculture at that time and a great number of products used as animal feeds[378]. In his opinion, the supply of food was so abundant that no famine had occurred in the country till that date[379]. Regarding the absence of famines, Megasthenes offers another explanation. This was the prevalent practice in the country of keeping the husbandmen inviolable during the wars when neither they nor their fields were ever violated by the combatants from either side. This exemplary practice—we do not know since when had been in vogue—kept the economy of the country completely undisturbed and periods of turmoil could leave no strain on the life of the common people. This similarly applied to the cities which were never razed to the ground by the winning army. In the estimation of Megasthenes, the Indians in those days had a high stature and a good body-build both of which, in his words, were largely attributable to the great abundance of nourishing food, the pure air and the finest drinking water of the land[380].

Agriculture made the principal means of livelihood in Kautilya's time. There were lands directly belonging to the State; the latter having full responsibility of agricultural operations with slaves and labours employed in the State Service[381]. Where the State could not cultivate the land directly, the land used to be leased out to the share-croppers[382]. Besides these two types, the remaining arable land of the country belonged to the farmers who, living in villages, were free to choose what types of crops to be raised, though in times of exigencies the State had the right to intervene. The regions receiving 35" to 48" of rainfall produce crop without irrigation[383], the latter being required in the regions having lesser rainfall, such as in Maharastra receiving about 24 to 27 inches[384]. Construction of irrigation works remained with the State, though private enterprise was also perhaps involved. Two types of irrigation were generally practised: (a) irrigation from tanks, fed by natural springs, lakes and wells; (b) irrigation by canals drawing water from reservoirs artificially constructed by raising embankments, or rather dam, across the rivers. Of these two, the former was more popular than the latter[385]. The farmers were required to pay for the water drawn for irrigation at different rates, such as, one-fifth of the produce for water lifted by hand even from their own water-works, one-fourth when the water is lifted by bullocks, etc., and one-third where the water was set flowing by any mechanical device[386]. Kautilya refers to three sowings, with succession of crops from season to season, and crops mentioned by him are rice, wheat, barley, different types of oilseeds, pulses, sugarcane, fruits, medicinal plants and herbs, perfume-plants, etc.[387] In his days, animal husbandry had an important place in the State's economy. Land not suited to cultivation was given over to pastures[388] and as it appears, all the grasslands belonged to the State. Like the 'Director of Agriculture'[389], the 'Superintendent of

Pastures' held tremendous responsibility in maintaining them, besides constructing tanks and wells for the animals and also making orchards and flower gardens in the pasture lands. The State maintained a large number of cattle and other animals in the charge of a separate official, the 'Superintendent of Cattle' who had to keep complete records of the State-animals, while the records of the village animals owned by private individuals were maintained. by the district officials[390]. The animals, apart from being used for draught purpose, provided a rich source of food with meat, fresh and dried, milk and milk-products, and their hide was a great source of State revenue[391].

Land was still the primary source of living in the days of Patanjali—in the middle of the second century B.C. —though in his opinion, people had become more prosperous and with increasing demands were taking greater interest in different types of activities other than agriculture[392]. Agricultural process seems to have had remained the same all through the centuries. Property right on land was in vogue and individual fields were carefully measured off the State officials. Scrupulous care was taken for dividing land into different types, both, perhaps, for agricultural and non-agricultural uses and great interest was displayed in the methods of sowing, agricultural implement, seeds and nature of crops and also in the storage of gram after harvest[393]. Patanjali refers to 'Grama' (village) and the 'Ghoshas' or the settlement of animal herders similar to those mentioned by Panini some three hundred years ago. Patanjali further mentions large village units[394].

Agriculture, constituting the backbone of the country's economy, is amply evidenced by its reference occurring in the writings of the foreigners. Eratosthenes, writing some time in the middle of the third century B.C.[395], points to the striking regularity of the copious rainfall in India, in both summer and winter, guaranteeing double crops in great abundance every year[396]. Among the crops mentioned by him are rice, flax, millet, sesamum, bosmoron (perhaps wild barley or millet), wheat, barley, pulse, cotton and abundant fruits. Strabo (60 B.C.-19 A.D) refers to the country lying between the Indus and Jhelum, around Takshasila, as extremely fertile and thickly populated[397]. He believes the land beyond the Beas to be equally fertile[398]. In either the Periplus or in the account of Ptolemy we do not find any direct reference to the economic life of the country. But the names of merchandise figuring in the list of trading articles gives a vivid picture of agricultural as well as the industrial affluence of the country.

Hiuen Tsang, visiting India in the middle of the seventh century A.D., makes copious reference to the agricultural condition of the country. The wide difference in the climate and soil made a great variety of produces[399]. Major among the crops grown at that time were rice and corn, many types of fruits, edible herbs and plants, including ginger, mustard seeds for oil, melons, pumpkins, etc. The most common food of the people included milk butter, cream, soft-sugar, sugar-candy, mustard oil and cakes made of corn. Fish, mutton, gazelle and deer were eaten fresh or salted. But, people eating onion and garlic, or beef and pork were treated as out-castes, living beyond the city-gates[400]. Hiuen Tsang found Kashmir famous for the production of fruit, flower and medicinal plants[401]; in the plains of Beas rice and late-sown corn were the principal crops[402]; the country lying between the Ravi and the Sutlej produced abundant harvests;[403] the land around Jullundur yielded cereals, including a large amount of rice, fruits and flowers[404]. Similar references are available for the lands stretching from the Ganga-Jamuna plains to the western coastal areas producing rich harvests of a wide variety of agricultural crops produced in the different seasons of the year. All these facts indicate the high level of agricultural development in the country; remaining undeterred through the passage of centuries.

B. Industry

Industry, as compared with agriculture, played, no doubt, a much lesser role in providing a means of living, but its significance in the economy of the country and in the social life was greater than agriculture. Its various products, giving rise to a tremendous traffic—both inlands and overseas—not only helped the royal exchequer but at the same time initiated the first major movement of people. It is not that the merchants were the only people moving from place to place; the artisans and the craftsmen changed their homes, settling down at distant place offering markets for their skill and talents. Instances of Indian trading colonies in West Asiatic countries, as mentioned before, are reported from very distant past. Similar instances of foreign colonies on Indian soil may not be found till a later date. Yet, a mixture of Indian population, beginning from the early part of the historical period, may be traced through a proper sociological scanning. All these had a direct impact on the urbanisation of the country where the growing stature of non-agricultural activities boosted up the rate of urban development and influenced its spatial character.

It should, however, be borne in mind that industry in those early days was pot an absolute monopoly of the urban centres. At least, a part of it was carried on in the villages having direct contact with urban places. Villages of this specialised character were invariably located in or near the immediate neighbourhood of the urban centres which, apart from providing the market for their products, also supplied the necessities of life of these villagers. Reference to such industrial villages occur in the old Buddhist literature. A carpenter's village, for example, situated near the city of Varanasi had five hundred carpenters who, shaping wood for the construction of houses and sign-posts, used to go with their produce to the city and built one or two-storey houses for whoever wanted them[405]. Instances of 'Professional Villages' are also found from these records which mention two smiths' villages, grown side by side in the rural area, one of which contained a thousand huts and they were supplying things like axes, hatchets, ploughshares, spikes and other implements to the villages lying around them[406].

In spite of these facts, the point need not be stressed further that industry actually could develop without urban backing, and far beyond the urban areas. Industrial villages mentioned above developed was directly focused on urban needs. Presumably, a number of industries had developed in rural environments. Most important among them was the pottery. Besides, various branches of the textiles and food industries were also located in villages. This is true still now with the handicraft industries, mostly concentrated in the rural areas of India. A closer scrutiny of the famous centres of rural industries of the present-day India, in fact, will give a more accurate idea of the urban development of the past, offering a concrete evidence of the existence of urban life in the nearby areas. But the fact should not be lost sight of that in every case, whether in those days or today, the very existence of the village industries—a specialized one—is dependent of the demands of the urban market. As such these industries at all times had sought location near the urban centres where from they could maintain easy contact with the urban market. It is not difficult to imagine that the market played the most important role in the development as well as the geographical distribution of the industries where the rural economy in those days, as today, had no means of sustaining the industrial activities without urban support. On the other hand, many of the industries found a strong foothold in the urban centres, bringing them time-old fame in their wide range of manufactures of inimitable quality.

That industry had carved out itself an important place as a main source of living in the sixth century B.C. cannot be disputed when a number of 'Guilds' had already formed on the basis of workers engaged in different types of industrial activities. At least four of them are mentioned in the old Buddhist literature[407] and the number, according to Rhys Davids, increased afterwards to eighteen[408], consisting of the following with specialisations in their precise fields:

1. The Wood Workers; 2. The Metal Workers; 3. The Stone Workers; 4. The Weavers; 5. The Dyers; 6. The Leather Workers; 7. The Potters; 8. The Ivory Workers; 9. The Jewellers; 10. The Painters; 11. The Fishermen; 12. The Butchers; 13. The Hunters and Trappers; 14. The Rush Workers and Basket-Makers; 15. The Cooks and Confectioners; 16. The Garland Makers arid Flower Seller; 17. The Sailors; 18. The Barbers and Shampooers.

The names of different guilds make it clear that people offering different professional service formed voluntarily or by economic as well as political necessity[409] into separate societies of their own, in which family tradition became the guiding feature of one's future activities. All these guilds, however, do not represent industrial workers in the true sense of the term. But the formation of guilds very strongly suggests the survival of a long tradition, built over a period of several centuries. Further, it also gives an idea about the market which seems to have had an extremely sophisticated character. The division of work between the weavers and the dyers means that the produce needed specialised knowledge. The picture obtained from the formation of these guilds points directly to the prevailing attitude of the society in putting more value on specialisation than on works of ordinary standard. Demands of such higher order could not have a rural origin; as a matter of fact, the products and services of these guilds, whether they were the residents of rural or the urban areas, were mostly to satisfy the urban needs. An analysis of the specialised nature of the work and the produce of the individual guilds may substantiate this.

Among the various guilds, those of the Wood Workers, the Metal Workers, the Stone Workers, the Weavers, the Dyers, the Jewellers, and the Painters were involved directly in the production of goods required by an urban society alone. As for instance, apart from their general types of activities, building of houses, ships and vehicles of all types were the specialised fields of job for the Wood Workers[410]; the Metal Workers made a fame in gold and silver work of "great delicacy and beauty"[411]; the Stone Workers made the stone staircases of the houses and the reservoirs and also laid the foundation of the houses, the upper parts of which were made of wood, carved pillars and bas-reliefs and mady crystal bowls of exquisite varieties[412], the weavers manufactured fine muslins and choiceable fabrics of silk and woollen rugs, blankets, coverlets and carpets[413]; the Dyers dyed clothes made by the Weavers[414]; the Leather Worker made a large variety of foot-wear and also expensive types of embroidered articles[415]; the Ivory Workers carved out a wide range of high-priced articles, including ornaments of extraordinary beauty; the work of the Jewellers, though not described anywhere, may be assessed from the intricate designs of the ornaments worn by the figures on the bas-reliefs, nothing at the same time that even today, such designs are in vogue in gold ornaments used by the Indian ladies; the job of the painters was to apply a plaster of lime on the wooden walls of the houses and decorate them with fresco-paintings.

Other guilds, directly serving the urban communities, were (*a*) the Cooks and Confectioners, the latter probably preparing different types of snacks consumed by the urban population; (*b*) the Barbers and Shampooers also dealt in perfumes needed by the sophisticated urbanities; (*c*) the Garland Makers and Flower-Sellers presumably fulfilled the artistic demands of the well-to-do classes of the urban resident; (*d*) the Butchers, with their shops and slaughter houses, naturally supplied the urban market.

On the other hand, guilds formed by the Fishermen, the Hunters and Trappers; the Rush Workers and the Basket Makers, and the

Potters were engaged in occupations which served both the rural as well as the urban markets. Of them, the Hunters and Trappers, supplying valuable articles like fur, ivory, venison and games collected from the vastly stretching forests largely catered to the urban rather than rural needs. The last of these guilds formed by the sailors, was not involved in any productive activity, but engaged in the traffic on the great rivers and the sea which played a significant part in the economy of the country.

Similar references to artisan classes are also available in Panini. He actually divides the artisans into two major classes — the village artisans (grama-silpins)[416] and the artisans; probably employed or patronised by the King (raja-silpins). Each village contained at least five types of artisans—the potter, the blacksmith, the carpenter, the barber and the washerman. Panini refers to eleven types of artisans classes in the country as follows:

1. The Potters; 2. The Carpenters; 3. The Bow Makers; 4. The Dyers; 5. The Miners; 6. The Weavers; 7. The Blanket Makers; 8. The Leather Workers; 9. The Blacksmith; 10. The Goldsmith; 11. The Lifters.[417]

While some of the important guilds of workers are missing from the list, like, the Ivory Workers, the Painters, etc., a number of new names appear on the list, such as, the Bow Makers, the Miners and the Lifters. The short list does not mean that industrial activities, by this time, had shrunk. In making reference to the different types of artisans, Panini mentions the major classes serving the society at his time. And in doing so, he probably ignores those which do not make it a skilled job. As a matter of fact, referring to 'raja-silpins', he uses the word 'skilled'[418] to identify them from the non-skilled. Taking this as the possible basis of his classification, one cannot fail to note that, at least three types of industrial functions have found no place in his list. It is not presumable that the Ivory Workers and the Painters had ceased to function in Panini's time since the former class still exists in India making a flourishing business. Similarly, the practice of decorating houses with paintings on lime-plastered walls done by a class of artisans specially trained and experienced in the art could not have stopped altogether in the days of Panini which is prevalent in some form till this date in the country.

On the other hand, the classes of craftsmen like the Miners and the Bow Makers, mentioned by Panini merit special consideration in view of the fact that the former, dealing in a wide range of precious stones and non-precious minerals like, iron, bell-metal, tin, etc., needed highly specialised knowledge in the identification as well as the intricate processes of collection or mining involved. Likewise, bow-making was an equally specialised trade in those days, making it one of the principal weapons of warfare. But the craftsmanship involved in the activities of the Lifters is not very clear. The Lifters, performing the construction of scaffolding—probably required for building works and repairs in the towns and cities—made it a work of specialised nature and hence figure in the list. A comparative study of the early list of guilds and that provided by Panini establishes beyond doubt that the prominence of industry as a principal means of livelihood had not waned in anyway. Industrial activities as performed by specialised group of artisans, continued to maintain their specialities in the different fields of production. Panini does not make any direct reference to industrial places. It is, however, quite apparent from his accounts that most of the industries carried on by the 'raja-silpins' or the skilled craftsmen were located in the urban centres of his days. This will be more clear from the accounts left by Kautilya.

The existence of guilds formed by craftsmen, representing different crafts, is mentioned by Kautilya, though he does not give any details about them[419]. But it is clear from his statement that the State Economy derived a large share of its revenue from the various types of industries functioning at his time. The chief among them were the Mining and the Manufacturing industries. Mining occupied a very important place and was mainly a State activity assigned to the charge of 'Director of Mines' (Akaradhyaksha) who was to be an expert in geology as well as metallurgy[420]. Equipped with skilled workmen and implements[421], he was to work the larger mines while the weak and expensive mines were to be leased out on a share-basis to the private enterprises[422]. Kautilya makes only stray reference to the availability of one or two minerals, such as Diamonds from Vidarbha, Kalingas, Kasi near Jabalpur, etc. In mining, gold and silver took the most important place, these two having been separately placed under the direct supervision of a 'Superintendent'[423] whose duty was to see to the manufacture of gold and silver articles by a skilled royal goldsmith in large workshop specially built in the middle of the market-places. Employees in these workshops were subjected to strict vigilance. Other industries associated with mining and mentioned by Kautilya are those concerning the smelting and manufacture of metalware made of copper, lead, tin, Vaikrantaka, brass, steel, iron, bronze and bell-metal[424]. The minting of silver and copper coins also formed an important industry. Factories manufacturing articles of conchshells, diamonds, gems, pearls, corals and caustics[425] figure in the list. Besides, salt manufacturing, probably from sea water involving the process of crystalisation, seems to have been widely practised in the country. The most important industry in Kautilya's time, however, appears to be the textiles for which much information is available in his text. Separate factories for the production of cotton, linen, silk and woollen materials are referred to, though it cannot be said for certain that the entire industry was a State monopoly[426]. A special cell was to function in charge of a Superintendent, for directing and controlling the operations and for keeping the quality of products high. The raw materials used for spinning yarn were cotton and silk cotton, silk, hemp, flax and wool, including hair of deer, and barke-fibre[427]. Among the most famous textiles mentioned by Kautilya are three different varieties of 'Dakula' from Bengal of which that from the Vangas was white and smooth; that from Karnasuvarna of Murshidabad and Rajmahal was of the colour of sun and smooth like a gem; that from Pundras was dark in colour and smooth like a gem[428]. Silk from Varanasi and the Pundras[429]; the Eri or Muga Silk from the Magadha, the Pundras and Karnasuvarna, the latter supplying the best in quality; silk and silkcloth from Gilgit[430]; cotton fabrics from Madurai, Varanasi, the Vangas, the Vatsas and Mahishmati being the best in quality[431]. Reference to the existence of a great variety of woollens, including white and coloured blankets, are also made without naming their places of origin. Over and above this, manufacture of ropes, throngs and straps meant for various uses, were carried on. Another industry functioning in those days was the manufacture of Chariots and carriages required for both war and for ceremonial occasions[432].

There is no way of knowing where the industries were located. But what appears from Kautilya's accounts, the industries, functioning mostly under State supervision, were mainly concentrated in the towns and cities where they could easily be supervised by the State's

Administrators. Kautilya nowhere mentions rural sector playing any important role in the industrial functions of the State. His villages, as has been examined earlier, are simple rural settlements making a living entirely out of cropping and posturing. In contrast in his City-Plans, particular sector is reserved for the factories.

Megasthenes, speaking of the same period, refers to the existence of artisans as a separate class of people in the country who made implements for the use of agriculturists and others. They, according to Megasthenes, enjoyed great privileges in the society. They were exempted from paying taxes for their products and in many cases received maintenance from the State[433]. Megasthenes refers to the Indians loving colourful dresses and ornaments. The dresses were made of materials woven in gold threads or the finest muslins, beautifully decorated with flowery designs. This particular reference to the materials of matchless beauty in those days speak of a high technical knowledge and taste in weaving.

Patanjali does not refer to any guild, but there is no reason to believe that the practice had ceased to exist in his time as the different classes of artisans mentioned by him corroborate with such classes making living in the earlier periods. According to the 'Mahabhashya'of Patanjali, life had become more prosperous and there was a greater demand for larger variety of products. Patanjali mentions five types of artisans in a village; the potter, the blacksmith, the carpenter, the barber and the washermen. He does not, however, make any special reference to the artisan classes living outside the rural areas. But it is clear from his statement about the functions of some of them that he was, in fact, speaking of the artisans working for the urban rather than the village markets. As for instance, referring to the blacksmith, he makes a distinction between the 'ayaskara'[434] or coppersmith and 'lohakara'[435] or ironsmith. They are classed by him as 'silpin'[436] or craftsman who worked on daily wages unlike the 'dasakar maker' or slave-blacksmith working on food and clothing only. It is interesting to observe that both these classes fit in more properly with the urban than the village economy, while the blacksmith belonging to rural areas subsisted more likely on the direct sale of their products to the villagers. Besides, the blacksmith producing arms[437] among other things had no useful place in the village.This becomes more obvious from the classes of artisans like, the Metal Workers, the Masons and

Architects, the Cooks and Confectioners, and the Weavers who could not have any foothold in a village economy. Among the Metal Workers, the goldsmith, making a flourishing business, had necessarily found his clients among the urban population and naturally functioned in the towns and cities. The Masons and Architects, forming another class of artisans, similarly could not have any place in a village economy. The 'Nagarkara'[438] of Patanjali means City-Architect, implying that his activity was entirely confined to the cities, taking part, probably, in the construction of buildings, Patanjali further refers to 'Kup-Khankaka' or Well-Diggers, the digging of well having been an important function in the urban centres in those days for supplying drinking water. Likewise, confectioners, dealing in baked cakes or pastries, called 'sashkuli' and 'mandakika',[439] made a living in the cities. Patanjali considers weaving of both vegetable and animal fibres as a low profession, graded with the mat-makers[440]. But his reference to famous fabrics named 'kasika' from Varanasi, 'madhyamika' from Chittor and 'satakas' from Mathura[441] make more than certain that textiles still maintained their earlier reputation of specialised branch of industries.

It does not escape notice that both Kautilya and Patanjali, living nearly four centuries apart, found agriculture as the primary source of occupation of the people of the country. Kautilya calls the principal occupations of his days—agriculture (krisi), cattle rearing (pasupalaya), and trade (vanijya)—as 'Vartta' or livelihood in which industries were not included[442], in spite of the fact that a considerable section of the population earned their living from the latter. Kautilya refers to a number of industrial professions and does not fail to observe the importance of their functions in the society. His details on the different branches of the mining activities, the emphasis laid on the various branches of metal-ware industries, and his particular reference to a large group of other industries producing luxury goods of high order, and the special importance attached by him to the different branches of the textiles distinctly indicate the solid base of the industry that it enjoyed with unique specialisation. This does not, however, mean that industry engaged a substantial section of the population. Kautilya does not treat it as one of the principal 'vratta' or means of livelihood at his time for the simple reason of its not being one of the major employers. But that particular fact does in no way belittle the importance of the industries. The total employment in the industries could not be large enough to compete with that in agriculture or even in trade. It holds true till today in spite of the great stride in industrial development made since Independence. It should not be forgotten that the major share of the country's wealth had always come from its great and varied agricultural resources, providing the principal basis for Indian Industries which, oriented to market needs, were concentrated largely in or near the market areas. It is not difficult to imagine that the industrial specialisation grew out of the special needs and backings of the urban centres and as such, most of the industries found their natural locations in or near their area of influence.

This flourishing condition of the industries does not appear to have dimmed during the succeeding centuries when Patanjali writes about the country. The specialisations still were there and his casual reference to expensive fabrics give a rare glimpse of the continued fame of India in her specialised products. This is further substantiated by a great variety of products put on sale as trading articles in the days of Patanjali. Without going into a long list and excluding the food products[443], Patanjali mentions only the important items like, the fabrics of silk, wool, flax, hemp, cotton, blanket of a defined standard, white woollen garments, dye stuff, leather goods—such as, sandals and shoes, iron chains, agricultural implements, pottery utensils, wines, perfumes, gold images, and vehicles like cart, chariot and boat[444].

Turning now to foreign sources giving, information about the brilliant industrial records of these early times we may refer to Strabo who, depending largely on Megasthenes as his source of information, mentions the carpenters, the blacksmiths, and the miners. Besides, he refers to the existence of six classes of urban workers, the first one of them being responsible for looking after everything relating to articles and seeing to their sale through public notices[445]. From all appearance, therefore, industry played a vital role in the economy of the urban centres.

Perhaps, a more accurate and direct source proving invaluable information about India's industrial glory is presented by the Periplus. It gives an exhaustive list of articles of trade, imported and exported to and from the country. Among the items of export many are manufactured articles, produced by different branches of industries functioning with a high degree of specialisation in their individual fields. The specialised products included coloured lac[446], peral of superior quality exported in considerable quantity[447]; silk thread[448], gum used both as incense and medicine[449] beams of wood including Ebony logs[450], oil of sesame[451], indigo[452], cane sugar[453], muslins of finest quality and of a great variety[454], including perhaps, muslin robes with pearls interwoven[455]; large quantities of coarse cotton fabrics[456] and coarse cotton, the latter used for stuffing mattresses and cushions[457]; long pepper[458]; iron, iron utensils, and swords[459]; among the valuable stones, gems[460], diamonds[461], goldstoné[462], sapphire[463]; agate in vast quantities[464]; porcelain or vessels made of flour-spath fetching extravagant prices from the Roman markets[465].

Without making the list longer it can be said that the items taking important place in the volume of external trade give a concrete idea about India's industrial prosperity. The industry was diversified in character, producing large surplus for export to the foreign countries and this constant flow of finished goods to the markets abroad justifies the high quality of the produce as well as the permanent character of the industries functioning over centuries. The author of the Periplus does not refer directly to the exact places of their production. In certain cases, however, he points to the places of their origin, though not giving the exact locations where manufacturing took place. It is, thus, not possible to know about the actual distribution of industries in those days. But it is quite evident that industrial functions were carried on extensively throughout the country which, in turn, gave rise to the most widespread nature of trade involving a large number of ports exchanging goods with numerous countries of the West.

Unlike the author of the Periplus, Ptolemy remains silent about the industrial performances of the country. He mentions marts, harbours and emporiums, thereby indirectly referring to the trading activities which naturally dealt largely in the products of the manufacturing industries.

Industrial activities do not similarly feature very prominently in the writings of Hiuen Tsang. But his stray references made at certain instances to particular kinds of activities give sufficient hint about the flourishing stage of the industry. To cite examples, Hiuen Tsang refers to the land of the Beas producing gold, silver, copper and iron, and the people wearing very shining white silk[466] and other fabrics which definitely were made in the country. Elsewhere he mentions people living in the Sutlej Valley also wore beautiful, bright silk stuff[467], and the kingdom of Mathura is famous for the production of fine species of cotton fabrics[468]. Hiuen Tsang finds Hardwar producing native copper, pure crystal and precious vases[469]. At Thaneswar[470], Kanauj[471] and at Valabhi[472] in Gujarat rare and valuable merchandise are collected in great quantities from different parts of the country. The people at these places were rich and at Valabhi there, were some hundred houses each possessing wealth amounting to a 'hundred lakhs'[473].

Trade and Commerce and Transport

Beginning from early times trade and commerce had a well defined place in the country's economy. This is amply evidenced by the existence of a merchant class, forming one of the leading castes of the society, and the large scale movement of goods irrespective of physical as well as political barriers within the vast subcontinent. Fick traces the existence of trade associations to the early period of Indian culture, maintaining further that such associations or guilds were formed with a specific purpose of making better employment of capital and for protecting the legal rights of the class; and different guilds kept close contact between themselve[474]. According to Rhys Davids, silks, muslins, brocades, embroideries, rugs and the finer sorts of cloth, cutlery and armour, perfumes and drugs, ivory and ivory products, jewellery and gold featured as the principal articles of trade[475] that were in movement from place to place within and outside the country. It may be interesting to note that each of the articles mentioned above was an expensive one, and trade only in them may give a wrong impression that non-expensive items were not in demand. As a matter of fact, trade itself was a highly expensive business in those days as taxes and entry fees to be paid in every country had to be borne by the merchants for their merchandise, armed guards had to hired by them for security against robbers during journeys overland and also the time involved was too great as the pace of the caravans on land "never exceeded two miles an hour"[476]. All these added to the expenses on transport and only the high priced articles could afford to bear such high expenses. The merchants, in fact, used to earn profits out of the sales, receiving two to three times the actual value of the articles[477] which alone compensated for the great risks and hardships undertaken by them. This particular fact may lead to a logical conclusion that the demands for such goods being so high in the country presupposes the existence of sufficiently wealthy community, providing a rich market, functioning at many places of the country. The trade in the items mentioned above was long-distance in character and it does not rule out the possibility of short-distance trade in less expensive articles.

The merchants carried the merchandise up and down the rivers, along the coasts and across the country by roads running in different directions. On the land goods were taken in two-wheeled carts drawn by two bullocks, travelling in long caravans. Fick, referring to the 'Jatakas' or Buddhist literature written between pre-Buddhist era and 300 B.C. at the latest[478], gives instances of trading activities of that period. According to him, overland trade was of much greater importance than sea-borne trade. Important trade-routes traversed the country in all directions and goods were taken-routes traversed the country in all directions and goods were taken over long distances, the transactions being most frequent between the eastern and the western parts of the country. Fick cities two examples to impress upon the hugeness of the caravan trade. In one case, a caravan-leader going from east to west takes 500 wagon-loads of articles[479]; in another case, a merchant, residing in Varanasi, engages 500 wagons in a single caravan[480].

The 'Jatakas' mention traders going from Videha to Gandhara, from Magadha to Sovira (Surat), from Bhrgukachha—round the coast—to Burma, and from Varanasi — down the river and across the sea or along the coast — to Burma. Similar trips were also made from Champa on the Ganga to Burma. It is highly curious to note that caravans crossing the Indian desert did the journey only at night-time—obviously to avoid the great heat of the day—and employed 'land-pilot' for guiding them along the correct routes. The pilots used to take the help of stars for keeping to right directions[481].

The importance of trade as a profession is distinctly manifest in the writings of Panini who has different terms to use for the different facets of this activity. For instance, he makes a clearcut distinction between larger business, comprising export and import, and smaller one, comprising local sales and purchases. He has different names for the merchants based on that type of business and the amount of capital invested by them on the one hand[482]; and for the merchants engaged in carrying goods outward or inward on the other[483]. He also refers to the customs and octroi duties charged on the trading articles. Regarding trading articles, Panini offers a long list in which the most prominent are — salt; five types of perfumes; silk fabrics; wool and woollen stuffs; linen and linen goods; hemp; cotton; cloth; blankets of standard varieties; animal skins used as upholstering material; four varieties of dye stuffs, including lac and indigo; leather goods, including containers and shoes; iron goods, including chains, spikes, ploughshares, yoke, axle, spade, etc.; food stuffs; utensils; intoxicating drinks; gold and silver ornaments; precious stones; metals like gold, silver, copper, lead and tin; weapons; musical instruments; weights and measures; wagons, chariots and boats; animals, like, cows, bulls and horses[484].

It is quite obvious that articles mentioned above include both the items of export and import. But the list, summarised from the accounts of Panini, points to the enormity as well as the great variety of the traffic.

The presence of the 'Director of Trade' as mentioned by Kautilya and the 'Superintendent of Market' in the city indicate the importance of trade among the leading professions of the society at his time. It is highly interesting to know that the duty of the Director of Trade was to encourage imports from foreign countries. For this purpose certain concessions were allowed, such as, the traders' dealing in imported goods were exempted from paying taxes and no law suit could be instituted against foreign traders[485]. In general however, duties and tolls to be paid on goods exported as well as imported were clearly defined. The duty levied, for instance, was one-fifth of the actual price. But it is not at all clear if there was a large variation between the duties payable for the imports and the exports. What we get from Kautilya is information on different rates of duties as charged for different types of goods widely varying from one-sixth to one-twentieth or one-twentyfifth of the price[486]. In any case, the names of items given by him having different rates of duties to be paid for sale, convey distinct idea about the high level of trading activities of the country. The idea becomes further strengthened from what we know about the responsibilities of the Market Superintendent. He had to keep strong vigilance on the use of correct weights and measures, having the right to fine the wrong-doers. Fines amounting to eight times the price were imposed upon the traders dealing in spurious goods and those selling goods of inferior quality, and those hoarding or charging a higher price were severely dealt with[487].

Patanjali's *'Mahabhashya'* mentions about risky journeys undertaken by traders, both inland and overseas, for selling a wide variety of articles in markets distant from the areas of production. He refers to long-distance inland as well as foreign trips made by merchants in his days. According to him, direct trips were made between Videha and Gandhara, Magadha and Sovira, from Bhrgukachha round the coast of Burma, from Varanasi and Champa by the Ganga and then across the sea to Burma[488]. Patanjali names a number of such articles mentioned in the foregoing paragraphs and, according to him, strict regulations were observed for the maintenance of quality, price and correct weights and measures of goods sold in the market. In his days, the villages maintained a closer link with the towns mainly for commercial purposes.

India's fame in trading activities had not diminished even in the opening of the Christian era when we find a long chain of ports—as mentioned earlier—making a busy life on the western coast. Ports of this kind were also present on the eastern coast and further inland all over the country along the great rivers, all of them taking an important part in the movement of merchandise. The Periplus provides a mine of information about the nature of goods, their origin and destination and their ports of embarkation. The picture emerging from all these accounts is one of a very large trade done on an extensive scale. It is significant to note that the character of the articles in trade did not change much during the intervening centuries. A comparative analysis of the list provided by Panini or Kautilya and the Periplus brings out a strange similarity between them in the nature of articles and this alone justifies our conviction that the foreign market for Indian products still went unchallenged. Hiuen Tsang does not give us much information in the context. Nevertheless, stray references made by him to certain places like, Thaneswar, Kanauj, Valabhi, etc., make it amply clear that trade and commerce took an important role in the economic activities of the country.

Among the articles, luxury products took the most important place in long-distance trade. They were ivory, precious stones and pearls, perfumes, spices, cotton and silk fabrics and fine wood. Apart from the internal market, ivory was in great demand in foreign countries for its multifarious uses as 'bed and table legs', handles and knobs of mirrors, flywhisks and sceptres, ornamentation for chairs, ceremonial carriages, the walls of elegant houses, sword hilts and scabbards, combs, bindings for manuscripts, musical instruments, etc.[489] India was equally famous for the production of precious stones and pearls, and the quality of Indian gems remained unsurpassed till then. The gems generally came from South India and there were largescale pearl-fisheries on all parts of the Indian coast as well as in the Ganga estuary. Barygaza was one of the chief ports exporting gems and pearls to the western world. Among perfumes and incense, sandalwood took the most important place for export; besides; the country also exported different types of gums and resins—myrrh, balsam, aloes, cinnabar, etc.,—serving as colouring matters, condiments or medicaments[490]. One of the most prized perfumes was musk, available from the northern mountainous regions of India. Similarly important was the market for the spices of which both pepper and ginger were most popular among the western nations. Produced mostly in the coastal regions of Malabar and Kerala, pepper was exported chiefly to Alexandria from where it used to be redistributed in the Mediterranean countries. The monopoly of trade in Indian ginger was in the hands of the Arabs. Other luxury spices exported from India were cinnamon—camphor as well as cinnamon-bark, cardamom, etc. But among all the exportable items particular reference should be made to cotton and silk manufactures for which India enjoyed the largest market in those days. Cotton grown locally was woven into exquisitely fine and beautiful fabrics—such as, the white and soft fabric 'Dakula' or Bengal, muslins, dyed in beautiful colours, from lower Bengal, best quality cotton fabrics of Madurai, Konkan, Varanasi, Kausambi and Mahishmati[491] and also from Trichinopoly (Triuchirapali), Tanjor (Tanjavur), Masulipatam (Machilipatnam), etc.,[492] along with carded cotton used for stuffing cushions and mattresses went to Egypt for further resale. Silk, obtained from China, was transformed into luxurious fabrics mainly at Varanasi and North-West India for export in vast quantities. There was also the export of woollen fabrics made of goat's hair or sheep's wool available in Bhutan the Tibet and woven in Kashmir. Precious woods formed another important export item. Teak grown along the coast of Malabar, in Kerala and Gujarat, Rosewood grown on the Coromondal coast and Ebony from Southern India were in high demand for construction purposes while Sandalwood available from Mysore, and Salem was much sought-after for its use in wood-carving industry as well as for its essence in making perfumes. Metals also used to form a very important item of trade. Brass, including a white variety resembling silver, and large quantities of good quality gold and iron, the latter much esteemed for its purity and hardness, are noteworthy. Besides, certain food-stuff, like, sugar, rice and ghee listed among the items of long-distance trade. There was also the export of dye-stuffs, such as, lac and indigo and live animals and birds. It is interesting to note that elephants, lions, tigers and buffaloes were imported from India in large numbers required for staging wild beast shows by the Roman Emperors. The export of large animals were usually made by landroutes, but the smaller animals like, monkeys, parrots and peacocks went in much larger quantities by sea-routes to Rome where they found a large market among the wealthy Roman ladies as their pets[493].

In return, India imported sweet wine, dried figs—both being great favourites of the Mauryan Emperors in the third century B.C. —costly vessels of silver, thin clothing, choicest ointments, metals like, tin and lead, coral, singing boys and beautiful maidens for the harems[494]. The great demand for the Indian luxuries gave rise to a number of Roman colonies in Southern India during the first two centuries of the Christian era. Such colonies did exist also at Kaveripatnam—a busy port on the mouth of the northern branch of the Cauvery[495].

Thus, India maintained a unique position in the commercial world as the main supplier of the world's luxuries. Throughout she had the balance of trade in her favour, exports exceeding imports as India had the advantage of producing all its essential commodities, leaving a large surplus for meeting the foreign needs[496]. The unfavourable balance of trade resulted in a huge drainage of gold from the Roman Empire, the value of which Pliny in the first century A.D. put at 100 million sesterces, or Roman coins[497] (Paul Masson puts it at 50 million). The magnitude of trade can further be gauged from the fact that there was a separate 'Board of Trade and Commerce' in Pataliputra as early as the fourth century B.C. the functions of which are defined in clear terms by Kautilya[498].

The development of a highly organised trade carried on through centuries naturally needed a well-knit transportation system lacing up the far-flung regions of the country. There is no mention of trade-routes in the pre-Buddhistic literature and so far no concrete evidence is available for markets existing in Vedic times. All we can presume is that, towns and cities and villages already flourishing in Vedic period were linked up by tracks with wells at intervals[499], the latter supplying drinking water for the travellers. The first mention of internal roads, operating as important trade-routes is found in the Buddhist literature, mainly the 'Jatakas'. From the copious references made therein it is found that already by the time of Buddha well-established trade-routes—both land and water—covered most parts of the Northern India, and by 300 B.C. the Mauryan Empire had extended them further into the Peninsular India.

The most important among them was the Imperial Highway, variously called as the 'Northern Route' or the 'Royal Road' by the Greek Geographers[500], the 'Uttarapatha' by Panini[501], which, running for about one thousand miles (10,000 stadia[502]), traversed the whole of the great North Indian Plain. Constructed in eight stages, the road ran from the port of Tamralipti or modern Tamluk in West Bengal, up the river to Champa and from there it went via Pataliputra and Varanasi to Kausambi; from there the road, proceeding along the south bank of the Jamuna, reached Mathura and then extend up to Delhi; from Delhi it crossed five rivers of Punjab and led up to the City of Pushkalavati via Takshasila, continuing therefrom up the Kabul Valley into Central Asia. The renowned cities touched by this great highway were Tamralipti, Champa, Pataliputra, Prayaga, Kanauj or Kanyakubja, Ramaganga, Delhi or Hastinapura, Sakala or Sialkot, Takshasila, Pushkalavati, Kapisi and Bahika. This particular route was extremely popular in the third century B.C. and continued farther by way of Oxus, the Caspian Sea and the Black Sea into Europe. Indian goods, as mentioned by Strabo and Pliny, entered into the European markets by this ancient highway[503]. The principal commercial artery of the North Indian Plains, closely following the Ganga-axis, gave rise to two important branch routes giving direct access to a large part of the country. One of them, branching off at Kausambi, led to Bhrgukachha or modern Broach, connecting on its way the great cities of Vidisa and Ujjain. Rhys Davids refers to another very important road of this time—sixth century B.C.—which, beginning at Sravasti, went straight southwards to Paithan in South India. On this route lay the important cities like, Saketa, Kausambi, Vidisa, Ujjain and Mahishmati. The second important branch of the great Northern Highway emerging at Mathura crossed modern Rajasthan and the Thar desert and extended up to the port of Patala, near the mouth of the Indus. Another road, not less important, took origin at Sravasti and closely following the foot of the mountains in the north emerged at Vaisali from where it turned southward and proceeded towards Rajagriha. The road might have extended on to Gaya to join the Northern Highway leading from Tamralipti westward. The important halting places along this road were Setavya, Kapilavastu, Kusinagara, Pava, Hatthi-gama, Bhandagama, Vaisali, Pataliputra and Nalanda[504]. Similar trade-routes and also developed in South India of which the Eastern Route—from Pataliputra to Orrisa—must have existed before the Mauryan period, that is, before the early part of 400 B.C., and the Western Route, connecting Ujjain with the City of Paithan in the Upper Godavari Valley and from there crossed the plateau to reach the cities of Kanchipuram and Madurai. This road came into existence in about the beginning of the Christian era. In all likelihood, a network of roads, linking all the important cities of the Peninsular India had developed by this time[505].

Trade relations between India and China had also been established before the Christian era. The trade route that went via Oxus River into Central Asia was met by another route running from west to east which, passing round the north of Hindukush, crossed the Pamir and went through the Tarim Basin into Chinese Turkestan and Yarkand. Silk from China travelled by this route to Syria[506].

The construction of these roads needed the cooperation of a whole army of technicians, architects, engineers and carpenters asisted by a host of woodcutters, ropemakers, roadmenders and labourers, etc., and from the Mauryan period onwards the emperors used to attach great importance to this, supervision the construction of the major routes personally[507]. The Mauryan Emperors especially used to take great care of these roads, constructing pillars at every ten stadia, indicating thereon the by-roads and the distance[508], wells and rest houses for the caravans at regular intervals along them; besides, regular ferry-services were also maintained at large river crossings. Both Panini and Patanjali refer to this wide network of roads, provided with resting places at regular intervals for the travellers[509].

The road system seems to have improved further in the following centuries, though direct reference to their construction and maintenance is not available in plenty in the contemporary Writings. The travel accounts of Fa Hian and Hiuen Tsang do not contain much information about the transport system in the country. But the extensive nature of travellings made by Hiuen Tsang in the major part of the country in those days gives an indirect clue to the existence of well-established road, and water ways. Further, in most of the cases of his visits Hiuen Tsang mentions the distance between different places. This, quite naturally, was calculated on the basis of pennanent routes, either land or water, and without doubt he obtained this knowledge from the local sources.

River-routes were, in no way, less important in those days. The main rivers like, the Ganga, the Indus and those in the south along with their tributaries constituted some of the principal commercial arteries of the country, carrying both goods and passengers in large and small vessels. Among the river-ports were Sahajati in Central India, Kausambi on the Jamuna, Varanasi, Champa and latterly Pataliputra on the Ganga were famous[510]. The boats plying on these rivers were available for hire and express boats are also mentioned[511]. According to the earlier 'Jatakas', river-traffic on the Ganga was probably limited down to Magadha, or at best to Champa wherefrom boats plied upstream upto Kausambi, the latter making the most important transhipment point. From Kausambi the goods were transferred on to carts for transporting by land-routes radiating out to the south-west and north-west. River traffic along the Ganga extended further in later times, the boats going down to the mouth of the river in the east, while in the west, the boats reached as far as Sahajati[512] by way of its principal tributaries draining the southern edge of the plateau.

The sea-borne trade needs a special mention as it directly focuses on the extensive foreign relations of the country in the early times. The antiquity of sea-trade may be traced back to the period of the Harappans, but it ceased altogether thereafter for some centuries and was resumed by the Aryans. The Rigveda contains several references to sea voyages, and the trade was very possibly carried on with such distant countries like Chaldaea, Babylon and Egypt[513]. A number of passages in the Ramayana also refer to maritime contacts with China, Java and Sumatra, while one passage distinctly refers to the Red Sea[514]. The contacts were usually commercial in nature as the Ramayana mentions merchants going beyond the sea and bringing presents to the King[515]. Similar references also occur in the Mahabharata and other religious Vedic literature like, the 'Sutras', 'Smiritis' and the 'Samhitas'[516].

Direct evidences of sea-borne traffic, however, are available for the later periods, that is, from about the beginning of the seventh century B.C. The fact that Indian Cedar wood was used in the palace of Nebuchadnezzar (604-562 B.C.) at Birs Nimrud, a block of wood—most probably Cedar of Indian origin was used in the temple at Ur, rebuilt by Nebuchadnezzar and Nabonidas (555-538 B.C.) and that certain Indian commodities—such as, rice, peacocks and sandalwood—were known to the Greeks and other nations of the West under their Indian names in the fifth century B.C., undoubtedly indicate a close commercial contact[517]. Similar trade relations were also established with the East Asiatic countries and, in Buddha's time, Indian commodities were already reaching Burma, Malaya and the Islands of Indonesia.

An international trade of this nature by water-routes naturally depended on the efficiency in building ships. In fact, as early as 325 B.C. — from the beginning of the Mauryan Rule in India—shipbuilding was a very regular flourishing industry with a large output. The Greek writer Arrian makes pointed reference to the construction of dockyards and in some ports of South India there were lighthouses made of brick and mortar with blazing lights for guiding the ships at night. According to Ptolemy, Alexander, the son of Lagos used a huge fleet of 2,000 vessels during his campaign down the Indus and other rivers and the entire fleet was built of Indian wood by Indian craftsmen[518] which proves that even before the Mauryas came to power, the industry was highly developed. Shipbuilding was a monopoly of the State. The first Maurya Emperor, Chandragupta (321-297 B.C.) maintained a 'Board of Admiralty' and a 'Naval Department' for this purpose, the latter headed by a 'Controller of Shipping' and the 'Superintendent of Passports'[519]. The existence of such a large organisation is a conclusive evidence supporting the idea that Maurya India was in constant intercourse with foreign States and that large number of foreigners visited the capital on business transactions[520]. Foreign commerce was so great that mere taxes on imports made a very big share of the total revenue of the State[521]. During the reign of Asoka (268-233 B.C.), trade relations became more direct and frequent with such countries like, Syria, Egypt, Cyrene, Macedonia and Epirus[522]. India, as Masson-Orsel says, was "one of the greatest marine and colonizing power of the past"[523].

The dates of Indian colonisation in South-East Asia, spreading from Southern Cambodia and Cochin-China to Annam or Champa region, Sumatra or the Isle of Gold (Suvarnadwipa), Java or the Land of Barley (Javadwipa or bhumi) are still debatable. But there remains no doubt about the expansion of Indian trade to these lands and farther up to China in the north. The Indian ships started making regular visits since the fifth century B.C. to the ports of these countries with her rich merchandise and thus opened the opportunity for colonization in the succeeding centuries. The earlier centuries of the Christian era saw further expansion of these commercial contacts and this is known from the writings of the Greek, Roman and other foreign authors as well as from numismatic evidences. Strabo writes about witnessing 120 ships sailing from Myos Haromos—a Greek sea-port on the Egyptian coast—to India. But the most illuminating accounts on the maritime activities are found in the Periplus, corroborated subsequently by Ptolemy. The Periplus refers to the large Indian ships seen off the East African, Arabian and Persian ports. According to the same source, the Egyptian Greeks took a major part in the extensive trade in Indian goods and this is supported by the old Tamil poets of South referring to them as 'Yavanas' —a word derived from the Greek word 'Iaones'. Until the use of the monsoon winds was discovered by Hippalus in about 47 A.D., the shipping between the Indian ports and those in the Persian Gulf and the Red Sea mostly followed the coasts. In the early centuries of the Christian era, with a favourable south-east monsoon, the voyage from Arabia to Muziris, modern Cranganore on Kerafa coast, took forty days during July and August, and the traders were able to return in December or January after transacting their business[524]. During this period, the Tamil States of South India maintained powerful navies and were visited freely by ships from both east and west which brought merchants of various races eager to buy choicest commodities and to pay for them in gold, solver or artistic wares of Eurpoe[525]. The great degree of maritime trade carried on during this period is highlighted by the Periplus mentioning scores of ports and harbours, giving details of the nature of articles traded between India and the countries lying beyond the ocean-barriers. Ptolemy, writing still later, recognises many of these ports and emporiums. That the sea-borne traffic had not slackened is corroborated by Hiuen Tsang. Inferences can be drawn from his writings, making a few references to the flourishing trade of some ports of his time.

REFERENCES

1. Rao, *op.cit*,. p. 160.
2. Piggott, *op.cit*., p. 238.
3. Gordon, *op.cit*., p. 87.
4. Wheeler, *Civilizations of the Indus Valley, etc*. p. 84.
5. Wheeler, *op.cit*., pp. 85-86.
6. Gordon, *op.cit*., p. 184.
7. Rao, *op.cit*., p. 184
8. Majumdar, R.C., Ray Chaudhuri, H.C., Datta, K., *An Advanced History of India*, Third Edition, 1970, Macmillan, pp. 32-33.
9. Clarke, Grahame, *op.cit*., p. 214.
10. Havell, E.B., *The History of Aryan Rule in India*, K.M.N. Publishers, New Delhi, p. 22.
11. Havell, *op. cit*. pp. 22-23.
12. Majumdar, Ray Chaudhari and Datta, *op.cit*., pp. 26-27.
13. Bhargava, Monohar Lal, *The Geography of Rigvedic India*. p. 38.
14. Majumdar, Ray Chaudhari and Datta, *op.cit*., pp. *27*.
15. Majumdar, Ray Chaudhari and Datta, *op.cit*., pp. *39-40*.
16. *Statesman*, August 10, 1976 (Calcutta Edition).
17. Basham, *op.cit*., 39, and Kosambi, p. 91.
18. Kosambi, *op.cit*., 91.
19. Kosambi, *op.cit*., 92.
20. Wheeler, *Civilizations of the Indus Valley, etc*., p. 95.
21. Wheeler, *Early India and Pakistan etc*., pp. 129-131, and, Puri, B.N., *Cities of Ancient India*, Meenakshi Prakashan, Meerut, 1966, pp. 23-25.
22. Wheeler, *op.cit*., 131-132; and pp. 1-3.
23. Puri, *op.cit*., p. 47.
24. Puri, *op.cit*., p. 46.
25. Wheeler, *Civilization of the Indus Valley, etc*., p. 102.
26. Sinha, K.K., *Stratigraphy and Chronology of Early Kausambi a Reappraised, in Radio Carbon and Indian Archaeology*, (Ed.) Agrawal, D.P. and Ghosh, A., Tata Institute of Fundamental Research, Bombay, 1973, p. 234.
27. Sinha, *op.cit*., p. 235.

28. Puri, *op.cit.*, p. 45.
29. Wheeler, *Civilizations of the Indus Valley, etc.*, p. 102.
30. Basham, *op.cit.*, p. 41.
31. Piggott, *op.cit.*, p. 263.
32. Sastri, K.A. Nilakanta, *Cultural Contacts between Aryans and Dravidians,* Manaktalas, Bombay, 1967, p. 27.
33. Basham, *op.cit.*, p. 37.
34. Wheeler, *Civilizations of the Indus Valley, etc.*, p. 113.
35. Tripathi, Vibha, *Introduction of Iron in India—'A Chronological Perspective', in 'Radio-Carbon and Indian Archaeology'*, Agrawal & Ghosh, p. 277.
36. Kosambi, *op.cit.*, p. 90.
37. Bhargava, *op.cit.*, pp. 1-2.
38. Majumdar, Ray Chaudhari and Datta, *op.cit.*, p. 34.
39. Rai, Jaimal, *The Rural-Urban Economy and Social Changes in Ancient India.* Bharatiya Vidya Prakashan, Varanasi, 1974, pp. 152-155.
40. Havell, *op.cit.*, p. 38.
41. *Ibid.*
42. Piggott, *op.cit.*, p. 268.
43. Hawkes and Woolley, *op.cit.*, p. 458.
44. Kosambi, *op.cit.*, p. 89.
45. Wheeler, *Civilizations of the Indus Valley, etc.*, p. 14.
46. Rhys Davids, T.W., *Buddhist India,* Motilal Banarasidass, Delhi, 1971, p. 35.
47. Rhys Davids, p. 36.
48. Rhys Davids, p. 37.
49. Rhys Davids, p. 41.
50. Kangle, R.P., *The Kautilya Arthsastra,* 2nd Edition, University of Bombay, 1972, p. 68.
51. Rhys Davids, *op.cit.*, p. 39.
52. Majumdar, Ray Chaudhari and Datta, *op.cit.*, p. 53.
53. *Ibid.*, p. 56 and p. 82.
54. Basham, *op.cit.*, pp. 287-288.
55. Jayaswal, K.P., *Hindu Polity : A Constitutional History of India in Hindu Times,* 4th Ed., The Bangalore Printing Publishing Co., Bangalore, 1967, p. 21.
56. Misra, Sudama, *Janapada State in India,* Bharatiya Vidya Prakasana, Varanasi, 1973, p. 1.
57. Jayaswal, *op.cit.*, p. 24.
58. Jayaswal, *op.cit.*, p. 3.
59. Jayaswal, *op.cit.*, p. 158.
60. Misra, *op.cit.*, p. 15.
61. Misra, *op.cit.*, p. 160.
62. Misra, *op.cit.*, p. 163.
63. Misra, *op.cit.*, p. 160.
64. Agrawala, V.S., *India as Known to Panini,* 2nd Ed., Varanasi, 1963, p. 426.
65. Misra, *op.cit.*, p. 44.
66. Misra, *op.cit.*, p. 99.
67. Jayaswal, *op.cit.*, p. 23.
68. Jayaswal, *op.cit.*, p. 25.
69. Agrawala, V.S., *op.cit.*,., p. 467.
70. Jain, Ramchandra, Ed., *McCrindle's Ancient India as described by Megasthenes and Arrian*, Today and Tomorrow's Printers and Publishers, New Delhi, 1972, p. 40.

71. Kangle, *op.cit.*, p. 59 (Part III).
72. Kangle, pp. 125-126 (Part III).
73. Puri, B.N., *India in the Time of Patanjali*, Bharitya Vidya Bhavan, Bombay, 1968, pp. 68-79.
74. Puri, B.N., *op.cit.*, p. 68.
75. Agrawala, V.S., *op.cit.*, p. 479.
76. Misra, Sudama, *op.cit.*, pp. 277-278.
77. Agrawala, V.S., *op.cit.*, p. 479 and Misra, Sudama, *op.cit.*, p. 277.
78. Ray Chaudhuri; Hemchandra, *Political History of Ancient India*, University of Calcutta, 7th Edition, p. 89.
79. Ray Chaudhuri, p. 96.
80. Rhys Davids, *op.cit.*, p. 38.
81. Rhys Davids, *op. cit.*, p. 37.
82. Majumdar, Ray Chaudhuri and Datta, *op.cit.*, p. 56.
83. Ray Chaudhuri, Hemchandra, *op.cit.*, p. 107.
84. Ray Chaudhuri, p. 114.
85. Sircar, D.C., *Studies in the Geography of Ancient and Medieval India*, 2nd Ed., Motilal Banarasidas, Delhi, 1971, p. 99.
86. Sircar, D.C., p. 193, and Ray Chaudhuri Hemachandra, *op.cit.*, p. 128.
87. Fick, Richard, *The Social Organization in North-East India in Buddha's Time* (Translated by Shishir Kumar Maitra), Indological Book House, Delhi, 1972, p. 95.
88. Ray Chaudhuri, Hemachandra, *op.cit.*, p. 134.
89. Wheeler, *Civilizations of the Indus Valley, etc.*, pp. 90-92.
90. Gordon, *op.cit.*, pp. 133-134.
91. Wheeler, *Civilizations of the Indus Valley, etc.*, pp. 90-92.
92. Wheeler, *op.cit.*, pp. 128-130.
93. Bridget, *op.cit.*, pp. 188-189.
94. Wheeler, *Civilizations of the Indus Valley, etc.*, pp. 125-127.
95. Bridget, *op.cit.*, pp. 188-189.
96. Bridget, *op.cit.*, pp. 174-175.
97. Wheeler, *Civilization of the Indus Valley, etc.*, p. 95.
98. Basham, *op.cit.*, p. 198.
99. Wheeler, *Civilization of the Indus Valley, etc.*, p. 116.
100. Basham, *op.cit.*, pp. 198.
101. Kangle, *op.cit.*, pp. 69-70 (Part III).
102. Smith, Vincent, A., *The Early History of India*, Oxford University Press, 1962, 4th Ed., p. 128.
103. Rhys Davids, *op.cit.*, p. 68.
104. Rhys Davids, *op.cit.*, p. 74.
105. Rhys Davids, *op.cit.*, p. 78.
106. Rhys Davids, *op.cit.*, p. 204.
107. McCrindle, *Invasion of India by Alexander*, p. 112.
108. *Ibid.*
109. *Ibid*, p. 121.
110. *Ibid*, p. 133.
111. *Ibid*, p. 309.
112. Agrawala, V.S., *op.cit.*, p. 75.
113. Agrawala, V.S., *op.cit.*, p. 139.
114. Agrawala, V.S., *op.cit.*, p. 135.
115. Agrawala, V.S., *op.cit.*, p. 137.

116. Jain, Ramachandra (Ed.), McCrindle's *Ancient India as described by Megasthenes, op.cit.*, p. 68.
117. Kangle, *op.cit.*, p. 59 (III).
118. Kangle, *op.cit.*, p. 56 (II).
119. Christaller, Walter, *Central Places in Southern Germany*, Englewood Clifts, 1966.
120. Kangle, *op.cit.*, p. 57 (II).
121. Kangle, *op.cit.*, p. 62 (II).
122. Kangle, *op.cit.*, p. 68 (II).
123. Kangle, *op.cit.*, p. 75 (II).
124. Fick, *op.cit.*, pp. 279-280.
125. Kangle,. *op.cit.*, p. 61 (II).
126. Kangle, *op.cit.*, p. 68 (II).
127. *Ibid.*
128. *Ibid.*
129. *Ibid.*, pp. 160-161 (III).
130. Puri, *India in the Time of Patanjali,* p. 15.
131. Puri, *op.cit.*, p. 79.
132. Jain, Ramchandra (Ed), McCrindle's *Ancient India as described by Ptolemy*, New Delhi, p. X.
133. McCrindle, John W., *Ancient India as described in Classical Literature,* Philo Press, Amsterdam, 1971, p. 6.
134. McCrindle, John W., *op.cit.*, p. 19.
135. *Ibid.*, p. 42.
136. *Ibid.*, p. 22.
137. *Ibid.*, p. 35.
138. Jain, Ramchandra (Ed.), *McCrindle's Ancient India as described by Ptolemy*, p. X.
139. McCrindle, *Ancient India as described in Classical Literatures,* p. 107.
140. McCrindle, p. 109.
141. Majumdar, R.C., *The Classical Accounts of India*, Firma, K.L. Mukhopadhyay, Calcutta, 1960, p. 337.
142. McCrindle, *Ancient India,* p. 111.
143. Jain, R. (Ed.) McCrindle's *Ancient India as described by Megasthenes etc.* p. 204.
144. *Ibid.*
145. *Ibid.*, p. 184.
146. McCrindle, John W., *The Commerce and Navigation of the Erythraean Sea and Ancient India*, Philo Press, Amsterdam, 1973 pp. 157-158.
147. *Ibid.*, p. 159.
148. *Ibid.*, p. 5.
149. *Ibid.*, p. 10.
150. *Ibid.*, pp. 107-108.
151. *Ibid.*, p. 107.
152. *Ibid.*, p. 122.
153. *Ibid.*, p. 125.
154. *Ibid.*, p. 127.
155. *Ibid.*
156. *Ibid.*, pp. 128-129.
157. *Ibid.*, p. 129.
158. *Ibid.*
159. *Ibid.*, p. 132.
160. *Ibid.*, p. 136.

161. *Ibid.*, p. 139.
162. *Ibid.*
163. *Ibid.*
164. *Ibid.*, p. 141.
165. *Ibid.*
166. *Ibid.*
167. *Ibid.*
168. *Ibid.*, pp. 144-145.
169. Sircar, D.C. *op.cit.*, p. 215.
170. Jain, Ramchandra (Ed.), McCrindle's *Ancient India as described by Ptolemy*, p. IX.
171. *Ibid.*, p. 37.
172. *Ibid.*
173. *Ibid.*, p. 38.
174. *Ibid.*
175. *Ibid.*, p. 39.
176. *Ibid.*, p. 40.
177. *Ibid.*, p. 42.
178. *Ibid.*, p. 50.
179. *Ibid.*, p. 51.
180. *Ibid.*, p. 54.
181. *Ibid.*, p. 55.
182. *Ibid.*
183. *Ibid.*, p. 57.
184. *Ibid.*
185. *Ibid.*, p. 63.
186. *Ibid.*
187. *Ibid.*, p. 65.
188. *Ibid.*
189. *Ibid.*, p. 67.
190. *Ibid.*
191. *Ibid.*
192. *Ibid.*, p. 68.
193. *Ibid.*
194. *Ibid.*, p. 70.
195. *Ibid.*
196. *Ibid.*, p. 72.
197. *Ibid.*
198. *Ibid.*, p. 75.
199. *Ibid.*, p. 117.
200. *Ibid.*
201. *Ibid.*, p. 118.
202. *Ibid.*, p. 122.
203. *Ibid.*
204. *Ibid.*, p. 126.
205. *Ibid.*
206. *Ibid.*, p. 127.
207. *Ibid.*, p. 128.
208. *Ibid.*
209. *Ibid.*, p. 129.

210. *Ibid.*
211. *Ibid.*
212. *Ibid.*, p. 130.
213. *Ibid.*
214. *Ibid.*, p. 133.
215. *Ibid.*
216. *Ibid.*, p. 134.
217. *Ibid.*
218. *Ibid.*
219. *Ibid.*, p. 141.
220. *Ibid.*, p. 147.
221. *Ibid.*, p. 151.
222. *Ibid.*
223. *Ibid.*, p. 152.
224. *Ibid.*, p. 154.
225. *Ibid.*, p. 156.
226. *Ibid.*
227. *Ibid.*, p. 166.
228. *Ibid.*, p. 169.
229. *Ibid.*
230. *Ibid.*
231. *Ibid.*, p. 172.
232. *Ibid.*
233. *Ibid.*, p. 176.
234. *Ibid.*, p. 178.
235. *Ibid.*
236. *Ibid.*, p. 179.
237. *Ibid.*
238. *Ibid.*
239. *Ibid.*
240. *Ibid.*, p. 180.
241. *Ibid.*, p. 181.
242. *Ibid.*
243. *Ibid.*
244. *Ibid.*, p. 182.
245. *Ibid.*
246. *Ibid.*, p. 183.
247. *Ibid.*, p. 184.
248. *Ibid.*
249. *Ibid.*, p. 185.
250. *Ibid.*
251. *Ibid.*, p. 187.
252. *Ibid.*
253. *Ibid.*
254. *Ibid.*, p. 216.
255. *Ibid.*, p. 217.
256. *Ibid.*, p. 227.
257. *Ibid.*
258. *Ibid.*, p. 228.
259. *Ibid.*

260. *Ibid*.
261. *Ibid*., p. 229.
262. *Ibid*., p. 230.
263. *Ibid*., p. 234.
264. Majumadar, Ray Chaudhuri and Datta, *op.cit*., p. 1050.
265. Beal, Samuel, *Si-Yu-Ki : Bhuddhist Records of the Western World*, Oriental Books Reprint Corporation, 1969, p. 205 (X).
266. *Ibid*., p. 143 (III).
267. *Ibid*., p. 147 (III).
268. *Ibid*., p. 158 (III).
269. *Ibid*.
270. *Ibid*., p. 163 (III).
271. *Ibid*.
272. *Ibid*., p. 165 (IV).
273. *Ibid*., p. 166 (IV).
274. *Ibid*., p. 165 (IV).
275. *Ibid*., p. 167 (IV).
276. *Ibid*., p. 173 (IV).
277. *Ibid*., p. 175 (IV).
278. *Ibid*., p. 177 (IV).
279. *Ibid*., p. 178 (IV).
280. *Ibid*., p. 179 (IV).
281. *Ibid*., p. 183 (IV).
282. *Ibid*., p. 186 (IV).
283. *Ibid*., p. 190 (IV).
284. *Ibid*., p. 198 (IV).
285. *Ibid*.
286. *Ibid*., p. 199 (IV).
287. *Ibid*., p. 200 (IV).
288. *Ibid*., p. 201 (IV).
289. *Ibid*., p. 202 (IV).
290. *Ibid*., p. 206 (V).
291. *Ibid*., p. 210 (V).
292. *Ibid*., p. 224 (V).
293. *Ibid*., p. 229 (V).
294. *Ibid*., p. 230 (V).
295. *Ibid*., p. 235 (V).
296. *Ibid*., p. 237 (V).
297. *Ibid*., p. 239 (V).
298. *Ibid*., p. 1 (VI).
299. *Ibid*., p. 13 (VI).
300. *Ibid*., p. 18 (VI).
301. *Ibid*., p. 19 (VI).
302. *Ibid*., p. 26 (VI).
303. *Ibid*., p. 31 (VI).
304. *Ibid*., p. 44 (VII).
305. *Ibid*., p. 61 (VII).
306. *Ibid*., p. 63 (VII).
307. *Ibid*., p. 66 (VII).
308. *Ibid*., p. 78 (VII).

309. *Ibid*., p. 83 (VIII).
310. *Ibid*., p. 113 (VIII).
311. *Ibid*., p. 149 (IX).
312. *Ibid*., p. 191 (X).
313. *Ibid*., p. 194 (X).
314. *Ibid*., p. 195 (X).
315. *Ibid*., p. 199 (X).
316. *Ibid*., p. 200 (X).
317. *Ibid*., p. 201 (X).
318. *Ibid*., p. 204 (X).
319. *Ibid*., p. 205 (X).
320. *Ibid*., p. 206 (X).
321. *Ibid*., p. 207 (X).
322. *Ibid*., p. 209 (X).
323. *Ibid*., p. 217 (X).
324. *Ibid*., p. 221 (X).
325. *Ibid*., p. 228 (X).
326. *Ibid*., p. 230 (X) and Smith, Vincent A. *The Early History of India*, p. 472.
327. *Ibid*., p. 253 (XI) .
328. *Ibid*., p. 255 (XI).
329. *Ibid*., p. 259 (XI).
330. *Ibid*., p. 260 (XI).
331. *Ibid*., p. 265 (XI).
332. *Ibid*., p. 266 (XI).
333. *Ibid*.
334. *Ibid*., p. 268 (XI).
335. *Ibid*.
336. *Ibid*., p. 269 (XI).
337. *Ibid*., p. 270 (XI).
338. *Ibid*., p. 271 (XI).
339. *Ibid*., p. 272 (XI).
340. *Ibid*., p. 274 (XI).
341. *Ibid*., p. 275 (XI).
342. *Ibid*., p. 279 (XI).
343. *Ibid*., p. 280 (XI).
344. *Ibid*., p. 98 (II).
345. *Ibid*., pp. 136-137 (III).
346. Smith, Vincent A., *The Early History of India*, p. 369.
347. Beal, *op.cit*., p. 235 (V).
348. *Ibid*., pp. 1-12 (VI).
349. *Ibid*., pp. 13-14 (VI).
350. *Ibid*., p. 26 (VI).
351. *Ibid*., p. 32 (VI).
352. *Ibid*., p. 66 (VII).
353. *Ibid*., p. 78 (VII).
354. *Ibid*., p. 82 (VII).
355. *Ibid*., pp. 83 and 86 (VIII).
356. *Ibid*., p. 165 (IX).
357. *Ibid*., p. 166-167 (IV).
358. Thomas, Walters, *On Yuan Chawng's Travels in India* (A.D. 629-645), Ed. by Rhys

Davids, T.W. & Bushell, S.W., *Royal Asiatic Society*, London. First Ed., 1961, p. 258.

359. Smith, V.A., *The Oxford History of India*, p. 181.
360. Majumdar, Ray Chaudhury and Datta, *op.cit.*, p. 152.
361. Thomas, Walters, *op.cit.*, p. 195.
362. Beal, *op.cit.*, pp. 73-74.
363. *Ibid.*, p. 259 (XI).
364. *Ibid.*, pp. 200-201 (X).
365. *Ibid.*, p. (XIII).
366. Beal, pp. XXIII-LXXXV.
367. Rhys Davids, *op.cit.*, pp. 45, 49.
368. *Ibid.*, p. 49.
369. *Ibid.*, p. 34.
370. Agrawala, V.S. *op.cit.*, p. 143.
371. *Ibid.*
372. *Ibid.*, p. 195.
373. *Ibid.*, p. 144.
374. *Ibid.*, p. 204.
375. *Ibid.*, p. 206.
376. *Ibid.*, p. 209.
377. Jain, Ramchandra (Ed.), McCrindle's *Ancient India as described by Megasthenes and Arrian*, p. 30.
378. *Ibid.*, p. 32.
379. *Ibid.*
380. *Ibid.*, p. 31.
381. Kangle, *op.cit.*, p. 170 (III).
382. *Ibid.*, p. 172 (III).
383. *Ibid.*, p. 149 (II).
384. *Ibid.*
385. *Ibid*, p. 172 (III).
386. *Ibid.*, p. 151 (II).
387. *Ibid.*, pp. 150-151 (II).
388. *Ibid.*, p. 174 (III).
389. *Ibid.*, p. 148 (II).
390. *Ibid.*, p. 175 (III).
391. *Ibid.*
392. Puri, B.N. *op.cit.*, p. 108.
393. *Ibid.*, p. 112.
394. *Ibid.*, p. 179.
395. Jain, Ramchandra, McCrindle's *India as described by Ptolemy*, p. X.
396. McCrindle, John W., *Ancient India as described in Classical Literature*, p. 25.
397. McCrindle, pp. 33-44.
398. McCrindle, p. 44.
399. Beal, *op.cit.*, p. 88.
400. *Ibid.*, pp. 88-89.
401. *Ibid.*, p. 148.
402. *Ibid.*, p. 165.
403. *Ibid.*, p. 173.
404. *Ibid.*, pp. 175-176.
405. Fick, *op.cit.*, pp. 280-281.

406. Fick, *op.cit.*, pp. 281-282.
407. Rhys Davids, *op.cit.*, p. 90.
408. *Ibid.*
409. Fick, *op.cit.*, p. 263.
410. Rhys Davids, *op.cit.*, 90.
411. *Ibid.*
412. *Ibid.*
413. *Ibid.*
414. *Ibid.*, p. 93.
415. *Ibid.*, p. 92.
416. Agrawala, V.S., *op.cit.*, p. 237.
417. *Ibid.*, pp. 230-236.
418. *Ibid.*, p. 227.
419. Kangle, *op.cit.*, p. 185 (III).
420. *Ibid.*, p. 182 (III).
421. *Ibid.*, p. 105 (II).
422. *Ibid.*, p. 182 (III).
423. *Ibid.*, p. 111 (II).
424. *Ibid.*, p. 108 (II).
425. *Ibid.*, p. 109 (II).
426. *Ibid.*, p. 184 (III).
427. *Ibid.*, p. 187 (II).
428. *Ibid.*, p. 104 (II).
429. *Ibid.*
430. *Ibid.*, p. 105 (II).
431. *Ibid.*
432. *Ibid.*, pp. 184-185 (III).
433. Jain, Ramchandra (Ed), McCrindle's *Ancient India as described by Megasthenes and Arrian*, pp. 42-43.
434. Puri, B.N., *India in the Time of Patanjali,* p. 109.
435. *Ibid.*
436. *Ibid.*
437. *Ibid.*, p. 110.
438. *Ibid.*
439. *Ibid.*, p. 111.
440. *Ibid.*
441. Agrawala, V.S. *op.cit.*, p. 232.
442. Kangle, *op.cit.*, p. 166 (II).
443. Puri, B.N., *India in the Time of Patanjali,* p. 119.
444. *Ibid.*, pp. 119-120.
445. McCrindle, John W., *Ancient India as described in Classical Literature*, p. 54.
446. McCrindle, John W., *The Commerce and Navigation of the Erthrean Sea, etc.* p. 13.
447. *Ibid.*
448. *Ibid.*, p. 14.
449. *Ibid.*, p. 16.
450. *Ibid.*, p. 17.
451. *Ibid.*
452. *Ibid.*, pp. 17-18.
453. *Ibid.*, p. 23.

454. *Ibid*., p. 24.
455. *Ibid*., p. 14.
456. *Ibid*., p. 113.
457. *Ibid*., p. 26.
458. *Ibid*., p. 28.
459. *Ibid*., p. 31.
460. *Ibid*., pp. 31 & 34.
461. *Ibid*., p. 35.
462. *Ibid*., p. 36.
463. *Ibid*., p. 39.
464. *Ibid*., p. 37.
465. *Ibid*., p. 38.
466. Beal, *op.cit*., pp. 165-166.
467. *Ibid*., p. 178 (IV).
468. *Ibid*., p. 180 (IV).
469. *Ibid*., p. 197 (IV).
470. *Ibid*., p. 183 (IV).
471. *Ibid*., p. 206 (IV).
472. *Ibid*., p. 266 (IV).
473. *Ibid*.
474. Fick, *op.cit*., p. 263.
475. Rhys Davids, *op.cit*., p. 100.
476. Rhys Davids, *op.cit*., 98.
477. Fick, *op.cit*., p. 274.
478. *Ibid*., pp. IX-X.
479. *Ibid*., p. 271.
480. *Ibid*., pp. 261-262.
481. Rhys Davids, *op.cit*., p. 104.
482. Agrawala, V.S., *India as Known to Panini*, p. 238.
483. *Ibid*., p. 241.
484. *Ibid*., pp. 245-247.
485. Kangle, *op.cit*., p. 128 (II).
486. *Ibid*., p. 145 (II).
487. *Ibid*., p. 260 (III).
488. Puri, B.N., *India in the Time of Patanjali*, p. 130.
489. Auboyer, Jeannine, *Daily Life in Ancient India from Approximately 200 B.C. to A.D. 700*. Asia Publishing House, Great Britain, 1965, p. 81.
490. *Ibid*., p. 84.
491. Shamasastry, *op.cit*., pp. 82-83.
492. Auboyer, *op.cit*., p. 83.
493. Basham, *op.cit*., p. 239.
494. Majumdar, Ray Chaudhuri and Datta, *op.cit*., p. 130.
495. Smith, V.A., *The Early History of India*, p. 462.
496. Auboyer, *op.cit*., p. 81.
497. Basham, *op.cit*., p. 229.
498. *Shamasastry, op.cit*., pp. 104-106.
499. Masson-Oursel, Paul, Willman–Grabowska, Helena, and Stern Philippe, *Ancient India and Indian Civilization*, Routledge and Kegan Paul Ltd., London, 1967, p. 109.
500. McCrindle, John, W., *Ancient India as described in Classical Literature*, p. 16.

501. Agrawala, V.S., *op.cit*., p. 142.
502. McCrindle, *Ancient India as Described in Classical Literature*, p. 16
503. *Cambridge History of India*, Cambridge University Press, Vol. I., p. 433.
504. Rhys Davids, *op.cit*., p. 103.
505. Basham, *op.cit*., p. 224.
506. Masson-Oursel, Paul, etc. *op.cit*., p. 111.
507. Auboyer, *op.cit*., p. 70.
508. McCrindle, *Ancient India as described in Classical Literature*, p. 54.
509. Agrawala, V.S., *op.cit*., p. 142.
510. Puri, B.N. *India in the Time of Patanjali*, p. 130.
511. Rhys Davids, *op.cit*., p. 103.
512. *Ibid*., pp. 103-104.
513. Mookerjee, R.K., *A History of Indian Shipping*, Kitab Mahal, 2nd Ed., 1962, p. 59.
514. Mookerjee, R.K., *op.cit*., pp. 38-39.
515. *Ibid*., p. 40.
516. *Ibid*., pp. 40-44.
517. *Ibid*., p. 60.
518. McCrindle, John, W., *The Invasion of India by Alexander, The Great, etc*., Today and Tomorrow's Printers & Publishers, New Delhi (New Edition), p. 134.
519. Kangle, *op.cit*., pp. 162 and 181 (II).
520. Smith, Vincent, A., *Early History of India*, p. 134.
521. *Ibid*., p. 79.
522. *Ibid*.
523. Masson-Oursel, etc., *op.cit*., p. 110.
524. *Ibid*.
525. *Ibid*.

3

Urban Development During the Medieval Period

After Hiuen Tsang, the source of information on urbanization in the country again dries up. For a few centuries it is not possible to know what happened in the life of different urban centres and how they survived. In fact, nothing is known for certain till the arrival of Alberuni in India in the beginning of the eleventh century A.D. When the curtain draws again, making the Indian stage once more visible to the inquisitor. Born in Khiva, in the present Uzbek Republic of the U.S.S.R., Alberuni or Abu-Al-Rahim Muhammad Ibn-Ahmad Alberuni, came to India in 1017 A.D. and stayed for about thirteen years in different parts of the country, utilising his time "in the study of India"[1]. Taking keen interest in Indian life and customs in its great many details and going into the depth of the Hindu religion and its philosophy, Alberuni wrote about twenty books on India, covering various fields, including the geography of the country. His geography contains information about the orographic systems of Asia and Europe about the origin of the alluvial plains of North India[2], rainfall in India[3] and the animals of the country, and refers to many of the town and cities existing in his time, mentioning distance between them in specific cases. The towns and cities mentioned by Alberuni are as follows :

Multan; Kanoj (Kanyakubja); Mahura (Mathura); Teneshar (Thaneswar); Prayaga (Allahabad); Banarasi (Varanasi); Ajodaha (Ajodhya); Pataliputra; Mungiri (Monghyr); Gangasayara (Gangasagaṛa); Kajuraha (Khajuraho); Gwaliyar (Gwalior); Kalanjar; Tiauri (Tripuri); Rajauri; Bazana; Dhar; Mandagir (on Godavari); Ujain (Ujjain); Tana; Sommath; Aror; Dahmala; Mirat (Meerut);

Panipat; Bihroj (Broach); Rajavari (Rajaori); Banavasi; Baroi (Baroda); Subara (Sopara); Jimur; Vallabha; Panayavar (Tanjore); Kanci (Kanchipuram); Tezi; Adhishtan (Srinagar).

A closer look at the list will establish the identity of most of these urban centres having earlier origin. As for instance, (*a*) Kanayakubja, Mathura, Varanasi and Ajodhya belong to the first group of capital cities built by the Aryans in the early part of the first millennium B.C. (*b*) Five other cities—Ujjain, Prayaga, Pataliputra, Tanjore, and Tripuri—similarly claim an early origin though probably not as the first group of cities. (*c*) There are at least eight cities mentioned by Alberuni which were recognised by such writers as Pliny, the author of the Periplus and Ptolemy. They are — Rajaori, Sopara, Thaneswar Gangasagar or Gange of Ptolemy, Multan, Aror, Braoch and Banavasi. (*d*) In the seventh century A.D. Hiuen Tsang recorded the existence of Khajuraho, Dhar, Vallabha, Adhistana or Srinagar and Modagiri or modern Monghyr as prosperous cities.

The identity thus established in the case of so many cities leads to the most important fact about urbanisation in the country—that is, its unbroken continuity. In four cases, the cities have survived for more than two thousand years and five other cities are nearly as old as the former. It is true that, towns and cities mentioned by Alberuni are too few for a vast country like India where urbanisation has continued for such a long time. But, poverty in number is not conclusive as Alberuni was neither keen on taking notice of them, nor did his pursuits lie in that direction. In his study of India, Alberuni was more devoted to exploring the depths of Hindu philosophy in its various manifestations than the physical or economic conditions of the country. His 'Geography' in fact, includes more details on the customs, manners and festivals of the people and, apart from casually referring to them says little about the role of the existing towns and cities in the economic or political life of India. Besides, time was not favourable for him to make acquaintance with a large part of the country. Muslim rule, though making a strong headway, was still in its infancy with only a small part of North-West India having been included in the empire of Mahmud of Ghazni; of the remaining part of India; the Western and Central parts were under the rule of powerful Rajput Kings, while Cholas in the South the Palas in the East were the powerful rulers. Alberuni, being a Muslim, cannot be expected to have had been tolerated by the Hindus of his time. the latter still recoiling from the nightmarish experience of expeditions made by Mahmud of Ghazni who carried on wanton destructions of Hindu temples and massarcre of common people on seventeen occasions[4]. Hence, Alberuni could not have a safe passage through Hindu India as other travellers like Fa Hien or Hiuen Tsang had. It is, therefore, quite likely that he had no occasion of visiting most of the places he mentions and, in fact, towns and cities recorded in his sixteen itineraries were obtained largely from the military and civil officers of Mahmud, and also from merchants and sailors as well as from Hindu and Muslim travellers[5]. This is, perhaps, the only reason why he is so reticent and indifferent about the general condition of the urban centres. The same reason further explains the extreme poverty of his record concerning urban centres. A careful study of the list shows that the towns and cities mentioned in his writings mostly belong to the North-Central part and from there of Gujarat and its adjoining coastal areas. Both these parts formed the principal theatre of action during Mahmud's invasions. It can thus be observed that, many urban centres of Alberuni's time existing in the country, but lying off the course of the merchants and ordinary travellers, did not find place in his 'Geography' as he had no other source of information.

The inadequacy of information stands as the principal obstacle in constructing any workable picture of the state of urbanisation and urban conditions in the country. While it cannot be said for certain that urbanisation did make any visible progress during the span of about three centuries from the time of Hiuen Tsang's visit to this country to that of Alberuni's time, it is equally difficult to establish that there had been any appreciable retardation in its development. Besides, in the absence of any specific reference to urban activities, no definite idea can be formed about the origin or the functional character of the towns and cities. Alberuni, however, distinguishes some of these towns and cities as capitals—Khajuraho, Tiauri or Tripuri, Bazana, Dhar, Tana, Dahmla, Tez, Adhistan or Srinagar, and two others fortresses—Gwalior and Kalanjar. This qualifying statement does not help much in understanding the character of urban centres. Nevertheless, there seems to be little scope for the others to have had a different character except on the coast where a number of ports did really exist even in this period. Leaving those few, all the remaining centres obviously obtained their urbanhood as Seats of Administration

From the time of Alberuni, for about another three centuries, we have no positive information about the progress of urbanisation in the country and it is only in the fourteenth century that Ibn Battuta, another Muslim traveller, gives substantial testimony to the existence of a flourishing urban life in India. Ibn Battuta crossed River Indus in September 1333 on a travelling mission to India. Here, appointed by the Sultan of Delhi as the Chief Quazi of Delhi, he stayed for about nine years and visited different parts of the country mostly as a companion to the Sultan, lastly leaving India in July 1342 for China as an emissary of the Sultan to the court of China. It has to be admitted that Ibn Battuta is always treated as a traveller, and not as a geographer[6] and his travel accounts were not written by him, but dictated from memory in the manner of telling stories about his experiences and that too after a long time of his actual visits to the places. It will not be unfair therefore to point out that perhaps imagination crept into his narratives and his accounts about many places cannot be taken as fully correct. At the same time one needs to be cautioned about his descriptions, for he was more interested in persons than places. In spite of all these weaknesses of the accounts, one cannot ignore the fact that unlike Alberuni, his geographical knowledge about the places was gained entirely from his personal experience[7].

In giving his impressions about the towns and cities of India visited by him, Ibn Battuta becomes highly eloquent about the city of Dihhli (Delhi) "the metropolis of India, a vast and magnificent city, uniting beauty and strength. It is surrounded by wall that has no equal in the world, and is the largest city in India, any rather the largest city in the entire Muslim Orient"[8]. In another place he bestows on Delhi still more laurels calling it "one of the greatest cities in the world"[9]. In his time Delhi was made up of four neighbouring and contiguous towns—(1) Delhi Proper; (2) Siri; (3) Tughlaq Abad; (4) Jahan Panah—set apart for the residence of the refining sultan[10]. Besides Delhi, Ibn Battuta accords a number of cities and towns with the following comments:

The city of Multan; Sarasati (Sirsa)–"a large town"[11] city of Quinawj (Kanauj)– "a large, well built and strongly fortified city, surrounded by a great wall"[12]. Galyaror, Guyalyur (Gwalior)– "a large and well-built town"[14], Koel: Kajarra (Khajuraho)[15], Dhibar (Dhar) "the chief city of Malwa"[16], Uajyn (Ujjain)–"a fine and populous town"[17]; Dawlat Abad or Deogiri–"the enormous city which rivals Delhi, the capital, in importance and in the spaciousness of its planning"[18]; Saghar (Songarh)–"a large town on the great river" (Tapti)[19]; Kimbaya (Cambay)– "The city is one of the finest there is in regard to the excellence of its construction and the architecture of its mosques"[20] and at his time was one of the principal seaports of India; Qandahar (Gandhar)–"a large town"[21]; Quqa (Gogo, in Kathiawar)–"a large town with important bazaars"[22]; Manjarur (Mangalore)–"a large town at which most of the merchants from Fars (part of Persia) an Yemen disembark, and pepper and ginger are exceedingly abundant there"[23]; city of Qualiqut (Calicut) "is one of the chief ports in Mulaybar (Malabar) and one of the largest harbours in the world, visited by men from China, Sumatra, Ceylon, the Maldives, Yemen and Fars"[24]; Jurafattan (Cannanore); Fandaryana (Panderani)–"a large and fine town"[25]; city of Kawlam (Quilon)–"one of the finest towns in the Mulaybar lands. It has five bazaars. They (merchants) are immensely wealthy"[26]. It was visited by merchants from China. The city of Mutra (Madurai)–Capital, "a large town with wide street"[27], Sudkawan (Either Satgaona) — a runied town on the Hooghly lying north-west of Hooghly town and was the mercantile capital of Bengal from the days of Hindu rule until the foundation of Hooghly by the Portuguese; or, Chittagong, as identified by Yule")[28], "a large town"[29]. In many ways Ibn Battuta's accounts are invaluable in the study of Indian urbanisation during the medieval period. The towns and cities are not mere place-names as is customary with many travellers, including Alberuni. To him they carry a greater meaning than being either a capital or a fortress. He distinguishes between the size of the urban places, looks into their build, architecture and planning, observes their beauty, marks the width of the streets and remarks on the extensive trading activity of the important seaports of his days, giving an idea about the extent of trade as well as trading items in many cases. All these informations even if conclusive and may be exaggerations in certain cases, give a realistic view of urbanisation in general.

According to Ibn Battuta's accounts, in the first half of the fourteenth century there were a number of cities and large towns, some of them quite admirable in their size, wealth and magnificence. The flourishing state of urbanisation is further proved by the fact that India held an important place in the world-trade. maintaining direct relations with Arab countries in the west and China in the east. International trade as a very important index of urban development is another convincing proof of the stability attained by many of the seaports acting the same role for a long past.

But the picture is largely incomplete when the whole country is considered. A careful analysis of the list of urban centres will show that Ibn Battuta's narratives are mostly devoted to the places situated on the western coast; apart from a few centres like Multan, Sirsa, Delhi, Kanauj, Koel, Khajuraho, Ujjain, Madurai and Sudkawan, all the towns and cities mentioned by him belong to the Western Coast. This does not mean that urban development was entirely absent in the remaining part of India. As a matter of fact, in stating his personal experience. Ibn Battuta does not go beyond what he saw. For instance, on the Western Coast there were important seaports like Cambay, Surat, Broach and Chaul which do not enter into his narratives as he did not visit them personally. Similarly, capital cities like, Warangal and Dorasamudra (both established as capital cities after 1190 A.D.), Vijayanagara (established around 1336 A.D.) and Rajamundry (mentioned by Hiuen Tsang) figuring conspicuously both in the earlier and later political history of South India are absent from his list. For the same reason no town or city east of Kanauj has any place in his list although important cities like Prayaga, Varanasi, Monghyr, Lakhnauti, to name a few only, were already there maintaining a flourishing existence.

In order to get a better idea about the state of urban development in the country we have to refer to much later sources, available some three hundred years after the visit of Ibn Battuta. The most valuable works in this connection are those of Abul Fazl, a courtier of Emperor Akbar (1542-1605 A.D.), giving more accurate information about the towns and cities of his time. He producted two voluminous works—'Ain-i-Akbari' and 'Akbar Nama' of which especially the former may be considered as a mine of geographical information.

In the second volume of Ain-i-Akbari, Abul Fazl mentions that empire of Akbar—covering the whole of West and Central India—was divided into fifteen Subahs or provinces, sub-divided further into 105 Sarkars or districts and there were altogether 2837 townships in

1594[30]. He does not give the names of all these towns, many of which were undoubtedly small centres, but refers only to the larger ones. The names of towns and cities occurring in different Subahs and mentioned by Abul Fazl are as follows:

1. *This Subah or Province of Bengal* : Janatabad (Gaur); Mamudabad; Sonargaon; Chatgao (Chittagong)*; Katak (Cuttack); Puri (Purushottama); Tanda Fathabad; Khalifabad; Bhal; Tajpur; Nasratabad; Pinjarah; Barbakabad; Sylhet; Sulaimanabad; Jalesar; Ramuna; Raepur; Mednipur; Mandaran; Manak patan;
2. *The Subah of Bihar* : Gaya; Tirhut; Rohtas; Behar; Patna; Seor; Monghyr; Hajipur.
3. *The Subah of Illahabad (Allahabad)* : Illahabad; Baranasi; Jaunpur; Chanadah (Chunar); Kalinjar; Ghazipur; Manikpur; Kurrah.
4. *The Subah of Oudh* : Awadh (Ajodhya); Bahraich; Nimkhar; Lucknow; Kheri; Gorakhpur; Bilgram; Khairabad.
5. *The Subah of Agra* : Agra; (Fatehpur) Sikri; Mathura; Kalpi; Kanauj; Gwalior; Alwar; Kanori; Narwar.
6. *The Subah of Malwa* : Ujjain; Chanderi; Mandu; Dhar; Raisin; Garha; Sarangpur; Jalalabad; Handia; Nandurbar; Mandeso; Gogran; Kotri Parwa.
7. *The Subah of Dandes (Khandesh)* : Asir, Burhanpur; Adilabad; Dhamarni; Choprah; Thalner.
8. *The Subah of Berar* : Elichpur; Panar; Shahpur; Kallam; Mahur; Ramgir; Kherla; Basim; Pathri; Mehkar.
9. *The Subah of Gujarat* : Ahmedabad; Pattan; Champner; Mahmudabad; Gogo; Cambay; Sidhpur; Barnagar (Vadnagar); Surat; Rander; Daman; Tarapur; Mahim; Bassein; Broach; Hansot; Junagarh; Somnath; Manglor (Manglor); Diu; Porbandar; Korinor; Ahmadpur; Muzaffarabad; Mul Mahadeo; Dwarka; Bhuj; Nawanagar; Sirohi; Abugarh; Nandod; Baroda; Sinor; Godhra, Sarath.
10. *The Subah of Ajmer*: Ajmer; Udaipur; Chitor; Jodhpur Nagor; Bikaner; Jaisalmir; Amarkot; Jalor.
11. *The Subah of Delhi* : Delhi; Badaon; Sambhal, Hansi; Sahnah

* Chittagong was outside the domain of Akbar.

(Sohna); Hisar, Sarhind; Mirath (Meerut); Saharanpur; Rewari.

12. *The Subah of Lahore* : Lahore; Nagarkot; Jalandhar; Sialkot; Mankot; Rohtas.
13. *The Subah of Multan* : Multan; Bhakkar; Brahmanabad; Alor; Kobhar (Ramnagar).
    The Sarkar of Kashmir : Srinagar.

Besides those mentioned above, a few more names appear in Akbar-Nama : Ambala; Sirsa; Panipat; Chitor; Firozabad; Rajauri; Punch; Bhagalpur; Kul (Aligarh); Jalalabad; Peshwar, Hajipur; Ranthampur; Mirtha (Merta); Gadha; Khirar (Khera); Chunar; Kotah; Arrah; Akbarnagar (Rajmahal); Balghatta; Burdwan; Bareilly; Bishnupur; Bhadrijan; Dacca; Darbhanga; Jessore; Ludhiana; Pattan, Satgaon.

The list, including only about 180 names, is not exhaustive, if Abul Fazl's statement is to be accepted, nearly 93 per cent of the total number of townships do not find any mention in his writings. The question may arise here on the veracity of his statement on total number of townships. It is difficult to know the sources on which he based his assessment. There is no supporting evidence to justify that he had precise information for making such a definite conclusion about the actual number of urban places existing in his time. It is equally difficult to believe that there could be so many towns in the 'Dominions' of Akbar, covering only the northern and the central parts of India when even today the number is not so large in the whole of India. True that the region comprising Pakistan and Afghanistan was included in the dominions of Akbar; but south India and the mineral-rich region of Orissa and Southern Bihar have now a far greater number of urban centres than the former two States put together. The weakness of Abul Fazl's statement is further revealed in the absence of any sound basis for distinguishing between small towns and villages; it is not unlikely that places with even small forts were considered by him as urban places and similarly many of the flourishing villages renowned for spinning, weaving and other types of craft industries were taken for townships.

In spite of over-estimation, Abul Fazl brings forward the truth with all forcefulness that urbanisation was no longer an isolated phenomenon, but had become diffused throughout the country. The total number, however inflated, gives the impression of a high degree of urban development and his reference, though confined to the important towns and cities only, makes this further confirmed. Thus Abul Fazl's invaluable contribution to our knowledge in this field cannot be underestimated. Instead of getting piecemeal information for the centuries following the visit of Hiuen Tsang in the seventh century, again we get a more or less full picture of the spread of urbanisation. This offers the scope of making an assessment of the overall progress attained during the intervening thousand years and ascertain if pattern in the spatial distribution of urban centres had undergone any substantial change.

From Abul Fazl's writing we gather that there were at least 18 large cities in India at that time. They were—Agra, Sikri, Delhi, Ahmedabad, Lahore, Cambay, Elichpur, Burhanpur, Asir, Ujjain, Mandu, Ayodhya, Lucknow, Chittagong, Varanasi, Jaunpur, Raepur and Mednipur. From his descriptions we gather that

1. Agra, first made capital by Iskandar Lodi in 1504, lying on the left or the eastern bank of the river Jamuna, was a "matchless city"[31] during Akbar's time which "for its air and water makes Badgad ashamed of the Tigris and Egypt of the Nile"[32]. At this time the city sprawled on both the banks of the river for five *kos*. It contained more than five hundred masonry buildings of beautiful architecture. This large city, "the centre of Hindustan", was filled with people from different countries and turned into "the emporium of the traffic of the world"[33].

2. Sikri, or Fatehpur Sikri, previously a village, "rose to be a city of the first order"[34] during Akbar's rule, where on the summit of a hill large fort was built. Within it palaces, residence for the nobles, a college, benevolent institutions and baths and a large market were constructed. The plains surrounding the hill became studded with numerous mansions and gardens converting it into a great place of concourse "such as might move the envy of the world"[35].

3. Delhi : In describing Delhi as one of the greatest cities of antiquity[36], Abul Fazl traces its history from about 1200 A.D. onwards when it had been built time and again by different Muslim rulers magnificence of which were still recognizable in their ruins. In spite of ruinous character of the most part of the city, its cemeteries were populous[37] and Abul Fazl called this "wondrous city"[38] as a Metropolis[39].

4. Ahmedabad : Abul Fazl describes Ahmedabad as "a noble city in a high degree of prosperity"[40], unrivalled for the display of its choicest products of the entire world. The Metropolis—as called by him—had 360 purahs or wards[41] each of which possessed all the requisites of a city, 84 of them being in a flourishing state in his time[42].

5. Lahore : This was "a very large city"[43], being among the first in size and population[44]. As a seat of the Government, it contained many splendid buildings and gardens. People from different countries of the world resided here and their manufactures made a surprising display. There were more than a thousand workshops in the city[45] producing a large range of "masterpieces of workmanships"[46]. The traders and craftsmen of this "illustrious city"[47] had the capacity of easily supplying a large army.

6. Varanasi : Abul Fazl calls it a large city famous for being the chief seat of learning in Hinduism from time immemorial. Beautiful cloths were woven here[48].

7. Ajodhya or Awadh : It was "one of the largest cities of India"[49] at that time highly "esteemed as one of the holiest places of antiquity"[50].

8. Jaunpur : Founded sometime in the middle of the fourteenth century A.D. by Firuz Shah[51]. Jaunpur developed into a "great"[52] and a large city"[53] in Akbar's time where woollen carpets were manufactured[54].

9. Cambay or Kambhayet was "large city where merchants of divers kings reside and wherein are fine buildings and much merchandise"[55].

10. Burhanpur, described as a large city, was "embellished with many gardens", and "inhabited by people of all countries and handicraftsmen play thriving trade"[56].

11. Asir developed as the residence of the Governor with a fortress on a lofty hill with "a large and flourishing city" at its foot[57].

12. Ujjain.

13. Mandu, another large city, had a fort the circumference of which was 12 *kos*. "For some period it was the seat for government and stately edifices still recall their ancient lords"[58].

14. Chittagong was a large city "considered an excellent port and is the resort of Christian and other merchants"[59].

15. Raepur.

16. Mednipur.

17. Lucknow.

18. Elichpur.

Nothing much is said except calling them large cities.

It may not be out of place here to make a note of the agricultural and industrial prosperity of the country in those days forming the background to the development of urbanisation. In writing about the Subahs or the provinces, Abul Fazl makes passing references to their climate, and agricultural and industrial activities.

In Bengal the summer was temperate and the cold season very short. The rains, beginning some time in May, continued for over six months when the plains got inundated leaving only the 'mounds' above water. Rice was the principal crop followed by wheat and barley. Long pepper grew in Mahmudabad (now comprising parts of N.Nadia, N. Jessore and W. Faridpur) and great abundance of oranges were available in Barbakabad (mainly Rajshahi, S.W. Bogra and S.E. Malda). The District of Bazula (comprising partly Rajshahi, Bogra, Pabna and Dacca districts of Bangladesh) had extensive forests, supplying timber for the ship industry[60]. Fine pomegranates were grown in Satgaon and Hughli. The harvests of food crops were "always abundant"[61]. Silk and sack cloth—made of jute, were produced in the District of Ghoraghat (comprising S. Rangpur, S.E. Dinajpur and N.Bogra); a fine cloth called 'Gangajal' was produced in the District of Barbakabad, and very fine muslins, having a great demand, were produced in the district of Sonargaon (W. Tipperah and Noakhali).

The climate of Orissa was dominated by rainy season lasting over eight months; of the remaining months three were cold and only one hot. The main corps of Orissa were rice and fruits and flowers available in plenty. Principal manufactures were cloths[62].

In the Subah of Bihar the summer was intensively hot, but the winter was mild (temperate). The rains continued for six months. Throughout the year the country remained green and fertile. Stone ornaments and paper of a good quality were manufactured at Rajgir. Precious stones imported from foreign countries gave rise to a constant traffic at Gaya[63].

The climate of Subah of Allahabad was healthy. Agriculture was in a flourishing state here. A variety of fruits, flowers, and garden herbs were grown with an abundant supply of melons and grapes. "Cloths, such as Jholi, and Mihrkal and the like are beautifully woven, especially at Benares, Jalalabad and Mau. At Jaunpur, Zafarwal and other places woollen carpets are menufactured"[64].

The Subah of Oudh enjoyed a good climate where summer and winter were nearly temperate. Agriculture was in a flourishing state and especially the different varieties of rice for its "whiteness, delicacy, fragrance and wholesomeness are scarcely to be matched"[65]. Flowers, fruits and game were abundant.

The Subah of Agra had an excellent climate, almost unrivalled[66]. Agriculture was "in perfection. Fruits and flowers of all kinds abound"[67]. In the two cities of Agra and Fatehpur Sikri numerous handicraftsmen had full occupation, producing carpets and fine stuffs under the direct patronage of the Emperor. Sugar of extreme witness and indigo of the finest quality were produced in the towns of Bianah and Kalpi; another town manufactured excellent sugarcandy and Alwar produced glass and woollen carpets.

The Subah of Malwa with all its lakes and green meadows, the stately palaces and the fair country homes "breathe the tales of fairyland"[68]. The climate was temperate throughout the year and every part of it was cultivated. Harvest were excellent, especially that of wheat, poppy, sugarcane, mangoes, melons and grarpes. In Hasilpur the vine bore two crops a year, besides a fine quality of betel leaves. "Cloth of the best texture is woven here"[69].

The Subah of Dandes (Khandesh) had a pleasant climate. Abul Fazl does not mention anything about its agriculture. According to him, good cloth stuffs were woven there, some particularly notable varieties being manufactured at Dharanagar (Dhar). The city of Burhanpur was also a large industrial centre.

Information about the Subah of Berar is similarly too niggardly. The climate and agriculture are noted to be remarkably good[70] while the singular reference to the industrial activities occurs in the case of Lonar which produced saltpetre.

The climate in the Subah of Ahmedabad was temperate where the sandy character of the soil prevented it from turning into mud during the rainy season. The staple crops grown were Jowar and Bajra—a variety of millets, but the spring harvest used to be poor. The Subah had to depend on the imports of wheat and other foodgrains from the Subahs of Malwa and Ajmer, and rice from Deccan. Industrially the Subah was really prosperous. "Stuffs worked with gold threads and of the kinds Chirah, Fotah, Jamahwar (a kind of flowered woollen stuff), Khara (an undulated silk cloth), and velvets and brocades are here skilfully manufactured"[71]. Besides, limitations of products from Turkey, Persia and Europe were also produced. Painters, seat engravers and other handicraftsmen were countless. "They inlay mother–O'–pearl with great skill and make beautiful boxes and inkstands"[72]. Among other notable products were excellent swords, daggers, bows, arrows and jewellery.

In the Subah of Ajmer the winter was temperate but the summer was intensely hot. The sandy soil and the scarcity of water made the spring harvests inconsiderable. Nothing is said about the industries.

The climate of the Subah of Delhi was nearly temperate. Much of the land getting inudated during the rains produced, in some places, three harvests a year. The fruits of Iran, Turan and Hindustan were produced here and "it is scarce excelled for the choice productions of every clime"[73]. No comment is made on its industrial activities.

The winter in the adjoining Subah of Lahore though "more severe than in any other part of India"[74] was yet healthy and its agricultural fertility "rarely equalled"[75]. Irrigation was practised chiefly from the wells, and through the encouragement of the Emperor choicest products of Turkestan, Persia and Hindustan were found here. Lahore was a large industrial centre.

The Subah of Multan had a climate almost similar to that of Lahore, but with less rainfall and more heat than the latter. There is no remark about its agriculture and industry.

In writing about Kashmir, Abul Fazl refers to the manufacture of beautiful shawls and other woollen stuffs in Srinagar as well as to the production of silk.

The very nature of information, as mentioned above, makes it palpably clear that Abul Fazl maintains extreme brevity in his statements, particularly on the agricultural and industrial developments of the country. The reasons may be the lack of exact information that naturally curbed his otherwise unbridled pen, but it seems to be unlike his meticulous mind which never faltered probing into different subjects. What appears to be more likely is that Abul Fazl by and large an historian, and not a geographer, was much less interested in geographical facts and hence was less elaborate in stating more than what flitted through his mind at the moment of writing about the

Empire of Akbar. His greater concern about the historical aspects is reflected throughout in the volumes of both Ain-i-Akbari and Akbar Nama and when he goes to write about the Subahs his characteristic vivacity to details drops visibly—making that into a cut and dry account of few place names and rivers. True, one cannot expect regional details from him, but the absence of any reference of the agricultural activities of many areas, almost casual reference to the industrial activities, yielding nothing about many of the important places, lack of any positive information about a number of the 'Large Cities' and, lastly, mention of only a small percentage of the existing towns and cities certainly indicate his mind which was not effusive about geographic details.

The shortcomings and the briefness of information do not however conceal the agricultural prosperity of the country which formed the actual basis of industrial and urban development. Most of the provinces enjoyed abundant harvests and produced a variety of crops—including many of the delicacies produced in them. The only exceptions were the provinces of Ahmedabad and Ajmer while in view of the good climate Khandes was not probably agriculturally non-affluent. The poverty of the first lay in the food crops, but not in the industrial crops as Ahmedabad was already famous for its cotton and indigo. In Ajmer the winter crops were poor which does not mean that the summer crops shared the same fate. Besides, situated on the main transport route connecting the imperial cities of Agra and Delhi with that of the South Indian cities guaranteed her every opportunity of meeting her deficit—if there was any—from both sources. Thus, rich agricultural surpluses, industrial supremacy with unrivalled position In the production of many choice as well as essential items and an extremely efficient age-old commerce developed an urban system which became more dynamic and much too common a feature of the settlement geography of the country than ever before.

The pertinent question may arise here on the authenticity of Abul Fazl about the large cities which, lacking the role of primate cities, formed the foundation of future urbanisation in the country.

The probability of any exaggeration or over-estimation of the greatness of these premier cities by Abul Fazl is ruled out on the basis of information supplied by writer like (1) Ferishta (reached India in, 1589), (2) Emperor Jahangir (1605-1627), (3) Pelsaept (1620-

1627). (4) Francois Bernier (reached India in 1658 or in early 1659 and left India in 1667); (5) Tavernier (1641-1665); (6) Manucci (1656); and (7) Thevenot (1666).

Agra : Jahangir, as the Emperor of India (1605-1627), wrote his 'Memoirs' and in that he refers to a number of towns and cities. According to Jahangir there were twelve chief cities in India at that time and names four of them, such as Agra, Delhi, Lahore and Ahmedabad"[76]. He mentions Agra as "the depository of the world's resources"[77]. In his opinion Agra was "a great and populous place"[78] before the Lodhi Sultans first came to make it their capital in 1504 A.D. From that date, however, the population and prosperity of Agra increased uninterrupted. During the time of Jahangir the habitable part of the city extended on both sides of the river. The western bank, containing the greater population, had a circumference of 7 *kos* and a breadth of one *kos*, while on the eastern bank the circumference was 2½ *kos*, the length and breadth being one and one-half *kos* respectively. "In the number of its buildings it is equal to several cities of Iraq, Khurasan, and Manwaraa-in-nahr (Tansoxiana) put together. Many persons have erected buildings of three or four storey in it. The mass of people is so great, that moving about in the lanes and bazars is difficult"[79]. The only thing he does not praise about it is its warm and hot climate[80]. Tavernier, visiting India on five successive occasions between 1641 to 1665, found the summers of Agra exclusively trying. But he admits it to be the largest city of India where the houses of the nobbles "are beautiful and well-built"[81]. There was a large market "consisting of six large courts"[82] selling among other things an enormous quantity of cotton[83]. At that time, however, the capital had already been shifted to Delhi. Bernier, writing about the same time of Tavernier, found it larger than Delhi both in the number of buildings and stone or brick houses. Besides, it was an unwalled city and thus in his opinion was inferior to Delhi[84]. Besides, the city was not built to any "settled design"[85] lacking the uniformity of street pattern that so eminently distinguished Delhi. Ralph Fitch, visiting both Agra and Fatehpur Sikri in 1585 calls them very great cities, each being greater than London. According to Smith the comparison suggests that the population of Fatehpur Sikri at this time should have been around 200,000[86]. Pelsaert, who was in charge of the Dutch Factory at Agra from 1621 to 1627[87], writes about Agra and a number of other towns and cities which he came to know personally. He found the city of Agra "exceedingly large, but decayed, open and unwalled"[88]. The city extended for 6 *kos* (or 3½ Holland miles) along the bank of River Jamuna but it was not so broad as "everyone has tried to be close to the river bank"[89] which was in fact, occupied by the "costly palaces"[90]. Pelsaert gives a very clear impression about the build of the city. The streets and houses were built without any regular plan and as a result the palaces of the great princes and lord were hidden away in alleys and corners[91]. The city had grown enormously within a space of few decades since Akbar made it his capital. The entire area was closely built over and thickly inhabited, virtually leaving no space for the growth of any remarkable market place as in Lahore, Burhanpur, Ahmedabad or other cities[92]. Five gates build by Akbar for the security of the capital lay in the middle of the city at that time when the built up area extending beyond them were three times larger. In his opinion had it been the fixed residence of the Emperor, as it was at his father's (Akbar) time, the city would have grown into "one of the wonders of the world"[93]. Beyond the Fort there was a great market where, apart from different types of animals, cotton goods and many other things were sold. On the opposite bank of the river the city was called Sikandra (not the Sikandra where Akbar's tomb stands). Pelsaert describes it as well-built and populated chiefly by banian merchants. It was fully two *kos* long but not so broad and contained many buildings surrounded by beautiful gardens. The place was one of the principal points of transhipment for goods coming from eastern provinces[94]. Manucci also found Agra as a large city with a circumference of twelve leagues[95]. Thevenot, writing a few years after, held it to be the greatest town of the Indies[96].

Thus, City of Agra, ruined by Mahmud of Gazni[97] in the first quarter of the eleventh century, came to prominence again in the beginning of the sixteenth century when Sultan Sikandar Shah of the Lodi dynasty "founded a new town in 1504 on the site where the modern city of Agra stands"[98] and the place continued as the capital till 1526 when Ibrahim Lodi, the last in the line, was defeated by Babar who, after establishing Mughal supremacy over the Afghans, established his capital at Agra. But his son, Humayun, succeeding to the throne in 1530 shifted his capital to Delhi. Till that time the city had grown mainly on the eastern bank of the river. Revival of Agra did not take place until Akbar removed the seat of government to this place and built a fort here on the west bank of the river, renaming the city as Akbarabad after his own name. Thus began a new history of Agra : the imperial city sprawling on both banks of the Jamuna soon rose to the zenith of prosperity, attaining an unrivalled position among the cities of India. It may be noted here that Pelsaert's reference to the city of Sikandra, lying on the eastern bank, actually formed part of Agra. The testimony to this by Abul Fazl and Emperor Jahangir cannot be challenged. The growth continued uninterrupted during the succeeding decades and though it was populous and exceedingly large, the signs of decay were already visible in the first quarter of the seventeenth century. The main reason for its decline was that it did no longer enjoy the esteemed privilege of being the Imperial capital during Jahangir's time who left the city in 1618 permanently. His son Shah Jahan, however, rebuilt the Fort and established the royal residence here.

Delhi : Unlike Agra, Delhi claims a much grater antiquity. It was founded by the Aryans as a capital city and from that time Delhi has maintained its existence till today although its history before the last part of the medieval period is rather obscure. Such obscurity, however, applies to many other important cities of India surviving through ages and our lack of knowledge about their past is not a sufficient ground to deny the fact that they were sufficiently important to keep their life uninterrupted. It is rather unfortunate to underestimate the foresight and ingenuity of the founders in the selection of sites of these cities. Sites of some of the oldest cities like Delhi, Allahabad, Varanasi, Lucknow, Lahore, etc., could not be chance-selected and it would be wrong to assume that mere primacy—as stated by Hambly in the case of Delhi[99]—was the actual advantage on their part for being not usurped by other centres enjoying superior location. Besides, Hambly does not attach any importance to Delhi as a natural location for the heart of an empire[100]. The testimony of history, however proves otherwise. The primary selection of site for building the Pandava Capital of Indraprastha had its strategic significance even in those earlier days. The Kurus had by then established their Kingdom around Kurukshetra—the country lying between the Saraswati and the Drisadvati in the Karnal-Ambala region of Eastern Punjab[101] with their capital at Hastinapura on river Ganga. They were not in good terms with their Pandava cousins and led by cunning gifted them the land on the west bank of the Jamuna, about eighty miles south-west of their own capital so that the Pandava capital built on that site could act as the first defence against attacks from the non-Aryan barbarian tribes of the west, south-west and the north-west[102]. It is difficult to imagine that the Pandavas failed to devine the actual motive that lay behind such a generous offer; perhaps the question of dignity, power and self-confidence made them accept the challenge gracefully which ultimately resulted in the emergence of Indraprastha, the Capital of the Pandavas. The site thus selected proved to be one of the best for urban development in the long run, never once succumbing completely to the pressure off unwelcome circumstances. Time and again new cities sprang up, sometimes on the ruins of the previous one or sometimes a little away from the ruins, but always on the same site, though under a new name. Altogether fourteen such cities have been traced so far, the fifteenth being the modern representative of the original capital. The most important fact about its urban career is very much revealing : on many occasions during the period of about thirty centuries of its life it has functioned as a capital, either of a Kingdom or of an empire, and considering the total length of time, it is the oldest capital among all the urban centres of India. For instance, according to Ferishta, 'Delhi' was founded as a capital by Raja Dilu some time before the Macedonian invasion[103]. In the middle of the eleventh century, Delhi figured again as the capital of Ananga Pala[104], a Rajput Chief of Tomar clan who built his capital at the site occupied now by the Qutb Minar. His dynasty lasted for a century and was succeeded by Bisaldeo, a Chauhan Chief of Ajmer whose grandson Prithviraj built a new capital named 'Rai Pithora' at the site of Ananga Pal's capital. The ruins of these Hindu capitals are traceable today in Mehrauli and around Qutb Minar. Death of Prithviraj in the hands of Muhammad of Ghur in 1192 ended the Hindu rule of Delhi[105] and in 1206 it became the first Muslim capital of India built as the site of Lal-Kot by Qutb-ud-din Aibak who also laid the foundation of the famous Qutb Minar[106] .The Slave dynasty founded by him, ruled till 1290 when a new dynasty was established by the Khaljis. Ala-ud-din (1296-1316), the last but one in the line, a real empire-builder, did not remain satisfied with the capital of Lal-Kot and built a new capital at Siri with a reservoir known today as Hauz-Khas[107]. In 1320, the Khaljis were supplanted by the Thughluqus, the first of them founding another capital of Delhi known as 'Tughluqabad', some four miles east of Lal-Kot which as testified by Ibn Battuta, turned out to be the largest city of India between 1335-42. Muhammad bin Tughluq, the second in the line, built a new centre, called 'Jahanpanah' which, along with Lal-Kot, Siri and Tughluqabad, formed the 'four towns' of Delhi at the time of Ibn Battuta's visit. Muhammad, however, removed the Capital from Delhi to Daulatabad in Deccan, the latter having central situation was considered safer from Mongol invasions, leaving Delhi desolate with its magnificent architectural works and its bare unpeopled houses. The entire project being "a movement of misdirected energy"[108] proved a complete failure and the capital was reshifted to Delhi. Firuz Shah Tughluq, third successor to the throne, removed his capital to a new city founded by him—Ferozabad, situated north of the site of Indraprastha, occupying all the ground between the tomb of Humayun and the Ridge. For another hundred and fifty years Delhi remained the capital of the Sultans. But in 1504 Sikandar Lodi established his capital at Agra, though Delhi retained much of its former importance. Agra retained that prestigious status for some time until Humayun, ascending the throne in 1530, removed the capital to Delhi and built or restored the fort of Purana Quila on the site of Indraprastha. Sher Shah, the Afghan chief, defeating Humayun, occupied Delhi in 1540 which he enclosed and fortified with a new wall. Bounded on the east by Jamuna and extending northwards as far as Ferozabad with its southern limit formed by the enormous fort of Purana Quila, Delhi at Sher Shah's time emerged as the capital of a large empire. Both Akbar and Jahangir made their primary capital at Agra.

Unlike Sher Shah and other Muslim rulers, Akbar had little interest for Delhi. His predecessors, Babar and Humayun, did not get much time in rebuilding the city on a grand scale as it had been done in many cases from the beginning of Muslim rule in India. But Akbar, having both the time and the resources at his command, had little affection for that city far larger and splendid than Agra of his time and it was to the latter that he devoted much more attention. His apparent neglect of Delhi was, not doubt, born of bitter memories, associated with the city where his father, Humayun died, and where not long before his assassination was plotted and where the memories of Sher Shah's vigorous administration were still fresh. Besides, beginning with the Lodi dynasty the presence of Afghan influence imbibed through decades of Afghan, rule made Delhi less safe and attractive in the eyes of Mughal Emperor Akbar who chose Agra as better place for his capital[109]. His son, Jahangir, seems to have had an equal dislike for Delhi and followed his father's suit in keeping his capital at Agra. Apart from calling it one of the twelve chief cities of India[110], Jahangir skips any comment about Delhi. Neither Pelsaert is at all generous in that respect. But both Tavernier and Bernier refer to Delhi, the latter more profusely than the former. Tavernier saw the new capital of Jahanabad growing to eminence, while Old Delhi, separated from the new capital by a simple wall, gradually going into ruins and peopled only by the poor[111]. In speaking about Delhi, Bernier refers to the old as well as the new city. The latter included the suburbs "which were considerable comprising a long chain of buildings"[112] and three or four smaller suburbs extended for more than one and a half league. Ferishta, writing some time before Bernier and Tavernier, declares Delhi to the "envy of the world"[113] while Manucci, visiting Delhi in the middle of the 17th century, mentions the large and wellbuilt bazars or markets within the city "where are sold things of every kind"[114]. On the other hand, Thevenot refers to the pulsatory character of its large population which reduces greatly with the movement of the royal court[115]. But in spite of the splendour of Agra, enhanced further through the construction of monumental buildings from the time of Akbar to Shah Jahan, the latter shifted his capital to Delhi in 1648,[116] founding a new city after his own name — Shahjahanabad on the site of modern Delhi for which much of the material obtained from the ruins of Ferozabad and Purana Qila were utilised in building the walls and the gateways[117]. Since then Delhi remained as the permanent capital of Mughal India. Despite Aurangzeb's apparent neglect of the city—which he left permanently in 1681 for the conquest of South India[118] — Delhi remained the foremost city of the Empire. The prosperity did not wane even in the eighteenth century when Mughal administration was already disintegrating and new powers like the Jats, the Sikhs and the Marathas had emerged. The situation rather renewed the importance of Delhi "as the place where emperors could be made and un-made"[119]. This position was retained until the city was taken over by the English in September 1857 and placed under military administration for some time when the entire civilian population was expelled from the city. It was restored to the civil authorities on January 11, 1858[120]. In 1912 it was declared as the capital of British India and for this purpose a new city was constructed here, taking the name of New Delhi.

The brief history of Delhi's past, outlined above, reveals some of the intrinsic qualities of its geographical location making it an unavoidable site and inevitable choice for capital on eight successive occasions during the historic period alone. Beginning from the middle of the eleventh century down to the modern times, on at least five of these seven occasions Delhi has been as Imperial Capital. The small triangular piece of plain between the river Jamuna on the east and the Delhi Ridge on the west, measuring about 70 sq. miles in area, has been the site for the development of all these capitals. Physographically, Delhi Plain in a part of the broad corridor that links the Punjab to the Ganga plains and repeating the characteristic "alluvial monotony"[121] of the North India plain. This corridor has always stood as an agricultural contrast between the north-eastern extremity of the Rajasthan desert and semi-desert foothills of the Himalayas. Standing in the middle of this corridor, Delhi enjoys a much greater nodality than any other centre for the convergence of the most important routes originating from the north-west across the mountains, from the east—stretching through the rich Ganga plains, from the south and west connecting the resourceful regions of Deccan, Malwa and the international trading ports of the western coast. The geographical location of Delhi has given it a marchaland position[122], receiving the first shock of every invasion coming from the north-west. The end of Hindu rule took place in Delhi and the Muslim rule in India had its birth here. For the resource-hungry marauders of the Middle-East and Central Asia, Delhi was the primary target during medieval period. Delhi was the gateway for the rich heartlands of the country. Occupation of the city thus became the deciding factor in the case of every political or cultural intrusion into India. The importance of this unrivalled strategic location had been proved on more than one occasion. Shifting of the capital by Muhammad-bin-Tughluq in 1327 to Daulatabad turned out to be an historic blunder and re-shifting of the capital to Delhi after all the huge expenses involved in building the new capital at Daultabad and transferring the entire population both ways proved Delhi as the surperior location for the capital of an empire. This was proved once again during the later part of the Mughal rule in India when Shahjahan shifted his capital from Agra to Delhi. It should be noted here that Agra, growing as the Imperial Capital from the time of Akbar to Shahjahan for about a century (1556-1648), was at that time the largest, most populous and the grandest of all cities in India. Even Shahjahan, like his predecessors, further joined in the building spree. It is highly curious to note that in spite of the very strong intention of making Agra more magnificent, a policy adroitly pursued through the first twenty year of his rule (1628-48), Shahjahan, all of a sudden, left the city of Agra and founded his capital in that old environment of Delhi. The reason for this change given by Tavernier visiting India at that time, was the climate being "more temperature"[123] at Delhi than Agra does not seem to be strong enough because the short distance between the two places could not make an appreciable difference. The actual reason behind such a move was, perhaps, the better situation of Delhi in view of the growing Jat and Rajput powers near at hand and also its greater advantage in keeping a watchful eye on the disturbing north-western border of the Mughal Empire. The status of the Imperial Capital was retained by Delhi for the succeeding two centuries, losing only with the inception of British rule in India. But, after the consolidation of British rule in the subcontinent, Delhi once again emerged as the seat of the Government in 1912.

A careful review of Delhi's urban status as a city reveals that something much more vital and powerful than mere primacy made it the inevitable choice on each of the three successive occasions mentioned above. For instance, Daulatabad, enjoying a safer location and a less harsh climate, built in an imperial style providing all comfort and security of easy living, failed to keep the capital for long and the latter moved back to Delhi which by then had degraded to a desolate place. The rehabilitation of Delhi, attracting artisans, merchants and learned men from adjoining towns[124] was not an easy task and the city did not regain its former glory and grandeur until long after this episode. The shifting of capital to Agra in the earlier part of the Mughal rule naturally relegated Delhi to an inferior position. At about Fazl's time even the latest Delhi was mostly in ruins[125] while, apart from referring to it as one of the largest cities of India. Jahangir does not say anything about the city although writes a lot about Agra and some other cities of his time. Pelsaert, visiting India, during the rule of Jahangir, is completely silent about it. Silence or neglect on the part of the writers was obviously caused by its unimportant position as a city and this is amply proved by the fact that a new city had to be built by Shahjahan when Delhi was once again re-selected for his capital. This was also the case when the capital of British India was shifted from Calcutta, the largest city of the country, to Delhi—then only a mediocre city.

All these facts illustrate the unchallenged position of Delhi's geographical location which neither bad time nor worst events could affect. The strategic significance of its location from the very date of its selection in the dim past never lessened but assured greater importance with time in the face of growing violation of India's frontier from the north-west. It is highly interesting to observe that the small triangle of 70 sq. miles has witnessed the birth of fifteen cities in succession, at least nine of them as capitals. The fact that on most of the occasions the city was built anew, away from the previous one, does not indicate virtual discontinuity, but a real slackening of urban life between the intervening periods when the older city going of urban life between the intervening periods when the older city going into ruins was incapable of containing the new capital. Urban continuity at least from the middle of the eleventh century therefore was not the actual factor in attracting capital functions to this site; cities as old as Delhi enjoying spells of greater prosperity than it and acting as Imperial Capitals sometimes were rather ignored in preference to Delhi which further strengthens the view that the site was the chief attraction.

The repetitive efforts of the capital-builders choosing the same site every time throughout the period of about three thousand years establish its overwhelming superiority beyond and doubt.

Lahore : Emperor Jahangir refers to Lahore as one of the greatest places in Hindustan[126]. In Pelsaert's opinion, it was great centre of trade before the arrival of the English merchants at Agra in the beginning of that century when Lahore was the chief market for indigo supplying the European and the Middle East countries. In his time business greatly dwindled, the exports—mainly in fine cotton goods—

were confined mainly to Persia and Turkey though as a provincial seat of the Government the city under the care of the Mughal Emperors had greatly recovered in view of "more splendour, royal buildings, places and gardens than in point of wealth"[127]. Few year later to Pelsaert's visit, Tavernier found it as a large town, extending for more than *kos* in length though many of its buildings, taller than those in either Agra or Delhi, were already "falling into ruins"[128] because of excessive rains. Bernier, giving the same reason, ascribes the decline of the city of the abandonment of it by the royal court after Jahangir's death[129] who frequently used to move his capital to this place. A contrasting view, however, is given by Manucci visting the city a few decades after Bernier. In his time the city was inhabited by great and rich merchants and it crammed with foreigners[130] and was "well provided with provisions"[131]. But Thevenot, writing shortly after Manucci, almost corroborates the statement of Bernier, though he does not deny the greatness of the city.

Ahmedabad : Ferishta takes Ahmedabad as the "handsomest city in Hidustan and perhaps in the world"[132] with its 360 mahullas or wards and principal streets which were sufficiently wide to allow ten carriages abreast.

Pelsaert gives an impressive account of the manufacturing and trading of this great city of India. It received a large amount of Patna silk, the latter producing annually 1000 to 2000 maunds, most of which was consumed in Ahmedabad[133] for the manufacture of "ormesines, satins, velvets and various kinds of curious stuffs"[134], carpets were also woven here using silk and gold threads. It was great emporium of trade, collecting goods of all descriptions from different parts of the country and exporting them to foreign lands from where a great variety of articles were imported to Ahmedabad for their onward transmission to Delhi, Agra and other inland places. Tavernier calls it "one of the largest town in India"[135]—carrying on a considerable trade in a wide range of items, silk stuffs taking an important position among them. But the most disheartening comments are made by Jahangir about this city. He calls it in various names like a dustbin, an abode of sickness, the thorn-bed, the house of hell[136] and is amazed to think "what pleasure or goodness the founder of the city could have seen in a sport so devoid of the favour (of God) as to build a city on it"[137]. Scathing remarks, born of unpleasant experience of an Emperor cannot, however, be taken seriously in understanding the greatness of the city. In spite of being a dust-bowl, made by its hot and dry atmosphere, it emerged as the principal industrial and commercial place of Western India, recorded so emphatically by widely travelled European merchantmen like Pelsaert and Tavernier visiting India at the time of Jahangir or little after his death. Thevenot also found the city as "most carefully kept in order"[138].

Cambay : In Jahangir's memoirs Cambay appears as "one of the largest ports in Hindustan"[139]. It was a walled city with fine houses where many merchants of distant origins came and settled. There was a mint for gold and silver coins. But signs of decline were already visible, as noted by Pelsaert, largely due to decreasing trade which was "nearly, or almost wholly at an end"[140]. A few caravans arrived at that time and that too carried goods of small value. Tavernier, making similar statement, holds the receding sea responsible for vast erosion in trade. In fact, this is also mentioned indirectly by Jahangir stating that the ships could not come directly to Cambay, but had to anchor at the port of Gogo, lying opposite on Kathiawar coast, from where cargos were carried in small boats to the former. Loss in trade was however largely made up by its industrial activities centred mainly on the cutting of beautiful agates and shaping them into various prize objects, demonstrating high workmanship; these along with indigo of a superior quality had a wide market. Thevenot recording his impression about a decade or so after Tavernier, notes that "the shops are full of aromatick perfumes, spices, silken and other stuffs. There are vast numbers of ivory bracelets, agatecups, chaplets and rings made in this town"[141].

Varanasi : Tavernier found it as "a large and very sell-built town"[142] where the majority of the houses were made of brick or cut-stone and loftier than in other Indian cities. The streets, however, were very narrow and inconvenient. Cotton and silk stuffs and other merchandise were produced locally and sold in the market. Pelsaert gives a list of articles manufactured in the city among which textiles and copper-wares were important. Bernier, visiting the city on one occasion in 1665 with Tavernier as his companion, pays great tribute to this place, having a "beautiful situation in the midst of an extremely fine and rich country"[143], developed into a renowned seat of learning. He calls it the Athens of India where learners from all parts of the country used to congregate. According to Manucci, "in this city is made much cloth worked in gold and silver which is distributed hence all over the Mogul realm, and is exported to many parts of world"[144].

Burhanpur : Founded about 1400 A.D. Burhanpur was a very large city at Pelsaert's time extending for 12 *kos* or more[145]. Tavernier found this big city in a rather much runied condition, though having a large trade in an enormous quantity of transparent muslins made in the city as well as in other centres of the province which were then exported to Persia, Turkey, Russia, Poland, Arabia, Egypt and other place[146]. The greater abundance of cotton, compared with any other province of India, started a flourishing industry in textiles which included among other things famous fabrics like those mentioned above. Some of the muslins were dyed in various colours; fabrics having stripes of gold and silver silk flowers on both sides, fabrics banded half with cotton and half with gold or silver enjoyed a large market in Persia and Turkey[147]. This is further corroborated by both Manucci[148] and Thevenot[149].

Similar accounts of affluence are not available from the writings of most foreign visitors for the remaining eleven large cities of Abul Fazl. They are Sikri, Elichpur, Asir, Ujjain, Mandu, Ayodhya, Lucknow, Chittagong, Jaunpur, Raepur and Mednipur. Thevenot, however, mentions Chittagong as "very rich"[150]. and Mandu as "one of the fairest ornaments of the province is of moderate bigness"[151] though from its ruins all about it appears to have been "much greater than it is"[152] in his time. Presumably the cities not talked of by the foreign visitors declined in importance during the succeeding decades. This does not mean that they discontinued to function as urban centres. On the contrary, except one or two like Asir and Raepur, most of the others survivings to this date prove the inherent qualities of their strong urban foundations. But the characteristic absence of any positive information in the writings of so many visitors like Ferishta, Bernier, Pelsaert, Tavernier, Manucci, Thevenot and Careri, supporting the pride of position once they enjoyed in the days of Abul Fazl conclusively proves their degradation.

Instead, a number of different centres acquired a greater importance by this time and grew into large cities. Important among them were as follows:

Patna, a provincial capital at Jahangir's time, "was one of the largest town in India not less than 2 *kos* in length"[153], producing annually

1000 to 2000 maunds of silk and also a large amount of coarse muslin. Manucci found it as "a very large city with bazars"[154], producing much white cloth of fine quality, fine mild cloth, a huge quantity of saltpetre, bottles, "cups of clay, finer than glass, lighter than paper"[155] which as curiosities are "carried all over the world"[156]. Thevenot also records it "as a very large town"[157] with a large production of cotton, silk and several other commodities.

Allahabad, a large city [158], being the seat of the Governor and having little trade became rather a pleasure resort where Emperor Akbar built a very fine fort. Manucci refers to the religious importance of this city where "multitudes of Hindus assembled"[159] and many people were stifled to death during such congregations.

Dacca, situated now in Bangladesh, the provincial capital of Bengal since 1657, developed into a large city extending over 2 *kos*[160] when Tavernier visited the place. Manucci calls it "the metropolis of the whole province of Bengal"[161] and it had many inhabitants including many foreigners.

Tatta, now in Pakistan, with its port known as Lahari Bandar received large vessels carrying merchandise from different countries of the world[162]. According to Tavernier it was one of the largest town in India[163], but the trade had already deteriorated in his time due to the rapid silting of the river. Manucci mentions Tatta as the principal city of the country of Sind[164], and Thevenot refers to its great trade and that of Lahari Bandar. In his opinion, the two-wheeled chariots made at Tatta had no parallels in the whole country[165].

Multan, the capital of the province of that time, developed an extensive trade with Persia in sugar produced in great volume in the city. Large quantities of cotton goods manufactured by it used to be exported to Kandhar[166]. Thevenot makes more or less similar statement, though, during the intervening years the trade had slumped due to the silting of the river[167].

Baroda, a city in Jahangir's days[168], had a considerable trade in Calicoes[169]. Thevenot found it as a "larger modern town"[170], inhabited by a large number of merchants and it was full of artisans"[171], manufacturing the finest stuffs of Gujarat.

Broach, another large urban centre, manufactured beautiful calicoes[172]. Careri found it "famous for its excellent white and stained calicoes, as also for ginger"[173].

Sironj was one of the notable centres making some of the finest types of muslin use of which was strictly confined to the Moghul Court. Besides, it had a large trade in all kinds of coloured calicoes "with which all the common people of Persia and Turkey are clad"[174]. Manucci gives similar view about its fame in the manufacture and trade in cotton products[175].

Goa grew into a "very large"[176] urban centre, considered to be one of the three finest ports in Eurasia[177]. Thevenot calls it "one of the fairest harbours in the world"[178]. Other large urban centres mentioned by Tavernier are Murshidabad and Nadia in Bengal, Gwalior, Nawar and Kalabagh. The names mentioned above do not complete the list of large cities and towns. There were still many centres, as mentioned by different authors, that had attained a prosperous stage of development both in size and function. Some of them may be mentioned here.

Feristha refers to Hyderabad, built as the new capital of the Qutb Shani Dynasty of Bidar in 1589[179], which "soon flourished to a very extensive degree"[180] with baths, hospitals run by learned physicians, and colleges. In his opinion, the city "not only bears a fair comparison with the cities in other parts of the world, in appearance as well as cleanliness, but it is superior to many"[181]. He further refers to Jahanabad—a city on the eastern bank of river Tapti. Feristha is highly impressed by the palace of the city of Srinagar in Kashmir which was twelve stories high and the Hindu temples having no parallels in the known world[182]. The city of Vijaynagar, fourteen miles in circumference in the days of Feristha[183] needs special mention. "The grandeur of the city, the splendour of the buildings, the wealth of the bazaars, the volume of trade and the density of the population are amply attested by a series of witnesses beginning in the fourteenth century, when Vijaynagar was only a few years old" [184]. Nicolo Conti, visiting the city in 1420, estimated its circumference to be sixty miles.

Abdur Raazaq, sent as Ambassador by the son of Timur to the Court of Calicut, describes it as "exceedingly large and populous"[185] and "is such that eye has not seen nor ear heard of any place resembling it upon the whole earth"[186]. The city had seven fortified walls built "one with the another"[187]. Domingos Pass, a Portuguese, visiting the city in 1552, considered it as large as Rome. According to him, there were more than 100,000 inhabitants and it was the best provided city in the world[188].

According to Manucci, Surat was a very populous city and the largest port in India visited by "ships from different parts of Europe, Persia, Mecca, Bassora, the coast of Malabar and Choramandal, Massulapatao (Machilipatnam), Bengal, Siam, Acheen, Queddah, the Maldives, Malacca, Batavia, Manilla, China and any other parts of the world"[189]. Besides "very fine lofty ships"[190] were used to be built in Surat "in a very short time, everything necessary being found, principally excellent timber, for which reason these ships last much longer than made in Europe"[191]. The importance of Surat may easily be conceived from the writings of Thevenot. With a population of 400,000 or above in 1773, it was more populous than either Paris or Bombay[192]. Manucci was highly impressed at the sight of Gwalior Fortress, "having a circuit of three leagues"[193] with its big palaces built on the crest of the hill. The fortress produced the best type of jasmine oil in India and the city spawling on the foot of the hill was famous for its musicians. Patan is another "great town"[194] mentioned by Thevenot where silk-stuffs were manufactured in abundance and exported therefrom. Ajmer, apart from being a fortress town and provincial capital, was the chief manufacturing centre of salpetre[195]. Pipli, near Balasor in Orissa, Satgaon and Kassimbazar in Bengal were "very rich"[196]. Lakshmanavati or Gaur and the city of Nadiya in Bengal were two more flourishing cities in those days. The city of Aurangabad, built by Emperor Aurangzeb, was "great town"[197]. Daulatabad was moderately large city, and its great trade was declining since the founding of Aurangabad[198]; Indore was famous for the production of swords, daggers and lances which had market all over India[199], Bidar was a "great town"[200]. Bijapur, the chief city of the kingdom of the namesake was above four or five leagues in circumference, with several large suburbs full of goldsmiths and jewellers' shops[201]. Apart from these, Thevenot also mentions Braoch, Mahamudabad, Debal, Bikaner, Daman, Bassien, Chaul, Calicut, Cochin, Vellore, Masulipatam, Negapatam, Pulicat, Bimlipatam, etc., as important towns.

The comparative study of the large urban centres existing between the times of Abul Fazl and the writers of the succeeding decades establishers beyond doubt that urbanisation became more dynamic and stable than heretofore. It is true that some of the cities, prosperous in the days of Abul Fazl, declined appreciably in the following decades, while centres, not so important in his time recorded impressive growth during the same period. This is not at all unlikely when urban prosperity was entirely dependent upon the stability of economic functions, such as, commerce and industry, both of them thriving best under the royal patronage. A close look at all these urban centres reveals that most, if not all, of them enjoyed that special privilege. Subsequent prosperity of decline was due to the change or entire shifting of that privilege. Sikri, Elichpur, Asir, Ujjain, Ajodhya, Lucknow, Jaunpur, Raepur and Mednipur offër concrete examples to this effect. But this does not mean that urban situation worsened in any respect; on the contrary, under the stable administration of the Mughal Emperors the overall situation greatly improved for the development and spread of urbanisation.

Urban growth and its countrywide development appear to have had taken a significant role, at least, from the middle of the medieval period. A great number of new towns and cities were founded during this period at different location spread all over the country. Important among them were—Daulatabad (1327), Vijaynagar (1336), Gulbarga or Ahsanabad (1347), Firozabad (around 1350), Jaunpur (1359), Hissar (1361), Jehanabad (1417), Burhanpur (1417), Ahmedabad (1412), Bidar (1430), Ahmadnagar (1494), Agra (1504), Golconda (1518), Hyderabad (1589), Fatepur Sikri (1571), Murshidabd (as capital in 1704), and Aurangabad (around 1636). Many of them look a leading role in the political and economic history of the country in the following centuries. Most notable among them were Ahmedabad, Agra and Hyderabad of which Hyderabad and Ahmedabad have grown into the fifth and sixth largest city of India today while Agra became an Imperial Captial, retaining that position for a considerable period.

Some of the Muslim rulers took an active interest founding new urban centres and this is proved by the Islamic derivation of the place-names, ending with the suffix 'abad'. They are Hyderabad, Ahmedabad, Daulatabad, Murshidabd, Agra—renamed by Akbar as Akbarabad, Delhi—rebuilt by Shahjahan under a new name of Shahjahandabad, etc. In fact, a scrutiny of the place-names will give a strong clue to the origin of Indian towns and cities and indicate the period as, in many cases, the prevailing practice of the founder was either as suffix or prefix. The are repetitions in names in certain cases, such as both Mathura and Chittagong were re-named as Islamabad. but unlike Alexander who gave the name of Alexandria to about twenty cities founded by him during his invasion of India, such repetitions are not common in naming important towns and cities in either the Hindu or the Muslim period.

In contrast to the prevailing Muslim practice, urban centres originating in the early or late Hindu periods generally ended with a suffix of 'nagar' or 'pur', or having a Sanskrit derivation, such as, Srinagar, Mulasthanapur (modern Multan), Lavapura (modern Lahore), Indraprastha (modern Delhi), Lakshmanavati (modern Lucknow and Gaur), etc. But such an identification it self becomes difficult if one is not well acquainted with the regional languages. This is more true about the South Indian names of towns and cities where the original Sanskrit derivation has been completely masked by local language or later transformations. For instance, modern Madurai was originally known as Mathura. Besides, the Muslim rulers changed the name of many urban centres during their rule in South India.

Medieval India saw the emergence of new towns and cities under the direct initiative of the Muslim rulers. The most illustrious record on this account was made by Firuz Shah (1351-1388) who, according to Ferishta, founded 200 towns[202] and established 1200 gardens in the vicinity of Delhi[203]. Among them are the city of Jaunpur, situated north-west of Varanasi, the city of Hissar Firozah or modern Hissar occurring north-west of Delhi, and the city of Firozabad or another new Delhi, covering all the land between "the kasba of Indarpat to the Kushk-i-shikar, five *kos* apart"[204]. The eight public mosques built by him in the city had a capacity of accommodating 10,000 prayers each[205]. From the beginning of the medieval period around the twelfth century, coterminous with the rise of Muslim power in India, this spirit of town-building is discernible with many of the rulers. Qutb-ud-din Aibak, the first Sultan of Delhi (1193-1210), built the famous Qutab group of buildings in Old Delhi; Iltutmish (1211-1236). The successor of Qutb's son, completed the Qutb Minar (Tower) started by Qutb-ud-din. He also made important additions to the Qutb group of buildings[206]. Fresh attempt at town-building did not take place until Ala-ud-din-Khalji came to the throne (1296), the intervening decades being a period of political confusion and disorder ultimately leading to the fall of the dynasty. Ala-ud-din "loved buildings and executed many magnificent works"[207]. He built a new Delhi called Siri, made extensive additions to the Qutb group of building and started the construction of a new Minar, double the size of the old one. The Minar, however, was never completed due to his untimely death in 1316. The real adventurous step in town-building was taken by Muhammad-bin-Tughluq (1325-1351). In 1327, he built the magnificent city of Daulatabad to which the capital from Delhi was shifted. Sikander Lodi founded a new city in 1504 at the site of Agra.

During the period of nearly three hundred and a quarter centuries (1206-1526) of the rule of the Delhi Sultanate many instances of important cities emerging in South India under the Muslim influence are available. Mandu in Malwa, Ahmedabad, Gulbarga, Bidar, Ahmadnagar, Burhanpur, Bijapur including its mausoleum having the second largest dome in the world built at the time when Taj Mahal was under construction[208], are some of the examples and all of them were capital cities.

Babar and his son Humayun, the first two Mughal Emperors in India, having been rather busy in consolidating their power, took little interest in town-building. Sher Shah, during his brief spell of reign (1539-1555), built a new city at Delhi, on the site of the old Indraprastha, known today as Purana Quila and founded Rohtas town in Punjab. Akbar re-built the city of Agra and fortified Agra Fort with magnificent walls and hundreds of buildings. But his unique creation was the place-city of Fatepur Sikri, occupied as the capital of his Empire for about fifteen years, though later abandoned by him. He also built the famous fort of Allahabad and established the town of Rajmahal in Bihar. Among the other Mughal Emperors, Jahangir has a poor record on this account. Apart from adding some buildings to the Fort of Agra and a few mausoleums he did not make any important contribution to the building of new towns. Shahjahan, on the other hand, build the Fort of Agra, and constructed the most beautiful mausoleum of Taj Mahal. He also founded a new Delhi after his own name—Shahjahanabad, to which the capital was transferred in 1648. Aurangzeb established the city of Aurangabad but, strangely enough, failed to show any enthusiasm about it during his long reign, spent mostly in wars. The last nine Mughal Emperors had little to do when the large empire was already falling to pieces; the epoch of Muslim rule in India ultimately closed in 1857 and the English finally assumed power.

The inventory made above may not be complete. but it is palpably clear that the role of the Muslim rulers was not a very great one in building new towns and cities. New centres founded by them are quite handful when compared with the length of time spread over more than six centuries at a stretch. Here also the initiative lay concentrated in the capital which again, on several instances, was built anew at the same site repeatedly by different rulers through centuries, as in the case in Delhi, or rebuilt with further additions, as in Agra. Even Mughal Emperor Shahjahan, the greatest of all the Muslim builders, is not an exception to this general rule. His entire work remained confined within the bounds of the twin capitals—Delhi and Agra.The political as well as social significance of this particular attitude, having a direct bearing on the urban development of Inida, cannot be overlooked.

Between 1206 and 1526, there had been thirty-two Sultans on the throne of Delhi and except Firuz Shah, none showed any exemplary zeal in town-building. The only positive aspect of town-building spirit shown by a few of them was again restricted to their capitals. On the negative side, they destroyed many of the existing towns and cities through innumerable raids carried on in the name of building an empire. This is not unlikely in a country where they still foreigners, and in the process of buildings up their power and wealth, sacking of the fallen city belonging to the alien Hindus was nothing unnatural. This does not explain why they were less enthusiastic about founding new urban centres within their own kingdoms. The simple answer may be that—being completely satisfied to live in pomp and grandeur in the capital-cities, sometimes built by themselves. they lacked any further energy or initiative for foundings newer centre. Besides, one builds where he is sure of his footing. Did the Sultans had that feeling of security? The answer is more to the negative. With constant warfare. the Sultans were likely to have been most reluctant at imposing more burdens on the fast-eroding exchequer. The existing town and cities supplied their needs and acted as political headquarters carrying on industrial and commercial functions, sometimes under their own initiative. In contrast, Firuz Shah towers above all of them, including even the later Mughal Emperors, in the work of new constructions.

His reign was not less peaceless than any of his predecessors or successors. But. building was is his blood. According to Ferishta. he built not only 200 towns and cities, but also constructed 50 dams and 30 reservoirs. 100 caravan-sarais for the travelling merchants, 150 bridges, 100 hospitals, 100 public baths, 30 colleges with mosques attached to them[209]. Even the Mughal Emperors cannot claim such an achievement at least in the field of town-buildings. In South India, cities like, Ahmedabad and Hyderabad came into existence at the initiative of the Muslim rulers though they displayed no interest no interest that went beyond the capital-city.

Urban Set-up : From the Medieval Period to the End of the Muslim Rule

The fact that sticks out is that, Urban development in medieval India owed little to the direct initiative of Muslim rulers.

It was more a product of the country's existing economy and had its roots, in many cases, in the distant past, receiving, at best, from time-time the caring protection of the rulers. It is rather strange to observe that the struggle for power during the medieval period between the different warring factions turning the entire country into a veritable battleground did not weaken the foundation of the urban economy to a large degree. It is to be noted here that, not a single important urban centre was spared of going through this extremely difficult situation on one or innumerable occasions over a period of six-and-a-half centuries; they had been the scene of battles, the victorious army often gathering its spoils through loot and pillage or inflicting destruction to the city. But, as in the Hindu period, most of the cities overcame this temporary set-back again and again in the Muslim period too and embarked on a vigorous, flourishing career. This indomitable life-force so characteristic of Indian urban centres is gathered from the unique location as well as the rich economic situation enjoyed by them. Political disturbances, much shorter in duration than spells of peace, could hardly affect those inherent qualities so that the cities could easily spring back to normally as soon as the difficult time passed off.

In order to understand the basic vitality of the urban centres, surviving and careering through the most turbulent times of Indian history, one needs to assess the attitude of the Muslim rulers if providing any prop to support the system or coming to its aid in any form whatsoever. The Muslim rulers came to stay in India; the innumerable invasions conducted by them within the country were aimed at widening their territorial power. But once subjugated, the towns and cities were never pillaged again, not at least by the victor, and were left undisturbed to prosper. Even the destruction, directed in most cases to temples and edifices, though temporarily slowed down but did not halt the material progress of those centres. This was unlike the actions of the invaders like the Sultan of Ghazni, Timur or Chengis Khan who razed the cities to dust, putting the inhabitants in thousands to the sword. Besides, the Muslim rulers could not fail to understand that urban prosperity ultimately enriches the royal exchequer, and this is only possible under an able administration, taking care of the country's productive organs and helping the safe movement of goods from one place to another. The Muslim rulers, in general, however, had not taken greatly to town-building and many of them were less inclined to the general welfare of the people. But it is far from true that all of them were impervious to the fundamental rules of economics. This is at least proved by the measures taken by some of them for the improvement of the material conditions of the country. During the rule of Ala-ud-din Khalji, for example, all the cultivated land was measured and the government took half the produce as tax;[210] the prices of all the articles were permanently fixed and a central granary was established at the capital for supplying grains to the markets in times of stress[211]. Baruni further states that, at that time there was safety on the roads in all directions and honest dealings for the merchants were guaranteed. Agriculture received special encouragement during the rule of Ghiyas-ud-din Tughluq when "canals were constructed to irrigate the fields, gardens were planted and forts were built to provide shelter to husbandmen against brigands"[212]. According to Baruni, the officers were instructed "to be careful that cultivation increased year by year... . The revenue was to be collected in such a way that the raiyats (peasants) should increase their cultivation; that the lands already in cultivation might be kept so, and some little be added to them every year"[213]. The measures adopted by Firuz Shah for improving the eceonomy of the country have already been mentioned. Shams-i-Siraj Afif notes that the peasants "grew rich and were satisfied"[214]. The grain was very cheap. "Fabrics of all kinds were cheap, and silk goods, both white and coloured, were of moderate price... such was prosperity that. throughout the Doab (Ganga-Jamuna Doab)... not one village remained waste, even in name, nor one span of land uncultivated"[215]. Sher Shah, during his brief reign of five years, introduced land revenue reforms, emulated as models in the succeeding centuries. A careful and proper survey of the lands was made and the land revenue was directly settled with the cultivators, the State-demand being fixed at one-fourth or one-third of the average produce payable in cash or kind. The rights of the tenants were thus duly recognised and rent was either remitted or loans advanced to the peasant when crops were damaged either by the encamped soldiers or drought[216]. Besides, Sher Shah contributed largely to the improvement of the communication system, connecting important places of his kingdom by a network of excellent roads. The longest of these, known as Grand Trunk Road today, extended for 1500 *kos* from Sonargaon in Eastern Bengal to the Indus. There is every reason to believe that this road followed the same route laid earlier, known as the Northern Route, which was improved by Sher Shah, extending it further to Sonargaon. Roads were also constructed connecting Agra with Burhanpur, Agra with Jodhpur and Chitor, and Lahore with Multan. Fruit trees were planted; caravan-sarais and wells were constructed at short distances along these roads and its was ordered that all strangers "without distinctions of country or religion"[217] be given entertainment at public expense. There was great safety on these road for the travellers. Akbar, the great Mughal Emperor, also took important measures towards the improvement of agriculture. "An order was promulgated for improving the cultivation of the country and for bettering the condition of the raiyats"[218].

The most important revelation made by all these accounts is the complete absence of any particular reference to any of the Muslim rulers taking a direct hand at improving the general urban conditions, improvement of industrial situation, establishment of any particular industry or adopting measures for furthering the benefits derived from commerce. Neither the Muslim historians nor the European travellers visiting India at the time of different Muslim rulers mention anything that might lead us to believe that they were positively keen on urban development in the proper sense of the term. In spite of that urban development reached a flourishing stage and does not appear to have had slackened at all throughout the entire stretch of the medieval and the later period. It, therefore, becomes necessary to find out the source of this driving force that kept urban life and functions uninterrupted. The basic functions of the town and cities of this period were either industry or trade and commerce, and they were located on the important trader routes—both land and water—generally in the riverine plains. There was no largescale industry at that time; the entire industrial structure was built upon the solid ground of different guilds and crafts of both the village and urban communities having long traditions in their individual sphere of activities. The important industries, developed on the basis of this traditional skill, could withstand every political upheaval as the producing units being house-bound were invariably small in size and thus easily movable or could remain obscure at the time of unrest. Besides, supplying the needs and luxuries of daily life, and producing exportable items that brought fresh wealth to royal treasury they were never made the targets of the warring factions. Thus, the absence of State guidance or support to the industrial and commercial activities did not hamper their normal progress and places, whether urban or rural, performing such functions could survive similar shocks of political changes. The result was of far reaching consequence. The industrial and commercial activities were no longer the absolute monopoly of the State capitals; in other words, capital function was no more the only decisive factor for giving rise to urban centres. The attainment of this independent character was not made overnight; even long before the medieval period the signs of adopting this distinctive character was visible in many of the towns and cities acting then as trading posts or ports and thereby maintaining a leading role in non-capital functions. The distinction between capital and non-capital centres became more pronounced during the medieval and later period, and the number of those with a predminance of economic functions both increased and became widespread in the country.

One may get some idea about the widespread nature of urban development from the accounts of Thevenot, travelling in India in 1666. Apart from describing the important places. Thevenot refers to many other towns in existence in different regions of India at that time. According to him, besides the large urban centres there were thirty more towns in the Province of Gujarat[219]; in the Province of Agra there were forty towns[220]; the Province of Multan had many good towns[221], the Province of Allahabad had "a great many good towns"[222]; the country, constituting Bengal and Orissa "is full of castles and towns"[223] and there were many towns on both coasts of the Bay of Bengal belonging to Bengal and Orissa[224]; there were great many trading towns in Rajasthan[225]; the country of Khandesh and Berar were "full of populous town and village"[226]; between Aurangbad and Kalvaral—a distance of about sixty leagues—there were eight towns[227]; in the kingdom of Bijapur their were "great many good towns"[228]; the east coast had several towns "some of which are good"[229].

The reference drawn here does not seem to be over estimation in view of the fact that Thevenot had named many of these places. The account, largely dealing with the important cities of his time, gives a clear picture of industrial and commercial opulence not perhaps attained by any other part of the globe till then. Almost the whole country abounded with a great variety of agricultural and industrial produces never found so handy in any other country in those days. This is partly revealed in the writings of Manucci as well, relating the conditions of the country as prevailing in his time (1656-1717). According to Manucci, the Province of Delhi was fertile in grain[230]. the Province of Agra was rich "in white cloth, silk stuffs, cloth of gold and silver of great fineness"[231] and indigo. The Province of Lahore produced fine white cloth, silk of all colour, embroidered materials, carpets, tents, saddles, swords, coarse woollen stuffs, boots and shoes, etc. The soil was fertile yielding rice and corn and a plentiful of sugar and great amount of rock salt ware available from the neighbouring mountains[232]. The famous products of the Province of Ajmer were very fine white cloth and great quantities of grain, milk, butter and salt[233]. In Gujarat the most important product was "a prodigious quantity of gold and silver cloth"[234] and flowered silks. Besides, gold and silver work and jewellery set with stones (diamond) were equally important. The country was "fertile in cereals" [235]. The Province of Malwa produced "white and coloured cloth abundantly"[236] and cereals in great amount. Plenty of fine white cloth, saltpetre and a rare quality of earthen pottery were the speciality of the Province of Patna. A great amount of printed cloth and also bows and arrows were manufactured in the Province of Multan. The Province of Tatta (Sind) was famous for its very fine white cloth, coarse and printed cloth, leather, grain and butter[237]. In the Province of Orissa much fine cloth was made and the land produced great quantity of rice[238]. The Province of Kashmir had earned its fame for producing woollen cloth, beds, ink-boxes, trays, boxes, spoons, etc. out of wood, and a plenty of fruits[239]. Benares and adjoining places lying in the Province of Allahabad were noted for their production of many types of silk stuff cloth of gold and silver, turbans, waist-belts and women's wear. Different types of vegetables and cereals were also grown in the province[240]. In and around Aurangabad large amount of white cloth and silk-stuffs were produced[241]. The Province of Berar was very much productive in cereals : corn, vegetables, poppy for opium and sugarcane were produced in plenty. The Province of Khandesh earned speciality in the production of very fine white and coloured as well as printed cloth for export in large amount. The soil was very productive for grain[242]. The vast region of the Province of Dacca produced the "prodigious quantity of fine white cloth and silken stuffs of which the nations of Europe and elsewhere transport several shiploads"[243]. The main products of the Province of Ujjain were grain and salt[244], that of Rajmahal very fine cloth and great quantities of rice, and the Province of Golconda offered the best variety of printed cloth in India[245]. Bernier, visiting India some time earlier, commented on the general conditions of India as follows: "It is important to observe, that of this vast tract of country, a large portion is extremely fertile; the large Kingdom of Bengal, for instance, surpassing Egypt itself, not only in the production of rice, corn and other necessaries of life, but innumerable articles of commerce which are not cultivated in Egypt; such as silks, cotton and indigo. There are also many parts of the Indies where the population is sufficiently abundant, and the land pretty well tilled; and where the artisan, although naturally indolent, is yet compelled by necessity or otherwise to employ himself in manufacturing carpets, brocades, embroideries, gold silver cloths, and the various sorts of silk and cotton goods, which are used in the country or exported abroad"[246]. At another place he remarks that the country around Delhi was extremely fertile, producing corn, sugar, indigo, rice, millet, three or four kinds of pulses in great abundance[247]. In his eyes the whole Kingdom of Kashmir wore the appearance of a fertile and highly cultivated garden with meadows and vineyards, fields of rice, wheat, hemp, saffron, many sorts of vegetable and fruit in abundance[248]. According to Bernier, Egypt no longer enjoyed the position of being "the finest and the most fruitful country in the world"[249], but it was Bengal supplying every necessity of life in great abundance. Among its products, enjoying both inland and foreign markets, the most important were rice, sugar, cotton and silk products, saltpetre as well as the best types of lac, opium, civet, long pepper, various drugs and ghee. In his words "there is in Bengal such a quantity of cotton and silks, that the kingdom may be called the common storehouse for those two kinds of merchandise, not of Hindustan (India) or the Empire of the Great Mogol only, but of all the neighbouring Kingdoms, and even of Europe"[250].

The picture of this affluence, derived from its rich agricultural background and a widespread industrial base, did not escape the notice of even Marco Polo, visiting some parts of South India in the early part of the medieval period (1288). He found the Province of Malabar as "the finest and noblest in the world"[251]. At that time ships used to come from many parts of the world for the purchase of pepper, ginger, cinnamon and beautiful cotton cloth produced in plenty in the Kingdom[252]. Merchants from different nationalities congregated at the ports like, Tana[253], Cambay, etc. for collecting the rich merchandise.

All these facts actually reveal the unique position that India enjoyed in the eastern hemisphere over a period of tens of centuries and the inevitable role of the Indian ports in the handling of the merchandise, obviously enormous both in quantity as well as quality, to feed such a large market. The fact that India, in spite of the chain of political turbulances inside the country, could retain her glory of being the veritable mercantile paradise for the merchants of the West and the East, irrefutably establishes mercantile superiority of the country. That no other country in the world enjoyed this position for such a long time as India did, proves the stability of her urban functions which continued through all vicissitudes of fortunes. One cannot ignore the background of these mercantile activities where India had been the bone of contention among the trading countries of the world. The entire framework of this external trade of India could not have developed on the basis of ports alone; it depended upon a far more gigantic infrastructure composed of a transportation system developed all over the country, highly skilled artisans producing quality goods, intermediaries and merchants collecting the produces from distant places, markets acting as collecting and distributing points, etc. and above all, the facilities, including protection and patronage offered by the rulers of the respective areas. The combination of all these factors and the sustained efforts of this nature were not possible from an agrarian base; urban backing was an absolute necessity for that. To be specific, the constructions of roads and their maintenance, the manufacture of articles of extremely high quality and the marketing, assemblage of raw materials needed for such industries, activity of the merchants arriving from distant quarters, etc., always prefaced an urban environment. About the roads of his days Ibn Battuta observes as follows : "It (Dhar) is twenty-four day's journey from Delhi, and all along the road between them there are pillars on which is engraved the number of miles from each pillar to the next"[254]. Manucci, visiting the country in 1756 and threreabout, pays glowing tribute to the system of 'sarais', or resting places for the travellers, the latter mostly being the trading merchants. The sarais were fortified places, built of stone or brick, offering accommodation to 800 to 1000 persons or more in many cases along with their "horses, camels and carriages"[255]. They were built throughout the Mughal Empire on every route and this alone gives an idea about the tremendous traffic on the roads in those days.

The innumerable items of manufacture referred to above, the speciality of Indian products regarded as rarities by foreigners, gave India a highly esteemed position which could not have been achieved without a strong urban foundation. Industries however small in size could not function in a purely agrarian surrounding. The economy of the country was basically agricultural, no doubt, but the extensive nature of industrial development presupposes an urban background. The extremely large variety of high quality and expensive goods were not the needs of the ruralites, forming the vast majority of the country's population. The royal courts and the nobilities enjoyed a large share of such products; still another large, if not the larger, share was exported to the foreign markets extending from China in the East to Europe in the West. The ever-growing demands of the European markets for Indian goods. the rivalry between European and Arab merchants, the latter ultimately getting dislodged in the race. establish the supremacy of Indian merchandise beyond any question. The entire industrial structure, even if largely localised in the rural areas, was mainly oriented to urban needs. This offers an indirect proof of the extent of urban development that had taken place in the country. Movement of goods, their long haulage in great bulk over hundreds and thousands of miles both inside and outside the country by land and sea routes could not be possible without chains of stations functioning as trading posts and ports. Thevenot, for instance, found a caravan of over a thousand oxen carrying cotton cloth from Agra to Surat[256]. Such a scale of industrial and commercial development cannot be the product of rural economy. A widespread and well-developed urban super-structure formed the necessary base for that.

All these facts indicate the height urban development reached as early as the medieval period when town and cities were no longer an isolated phenomenon of the settlement geography of the country. But however large the number was, the urban system does not see to have had undergone any material change during the intervening period. The capital-cities still dominated the scene; non-capital cities, functioning as commercial or industrial centres, were subsidiary to the former; barring the fortress cities, the entire urban development remained largely concentrated in the river-valley zones, providing both land and water routes; centres situated on the navigable rivers, principal trade routes and the coasts enjoyed a greater rate of prosperity than those situated farther away; the principal industries being agro-based, the fertility of the land with a greater variety of products had an important part in contributing to the prosperity of the urban centres. Convergence of routes further added to this prosperity. Thus, urban system that developed in those days was primarily the product of the soil, the advantage of transport taking an important role in determining the functions as well as size of the urban centres. While it is not possible to know the size of the individual centres as expressed by population, it can well be presumed that graded development was not yet in sight.

There is, however, no doubt that some of the cities were quite large. Bernier, for instance, refers to a fire in 1662 consuming over sixty thousand houses of the common people of the city of Delhi[257]. On this account alone the population of the city would be about 300,000, taking five heads for each family; to this one has to add the royal household containing thousands of soldiers, servants, etc. This however, does not include the large number of people doing higher jobs, their families, and the merchants. On a modest estimation therefore the population would be around 400,000. According to the Imperial Gazetteer, the population of Ahmedabad would have been nearly 900,000[258] in the time of Abul Fazl when the city had 84 wards[259], Manrique, the Augustinian missionary, wrote in 1649 that the population of the city of Agra was 600,000 in 1640[260]. Apart from these stray, sometimes indirect, references such figures cannot be constructed for other cities.

In spite of the widespread nature of urban development in the country, the material standard of the urban centres—in respect of their houses and streets—was not very high. Besides the capital-cities, others were not so well built, generally giving a very poor look with ramshackle structures. In Babar's opinion, Indian towns were extremely ugly[261]. Ferishta, visiting the country in the end of the sixteenth century, was of the same opinion. He considers Indian towns and cities very unclean and filthy, though he does not fail to appreciate the beauty and splendour of some of the cities. According to him, Hyderabad was the best city in the world for its appearance and cleanliness where the shops and private houses were built of stone and mortar[262]. Another city, Ahmadnagar, founded in 1494, soon came to rival Bagdad and Cairo with its buildings[263]. The same author mentions elsewhere that most of the houses in the city of Ahmedabad were built of brick and mortar, and the main streets were as wide as to allow ten carriages to pass abrest[264]. Ferishta also refers to Kanauj and Mathura which were magnificent cities when Mahmud of Ghazni invaded them in 1018. Mahmud found the city of Kanauj raising "its head to the skies and which in strength and beauty might boast of being unrivalled"[265], at that time the city of Mathura, with a thousand of edifices of marble "teeming with imposing temples, the glittering spires of which towered above the house-tops"[266] made a unique spectacle. The opinion of the European travellers are not encouraging either. Bernier, for instance, states that most of the Indian towns are "made up of earth, mud and other wretched material"[267], and there was no city which did not show the signs of decay.

Such conclusions are too sweeping to reveal the actual urban condition prevailing in those days. Babar's association with India—the last twelve years of his life having been spent mostly in wars—was too short to allow him any real respite for knowing the country, least to love it. Moreover, his knowledge of the country, limited to a small part of North-West India, cannot be conclusive. Like Babar, Ferishta was similarly not acquainted with a large part of the country. Further, he was more concerned with the history of the country and paid less attention to the urban conditions for which his information is extremely incomplete. Even Bernier himself mentions at another place that he was astonished to hear the contemptuous remarks of the Europeans about the beauty of the Indian towns. Their complaints about the buildings is refuted by Bernier with the remark that, European type of buildings were not suited to Indian climate. But his comment about the general decadence of the cities needs further explanation. During the expansion of Muslim rule in India many of the existing cities had been the main scenes of battle; with their fabulous wealth they were made the principal targets of the invaders for plunder and destruction. Bearing the signs of time-long ravages, the cities would thus give a ruinous look in the eyes of a visitor. Besides, many of them had been built anew time and again on the same site by the ruling King or Emperor, leaving the old city to gradual decay. Delhi provides the most illustrious example for this. Otherwise, Bernier is rather correct about the general poverty of the urban scene. Houses made of flimsy materials, narrow streets, and absence of general urban amenities speak of poor living conditions in most the towns and cities. But that does not mean that better living condition was altogether absent in all of them. Reference to better housing and street conditions are available from the writings of some of the foreign travellers. Thevenot reports that the market places of the city of Broach were located on a broad street[268]. According to the same source, Ahmedabad was a very well-kept city[269]; in Cambay the houses were made of bricks and were very high[270]; in the city of Surat the houses of the rich people, made of brick, lime and wood, were pretty well-built[271]. in the Imperial Capital of Agra the entire river-front was thronged with beautiful palaces and mansions of the rich people and the streets were wide[272]; the two main streets of the principal market area of Delhi were wide, straight and very long, providing a beautiful sight[273]. The entire market place with innumerable shops, warehouses and the houses of the merchants were made of brick. Lahore looked picturesque with its mosques, public baths, caravan-sarais, squares, palaces and gardens[274]; the building of the city of Aurangabad were made of free-stone and they were pretty high. There were public places, caravan-sarais, public baths in the city[275]; in Daman the houses were built of white stone and the streets were fairly large[276].

Information of this nature are not available for many of the towns and cities, though it cannot be doubted that better living conditions prevailed at least in some more of them. Brick and mortar, used profusely by the royalties and the rich classes, were not in common usage. The ordinary citizens, including a large section of the rich people, were not much alive to a high standard of living. Thus, the urban scene, as typified by extremely poor housing conditions, giving almost the appearance of overgrown villages, the narrow streets without any symmetry in their layout, wore an unimpressive look in the eyes of the foreign visitors. Imperial cities like, Delhi and Agra, were no exception to this rule either. Apart from the two main streets of Delhi, the seat of the then Mughal Emperor, the remaining five streets, not so long or straight as the former were joined by numberless smaller roads running from every direction, following no general principle. Only a handful of the houses occurring within this labyrinth and belonging to the rich merchants as well as the Emperor's middle-ranking Officers were made of brick or stone[277]; the rest were of mud and thatch. It was for these mud and thatched houses that Bernier calls Delhi "a collection of many villages"[278]. Similarly, Agra, though greater in extent than Delhi with a larger number of residences and good stone or brick houses of the private individuals, was inferior to the latter in the absence of uniform and wide streets[279]. Besides the houses on the principal streets, the majority were like those in other towns of India[280]. According to Bernier, Agra looked more like a country town than Delhi[281]. The overall picture that emerges pointedly refers to these pre-industrial slums present in almost every city, providing residence for the mass of the urban dwellers. The city was thus sharply divided into two constrasing sections; the smaller one usually contained the royal and other palaces, the Fort and sometimes, the principal market, while the large section formed a vertiable mess of low, poorly built houses, crowded along the narrow lanes and bye-lanes. Such a distinction brings into light the second most important characteristic feature of the urban life, that is, there were only two classes of people constituting the urban population of the period stretching from the Middle Ages to mid-nineteenth century; the dividing line was sharp enough to exclude completely the middle class from the scene. This is corroborated by Bernier who observes as follows: 'In Delhi there is no middle state. A man must either be of the highest rank or live miserably"[282]. Delhi, as the Imperial Capital, naturally set the tone of life which cannot be expected to have been different in the remaining towns and cities of India. The economy was controlled by two hands : the royal houses and the big merchants. Beyond them wealth never accumulated in the hands of the commoners.

The impressions of the foreign travellers, however, do not convey the full picture as an underlying contempt for Indian life in its various manifestations expressed indirectly in comparing local urban conditions with that of Europe which often carried away the writer on many instances from the actual truth. It is true that until then Indian towns and cities developed without any plan; the streets were narrow and crooked; the houses belonging to the common working mass were mostly of mean structure and extremely crowded; the shopping areas were equally crowded places without having any provision for displaying their exhibits. But, out of this crowd and squalor came a large number of classic products which set the minds of European merchants afire, culminating in the establishment of European settlements in India. If the standard of manufactured goods is any criterion for judging the scale of urban development, India, at that time, was not behind any country of the world. The splendour and wealth of cities like, Agra and Delhi, reflected in their matchless magnificent structures dazzled the eyes of the European visitors. These, along with the great number of cities and towns spread over the vast canvas of the country made urbanisation far more stable than it was in the earlier centuries.

A fuller picture of this urban development cannot be obtained without referring to the growth of European settlements in India and the significant role played by them in the succeeding centuries.

REFERENCES

1. Sachau. Edward. C., Alberuni's India. S. Chand and Co.. New Delhi. 1964. p. XVI.
2. *Ibid.*, pp. 197-198.
3. *Ibid.*, pp. 211-212.
4. Majumdar, Ray Chaudhuri and Datta. *op. cit.*, pp. 173-174.
5. Sachau. *op. cit.*, pp. 316-317 (Annotations).
6. Gibb. H.A.R.. *Ibn Battuta: Travels in Asia and Africa.* Routledge and Kegan Paul. London. 1969. p. 15.
7. *Ibid.*, p. 12.
8. *Ibid.*, p. 194.
9. *Ibid.*. p. 205
10. *Ibid.*, p. 194.
11. *Ibid.*, p. 193.
12. *Ibid.*, p. 223.
13. *Ibid.*, p. 224.
14. *Ibid.*, p. 215.
15. *Ibid.*, p. 226.
16. *Ibid.*
17. *Ibid.*, p. 227.
18. *Ibid.*
19. *Ibid.*, p. 228.
20. *Ibid.* p. 229.
21. *Ibid.*
22. *Ibid.*, p. 230.
23. *Ibid.*, p. 233.
24. *Ibid.*, p. 234.
25. *Ibid.*
26. *Ibid.*, p. 238.
27. *Ibid.*. p. 264.
28. *Ibid.*, p. 366.
29. *Ibid.*, p. 267.
30. Jarrett, H.S. and Sarkar, Jadunath, *Ain-i-Akbari of Abul Fazl-i-Allami,* Vol. II. 2nd Ed., Royal Asiatic Society. Calcutta. 1949, p. 129.
31. *Ibid.*, p. 191.
32. Beveridge. H., *The Akbar Nama of Abul-i-Fazl,* Asiatic Society of Bengal, 1972, p. 117, Vol. II.
33. Jarrett and Sarkar, *op. cit.*, p. 191.
34. *Ibid.*
35. Beveridge. *op. cit.*, p. 531 (II).
36. Jarrett and Sarkar, *op. cit.*, p. 283.
37. *Ibid.*, p. 284.
38. Beveridge, *op. cit.*, p. 104 (II)
39. Jarrett and Sarkar. *op. cit.*, p. 292
40. *Ibid.*, p. 247.
41. Beveridge, *op. cit.*, p. 12 (III).
42. Jarrett and Sarkar. *op. cit.*, p. 283.

43. Beveridge. *op. cit.*, p. 80 (II)
44. Jarrett and Sarkar. *op. cit.*, p. 317.
45. Blochmann. H., *The Ain-i-Akbari,* Vol. 1. Asiatic Society of Bengal. Calcutta. 1927, p. 98.
46. Blochmann, H., p. 93.
47. Beveridge, *op. cit.,* p. 624 (I).
48. Jarrett and Sarkar. *op. cit.*, p. 169.
49. *Ibid.*, p. 182.
50. *Ibid.*
51. Majumdar, Ray Chaudhuri and Datta. *op. cit.*, p. 324.
52. Beveridge, *op. cit.*, p. 215 (II).
53. Jarrett and Sarkar, *op. cit.*, p. 170.
54. *Ibid.*, p. 169.
55. *Ibid.*, p. 248.
56. *Ibid.*, p. 232.
57. *Ibid.*
58. *Ibid.*, p. 208.
59. *Ibid.*. p. 137.
60. *Ibid.*, p. 136.
61. *Ibid.*, p. 134.
62. *Ibid.*, p. 138.
63. *Ibid.*, p. 162.
64. *Ibid.*, p. 169.
65. *Ibid.*, p. 181.
66. *Ibid.*, p. 190.
67. *Ibid.*
68. *Ibid.*, p. 206.
69. *Ibid.*, p. 207.
70. *Ibid.*, p. 236.
71. *Ibid.*, p. 247.
72. *Ibid.*
73. *Ibid.*, p. 283.
74. *Ibid.*, p. 316.
75. *Ibid.*
76. Rogers, Alexander and Beveridge, Henry, *The Tuzuk-i-Jahangiri or Memoirs of Jahangir,* Munshiram Manoharalal, Delhi, 1968, 2nd Ed., p. 128.
77. *Ibid.*, p. 73.
78. *Ibid.*, p. 4.
79. *Ibid.*. p. 3.
80. *Ibid.*, p. 4.
81. Ball. V., *Travels in India by Jean Baptiste Tavernier,* Macmillan and Co. London, 1889, p. 105.
82. *Ibid.*, p. 109.
83. *Ibid.*
84. Bernier. Francois, *Travels in the Mogul Empire,* S. Chand and Co.. New Delhi, 1972 (3rd Ed.), p. 284.
85. *Ibid.*, p. 285.

86. Smith. Vincent A., *op. cit.*, Akbar, p. 77.
87. Moreland. W.H and Geyl P., *Jahangir's India, The 'Remonstrantie' of Francisco Pelsaert,* Cambridge. W. Heffer and Sons Ltd., 1925, p. IX.
88. *Ibid.*, p. 1.
89. *Ibid.*, p. 2.
90. *Ibid.*
91. *Ibid.*, p. 1.
92. *Ibid.*
93. *Ibid.*, p. 2.
94. *Ibid.*, p. 4.
95. Manucci, Niccolao, *'Storia do Mogor' or Mogul India,* Translated by William Irvine, Editions Indian, Calcutta, 1965, p. 130 (I).
96. Sen, Surendranath, *Indian Travels of Thevenot and Catreri,* National Archives of India, New Delhi, p. 46.
97. Smith,
98. Majumdar, Ray Chaudhuri and Datta, *op.cit.*, p. 333.
99. Humbly, Gavin, *Cities of Moghul Indian*, UBS Publishers, Distributors, Delhi, 1968, p.13
100. *Ibid.*
101. Sircar, D.C. *op. cit.*, p. 99.
102. Mitra, Asok, *Delhi Capital City,* Thomson Press (India) Limited, New Delhi, 1970, p. 1.
103. *Imperial Gazetteer,* Vol. XI, p. 233.
104. *Ibid.*
105. Majumdar, Ray Chaudhuri and Datta, *op.cit.*, p. 270.
106. Hambly, *op. cit.*, p. 15
107. *Ibid.*, p. 16.
108. Lane-Poole, Stanley, *Medieval India under Mohammedan Rule,* A Universal Publication, Delhi, 1963.
109. Hambly, *op. cit.*, p. 64.
110. Rogers and Beveridge, *op. cit.*, 128.
111. Ball, V., *op. cit.*, p. 96.
112. Bernier, *op. cit.*, p. 242.
113. Briggs, John, *History of the Rise of the Mohomedan Power in India,* Translated from the original Persian of Mahomed Kasim Ferishta, Editions Indian, Calcutta, 1966, p. 242 (I)
114. Manucci, *op. cit.*, p. 177.
115. Sen, Surendranath, *op. cit.*, p. 60.
116. Smith, V., *op. cit.*, p. 211.
117. Hambly, *op. cit.*, p. 103.
118. Majumdar, Ray Chaudhuri and Datta, *op. cit.*, p. 484.
119. Hambly, *op. cit.*, p. 131.
120. *Imperial Gazetteer,* Vol. XI, p. 236.
121. Spate, O.H.K. and Learmonth, A.T.A. *India and Pakistan,* Methuen & Co. Ltd., 1967, p. 535.
122. *Ibid.*, p. 541.
123. Sen, Surendranth, *op. cit.*, p. 96.

124. Majumdar. Ray Chaudhuri and Datta. *op. cit.*. p. 313
125. Jarrett and Sarkar. *op cit.*, p. 284.
126. Rogers and Beveridge. *op. cit.*, p. 63 (I).
127. Moreland and Geyl. *op. cit.*, p. 30.
128. Ball. *op. cit.*, p. 94.
129. Berniers. *op. cit.*, p. 384.
130. Manucci. *op. cit.*, p. 174.
131. *Ibid.*
132. Briggs. *op. cit.*, p. 8 (IV).
133. Moreland and Geyl. *op. cit.*, p. 7.
134. *Ibid.*, p. 19.
135. Ball *op. cit.*, p. 72.
136. Rogers and Beveridge. *op.cit.*, p. 13 (II).
137. *Ibid.*
138. Sen, Surendranath. *op.cit.*, p. 17 (I).
139. Rogers and Beveridge. *op.cit.*, p. 416.
140. Moreland and Geyl, *op.cit.*, p. 19.
141. Ball, *op. cit.*, p. 17.
142. *Ibid.*, p. 118.
143. Bermier, *op. cit.*, p. 334.
144. Manucci. *op. cit.*, p. 77 (II).
145. Moreland and Geyl. *op. cit.*, p. 12.
146. Ball, *op. cit.*, p. 51.
147. *Ibid.*, p. 52.
148. Manucci, *op. cit.*, p. 65 (I).
149. Sen, Surendranath. *op. cit.*, p. 101.
150. *Ibid.*, p. 95.
151. *Ibid.*, p. 97.
152. *Ibid.*, p. 98.
153. Ball. *op. cit.*, p. 121.
154. Manucci. *op. cit.*, p. 77 (II).
155. *Ibid.*
156. *Ibid.*
157. Sen, Surendranath. *op.cit.*, p. 95.
158. Rogers and Beveridge. *op. cit.*, p. 204 (I).
159. Manucci *op. cit.*, p. 76 (II).
160. Ball. *op. cit.*, p. 128.
161. Manucci, *op. cit.*, p. 80 (II).
162. Moreland and Geyl. *op. cit.*, p. 31.
163. Ball, *op. cit.*, p. 10.
164. Manucci, *op. cit.*, p. 59 (I).
165. Sen. Surendranath, *op. cit.*; pp. 74-75.
166. Moreland and Geyl, *op. cit.*, p. 31.
167. Sen. Surendranath. *op. cit.*, p. 77.
168. Rogers and Beveridge. *op. cit.*, p. 431.
169. Ball. *op. cit.*, p. 71.
170. Sen. Surendranath. *op. cit.*, p. 44.

171. *Ibid.*
172. Ball. *op. cit.*, p. 71.
173. Sen. *op. cit.*, p. 164.
174. Ball, *op. cit.*, p. 56.
175. Manucci, *op. cit.*, p. 66 (I).
176. Ball, *op. cit.*, p. 186.
177. *Ibid.*
178. Sen, *op. cit.*, p. 129.
179. Smith, Vincent, *Oxford History of India*, p. 294.
180. Briggs, *op. cit.*, p. 272 (III).
181. *Ibid.*, p. 313 (IV).
182. *Ibid.*, pp. 258-260 (IV).
183. *Ibid.*, p. 318 (IV).
184. Smith, Vincent, *Oxford History of India*, p. 310.
185. Elliot, H.M. and Dowson, *The History of India as Told by Its Own Historians*, Kitab Mahal. Allahabad. Vol. IV, p. 105.
186. *Ibid.*, p. 106.
187. *Ibid.*
188. Smith, Vincent, *op. cit.*, p. 312.
189. Manucci, *op. cit.*, p. 60 (I).
190. *Ibid.*
191. *Ibid.*
192. Spear, Pereival, *The Nabobs, A Study of the Social Life of the English in Eighteenth Century India*, Oxford University Press. London. 1963, p. 66.
193. Manucci. *op. cit.*, p. 68 (I).
194. Sen, *op. cit.*, p. 45.
195. *Ibid.*, pp. 68-69.
196. *Ibid.*, p. 95.
197. *Ibid.*, p. 103.
198. *Ibid.*, pp. 107-108.
199. *Ibid.* p. 112.
200. *Ibid.*, p. 113.
201. *Ibid.*, p. 128.
202. Elliot & Dowson, *op. cit.*, Vol. III. p. 269.
203. *Ibid.*, p. 345 (III).
204. *Ibid.*, p. 303 (III).
205. *Ibid.*
206. Smith, V., *op. cit.* p. 237.
207. *Ibid.*, p. 246.
208. *Ibid.*, p. 302.
209. Briggs. *op. cit.*, pp. 269-270.
210. Smith, V., *op. cit.*, p. 246.
211. Elliot & Dowson, *op. cit.*, Vol. III, pp. 192-193.
212. Majumdar, Ray Chaudhuri and Datta. *op. cit.*, p. 307.
213. Elliot & Dowson. *op. cit.*, p. 230.
214. Majumdar, Ray Chaudhuri and Datta *op. cit.*, p. 290 (II).
215. *Ibid.*, p. 345 (III)

216. *Ibid.*, pp. 433-434.
217. Briggs. *op. cit.*, p. 78.
218. Elliot & Dowson *op. cit.*, Vol. V. p. 513.
219. Sen. Surendranath. *op. cit.*, p. 44.
220. *Ibid.*, p. 56.
221. *Ibid.*, p. 77.
222. *Ibid.*, p. 92.
223. *Ibid.*, p. 96.
224. *Ibid.*, p. 97.
225. *Ibid.*, p. 98.
226. *Ibid.*, p. 99.
227. *Ibid.*, p. 108.
228. *Ibid.*, p. 127.
229. *Ibid.*, p. 147.
230. Manucci, *op. cit.*, p. 396 (II).
231. *Ibid.*, p. 398 (II).
232. *Ibid.*, p. 399 (II).
233. *Ibid.*
234. *Ibid.*
235. *Ibid.*, p. 400 (II).
236. *Ibid.*
237. *Ibid.*, p. 401 (II).
238. *Ibid.*, p. 402 (II).
239. *Ibid.*
240. *Ibid.*
241. *Ibid.*, p., 403.
242. *Ibid.*
243. *Ibid.*, p. 404.
244. *Ibid.*
245. *Ibid.*
246. Bernier, *op. cit.*, p. 202.
247. *Ibid.*, p. 283.
248. *Ibid.* p. 397.
249. *Ibid.* p. 437.
250. *Ibid.* p. 439.
251. Yule. Henry, *The Book of Ser Marco Polo The Venetian, Concerning the Kingdoms and Marvels of the East,* John Murrary, London, 1871, p. 267 (II).
252. *Ibid.*, pp. 324-325 (II).
253. *Ibid.*, p. 330 (II).
254. Gibb, *op. cit.*, p. 266.
255. Manucci, *op.cit.*, 67 (I).
256. Sen. Surendranath. *op.cit.*, p. 103.
257. Bernier, *op. cit.*, p. 246.
258. *Imperial Gazetteer,* Vol. V. p. 106.
259. Jarrett and Sarkar. *op. cit.*, p. 247.
260. Lane-Poole, *op. cit.*, p. 236.
261. Beveridge. A.S., *Babar Nama,* Orient Books Reprint Corporation, New Delhi. 1970, pp. 487-488.

262. *Ibid., op. cit.*, p. 313 (IV).
263. *Ibid.*, p. 123 (III).
264. *Ibid.*, p. 8 (IV).
265. *Ibid.*, p. 33 (I).
266. Nazim, M., *The Life and Times of Sultan Mahamud of Ghazni,* Munshiram Manoharlal, New Delhi, 2nd Ed., 1971, p. 107.
267. Bernier, *op. cit.*, p. 227.
268. Sen, Surendarnath, *op. cit.*, p. 9.
269. *Ibid.*, p. 11.
270. *Ibid.*, p. 17.
271. *Ibid.*, pp. 22-23.
272. *Ibid.*, p. 49.
273. *Ibid.*, p. 60.
274. *Ibid.*, p. 85.
275. *Ibid.*, p. 103.
276. *Ibid.*, p. 116.
277. Bernier, *op. cit.*, p. 246.
278. *Ibid.*
279. *Ibid.*, pp. 284-285.
280. Ball, *op. cit.*, p. 105.
281. Bernier, *op. cit.*, p. 285.
282. *Ibid.*, p. 252.

4

The Rise of the European Settlements
A New Element in Indian Urban Development

In the absence of any other direct source yielding positive information about the nature of urban growth as well as its development in the entire country we have to turn our attention again to its trading activities throwing light on the history of Indian urbanisation. As has been mentioned earlier, Indian merchandise — both manufactured and unmanufactured — enjoyed a world-wide reputation since the days of Indus Civilisation, and from time-to-time countries lying west of India keenly contested among themselves for monopolizing this trade. The monopoly of commerce, changing hands many times through centuries, came to rest for a while with the Arabs some time after the death of Mohammad when they subdued Persia and Egypt. This ultimately dislodged the Greeks from their direct intercourse with Alexandria which had for a long time been their principal emporium for Indian goods. Realising the enormous advantages derivable from the 'Eastern Commerce', Khalif Omar founded the city of Bussora, on the west bank of the Shat-el-Arab, between the junction of the R. Tigris and R. Euphrates and the Persian Gulf, to deal with the shipping engaged in the Indian trade. Although the Arabs made several visits to Gujarat, the Gulf of Cambay and the Malabar Coast in the seventh and eighth centuries, besides a few merchants, they did not settle down permanently anywhere in India. The Arab Empire then included the whole of the north coast of Africa, beginning from the Delta of the Nile to the Straits of Gibraltor, together with a great part of Spain—thus cutting off the Christian world from the Eastern commerce. The rise of Venice, however, established a closer intercourse between the Christians and Mohameddans, and opened the ancient channel of intercourse with India and Egypt whereupon Venetian merchants became the distributors of Indian merchandise over the west of Europe.

The decline of the Arab Empire from about the middle of the eleventh century, followed by invasions of Turks, revived the old hostility between the Christians and the Mohameddans. The western countries seized the opportunity and allowed their adventurous merchants to settle at Acre, Aleppo, and other trading centres on the coast of Syria with commercial privileges and, in course of time, the cities of Venice, Genoa, Amalfi, Pisa and Florence came to monopolise the Indian trade. But soon a strong competition arose between the Geonese and the Venetians for the exclusive control of this trade and the former, combining with Greeks, drove the latter from Constantinople. The Venetians, on their part, obtaining the help of the Pope, finally succeeded in establishing their intercourse with India upon a more solid basis than they ever enjoyed before. The conquest of the Greeks by Mohammad II in 1453 expelled the Geonoese from Constantinople and the city ceased to be the principal mart for the supply of Indian commodities to the European market. After that this trade was completely monopolized by Egypt and partly by Syria, while the Venetians, making commercial treaties with the Mohameddan princes, secured a position to monopolize the supply of Indian products to the countries of the West and this was maintained by them till the close of the fifteenth century.

The opening of the sixteenth century is extremely significant in the political as well as economic history of India with its deep impact on the later course of urbanisation in the country. The beginning of this century saw European merchantmen arriving in India for the first time and in no time establishing their supremacy over the Arabs in the monopoly of the West-bound trade. The monopoly was not easily earned. Before the last quarter of the fifteenth century, the Indian Ocean was a closed sea to the Europeans, the Cape of Good Hope was not known to them, and the overland routes from the Red Sea and the Persian Gulf were in the hands of the Arabs. Meanwhile during 1400's the techniques of shipbuilding and the science of navigation had improved greatly. The Portuguese and the Spaniards made sea-worthy ships, much lighter and faster, capable of sailing in rough weather. In addition, the discovery of the new route *via* the Cape of

Good Hope opened immense possibilities for the Europeans and this, in the long run, struck the final blow to the century-old Arabian supremacy in the Indian waters. The fact, however, cannot be lost sight of that the journeys round the southern tip of Africa in sail-boats were not only longer ones, but taking about six months each way they were extremely time-consuming and highly hazardous too. Besides, the country which they came to was not very much hospitable, and each European country, employing every skill as well as duplicity for getting into advantageous terms with the Indians and thereby ousting other competitors, had an uphill task. This palpably risky involvement on the part of these foreign countries, made at the huge cost of both fund and personnel, cannot be fully explained without going into the characteristic speciality of the Indian merchandise on the one hand, and the ulterior motive of getting a permanent foothold in the country on the other.

For nearly four thousand years or so the people living around the Mediterranean Sea and especially those living in the cold climates of Europe had a special fascination for the Indian products and craved to have a share of the trade. Among the most important products were a wide range of spices, high quality textiles, metal objects, perfumes, pearls and precious stones, sugar, wood and a large number of other luxury items. It is difficult for someone living in the present day to appreciate exactly what the spices and other products meant to the people of the West. In those days, excepting few privileged ones, the vast majority of the people had to depend on meat either dried or smoked and the only way that meat could be made palatable was by the lavish use of spices. Cloves, nutmeg, cinnamon, ginger and pepper were of great value as preservatives of food. Meat without spice was virtually inedible. "Spices had a considerable place in life; men were prepared to die in search for them, and many did; no gift was more acceptable, and to be well supplied was a mark of status"[1]. Pepper was so highly valued that in the days of the Romans, like gold it used to be a medium of exchange. Some of the species were also in great demand for their medicinal powers. Indian fabrics were much lighter in comparison to the coarse woollen garments worn by the Europeans and they could be washed and easily dried. Furthermore, the extremely high quality of the Indian cotton and silk textiles were greatly admired by the rich classes in the West. The wealthy people could afford to buy beautiful carpets to replace the ugly rushes that were then used to cover the flagstones. Not for the quality alone, but also for their special character these different articles had an unrivalled place in the European market.

The lure of Indian merchandise drew the attention of the Portuguese, and in May 1487, Dom Joao II, King of Portugal, sent Joao Peres de Covilhao to "discovered the lands whence spiceries were procured"[2]. The latter, making a long detour *via* Constantinople, Alexandria and Cairo arrived in India in an Arab ship from Aden. He reached Cannanore, on the Malabar Coast, in the late summer of 1488, and thereafter visited Calicut and Goa. Covilhao found Calicut as a busy port with craftsmen working everywhere. The shops provided work places for the silversmiths, the coppersmiths, the shoe-makers and leather-workers. The markets were crowded with tradesmen selling fruits, honey-drenched sweetmeats, spices, sild, tin, tea, cutlery, and many other kind of merchandise[3]. He also found the city of Goa as a thriving port, specialising in the import of Arab horses then were in great demand in India[4]. From Goa, Covilhao returned home carrying information about the huge trade, especially in ginger, pepper, cloves and cinnamon. The actual arrival of the Portuguese did not however take place till Vasco da Gama, discovering the new route *via* the Cape of Good Hope, arrived in India on the 17th May, 1498 and anchored off Kappat, a small village, eight miles north of Calicut.[5]* After visiting Calicut, Cannanore and Anjediva — a small island lying off the coast of N. Canara, Gama left India in November, 1498, returning to Lisbon in September, 1499[7]. Gama carried back a huge amount of cargo and after meeting all the expenses of the voyage and rewarding all who had taken part in that great enterprise, the net profit was sixty times the actual investment[8].

Such a fabulous gain had a tremendous effect on the mercantile minds of Portugal which behaved like coming "into a sudden fortune beyond the sea"[9]. No time was lost in arranging the next expedition which took place in the following year of Vasco da Gama's return to Lisbon. Pedro Alvarez Cabral, sent by King Emmannuel to establish commercial intercourse with the Zamorin of Calicut*

* Danvers gives a different date : August—1498[6].

* Zamorin called by Ibn Battuta the 'Samari' — a word familiar to theologians as the legendary ancestor of the Samaritans — is the Malayalam word 'Samuri' meaning 'Sea-king' turned into Portuguese tongue to Zamorin[10].

was given a more elaborate and fully armed fleet that Gama, consisting of thirteen ships and 1200 men on board necessary to frighten the Arabs[11]. Cabral arrived at Calicut on the 30th August, 1500, about six months after his departure from Lisbon, and was successful in making a treaty of peace and friendship with the Zamorin, and in establishing the first Portuguese Factory or Agency at Calicut. in the same year, Cabral founded the second factory at Cochin. The hostility of the Arab merchants experienced by both Gama and Cabral, and the serious brushes between Cabral and the Arabs finally compelled the King of Portugal to choose the path of "armed monopoly"[12]. Accordingly in 1502 he sent Gama with a large fleet of twenty ships, with the object of securing a "permanent foothold on the Indian coast for armed commerce"[13]. This was fully accomplished; two factories were established, one at Baticala, and the other at Cannanore, and within the next two years of Gama's return, that is, by 1505, Arab traders were completely routed by the Portuguese, the latter consolidating their position on the Malabar Coast. The determination of Portugal to hold on to what has already been won is further proved in the appointment of the first Portuguese Viceroy to India in 1505. The following years saw more success attained in the expansion of their territorial jurisdiction as well as in obtaining an overall control of the Indian Ocean. Territorial aims did no longer remain confined to the Malabar Coast, but were directed towards the northern parts of the western and the eastern coasts. The result of this was the growth of Portuguese settlements all over the coast as follows :

> Calicut (1500)[14]; Cochin (1500)[15]; Baticala (1502)[16]; Cannanore (1502)[17]; Quilon (1503)[18]; Goa (1510)[19]; Dhabol and Chaul (1522)[20]; Ponnani (1525)[21]; Thana (1528)[22]; Daman (1530)[23]; Gogo, Bulsur, Agashi and Surat (1531)[24]; Mahim and Bombay (1532)[25]; Cambay and Bassien (1534)[26]; Diu (1535)[27]; Mangalore (1537)[28]; Chittagong (1537-38)[29]; Masulipatam (1570)[30]; Hooghly (1579)[31].

The time and place could not be more propitious for the arrival of the Portuguese in India. The great empire of the Mughals was still a far cry. The whole of India was divided into a great number of independent kingdoms and principalities. The division was of more serious nature in the western coast where each of the important seaports had given rise to an independent State. These petty kingdoms thrived entirely on the revenues earned from ocean traffic and, as a rule, they fought among themselves for obtaining a larger share of that. The Portuguese, arriving on the scene, took full advantage of the disturbed situation. The geographical distribution of the Portuguese settlements shows that, except three (Masulipatam, Hooghly and Chittagong), all their settlement were on the western coast and the vestige of the Portuguese Empire that remained till 1961 was also confined to that region.

The Portuguese achievements in India did not, however, go unnoticed for a long time. Both the Dutch and the English "almost simultaneously took measures to contest the claim of Portugal to the monopoly of Oriental Commerce"[32]. Within a space of little over a hundred years of the appearance of the Portuguese, the Dutch established their first factory at Masulipatam in 1605 and by the middle of the seventeenth century they succeeded in establishing themselves in Gujarat, on the Coromondal Coast, in Bengal, Bihar and Orissa, besides entering deep into the interior of the lower Ganga Valley. They settled at the following places:

> Masulipatam (1605)[33]; Devenampatam (1608)[34]; Pulicat (1609)[35]; Surat (1618-1620)[36]; Broach (1620)[37]; Cambay (1620)[38]; Ahmedabad (1620)[39]; Agra (1620)[40]; Burhanpur (1620)[41]; Gogo (1631)[42]; Bimlipatam (1641)[43]; Karikal (1645)[44]; Chinsurah (1653)[45]; Hugli[46]; Negapatam[47]; Balasor (1658)[48]; Kassimbazar (1658)[49]; Patna (1658)[50]; Baranagar (1658)[51]; Tuticorin (1658)[52]; Golconda (1660)[53]; Quilon (1661)[54]; Cranganore (1661)[55]; Cannanore (1663)[56]; Porto Novo (1680)[57].

Throughout the seventeenth century the Dutch, supplanting the Portuguese, enjoyed the monopoly of the spice trade in the East. This did not, however, last long in the fact of strong rivalry of the English. The latter, arriving close to the heels of the Dutch, made their first settlement at Pettapoli (Nizamapatam) on the eastern coast in 1611 and their first factory at Surat in 1612. This was followed in a quick succession by the emergence of English factories at other places :

> Cambay (1612)[58]; Ajmer (1614)[59]; Ahmedabad (1616)[60]; Baroda (1618)[61]; Borach (1618)[62]; Agra (1618)[63]; Pulicat (1620)[64];

Masulipatam (1614)[65]; Armagao (1626)[66]; Hariharpur (1633)[67]; Puri (1633)[68]; Pipli (1633)[69]; Balasor (1633)[70]; Rajapur (1637-38)[71]; Carwar (1638-40)[72]; Baticala (1638-40)[73]; Madras (1639)[74]; Hugli (1651)[75]; Kassimbazar (1651)[76]; Patna (1651)[77]; Bombay (1661-1665)[78]; Vizagapatam (1668)[79]; Burhanpur; Rajmahal (1688)[80]; Malda (1688)[81]; Dacca (1668)[82]; Thana (1774)[83]; Tuticorin (1781)[84]; Calcutta (1690)[85].

By this time Portuguese influence got vastly eroded and was gradually being replaced by the English who contended with the Dutch for obtaining supremacy in the Indian trade. In the first quarter of the seventeenth century another European power, the Danish, appeared on the Indian scene and made a feeble attempt at taking a part in the scramble. They founded two factories in India, the first one at Tranquebar on the east coast in 1620, and the other at Serampore in Bengal in 1755[86].

The last of the European powers was the French who arrived in India in the later part of the seventeenth century and had their first factory established at Surat in 1668, followed by others Masulipatam (1669)[87]; St. Thome (1672)[88]; Pondicherry (1673)[89]; Chandernagore (1690)[90]; Mahe (1721)[91]; Yanam (1773)[92]; Calicut (1722-23)[93]; Karikal (1738-39)[94]. The growing contest between the Dutch and the French, enticed by the English, and later on between the French and the English greatly weakened the commercial position of the French, leading subsequently to the abandonment of its factories at Surat and Masulipatam in the early part of the eighteenth century. Thus, by the middle of that century the English earned unquestionable supremacy over all the foreign competitors in the trade of Indian merchandise.

The ultimate failure of the Portuguese, the Dutch and the French is not difficult to understand. The Portuguese "had the advantage of the start in the race for the control of the Indian trade"[95]. But "the emergence of powerful dynasties in Egypt, Persia, and north India (the Mughals) and the appearance of the turbulent Maratha power as neighbours reduced the local advantage of the Portuguese in India. Political fears roused by the activities of Jesuit missionaries and hatred of persecution such as the inquisition practised, caused reaction against the Portuguese spiritual pressure. Greed, selfishness, and corruption weakened the administration. But the system still worked and produced wealth. It was destroyed by the Dutch and the English, two nations with wider resources and greater compulsions to expand than the Portuguese in the Indies failed to resist"[96]. The Dutch, on the other hand, making a flourishing trade in India could not continue for a long time in the face of the stiff resistance from the French and the English and wisely quitted the scene for Java where they had their main centre established before coming to India and concentrated on utilising immense resources of the spice trade of the adjoining islands. The French, on the other hand, were too late to come when the other foreign powers were already established in most of the important trading stations of the country. Unlike others, they were less enterprising, less organised and received little backing and encouragement from their own Government in Europe[97]. In contrast, the pluck and courage of the English, the unfliching determination of the Company's personnels and, above all, the strong political support at home paved their way to the final success.

The political motive behind the establishment of 'factories' or agency houses in India by the foreign powers cannot be ignored. "The factory was a compact little nest of buildings, consisting of the lodgings of the Chief or President and his subordinates, warehouses, godowns and offices, the whole surrounded by the ramparts of the 'fort'"[98]. A fortified factory naturally led to the emergence of permanent settlements and in many cases the entire town or the city came into the possession of the Europeans. It is, therefore, erroneous to call such settlements as factories: they were nothing but European colonies in India. In fact, as early as 1671, Bombay was referred to as a colony by the English in a despatch to the home Government[99]. It is true that even in the heyday of Portuguese rule in India, their colonial possession did not consist of more than a small strip around Goa and a few more towns along the west coast, which amounted to about 1605 m^2. Similarly, the British territory in India during the period of the Mughals was too negligible, comprising only a few square miles in the island of Bombay, Madras and Calcutta. The French possession was equally small, confined to a small number of towns and cities like Pondicherry, Chandernagore, Mahe, Karikal and Yanam. The growth of European settlements in India, howsoever small in number or total area at that time, carried immense importance in historical perspective. They offered, for the first time, a permanent foothold for the European powers on Indian soil which went to determine later on the course of the political and also the economic history of the country. What in the beginning was merely a commercial ambition gradually developed into colonial aspirations, fulfilled during the following centuries.

Those settlements from the very commencement made positive contribution to the urban development of the country. The factories or agency houses establishing direct contact between the city and foreign traders undoubtedly strengthened the economy. This is more clearly seen in the case of some hitherto obsolete centres which, through the activity of the foreigners, burst forth into a new life. Goa is one of them. In 1641-48, Tavernier observed as follows: "All those who have seen both Europe and Asia thoroughly agree with me that the port of Goa, that of Constantinople, and that of Toulon, are the three finest ports of our great continent"[100]. The city "combined the riches of commerce with the splendour of ecclesiastical pomp and a powerful military court"[101]. Another example is provided by Pondicherry, founded by Francois Martin in 1674 on a small piece of territory ceded by a native ruler[102], which turned out to be the capital of French colonies in India. This flourishing and populous centre was, however, occupied by the English in 1761 who deliberately destroyed it and when, after four years, it was restored to the French in 1765, everything was in complete ruins[103]. Once re-established, it did not take the French long to rebuilt Pondicherry and within another three years it grew into a beautiful, planned town with a total population of about 61,200[104]. Similar instances can be drawn from places like Chandernagore, Mahe, Yanam, Karikal, etc., each of them embarking upon a new career. All these cases, however, become really insignificant when compared to the achievement of the European settlements in giving rise to Calcutta, Bombay and Madras.

Threshold to an Empire-Building Process

Historically, Bombay is the oldest of these three places. The earliest inhabitants of Bombay, originally consisting of seven islands, were the Kolis, an aboriginal tribe of husbandmen and fishermen, and it is from their goddess 'Mumba' that the place derived its present name. The temple of Mumba, a form of Hindu goddess Parvati, lay near the site at present occupied by the Victoria Terminus. The Bombay islands formed a part of the Maurya Empire at Asoka's time (273-232 B.C.), but the place did not come into any prominence till the end of the thirteenth century when Raja Bhima founded the town of Mahikavati or Mahim and his followers spread over the island. The Hindu rule ended in about 1348 when Bombay and Salsettle were won over by the Sultan of Gujarat, ceded later on to the Portuguese in 1534. Although they remained in the possession of the Portuguese for over one and a quarter of a century, the latter failed to make a successful colonisation of them. The lands were divided into manors or fiefs and were granted as rewards to individuals or religious orders on a system of 'a foramento' under the condition that the rewardee will have to furnish military aid to the King of Portugal. In course of time the Franciscans and Jesuits built a number of beautiful churches in the northern districts, but the intolerance of the Portuguese largely hindered the growth of the settlement, having only a population of about 10,000 when the Port and the Island of Bombay were transferred to the English on June 23, 1661[105] as a marriage dowry from the Infanta of Portugal to King Charles II of England. The actual possession by Humphrey Cook, on behalf of the King of England took place four years later in 1665. It was, however, not until 1720 that the English were successful in dislodging the Portuguese religious orders from the northern portion of the islands and incorporate Mahim, Sion, Dharavi and Vadala into their own territory in India.

The real founder of the city was Gerald Aungier (1669-1677) who resolved to make it a "place of safety for shipping and trade"[106]. In order to guard it from the Marathas inland, the Malabar pirates from the south coast, the Dutch by the sea and the Portuguese, who still then retained the adjacent island of Salsette, Aungier built the main fortress. Since chief English import at that time was bullion, a mint was set up at Bombay[107] and in order to promote manufactures it was arranged to distribute cotton directly from the Company's own stores[108]. The settlement of the land revenue, establishment of law courts, freedom of trade and religion, and above all, the security guaranteed by its strong defences invited new settlers among whom the most important were the Banias, the Armenians and the Parsis. But before Aungier's efforts could show any result, Bombay plunged headlong into a chain of troubles culminating into a war with the Mughal Emperor. Peace was made with the Emperor, but internal squabbles among the members of the East India Company, the steady unfriendliness of the Portuguese, occasional visits of the Mughal fleets and, lastly, the piratical activities in the coastal waters left no real peace for a long time. Trade was hampered and the place remained the "unhealthiest, the poorest, and the most despised"[109] of all the English settlements in India. The situation did not improve even when the headquarters of the English Governor was transferred from Surat to Bombay in 1709. The continued hostilities of the Marathas and the Sidi pirates greatly endangered Bombay's existence. Secondly, the damp climate, the marshes on the land-ward side of the island, the presence of toddy trees, shutting out the sea breezes, and, finally, the system of manuring the trees with partly decayed fish giving a horrible stench made life quite unattractive for the foreigners. The political insecurity made it equally uninviting to the Indians as well. The unpopularity of Bombay, starting soon after Aungier had left the place, was the principal cause of its depopulation. "The population which had grown from about 10,000 in 1660 to an estimated 40,000 or 60,000 in 1678, had shrunk to 16,000 in 1716 and not until 1744 was it rather optimistically estimated at 70,000"[110]. During this entire period, however, the city-administrators did not remain completely idle. In 1718, the town was walled-up, attracting new settlers, especially from the troubled Gujarat. The functions of the city improved further through the establishment of a bank in 1720, and for streamlining the administration a criminal court was set up in 1727 and a mayor's court in 1728. In 1736, the dockyards were extended under the guidance of a Parsi ship-builder, Lowji Lassaramji Wadia from Surat. All these resulted in an increase of the population. The history of the ultimate prosperity of Bombay is different from that of either Calcutta or Madras, both of which had the advantage of blossoming as Military Centres. Merchants took it as a favour to reside in Calcutta and Madras; in Bombay they had to be attracted from still larger centre of Surat.

Since 1740 the situation started improving at a faster rate than ever before and in 1754 Bombay could be considered as a flourishing place[111]. During the following years the defences of the town were further strengthened and by 1756 pirates were completely destroyed; besides, two new docks were completed respectively in 1750 and 1762, and passenger boats started plying regularly between the island and the mainland; from 1748, building regulations were enforced.

Among the improvements that followed were the enactment of labour rates, enforcement of a better system of conservancy in 1777, erection of hospitals in 1768 and 1769, an accurate survey of the land and replacement of the old Bhandari Militia by proper police force in about 1780. The beginning of cotton trade with China in 1770 opened a new horizon for this town. Parsons, visiting the island in 1774, found it as an elegant town, nearly a mile in length and about a quarter of a mile broad, with well-laid streets and numerous handsome buildings[112]. By that time Bombay had become the headquarters of the English on the west coast. The secret of Bombay's ultimate success lay in the continued activity of their dockyards and the harbour. "The Parsi ship-builder rather than the English merchant was the true maker of Bombay"[113].

Unlike Bombay, Madras has a much later origin, founded by the English in 1639. The political as well as economic considerations concerning Masulipatam's strained relations with the King of Golconda, and the considerable distance of the former from the principal centres of weaving and dyeing compelled the English to find for a new place from where trade could be carried on uninterrupted. In August 1639, Francis Day, a member of the Council at Masulipatnam—then the Company's headquarters on the Coromondal Coast—and the Chief at Armagao, selected a spot, thirty miles south of Pulicat, with a roadstead, and taking the help of the local Hindu Chief, managed to obtain the grant for that small piece of land on the shore lying north of the friendly, but decaying, Portuguese settlement of San Thome, and was permitted to build a fort[114]. The Fort completed in the following year, was named after England's patron Saint as Fort St. George, and in accordance with the expressed desire of the local Hindu Chief, the settlement was called Chennappatanam[115]*. In the same year, 1640, a decree towards the exemption of taxes for thirty years attracted about three to four hundred families of weavers who settled round the fort. In establishing the settlement or in erecting the fort, Francis Day did not wait for permission from home for which even after six years he was not

* The English name is probably dervied from the Sanskrit name of a legendary King of lunar race, corrupted in Telegu to Mandaraz, and would be in full Mandaraz-patanam on the analogy Duragaraz-patnam, the alternative name of Armagaon[116].

forgiven by the Government in England for the expenses thus incurred[117]. In 1641, the headquarters were transferred from Masulipatam to Madras and by 1685, all the English settlements in Bengal and on the Coromondal Coast were placed under its care.

Madras gave the English their first piece of Indian soil and it was here that the earliest of the full-scale English settlements grew up; factories established by them before that elsewhere were mere plots offered by the Kings in their towns or cities. The growth of Madras was rather unfettered and it became "the richest and most populous town on the eastern coast"[118] with about 250,000 inhabitants living in the surrounding encampments and townships[119] when it succumbed to French attack in 1746, remaining in their possession for about three years. After reoccupying Madras in 1749, the English fortified the fort in such a manner that it could resist the French in 1759, after which the town remained free from any outside attack.

The Company gradually acquired more land around the fort and its immediate vicinity. Before this, however, Madras had already been raised to Presidency in 1653[120], and later on in 1687 a municipal government was formed.

Calcutta was the last of the three principal cities to appear on the map. Perhaps the earliest reference to Calcutta, as a village, occurs in a poem of 1495[121] when Satgaon, situated on R. Saraswati—little north of Hooghly town—was the principal emporium of trade. At this time there was another important market at Betor, situated near present Sibpur, on the west bank of R. Hooghly, which was the mercantile headquarters of the Portuguese. The gradual silting of R. Saraswati in the sixteenth century led to the decline of Satgaon and most of the deserters settled in Hooghly. But, some time in the middle of that century, four families of Bysaks and one Seth family founded the village of Govindapur, occupying the present site of Fort William. Shortly after this the Portuguese left Betor for Hugli (Hooghly) and the trade was diverted to Sutanuti, or, literally a 'Cotton Thread Mart'[122], which had already been carrying on a good trade in yarns and cloth. The original site of this village is now occupied by the northern portion of the city, extending from Chitpur in the north to Jorabagan Ghat, the latter lying a little below Nimtolla Ghat. To the south stood another hamlet known at that time as Dihi Kalikata, covering the area extending from Nimtolla Ghat to Babu Ghat, the southern boundary of which was formed by a creek originating from the Salt Lake in the east. Calcutta, perhaps, derived its name from the last-named village, though the possibility of another derivation—from the famous Hindu temple of antiquity, Kalighata, now forming a part of the present city — is not remote[123]. When the English arrived on the scene, the three villages — Govindapur, Sutanuti and Dihi Kalikata—were already there.

By the last quarter of the seventeenth century, both the political and economic situation of Bengal became too provocative for the English to resist their ambition for securing a permanent foothold any further. The opportunities came in succession. The destruction of the Portuguese and Arakanese pirates, infesting the head of the Bay of Bengal by the Mughal Governor of Bengal—Shaista Khan—in the 1660s opened a new area for trade. While the Portuguese were out of the picture, the Dutch had already exhausted much of their force in their constant struggles with the Portuguese in the beginning and with the French and the English at the later stages. Besides, the Dutch and the French had, till then, concentrated little on consolidating their position in Bengal. They had a few factories in some of the important trading stations in Bengal, no doubt, but none of them nurtured the idea of building an empire in India. In fact, unlike the Portuguese and the English, both the Dutch and the French interests in India were purely commercial which remained unchanged with the French till 1742[124]. In contrast, the English attitude was made clear in a note written by the Directors of the Company from home country as early as in December, 1687, asking its servants to make the foundation of a large, well-established and permanent English dominion in India[125]. Such a desire as well as its practicability was naturally prompted by their success in establishing two permanent settlements in Madras and Bombay. The commerce of Bengal in those days consisting of silks, muslins, saltpetre, sugar, opium, rice, jute and oil, was the most valuable in India[126]. In 1651, the English were granted a privilege of trading in Bengal against a token payment of Rs. 3,000 as annual duties, and in 1656 they were even exempted from paying this duty which was further ratified in 1672 and 1680. It is to be noted that neither the Dutch nor the French did ever enjoy such advantages, amounting to political protection from the rulers of the country. During this period English factories had been established at Hugli, Kassimbazar, and in the following years at Dacca, Rajmahal and Malda, which gave them all opportunities for collecting the huge merchandise of the region. Apart from occasional harassments at the hands of the local customs officers, trade facilities remained completely unburdened and free of any official interference. But peaceful commerce did not satisfy the English; their aim was territorial gain. In 1686, they sacked Hugli from where they were driven away by the Mughals and during their retreat down the river Job Charnock, the Agent of the Company at Hugli town, arrived on December 20, 1686, at the mud-flats with a deep water-anchorage, the site of modern Calcutta, and selected it as the much sought-after site for a permanent settlement necessary for making a stand against a land force[127]. As it proved later on, the selection could not be better and wiser than what Charnock did with his long experience of about thirty-three years in Bengal. The western bank and the adjoining countryside, besides remaining at the mercy of the turbulent rivers, were open to the attack of the bandits of Orissa and southern Bengal. The eastern bank, well-raised above the river, was much too narrow—about a mile wide—and then sloping down eastwards into the brackish waters, formed a "deadly region, long given up to malaria and crocodile"[128]. In spite of the unhealthiness, several reasons led Charnock to its selection. Its situation at the highest navigable point for sea-going vessels gave it added advantage over the Dutch and French factories located further inland. The place had the unique position of commanding the river approaches from the north, south and west. The swamps, spreading over a hundred square miles, made it unassailable by troops from the east[129]. This shut-off location of the place and the absence of any important settlement in the south and also in the north, for over hundred miles in the latter direction till Kassimbazar was reached, made it the most safe location for the English settlement. At the same time, it provided the best spot for the building of a port and dockyards with ship-building and repairing facilities.

Soon after his arrival, Charnock began erecting some temporary huts at Sutanuti and sought the permission of the Mughal Viceroy for building a factory. In February, 1687, the Viceroy sent an army to crush the new settlement upon which Charnock fled to Hugli. In September he again came back to the place to find no trace of the structures made by him on his earlier visit. He started fresh negotiations with the Viceroy for establishing a factory and set on making rough shelters along with some defensive works which gradually came up through the dogged perseverance and unaccountable sufferances of his men working in the hot whether and the drenching rains of 1688[130]. But all this was not appreciated by the Directors of the Company at home who obviously lacked the imagination and foresight of Job Charnock. A reproachful despatch reached him on September 20, 1688, ordering him to sail for the conquest of Chittagong[131]. After an abortive attempt at Chittagong, Charnock returned to Madras where, at last, his long cherished permission from the Mughal Governor of Bengal arrived. The English were permitted to settle at the site, originally selected by Charnock, and were allowed to have a free trade unhampered by local taxes against the old payment of Rs. 3,000 a year. Following this, on August 24, 1690, Charnock landed for the third time on the deserted river bank where, except a few mud-hovels, nothing remained of the previous settlement. Accompanied by thirty soldiers in all Charnock founded here Calcutta, the first permanent English settlement in Bengal, which gradually emerged as the future capital of British India. The task was not easy in the face of the strong reluctance of his followers who preferred the easy and comfortable life at Hugli where, at that time, the English were most welcome. With an iron determination for building a permanent stronghold for the English instead of 'fenceless factories'[132], Charnock, even at the old age, ignored all the displeasure, whether of his men or of his superiors at Madras, and went on building the place anew, securing for the first time, perhaps, a large sum form the Company at home in the middle of 1692. Early next year, January 10, 1693, Charnock died unthanked and unrewarded, but by that time he had given the English a sound footing at Calcutta which, within a decade of its founding, turned into a busy market with 1,200 English inhabitants[133].

Under the mature and able guidance of Charnock, trading was resumed and building operations of the simplest kind at first were started. The wealthy business people were attracted to the place and gradually the settlement extended southwards along the river bank, spreading over the villages of Dihi Kalikata and Govindapur. Of the three villages Dihi Kalikata was "probably the first to be supplied with buildings of a more substantial kind to serve as magazines for the Company's increasing wares and investments"[134].

In 1696, the rebellion of Sobha Singh, a zamindar in the District of Burdwan, against the Mughals gave the English an excuse to fortify their new settlement and a fort was completed during the years 1696-1702 on the site, west of the of the present Dalhousie Square occupying the area lying between Fairlie Place and Koliaghat Street. In 1698, the Mughal Governor of Hugli granted them the zamindari of the three villages of Sutanuti, Dihi Kalikata and Govindapur on a payment of Rs. 1,200 to the previous owners[135], thus establishing the position of the English further in Bengal. In December, 1699, the Board of Directors declared Bengal a separate Presidency, and placed all the English factories in Bengal under the charge of a newly appointed Governor. The fort, henceforward known as 'Fort William', was made his headquarters.

A Territorial Deam Fulfilled

Calcutta grew rapidly and with the expansion of business and population it became necessary to expand the territory. An emissary was sent to Delhi and in 1717 the Company obtained permission from the Emperor to rent thirty-eight villages in Bengal, which made up the area covered, later on, by the cities of Calcutta and Howrah. In spite of the initial opposition of the Governor of Bengal, the 'firman' of the Emperor granted extraordinary privileges which acted as the 'Magna Carta of the Company' — as called by Orme[136], giving the English an unrivalled position in Bengal. However, for many years from the time of Job Charnock's death, little is known of the progress of the town. Indeed in 1717 it remained a straggling village of mat houses; the whole of the area south of Chandpal Ghat was still thickly covered with jungle and forest. The present site of Chowringhee was occupied by villages of the most miserable kind, surrounded by marsh and jungle and although the town had extended by then to Chitpur Bridge, yet the intervening space was in no better condition than the rest; all was jungle and marsh[137].

But commerce, overcoming these handicaps, seems to have had grown up very rapidly. Captain Alexander Hamilton, who visited Calcutta in 1710, describes it as a market town for corn, coarse cloth, butter and oil, and other products of the country. On the side of the R. Hooghly he found docks "repairing and fitting their ships bottoms"[138]. According to Stewart, "success produced new adventures; and beside a number of English private merchants licensed by the Company, Calcutta was in a short time peopled by Portuguese, Armenian, Mughal and Hindoo merchants who carried on their commerce under the protection of the English flag: thus the shipping belonging to the port amounted to 10000 tons"[139]. By 1735 a prosperous native town had grown up around the English factory, warehouses and the Fort, accommodating about 100,000 people who had settled for many, occupations and security[140]. Aliverdi's strong grip on administration between 1740-56 as the Nawab of Bengal gave the English a peaceful time to settle in Calcutta which grew quickly as a trading centre. Outside the walls of the Fort they erected fifty buildings on the bank of the river which thronged with shipping[141].

In 1742, a wide ditch was dug, running in a semi-circle round the town as a defensive measure against the Maratha raiders. The scare caused by the raids as well as the growing trade increased the influx of new settlers who felt more secure in the well-defended town and according to an estimate of Holwell, the population rose to 409,000. This, however, seems to be an overestimate since the number of houses was, still then, about 15,000[142]. But there cannot be any doubt in the growth of the town which, by 1756, had reached such a stage of material progress that its trade is stated to have had exceeded one million sterling yearly and that about fifty vessels or more visited the port annually[143]. The territory of the town extended like a crescent along the bank of the river from north to south for about three miles[144]. The area between the river in the west and Mission Row on the east, Canning Street in the north and Hastings Street in the south was built up with offices, godowns, residential houses for the Company's employees and the Fort had about 230 masonry structures in 1753, meant exclusively for the Europeans; the Indians lived in the remaining part of the town, containing about the same number of masonry houses.

But during all these years the relation between the Company and the Nawab of Bengal gradually deteriorated. The Mughal 'firman' of 1717, giving them rights of free trade, was enjoyed much to the discontent of the local rulers. The English, however, did not keep strictly to these commercial concessions; time and again they overstepped their extensive privileges[145] naturally causing great displeasure of the Nawab. In fact, their territorial ambitions did no longer remain concealed; their activities in Madras, Bombay and in Calcutta became so much militant that commercial that it was not possible to have a closed eye to their ulterior motive. Close on the heels of all these came the news of further fortifications made by the French in their colonies. The English settlements having already inflamed the sentiment of the Nawab of Bengal led to the storming of Calcutta by the latter on June 16, 1756, who captured it after four days of small resistance. The English abandoned the town and it was not recovered until January 21, 1757, by Clive. After this the English hatched, under the leadership of Clive, the most heinous conspiracy with the dissidents of the Nawab's court. The Nawab was dethroned and killed and a new one was installed. As a prize the English won Calcutta as a free gift along with some of its adjacent villages and the zamindari of the 24-Parganas[146]. This made the real beginning of British rule in India.

The growth of Calcutta upto this period refers to its first phase of development. Exploiting its advantageous location, the settlement grew rapidly as the most important trading centre for the Company in the eastern part of India. Commerce and trade were its vital forces. Clive's victory, turning the tide in favour of the Company, made way for the establishment of British rule; and this having commenced in Bengal ushered in a new era in the life of Calcutta which, within a short time, became the Capital of British India. In the opinion of Martin, modern Calcutta dates from 1757 when, following its capture and destruction by the Nawab, reconstruction was started in full siwng[147]. It actually meant its second phase of development—a more vigorous and diversified in character. A mere trading station prior to 1756, it took Calcutta about forty years to blossom into the largest city of India, with five hundred thousand souls and a degree of prosperity unparalleled in any other quarter of the world[147]. Rennell, visiting Calcutta between 1764-76, comments as follows : "Within these 20 or 27 years (since 1756) Calcutta has been wonderfully improved both in appearance, and in the salubrity of its air : for the streets have been properly drained, and the ponds filled up; thereby removing a vast surface of stagnant water. Calcutta is well known to be the emporium of Bengal, and the seat of the Governor General of India. It is a very extensive and populous city, being supplied at present to contain at least 500,000 inhabitants"[148]. In the last quarter of the eighteenth century, Calcutta's trade was of an extensive nature and the R. Hooghly in consequence used to be covered with vessels, adding to the opulence and industry of the place where great many ships were built at the docks of the "richest town"[149] of India. Thus, before the turn of the country, Calcutta emerged as the premier city of India.

The Emperor's generosity, or rather the lack of farsightedness, in allowing the English to rent the thirty-eight villages around Calcutta came to be the most significant political recognition accorded to any other foreign power. The possession made their position more clear and firm than either at Bombay or at Madras. They became really established and the political atmosphere, with a weak Nawab on the throne of bengal surrounded by conspirators, could not be more favourable for fishing in troubled waters. This made a turning point in the history of India with its deep-rooted impact on the course of urbanisation in the country.

In retrospect, political supremacy of the English was not achieved in a day or by any single action. Even if the territorial ambitions of the English had taken form as early as the middle of the seventeenth century, consequent upon their successful colonization of Madras and Bombay, it remained far from a reality till they got a firm foothold in Bengal in the first quarter of the eighteenth century. It was only then that the idea got fresh winds on its sails and successive events steered it through a defined course of action.

The action and the path that they followed were not simple either. Nearly a century passed before the English could spread their territorial sovereignty over the whole of India. The change of the political map of India during that hundred years gives an interesting insight into the intense political turmoil that gripped the country—a long episode of the rise of British Power in India as a consequence of the fall and gradual disintegration of the kingdoms and Princely States.

The real beginning of the episode may be traced back to the year 1717 when Emperor Farrukshiyar of Delhi issued firmans giving the English right to rent land in and around Calcutta and a full privilege of duty-free trade in Bengal on payment of nominal annual fee to the Nawab's treasury, besides a few more trade-concessions in South India. All these were done by the emperor in return of the service of curing him of a painful disease by Surgeon Hamilton who accompanied the Emissary of the East India Company to the Royal Court[150]. The initial success may not appear much too significant at the surface, but it bore great value for Calcutta which, with its thirty-eight villages coming under the virtual possession of the English, could be utilised as the stronghold for future political manoeuvres. Indeed, it did not take them long to assure a direct part in Bengal's politics. In 1757, the battle of Plassey established the military supremacy of the English and made them the *de facto* masters of Bengal. With "sudden transformation of plodding merchants into the arbiters of Bengal politics"[151], the situation changed wheel "the Nawab became a suitor for British favour instead of the regulator of British activity"[152]. The English did not fail to make best of this changed situation. In the following years the Nawab became a figure-head while the supreme control of the administration gradually passed into the hands of the English. Having thus established their away over Bengal they looked for further ground for action. The opportunity was not long to come. The Emperor of Delhi was not in good terms with the Nawab of Oudh. As there was no power over the entire stretch of the country between Calcutta and Delhi to resist English arms, both of them sought their help for arbitration. Accordingly, the English concluded the Treaty of Allahabad in 1765 by which Oudh was restored to the Nawab while Allahabad and its surrounding tracts were detached from Oudh and handed over to the Emperor. In return the Emperor granted the Diwani of Bengal, Bengal, Bihar and Orissa to the English. According to the laws of the Mughal Administration "the powers of the government was divided into Diwani, or power of collecting revenue and administering civil justice, and nizamat, or power of commanding troops and dispensing criminal justice"[153].

The action, made of supreme fact, gave the English a legal recognition and market "the first great step towards the direct administration"[154] of a large part of the country. In 1773, the home Government, by a Parliamentary Act, elevated the post of Governor to the Governor General of Fort William in Bengal with authority over the other two Presidencies of Bombay and Madras. In addition, a Supreme Court was established in Calcutta.

The ascendancy of British Power in India, from 1765 onwards, cannot be understood without reviewing the political picture of the country. The principal object of the East India Company, in getting a monopoly of Indian trade unhampered by interference from other foreign competitors, still then was of supreme concern of the home Government in Britain. It was, so to say, an armed trade, no doubt, but the English were no exception either in this regard as they had to fight their way with other foreign contenders in the field equally armed. The home Government had no objection in establishing colonies in India as a means of furthering trading rights. The idea of establishing such colonies—like, Bombay, Madras and Calcutta—for a long time had no pretension to territorial claims. This is amply justified by the attitude of the home Government which expected from the Company nothing but prosperity in trade and commerce. The situation in India, however, was much too provoking for the Company to keep aloof from the common tide of events and finally, it got embroiled in the game of local politics. In the early year's the Company was mainly engaged in dislodging other foreign traders from the Indian soil and for that it carefully avoided any direct conflict with the Indian rulers. As long as Aurungzeb the last the Mughal Emperors, was in power the policy of the Company did not change. The death of Aurungzeb in 1707 brought the empire into complete disarray, the grip of the later Emperors' on the empire was lost in no time and independent powers rose their head on the ruins of the Mughal Empire, dividing the country into a large number of different camps with their swords drawn for greater spoils. In North India, Bengal and Oudh became virtually independent; the whole of Punjab was in the hands of war bands where Sikh Power was gradually taking form; Sind came under the rule of Afghans. The weakening of the Mughals further brought into the field new aspirants to power — such as, the Jats and the Ruhilla Afghans. The last vestiges of the Mughal Empire, already threatened by these ambitious rulers, were severely shaken further by the Afghans who, for some years, constantly swooped down on the north-west plains of India with an aim of conquering the throne. The catastrophe was, however, providentially avoided through the final departure of Ahmad Shah Abdali, the last of the marauding Afghan Chiefs, in 1767 after which the menace greatly abated, ceasing altogether by 1790.

The political instability, confusion and the great disorder were not confined to North India alone, the whole of India became a prey to power rivalry. The Rajpur States, for example, once strong confederates of the Mughals, were disunited and disorganised and were being constantly harassed by the Marthas. The latter, forming the largest power in Central and South India, were not in good shape either. In spite of having indomitable courage, unequal vigour and an admirable national spirit, they failed to keep united for long. Lust for power gave place to political wisdom; mistrust among leaders sowed the seeds of dissension and what could merge as an Empire replacing the Mughals, broke down into five separate independent units headed by the Gaekwar, the Bhonsle, the Sindhia, the Holkar and the Peshwa. Instead of fighting for a common cause, they fought among themselves. The chaos was not yet complete. There were still others to take advantage of the situation. Hyderabad shook off Delhi's influence and emerged as a new State. But the State was not free from Maratha raids which gradually sapped its energy for resisting foreign encroachments. Mysore, originally a Hindu State, came under Muslim rule. Besides, a large number of small principalities had arisen in South India, constantly changing allies for the furtherance of their own interests.

The disintegration of the Mughal Empire, the withdrawal of the Afghans and the enfeebled condition of the Marathas left no power in India to match the courage and fortitude of the English or to ignore their claims. The extreme political confusion of the period under review was not the only opportunity that the East India Company exploited directly, even incurring displeasure of the home Government at many stages. What got them really involved was the call for their help by different rulers in their struggle for power and this ultimately led to their conquest of India. It is not true that the Indian rulers were completely blind to the consequences. The last two independent Nawabs of Bengal — Aliverdi Khan and Sirajuddaula, the last two Nawabs of Mysore — Hyder Ali and Tipu Sultan, and so also the ruling Maratha Chiefs were fully alive to such a possibility. The resistance from Bengal and Mysore was too much delayed and isolated in manner, while the Maratha Chiefs could never unite for a concerted action for averting the eventuality.

The Emperor's firman of 1765, giving the English virtual control over financial administration, acknowledged their authority in Bengal, Bihar and Orissa. Once reliquished, there was no road back. Thenceforward Bengal became the primary seat of their political manoeuvres, while the two other subsidiary places of Bombay and Madras helped in furthering this end. Shortly before this the East India Company, deleting the French in the Third Carnatic War of 1759-60, had acquired a foothold for itself in the Northern Circars of the East Coast which left them the undisputed masters of the sea[155]. The role of the three coastal centres of Calcutta, Bombay and Madras — primarily English in origin — was decisive in deciding the fate of India for the following centuries.

The unfortunate example set by the Mughal Emperor and the Nawab of Oudh in seeking English intervention for solving their territorial problems soon started to be emulated by others. The rapid rise of Hyder Ali in Mysore excited the jealousy of the Marathas, the Nizam of Hyderabad and the Egnlish. In 1766, the last three entered into a triple alliance against Hyder, but this turned out to be abortive due to the vacillation of the Nizam and the circumstances forced the English to make a treaty with Hyder in 1769. The Company was severely reprimanded by the home Government which was not in favour of any further expansion of British territories in India[156]. This, however was not heeded to by the Company which already felt greatly tempted about the immense possibilities that lay hidden under such alliances. Between 1775 and 1782, the English made several teatics with the Peshwa, one of the Maratha Chiefs, and entering into armed conflict on his behalf obtained the Island of Salsette as a rightful possession. the last treaty of 1782, giving the English at least twenty years' peace with the Marathas, established once for all the absolute supremacy of English arms in South India. Meanwhile, the Nizam, by a treaty of 1768, placed himself under the protection of the English. The death of Mahadaji Sindhia in 1794, the most outstanding Maratha Chief of the period, destroyed all chances of Maratha supremacy in Central India and the English were left uncontested to build their own dominion. The situation had become more and more explosive during these years. In violation of the terms of the treaty of 1769 concluded between the English and Hyder Ali, the former did not come to the rescue of the latter when his kingdom was invaded by the Marathas in 1771. This naturally angered Hyder and he declared war against the English 1780. The latter were defeated in two battles but succeeded in detaching the Sindhia and the Nizam from alliance with Hyder. The conflict remained undecided due to the commencement of the rainy season and followed by the sudden death of Hyder Ali in

1782. Tipu Sultan, Hyders successor to the throne of Mysore, proved equally dangerous to the English; besides, both the Nizam and the Marathas thought him greatly prejudicial to their own interests. They entered into a triple alliance in 1790, and helped the English forces in their war with Mysore. This lasted for about two years, ending on the treaty of 1792 by which Tipu had to surrender half of his dominions to the Peshwa and the Nizam. The English obtained Malabar, and a few more districts in the South beside £ 3,000,000 as compensation[157]. Tipu was finally defeated and killed in another war in 1799 following which a large part of his kingdom, comprising Kanara, Wynaad, the districts of Coimbatore and Daraporam and some tracts in the east along with the capital of Seringapatnam were annexed to British possessions. The truncated State, losing some more portions to the Nizam and the Marathas was given over to the descendant of the early Hindu rulers. British territory in the south henceforth extended from the shores of the Arabian Sea to the Bay of Bengal across the base of the peninsula.

The consolidation of power went on unabated with the English during this period. In 1775, the Raja of Benares was forced into a treaty of English overlordship. In 1798, the English unjustly intervened in the case of disputed succession to the throne of Oudh and gave that to the wrong person who ceded the fort of Allahabad to them as a prize. The English, now, adopted a policy of subsidiary alliance with regard to Indian Powers. According to this policy the greater principalities were to maintain a native force under the command of a British Officer and had to cede certain territories to the English for meeting the maintenance of this force; the lesser principalities were to pay an annual tribute to the English—all in the name of political security. The feeble Nizam accepted it at once in 1798. This was made more permanent in nature two years after whereby the Nizam had to accede to the maintenance of a larger force and surrender all the territories obtained from Mysore. In 1801, a treaty was concluded between the English and the Nawab of Carnatak by which the entire civil and military administration was taken over by the former. Prior to this, in 1799, both Tanjore and Surat States were compelled to surrender their administrative authority to the English. The latter played the same trick with the Nawab of Oudh who was forced to sign a treaty in 1801, ceding half of this territory lying between the

Ganga and the Jamuna to be annexed to British possessions. This virtually ended his rule.

The Peshwa, one of the Maratha Chiefs, agreed to the terms of Subsidiary Alliance in 1802 and ceded permanently territories yielding a revenue of Rs. 2.6 million a year for the maintenance of British troops within his dominion. The surrender made by the Peshwa greatly wounded the feelings of the remaining Maratha Chiefs who foresaw in it the growing shadow of British suzerainty. The Scindhia and the Bhonsle united into an armed conflict with the English in 1803, joined later on by the Holkar. The war ended in the defeat of the Marathas. The Bhonsle had to give away the province of Cuttack, including Balasore, and the whole territory west of the R. Wardha went to the English: the Schindhia had to cede all his territories lying between the Ganga and the Jamuna, his forts and territories lying north of the Rajput principalities of Jaipur, Jodhpur, etc., and west of the Ajanta Hills. Further, he entered into a subsidiary alliance with the English. The Anglo-Maratha war gave the English an unrivalled position. Their possessions in Bengal and Madras being now linked up made a continuous stretch spreading from north to south. Treaties of alliance were also concluded with the Rajput States of Jodhpur, Macheri, Bundi and Bharatpur. In 1803, the Mughal Emperor sought English protection.

English claims on the Marthas were not yet complete. By the treaty of 1816, the Nagpur State was brought under subsidiary alliance, thus ending the independent rule of the Bhonsles for ever. The Peshwa could not swallow the humiliation he was put to by the previous treaty of 1802. He made fresh attempts at organising the disgruntled Maratha Chiefs against the English. But the latter took prompt measures to foil this and the Peshwa had to sign another treaty in 1817, renouncing his leadership of the Maratha Confederacy and surrendering the Konkon along with some important strongholds to the English. Soon after this, however, the Peshwa again rose in arms in the same after year, joined by both the Holkar and the Bhonsle. They were completely defeated by the English as a result of which the area lying to the north and south of the R. Narmada was annexed to the British territories and the Holkar was humbled to enter into a subsidiary alliance..

The extension of British territories in India went on unhindered during the successive years. The victory of the English in the Nepal

War of 1814-16 extended the northern frontier of their dominion to the Himalayas. The Garhwal and the Kumaon districts came into British possession. Following this, the remaining Rajput States and those of Central India entered into defensive alliance with the English.

By the year 1823, British control was firmly established over the greater part of India, the dominion extending from the Sutlej to the Brahmaputra and from the Himalayas to the Cape Comorin. The only challenge to their position came from the two frontiers on the east and the west. The high-handed acts of the British resident in Sind brought it into conflict with the English, and Sind was ultimately annexed to the British dominion in 1843. The English fought two wars with the Sikhs and by 1849 the boundary of the British territory was pushed to the base of the mountains of Afghanistan in the west. Similar action was also taken against the Burmese in the east. A treaty, concluded in 1852, extended the frontier of British India up to the banks of the R. Salween in Burma. There still remained, however, a number of minor Indian States to be brought under the direct control of the growing empire and this was done on various pretexts. For instance, the 'Doctrine of Lapse', introduced at this time, meant that the sovereignty of the dependent States would lapse in the absence of direct heir and the State would automatically become a part of the British possession. The 'Doctrine' started to be applied from 1834 onwards in full vigour. The axe fell, in one or other form on Cachar (1832) and Jaintia (1835) in Assam, Coorg (1834) and Gwalior (1843); the Doctrine was applied to the States of Madurai (1839), Kolaba and Jalaun (1840), Surat (1842), Satara (1848), Jaitpur and Sambalpur (1849), Udipur (1852), Nagpur (1853) and Jhansi (1854). In 1853, a part of Sikkim was forcibly taken over and in the south the Nizam of Hyderabad was compelled to surrender the Province of Berar to the English.

Thus, what began in the form of 'Diwani' in 1765, rapidly took the shape of an empire within the course of the following sixty years or so, making English the absolute power in India with unchallenged authority extended beyond the frontiers of the subcontinent. The success within such an extremely short period, however unprecedented, is not difficult to understand. The loosening grip of the Mughal Emperor and the consequent rise of opposing ambitions for power among the Indian Rulers revealed the fundamental weakness of the country to any intelligent eye. The English came as traders and for a century and a half did not aspire much for anything more than establishing a few colonies of their own, situated at distant places. This, apparently, placid attitude got a severe jolt at the happening of events in quick succession from 1757 onwards, and the traders changed their roles fast from mercenaries to arbiters, and finally to conquerors. The conquest of India is the most important achievement in the entire history of British colonialism since such a gigantic task was accomplished by only a handful personnel of a Trading Company. True, the Company had occasionally been severely criticised at home, forbidden or advised caution from time-to-time for actions of delving into Indian politics. As early as 1767, the Secretary of the East India Company told the Parliament that the Government did not want conquest and power but looked for only commercial interests[158]. Similarly, the 'Second India Bill of 1783' forbade the Company "to invade, or enter with any armed force, or in any hostile or offensive manner into the territory of any native, independent prince or State in India except upon intelligence", that, "such prince or state is about to attack or make war upon"[159] the Company's territories or independent princes. Pitt's 'India Act of 1784', cautions the Company against making "treaty to defend or guaranty either to declare war or commence hostilities, or enter into any treaty for making war, against any of the country princes or states in India"[160]. Yet, the imperial attitude of the home Government did never waver from its goal of getting free trading rights in the country politically subjugated than left to Indian Rulers. The commercial attitude, thus, in course of time, was replaced by imperial ambitions[161] and before the close of the eighteenth century the English in India swang into direct action. The preservation of the British territorial possessions in India was never objected to, and the primary objection too gradually mellowed down at the realisation of the immense prospects opened up by the new acquisitions. Important persons of the Company were called back from their services on occasions for their abuse of power; the Parliamentarians had lashed out at the cruel behaviour of the Government's representatives in India on several occasions; the British public became indignant at the Company's various activities in the country, but no intention of withdrawing from India was ever shown by the home Government. On the contrary, it met all demands for men and money and war materials needed by the Company in building up the empire which was never forced upon them.

The secret of British success thus lay greatly in the policy of understanding that remained unraptured throughout between the Company and its Directors at home. Besides, there were other causes contributing in no less degree to their success. The English, for instance, were superior to their Indian counterparts in both arms and military tactics. The defeat of the French made them supreme power on the Indian waters. Unlike the Indian powers, the Company maintained a strict discipline among its rank and file—both civil and military; a strong financial position enabled the Company to keep its soldiers regularly paid while troops under many of the Indian Rulers went unpaid for months. The last important factor contributing to the success of the Egnlish was their religious tolerance. Unlike the Portuguese, they never interfered with the religious faiths and beliefs of the people, majority of whom were constituted by the Hindus and the Muslims[162]. As a result, the common people had little to lose under the English rule during that period when anarchy and constant wars among the rival Indian Rulers had already made life of the common people utterly miserable.

The rise of European settlements in India beginning in 1500 A.D., with the establishment of the first Portuguese Factory at Calicut, ended ultimately in the subjugation of the country by the English within the succeeding three centuries. Such a political change is closely linked up with the course of urbanisation during that period. The European settlements added a new dimension to Indian urbanisation.

The Europeans brought with them a different sense of urban life which found expression in the buildings and the other constructions as well as in the layout of the settlements they established or reconstructed. The Portugese influence remained confined to the western coast and the State of Goa is a living example of this where most of the churches, both old and new, have preserved the architectural beauty till today. The French Pondicherry was built on a different plan, with straight and wide roads, with buildings in rectangular blocks interspersed with public gardens. The Dutch Negapatam was neatly laidout with squares and characteristic canals. But compared to all these foreign influences, that of English is much more significant in introducing new elements in the style of architecture and overall get-up of the towns.

The progress of English settlements in India makes an interesting study. At the beginning of the eighteenth century the English society was mainly confined to four principal settlements — namely, Madras (Fort St. George), Calcutta (Fort William), Bombay and Surat. Except Surat, all the remaining three towns were established at new sites and these small settlements were already becoming nuclei of Indian towns where Indian merchants settled for trade and security. Having, rather, a free-hand in building these settlements, the English tried their best to make these towns an exact replica of English towns at home country. This is most clearly observed in the architecture of that time where "the classical style was imported bodily"[163]. The gardens were similarly the exact imitations of English gardens then in vogue in England.

With increase in the size of the settlements, the internal spatial arrangement of the towns became more marked. The towns came to be divided into two distinct quarter — the White and the Black Towns, with garden houses of the English in the suburbs. In Calcutta, for instance, after 1757 such garden houses ran up and down the bank of the river from Barrackpore to Garden Reach,[164] each remaining, though not geographically, but socially distinct. The distinction was very sharp in both Madras and Calcutta, but was absent in Bombay due, perhaps, to "its royal origin"[165]. These cities, with White and Black quarters, Esplanades, Golf Links, etc., introduced something entirely non-Indian to the Indian cities of the time. The classical distinction of White and Black towns gradually gave place to the origin of 'Civil Lines' in many of the principal Indian Cities at a later age, while true replica of English towns emerged in the form of Hill Stations all over the country with typical residential buildings, hotels, restaurants, market-places including showroom facilities, the Mall, the Gardens and the Public Schools offering British system of education. Thus, the whole atmosphere in such towns breathed an English air. Introduction of the exotic style of architecture, adopted on a much larger scale by the well-to-do section of the Indians in the construction of buildings, whether public or private, and the emergence of Hill stations were the two most important contributions made by the European Settlements to Indian Urbanisation. This change did not, however, begin till about the middle of the nineteenth century. Besides, the psychological change of this nature was a slow one, restricted in nature, remaining confined generally to the large urban centres and there too a mixture of Indian and English style had never gathered sufficient momentum for an overall Europeanisation of the Indian Urban scene anywhere in the country.

But the real change took place elsewhere and it was here that the English settlements accomplished an historic task. The tide of urban development took a new turn; growth of the three coastal (or near-coastal) cities of Calcutta, Bombay and Madras made themselves the principal focus of future urban development in the country. The three centres, acquiring gradually more and more political and economic power, reshaped the urban history and the tide originating at these places in course of time reached farther and farther inland. Before their coming into existence. Delhi or Agra, as Imperial cities, dominated the scene and all other centres looked upon them as a source of inspiration. The spirit of urbanisation coursing down from the Imperial capital, made a different impact on the urban development in the country. The rise of the coastal cities changed this course in the reverse direction; instead of being from the centre coastward it became henceforward from the coast inward. At the same time, the predominance of commerce over political functions as the major factor in determining the size of urban settlements was established once for all. From that time urban future of India, for a considerable period, became closely bound-up with the activities of these ports.

Economic Transition and Urban Stagnation

The rise of the European settlements culminating in the territorial acquisition of the country by the English definitely had its impact on the course of urbanisation. Nearly a hundred years of complete anarchy and absence of rule keeping the country divided into hundreds of political camps could not be conducive to urban development. The war-machineries, whether of the Indian chiefs or of the English, thrived and operated from the towns and cities, when the latter were also the principal targets of the warring factions. Hence, they had to exist. No party wanted them fully destroyed, though partly damaged they could be, as they provided the footing for future action. The continued warfare did, indeed, curtail the economic activities of these centres as one can imagine, where not only safe traffic was out of question, but also the demands of goods for transport fell off considerably. The situation did not improve either during the later years when British rule was permanently established in India, giving peace and security of life. Towns and cities long famed for their specialised products faced a continually shrinking market; the entire industrial structure crashed down under stiff competition from imported goods; the activities of the commercial centres, including numerous ports, greatly slackened. All these spelt disaster for Indian economy which naturally slowed down urban progress considerably. A brief review of the situation leading to the slowing down of urban activities in India will bring out the facts in true perspective.

The political unrest of the country beginning from the closing years of Aurangzev's rule soon gave way to a virtual chaos. The incessant wars drained the exchequer heavily, and the bankrupt rulers made still heavier demands on their subjects. The natural consequence was a complete papuerisation of the common people. Political disorder, the loss of peace and security severely disrupted the economic life of the country. The Court could no longer patronise the industries producing quality goods both for the internal market and export. Even before the death of Aurangzeb, industries had started declining so much so that the East India Company could not procure sufficient amount of cloth for export during the years 1690-98[166]. The general deterioration of the industries was also due to the gradual disappearance of trading facilities. The roads and rivers did not remain safe for the movement of goods; prowlers were most active in the absence of a strong administration. The rise of the Maratha Power in the middle of the seventeenth century and the disappearance of Portuguese authority from the western coast gradually brought port activities to a standstill. The venue of trade shifted to the eastern coast, but there also the constant rivalry between different foreign trading powers slackened the course of commerce. Like industry and commerce, agriculture was equally hard-hit. The farmers no longer enjoyed the benign care of the rulers. Remedial measures for agricultural improvement as adopted by different Kings and Emperors in different periods were talks of the past. Besides, frequent outbreaks of famines and the occasional failure of seasonal rains caused untold miseries to the farming population.

Nevertheless, the agricultural and industrial position of the country was still enviable in respect of the speciality of her products. In fact, India held an important place in the world for her industrial products till about 1813[167]. Agriculture was, no doubt, the predominant occupation of the majority of the people. Yet, a large section of the population found employment in the industries, mostly agro-based, which were varied and extensive in character. Robert Orme, visiting India between 1743 to 1760 observes: "On the Coromandal. and in the province of Bengal, when at some distance from the high road, or a principal town, it is difficult to find a village in which every man, woman and child, is not employed in making a piece of cloth"[168]. Textiles, comprising both cotton and silk, were still the principal products of her industries, and Bengal had the most extnesive market. The Royal Court of Delhi used to have all its linen and silk from Bengal, while silk, both raw and manufactured, cotton textiles, sugar, opium, grain, etc., were exported from Bengal to Arabia, Persia and the European countries, the latter making largest investments here[169]. "The entire econo of Bengal was", in fact, "dominated by the needs of the European Market in 1760s, 1770s, and 1780s"[170]. Besides, there was the inland trade.

Textiles held the pride of place among all the manufactures and was most extensively developed in the country, producing an immense range of quality goods. According to Francis Hamilton, spinning and weaving were the great national industry of India next after agriculture[171]. From all accounts available, spinning and weaving of cotton was best developed in Bengal. Weaving was done in almost every village of Bengal and almost every district had its own speciality. The production of finer and valuable materials was concentrated in and around towns and cities. The prime position, however, was taken by Dacca, with her products of exceedingly high quality, till then unrivalled in the world. It was famous for different grades of muslins. The Bikrampur and Sonargaon paraganas of Dacca District produced such high quality muslins that those were sometimes sold at four to five hundred rupees a piece[172]. It was a great puzzle to Orme to see "how works of such extraordinary niceness"[173] could be produced in Bengal by such ordinary implements. According to him, the products of Dacca made specially for the Royal Household were of "such wonderful fineness as to exceed ten times the price of any linen permitted to be made for Europeans, or any one else in the

Kingdom"[174]. Among other important centres, Santipur in Nadia District produced a variety of plain muslins; Midnapur specialised particularly in dyeing, while Chandrakona and Khirpai in the same district excelled in the production of both coloured and plain muslins. Malda town and its vicnity had 4000 looms, specialising in thin plain muslins and calico. Cotton manufactures alone fetched about Rs. 1,674,000 a year[175]. Birbhum was famous for her coarse calico. Cotton spinning was the principal household industry of the womenfolk of Dinajpur district, turning out yarn to the value of Rs. 1,165,000 a year[176]. Some other centres with their specialisation in plain white muslin were Haripal, Golaghat and Farashdanga in Hooghly District and Baranagar in the District of 24-Parganas[177]. The importance of Bengal products can be ascertained from the fact that, towards the end of the 19th century, the East India Company had as many as nineteen commercial residences in the Bengal Presidency, namely, Dacca, Harial (Rajshahi Dt), Kumarkhali, Rangpur, Rampur—Boalia, Malda, Cossimbazar, Jangipur, Santipur, Haripal Golaghat, Radhanagar (Midnapore Dt), Midnapore, Khirpal, Sonamukhi (Bankura Dt), Chittagong, Lakhipur, Patna and Benares to which later on were added two more [178]. The total value of the cotton piece-goods exported between June 1797—May 1798 from the port of Calcutta alone was over 8,171,000 sicca rupees[179]*. The economic survey of Dr. Francis Hamilton made between 1800 and 1807, throws more light on the importance as well as the widespread nature of this industry. According to Hamilton, Cotton spinning was entirely done by the women and in the District of Bihar alone there were 330,426 heads engaged in spinning; number of weavers was also large and the total value of the spun thread and manufactures stood at Rs. 2,367,277 and Rs. 540,000 respectively[181]. In Sahabad District, spinning employed 159,500 heads, producing thread to the value of Rs. 1,250,000 a year and weaving was done in 7025 houses on 7950 looms[182]. Bhagalpur District had 160,000 women employed in cotton spinning and 7279 looms engaged in cotton weaving[183]. There were 10,000 looms producing coarse cloth in Purnea District worth at Rs. 1,089,500 and 3500 looms turned out finer cloth[184]. Fine cotton fabrics were also produced outside the Province of Bengal, such as

---

F.No. 100 Sicca Rupees=166 current rupees.[180]

in Patna and Gaya Districts, Benares and Allahabad, Jaunpur, Orissa, Surat, Gujarat, Malwa, Khandesh, Mysore and the northern parts of Madras Presidency[185].

Silk was another speciality of Bengal. Province Bengal silk used to be sent to Surat, Mirzapur, Benares, Nagpur and Poona; from Mirzapur, it went further to Multan and Lahore. Before 1770, the total export of silk from Murshidabad to surat alone was around 13,000 to 20,000 maunds* a year[186]. During Aliverdi's time (1740-1756), the customs's records at Murshidabad show an entry of Rs. 70 lakhs in raw silk, excluding European investment[187] which, in Bengal, amounted to ten million rupees in 1777 and Rs. 10,959,130 in 1793, comprising Rs. 2,586,847 in raw silk and Rs. 6,768,408 in raw silk and cotton piece-goods respectively[188]. The production of raw silk was mainly concentrated in eight centres *viz.*, Kumarkhali, Rangpur, Rampur-Boalia, Malda, Jangipur, Cossimbazar, Ganutia (Birbhum Dt) and Radhanagar of which Rampur-Boalia was the most important centre in the whole province. It was also the largest market for raw silk, having inexhaustible supplies. An idea about the size of some these silk filatures may seem interesting. Ganutia Factory, for instance, employed nearly 4000 workers and in the Kumarkhali Filatures the number of workers was 151,185 in 1812, 314,925 in 1813 and 289,769 in 1814[189].

Among the other notable industries were sugar, indigo, saltpetre and opium, each having significant place in external trade. The cultivation of sugarcane was extensively carried on in the area "from Benares to Rangpore; and from the borders of Assam to Cuttack"[190]. Till 1813, sugar was the third most important industry of Bengal. Almost every district made sugar and the important centres of production were Rangpur; Birbhum, Santipur, Haripal and Radhanagar. Outside Bengal, the industry was mainly concentrated in Benares, Patna, Shahbad, Tirhut, etc. In 1756, the total export of sugar from Bengal alone amounted to 50,000 mounds. The trade, however, slumped since 1805 with the entry of Mauritius sugar into the British market.

Indigo was another important article of export to the European Market. The industry flourished most in Gujarat and Agra. But the

* 1 Maund = 37 Kilograms

trade suffered a serious set-back, stopping altogether from 1724, due to competition from other quarters, *i.e.* W.Indies and America. It did not, however, take long for the latter sources to dry up and the English were compelled again to look upon the Indian market as a source of supply. From about 1780 onwards the East India Company took up[191] the cultivations of indigo plants in a serious manner and in no time the cultivation extended from Dacca to Delhi[192]. Large-scale production of indigo soon followed and the export, beginning in about 1790 increased to nearly 9 million lbs a year in 1829 form all the English factories established in Bengal Presidency[193]. The industry was highly concentrated in Bengal Presidency, and in 1830 there were about one thousand factories flourishing best in Pabna, Faridpur, Nadia and Jessore when practically no district was left without some manufacturing plants[194]. In Bihar, Tirhut was the most important producing centre followed by Purnea, Shahabad and Bhagalpur. Benares was another important centre of production. Some amount of indigo was also produced in Madras and Bombay. The total value of the export stood at £ 3,600,000 on its arrival in England[195].

Saltpetre, another important item of commerce, was in great demand among the European nations as the chief ingredient for the manufacture of gunpowder. During the Mughul period, Bihar was the most important producer and Patna was the chief market for this product of strategic value[196]. The factories concentrated at Fatwa (near Patna), Mau (Darbhangha Dt), Chhapra and Singhia (near Hazipur in Muzaffarpur Dt) were run under the supervision of the main factory at Patna[197]. In 1758, the East India Company secured a monopoly of saltpetre trade in Bengal[198] as a result of which all the manufacturers in Bengal and Bihar came under the direct control of the Company. The other foreign traders had to depend on the mercy of the English for a share in the trade of saltpetre and that too was allowed only in peace time. In Bengal, Malda was the principal producer of saltpetre; other important places of manufacture were Benares, Kanpur, Etawah and Lucknow. It was also manufactured in the Northern Circars and Mysore. Between 1764-76 and 1783-93, the Company sold 295,673 bags (591,346 mds.) and 331,301 bags (662,602 mds.) of saltpetre respectively in the European Market[199].

According to Firminger, trading in opium was one of the principal source of revenue for the East India Company[200] which established its monopoly in the trade of opium in 1761. Bihar was the largest producer, and the factories were mostly confined to the Districts of Patna and Gaya. The Bihar factories supplied the bulk of the production, amounting to about 8000 mds. in 1808-09[201]. Opium factories did also exist in Benares, with an annual production around 1500 mds[202]. Rangpur in Bengal was another important producer. China was the chief buyer, taking 4560 out of 4621½ chests in 1808-09, the rest going to Malaya and the East Indies. Small quantities went to England for medicinal purposes. In 1814-15, the total value of opium exported to China amounted to 7,171,000 sicca rupees[203].

A brief outline of the principal industries engaging the interest of the foreign trading companies does not exhaust the list of the trading items. As observed earlier, more articles were on the list of export, ranging from food grains to luxury goods. Initially, the immediate concern of the East India Company was to obtain a virtual monopoly of the trade between India and the foreign countries and thus to act as the principal supplier of Indian goods to both the European and the Far-East Asian market. The prevailing attitude being so did not, for a long time, collide with the economic prosperity of the country; on the contrary, progress in agriculture and industry helped the growing trade of the Company. But once territorially established, the outlook underwent a drastic change. Two important events of contrasting nature taking place almost simultaneously created a new situation for the changed outlook. The first one is the Industrial Revolution from 1760 onwards, making a start in the home country, and the second is the declaration of Independence by America in 1776 created a changed atmosphere. The significance of the Industrial Revolution lay in an increasing demand for markets abroad for the machine-made products of the home industries and this became irresistible with advancing time. On the other hand, prior to her independence America was a principal source of raw materials and also was one of the principal markets for British goods. The declaration of Independence closed the door permanently for this two-way traffic. They had, therefore, to look to the East instead of West for both raw materials and market. Even the newly opened colonies in the West Indies could not meet the multifaceted needs of the British industries. India, with her fabulous wealth of resources and her vast population providing the largest market of the time, fulfilled the two-sided needs admirably. The time for exploitation could not be more opportune than this. The British were already politically established on the subcontinent and it was easy from them to take any raw material they chose and force upon the Indians machine-made goods even if they were of poorer quality. At the same time, for increasing the marketability of the inferior goods it was necessary that the hand-made Indian quality products should be completely withdrawn from the market. This could not be done without the closure of Indian industries. Before long the rulers set on the task of methodical elimination of every branch of Indian industries which bore any threat of competition to the products of their machinal counterparts at the home country. It sound rather puzzling that in the process of elimination the English lost perpetually a vast market, at least in Europe, for the Indian classicial manufactures. Apparently it may seem quite inconsistent with the British merchant genius. Even if Indian industries had been allowed to stay, it was not difficult for the rulers to divert the entire product to the channels of export to foreign countries and thereby earn the total profits. The British Government in India was not entirely blind to such a likely business prospect; what restrained and compelled it to act differently was, perhaps, the deep fear of British industrialise in losing the market for their coarser goods in the face of a competition from much finer and durable products of Indian origin.

The decline and complete ruin of the Indian industries thus became a matter of time. The course was not abrupt, but it was systematic and unfaltering.

As early as 1769, the Directors of the EIC (East India Company) prohibited by a mandate the work of the silk-winders outside the English factories in India[204]. Silk weaving came to be greatly discouraged from that time which had its desired effect in the ultimate decline of silk manufactures. A series of important discoveries made between 1779-86 put the Lancashire Cotton Textile Industry in a stronger position to compete with Indian products. British manufactures put more and more pressure on the home government for stopping import of Indian goods and finer yarn; instead, they wanted imports of raw cotton increased[205]. As early as in 1700 and 1720, use of Indian cotton and silk products in Britain were prohibited by law passed by the Parliament[206]. The import of those articles into England at that time by the EIC was entirely meant for the European market where they were in great demand[207]. Legislative prohibition, barring entry of Indian goods into British market, high tariffs, the gradually tightening control on the weavers by various Government Regulations, the destruction of the Indian shipping, constant propaganda and the Charter Act of 1813 allowing British private traders in India the rights for free trade and purchase of landed property, besides preparing the Indian market for British machine-made products, were some of the means that paved the way for the extinction of Indian handicrafts.

In fact, the Charter Act of 1813 sounded the death knell for the Indian industries. Since the opening of the 19th century, the Indian industries had been maintaining a stifling existence. The Charter, giving unlimited right to the private British traders and free merchants and at the same time putting an end to the monopoly of the EIC in foreign trade, opened a new chapter. The private traders being "better salesmen for the merchandise of industrialised Britain"[207] were bent on destroying the Indian industries and convert India into one of the "depots of raw materials and markets for finished goods"[208]. The textile industry had already declined. In 1818, muslin had been omitted from the list of goods imported to the European market. The Company's factory at Dacca was closed down and the drastic reduction in the price of British cotton products finally ousted the Indian goods from the market[209]. From 1813 onwards, the concerted action of the free traders in preparing the Indian market for British goods succeeded greatly in thwarting any attempt of he Indian handicrafts to survive. The Charter Act of 1833, giving British free traders greater opportunity and freedom, perpetually sealed the fate of Indian industries and "the period witnessed the decline, and in some cases the end, of all the industrial arts of India"[210]. By the time of Indian Mutiny (1857), the famous Cotton Textile Industry had already degenerated and shrunk to a village craft[211].

No disaster could have shaken India's economy more greatly in any period than the decay of the Textile Industry. For centuries India held her place in the international market for her textiles which sold at high price for their exquisite qualities. It was, in true sense of the term, the national industry, most widely developed, giving employment to millions. This collapse almost became symbolic of the collapse of India's industrial supremacy enjoyed hitherto over a very long period. Whether the destruction of Indian industries was a natural course of action on the part of British industrialists is far from consideration here. What sticks out as a fact is that, Indian industries with their basis of handmade products, could not complete with the machine-made products of Britain. Mechanisation of the industries, beginning with the Cotton Textile, was soon to spread to other industries and the products of ordinary quality needed a stable market free of any competition. The whole of Europe was soon to follow this course. Besides, there is also another point to be judged. The ruin of Indian industries took place mostly in the production of high quality goods. The disappearance of the great patrons in the rulers of Indian Kingdoms greatly restricted the market. The closure of the European and Middle East markets did the final damage. In spite of that it will be an exaggeration of the actual truth to say that the traditional industries were completely ruined and disappeared for all time. In fact, some of them went out of the scene altogether, no doubt, but, many others substantially shrank in size, range of productions and worked in miniature forms in isolated manner. The hand-made silk of Bengal, Kashmir, Uttar Pradesh, South India, the hand-made cotton products of Bengal surviving till this date are remnants of the old houses. The import of British cotton goods, beginning some time about the 1780 rose to £ 18,400,000 a year in 1809[212]. In 1813, Calcutta alone exported cotton goods valued at two million pounds to England; seventeen years later, in 1830, Calcutta imported machine-made goods from England of the same value. Besides, woollen goods, copper, lead, iron, glass, earthenware, etc., were also imported. The entry duty of British manufactures at Calcutta port was 2½ per cent on their actual price whereas it ranged upto 400 per cent for Indian goods on entering England[213]. Internal trade similarly strained under the burden of heavy internal duties imposed by the EIC. According to Lord Ellenborough, in 1835 cotton goods, manufactured in India and consumed in the country, were subjected to a duty of 17½ per cent as against 2½ per cent paid by English cotton goods imported into India; leather goods and sugar had to pay a duty of 15 per cent each, and altogether not less than 235 different articles of trade were subjected to such high rates of inland duties[214] at different posts on their transhipment from one place to another.

Slump in trade as a consequence of the decay and ruin of Indian industries in combination with heavy taxation was directly reflected in the economy of the country, and urban development did not go unscathed. Towns and cities thriving on industrial and commercial activities felt the blow more severely than others making out a different living. It is true that a large part of the industrial activities were confined to rural areas. But as stated earlier, the industrial manufactures, whether textiles, sugar, saltpetre, or other luxury items made of wood, metal, leather or precious to semi-precious stones, etc., were made to urban tastes and meant for the urban markets or for sale abroad; rural life as too simple and too poor to afford them. Manufactures needed by the urban markets, whether inland or abroad, therefore, naturally preferred urban locations, and innumerable towns and cities bear evidence to that effect. Where the industries were located in villages, they were not far removed from important urban centres. The effect of industrial slump was more severely felt in the urban centres than the rural places as people engaged in industrial pursuits in the villages had it, in many cases, as their part-time occupation, or, even if it was a whole-time occupation, they could revert to farming at times of dire distress. This was not possible for industrial workers or people engaged in trade in the urban centres. Loss of occupation threw them out of the only means of living. This meant large-scale unemployment, impoverishing urban life as a whole and leading to urban depopulation.

Urban India at the Beginning of the Nineteenth Century

Walter Hamilton writing his 'Description of Hindostan' in 1820, refers to the towns and cities of India existing at the beginning of the nineteenth century. In all, he has referred to little over fifteen hundred towns and cities. According to his account, the Provinces of Gujarat and Bengal had the largest number of urban centres, having about 138 and 118 respectively, followed by the Provinces of Madras (116), Malwa (82), Aurangabad (79), Agra (78), Bijapur (75), etc., the smallest number being in the Province of Kashmir (5). Majority of the urban centres were located in South India, and only about one-third were in the North Indian Plains. Altogether, sixteen centres are shown to have had a population of over a hundred-thousand each, and among them at least two, Benares and Calcutta, hit the mark of half-a-million. Eight of them were in South India and the remaining eight were in North India. They were as follows, showing their population within the brackets.

1. Benares (600,000); 2. Calcutta (500,000); 3. Surat (450,000); 4. Patna (312,000); 5. Madras (300,000); 6. Lucknow (200,000); 7. Hyderabad (200,000); 8. Dacca (180,000); 9. Bombay (170,000); 10. Delhi (150,000); 11. Moorshidabad (150,000); 12 Poona (120,000); 13. Nagpur (100,000); 14. Baroda (100,000); 15. Ahmedabad (100,000); 16. Cashmere (100,000).

The validity of the population figures given by Hamilton is not beyond question. The figures obtained by him from contemporary records were not the results of a systematic census, made at any particular time at all the places. In giving the figures of population of these cities Hamilton admits in the 'Introduction' of his book that the estimate "composed from a variety of documents must be considered only as in approximation to reality"[215]. On a closer examination it appears that the sources of the figures are not same in all the cases and different figures are given by the author for the same city at different places of his 'Description'. For instance, in the case of Benares an enumeration was made in 1803, placing the number of permanent inhabitants of the city at 582,000, instead of shown by him in the 'Introduction' as 600,000; the population of Calcutta has been placed by him at 500,000, assumed as "a tolerably correct approximation of the real number"[216] on the basis of calculations made between 1802 to 1810; for the population figure for Surat another assumption based on too higher but contradictory estimates made in 1796 and thereabout is presented[217]; the population of Poona shown as 120,000 in the 'Introduction' and that of Ahmedabad are similarly based on assumptions; the population figures shown for Patna and Murshidabad are also examples of another type of assumption where the number of houses existing then in each city has been multiplied by an average number of persons living in a house; in the case of Delhi and Hyderabad Hamilton has "reasons to believe"[218] or "suppose"[219] that the population varied between 150,000 and 200,000 in Delhi, though shown as 150,000 in the 'Introduction', and 200,000 at Hyderabad; the population of both Lucknow and Madras are rough estimates for 1800[220] and 1794[221] respectively; the population of Dacca estimated by the City Magistrate in 1801 was shown to exceed 200,000 though elsewhere Hamilton put it at 180,000; for Bombay a census was conducted by the Government in 1816, placing the population at 161,550[222] instead of 1,70,000 as mentioned by Hamilton in the 'Introduction'; for each of the three other cities, *viz.*, Nagpur[223], Baroda[224] and Srinagar or Cashemere[225], Hamilton simply mentions that the population was estimated at 100,000.

Apparently the figures do not appear to be fully convincing. In that case they should be either an over-estimate or an under-estimate. The chance for over-estimation is quite slim in view of the fact that the estimates were made by the Europeans at a time when they were already settled in India. As rulers of the country they had no special fascination for Indian towns and cities to show an inflated figure of population where size of urban centres indicate the rate of urban development. It would have been natural for them to make an under-estimation, as has often been done by European writers in those days in describing the urban life of India. Besides, inflated figures would have given rise to greater complications, as taxes actually realised from permanent residents would not tally with the actuals. There is at least one point going against any possibility of over-estimation : that is the manner of calculation where the total number of urban houses are multiplied by an average number of persons living in a house. On two instances the number of persons have been taken as 6 (Patna)[226] and 5 (Murshidabad)[227] respectively to arrive at the intended figure. Such a house-density, being normal even today, may be rather an under-estimation for that time when joint family ties were much stronger than today. The method, being direct and simple, is likely to have had been the basis of estimating the population of other cities, though not clearly stated by Hamilton in many other cases. Instead, he has referred to only the number of houses in some more towns and cities without giving the number of the total population. This, perhaps, is indicative of the prevalent practice of calculating the total number of houses for giving an idea about the actual population residing in the urban centres. Reliability of such a method depends on the sincerity of the counting authority. Since there is no way of judging this, it is safer to accept the figures nearing actuals, leaning towards an under, than an over-estimation.

The existence of at least sixteen cities including two half-a-million centres on the list, as recorded by Hamilton, at the opening of the nineteenth century is indicative of high urban development in a country which had passed through more than a century of extreme political turmoil when kingdoms and empires had fallen to dust, and the entire economic system became completely jeopardized under the pressure of intriguing interests. Peace and prosperity of the country had been at peril through the preceding centureis on several occasions during the Muslim rule by internal warfare and attacks of the marauding invaders. But they were of limited nature both in time and space; nothing was equal to what happened in the following century, witnessing the dissolution of the Mughal Empire and the establishment of British rule in India. Urban centres surviving such a difficult period speak of their intrinsic strength acquired through long period of sustained activity in the economic field of the country. Not that the cities thrived well, maintaining a flourishing career in every case; in fact, the signs of decay were already registered by many of the cities at the opening of the century.

A close scrutiny of the cities of this period make some important revelations in this regard. Of the sixteen cities, four are of most ancient origin. They are Benares, Patna, Delhi and Surat; another three, namely, Nagpur, Srinagar and Lucknow can claim antiquity if not equal, yet of considerable period; Hyderabad, Dacca, Murshidabad, Baroda, Ahmedabad, and Poona came into existence during the medieval period while the last three cities — Calcutta, Madras and Bombay — were the products of British colonisation in India. It is highly significant to note that in spite of being one of the earliest in origin. Benares held the most leading place among the cities of India in this period, containing over six hundred thousand permanent residents. According to Hamilton, such a large population is the result of "the most undisturbed tranquility"[228] enjoyed by the city from the time of its coming under British rule in 1781 since when the population had increased continually and "the buildings having expanded to the neighbouring villages"[229]. Peace led to prosperity, no doubt, but it could not raise the population figure so high within the space of a few decades if other factors had no part to play in contributing to its fabulous growth. The basic factors were its age-old industries producing goods of inimitable quality, its fame built-up over centuries as a principal trading centre for goods collected from a rich hinterland, its position in the country as a leading centre of learning and, above all, the place held by it in the minds of the Hindus as one of the most sacred centres of India. The multi-functional character had naturally made Benares a very large, populous city for centuries and, situated a long way from the passage of the invaders, it did not suffer much during any earlier period of its history. The peace offered by the British might have helped in keeping its activities undisturbed, but nothing more than that.

The third and fourth position among the largest cities of India at this time were held respectively by Surat and Patna. Like Benares. Both of them had maintained a distinguished career through centuries, holding that position almost unimpaired irrespective of vicissitudes of fortune. Surat, in spite of losing importance as a consequence of the drying up of its river during the preceding two centuries, was the leading commercial centre. Even in 1773, Surat, containing about 450,000 inhabitants, was more populous than London and Paris[230]. Patna, the capital of Kingdom and Empires, degraded politically, yet as a trading and industrial centre it regained its earlier status of having an eminent position among the prominent cities of the country. Unlike these three cities, Delhi, however, was in a decayed condition, with ruins covering an area of about twenty square miles. The loss of its status as the once Imperial Capital dealt a severe blow to its industry as well as commerce.

These four examples alone forcefully bring out the vigour of Indian urban life, its unique stamina and the power of survival. The cities mentioned above have stood the challenge of time through few thousand years of their existence. Kingdoms and Empires have vanished, the rulers have changed; interests of the people have swayed time and again when the vanquished cities have become the targets of pillagers sweeping them with death and destruction; normalcy of life had disappeared on such occasions threatening it with complete annihilation. But again and again cities have revived, and keeping the life-cycle uninterrupted they have proved their power of resistance, their invulnerable character, the unfathomable capacity of regeneration. All this stems from the country's rich economic heritage. The background of this sustained, continuous, urban development has been provided by an agricultural surplus which naturally has released a section of the people to work on the agricultural produces, thus giving rise to secondary occupations. Such activities always needed concentration of people at selected points or places where the products from the fields could be easily collected—that is, by means of water and land routes. The real origin of many of the craftsmanships involved in the working out of different types of essential to luxury goods from the agricultural products, and later on from natural products may be traced to rural areas. But for their perfection, standardisation, improvement in quality as well as in variety through exchange of ideas and experience different environments were needed where, under an organised system, the craftsmen could be assured of a constant supply of raw materials and devote their time exclusively to the production of various goods of higher order. The products of the secondary occupation brought markets into existence; the surplus in the manufactured products gradually extended the market from the confines of the place of production to other place of consumption. The activities related to the collection of raw materials and distribution of finished products gradually gave rise to tertiary occupations. The origin of different types of occupations, making division of labour more clearly defined, made the society more and more complex in nature and this could not happen in the absence of an organised system holding power as well as imagination for building up the entire system of settlements completely separate from the rural ones. These were the urban settlements that gradually took form on the basis of a surplus economy. The capital-cities, primarily taking origin for serving administrative needs, naturally were the first to attract people released from the rural areas. Once established, the cities, whether capital or non-capital in origin, continued to function and did not cease unless forced by extraordinary circumstances. The circumstances putting an end to many of the cities in the course of centuries were more economic and political, than natural. For instance, disappearance of a Kingdom naturally led to the decline and ultimate death of a city; again, the loss of political status, enjoyed by any city, curtailed its economic freedom and market, and the withdrawal of the Court's protection after the Kingdom was overthrown meant its complete decay in many cases; shifting of the seat of administration or change in the course of commerce did also equally affect the life of many cities, gradually pushing them into insignificance. Unlike political or economic factors, natural causes, like change in the river courses, drying up of riverbeds or floods, etc., were much less responsible for destroying cities in India. However strange it may sound, one cannot find many instances of important cities having disappeared like Mohenjo-daro due only to natural calamities.

Among the other cities, at least five showed similar signs of decay. They were Lucknow, Dacca, Murshidabad, Ahmedabad and Srinagar. All of them had been capital cities of independent kingdoms. The earlier prosperity was greatly derived from the status enjoyed. The introduction of British rule, depriving them of their political status, cut at the base of their foundation, thereby reducing the economic importance into insignificance. The removal of the capital of Oudh from Fyzabad to Lucknow in 1775 turned the latter into "one of the largest and richest towns of India"[231] with a population "roughly estimated at 300,000"[232] in 1700. But the rapid growth did not continue for a long time; the establishment of British rule and the consequent "waning splendour of the Nabob's Court"[233] hit it hard with a decrease in its population. The city of Dacca, spread over a large area, sprawling on the river bank for six miles[234] was not its oldself. Judged from the "magnificence of its ruins, such as bridges, brick causeways, mosques, caravan-serai, gates, palaces, and gardens, now overgrown with jungle"[235], the city was at the peak of its prosperity during the second half of the seventeenth century. The decline set in with the gradual weakening of the Moghul Empire; and this was further speeded up by the abolition of the Provincial Council established by the British Government in 1774 and the subsequent transfer of administrative functions to different districts[236]. The transfer of the capital from Dacca to Murshidabad in 1704 made it the Metropolis of Bengal, extending for eight miles on both sides of the river Bhagirathi. The decline of Murshidabad began in 1757 when the Nawab of Bengal was defeated by the English, and the city never recovered its old position. In the first quarter of the nineteenth century "the thick, impenetrable and yearly increasing jungle"[237] had swallowed up a large part of the city even though it was still then a place of great inland traffic"[238]. Ahmedabad, being one of the four largest cities in Jahangir's time and "from being one of the largest capitals in the east.... had contracted in 1780 to five miles and three quarters in circumference", while "tottering minarets, ruinous palaces, mouldering aqueducts and caravan-serais"[239] spread over an area of about thirty miles in circumference speak of its early grandeur. Since the fall of the Mughal Empire, the city changed hands many times and the loss of political status as capital on the one hand, coupled with constant wars on the other, led to the deterioration of its trade and commerce. The effect was continuous decay. Srinagar also was a declining city at this time due to similar reasons.

In contrast, the really flourishing cities of this period were Calcutta, Madras and Bombay, and according to Hamilton's account, the first two were occupying respectively the second and fifth position among the largest cities of India in the first quarter of the nineteenth century. It is highly interesting to note that, each of them owed its origin to English activities in the country and before a century elapsed Calcutta emerged as the second largest city, Madras fifth and Bombay ninth in position among the leading cities of the country. They rose to that eminence from an insignificant beginning and while the other big cities, belonging to the list of the big sixteen, had a long career spreading over a few thousands years in certain cases, those three of English origin were the youngest of the lot. What is really striking is that, though born in a disturbed period and careering through a difficult time, the cities of English origin gained in size and importance when during the same period most of the rest had suffered heavy losses in both political and economic status. The basic fact behind these contrasting results is not far to seek. The cities of English origin, acting as headquarters of British political and economic activities in India, were in a privileged position, enjoying a greater degree of freedom in functions and a greater amount of protection and care than the other cities. The prolonged political disturbances upsetting the economic life of other cities came to an end with the establishment of British rule over these cities, no doubt; but in no time it was replaced by a strong apathy of the rulers towards the revival of their economy in any large measure. The industries were discouraged; the market gradually shrank; the trade slowly passed hands from the local people to the English free traders. The result was disastrous. The cities degraded; the spectre of economic threat slowly depopulated them which can clearly be assumed from the shrinking size of many of these cities.

This, naturally, leads to the obvious conclusion that the cities, remaining in decayed condition at the beginning of the nineteenth century, were in better shape and position in the immediate or distant past, that is, before the installation of British power in India when they had a much greater amount of activity extending to various fields and, consequently, a larger population. Thus, the existence of only sixteen cities, each with a population of a hundred thousand or over, reveals the poverty of the urban scene. There is, of course, no way of giving an exact number of such cities existing prior to this period. It cannot be true that the reasons responsible for the degradation of cities like Delhi, Ahmedabad, Dacca, Murshidabad and Lucknow were not equally operative elsewhere. There are positive evidences to show that quite a number of cities had deteriorated from their earlier position of eminence. The city of Agra provides the most convincing example which, enjoying the status of an imperial capital during the Mughal period, had degenerated conspicuously during the following century, containing barely about 60,000 inhabitants, with extensive ruins all around at the first quarter of the nineteenth century. Lahore, though "still a town of considerable size"[240] in the early part of the nineteenth century, had been one of the most important and populous cities of the country in the seventeenth century. Vijayanagar, a great metropolis of the sixteenth century, was mostly in ruins[241]. Cambay, the sea-port of Ahmedabad during its flourishing days and one of the most important metropolices of India rising to that position from its trading activities going back to pre-historical period, had shrunk of an area of about three miles in circumference, representing "a collection of uninhabited streets, ruined mosques, and mouldering palaces"[242]. Among the other notable centres recording remarkable degree of retogression were Indore[243], Bijapur[244], Multan[245], Broach[246], Burhanpur[247], Elichpur[248], Coimbatore[249], Madurai[250] and many others of smaller stature. One cannot, however, be sure about each of them having actually attained the status of a larger city, housing over a hundred thousand inhabitants or more. But their fame as large and populous urban centres is beyond and dispute.

Without making the list long, it can be said with confidence that most of the cities commanding an eminent position for centuries were a poorer look at the opening of the nineteenth century. Instances, however, are not lacking about the decline or complete disappearance of cities in the earlier periods. But at no time such an end mass decline had taken place. The tremendous activity in trade and commerce, markets crowded by people of different nationalities of the world creating a cosmopolitan atmosphere, shops stuffed with goods of all descriptions from distant countries, beautiful palaces, magnificent structures of temples with their stores of treasures and colourful mosques adorning the city-scape, feverish speed of city's expansion into adjoining countryside, etc., giving a glimpse of the high pitch of urban dynamism and overflowing affluence were scarcely to be noticed in any part of the country. Urban proliferation became a myth; it was a period of urban stagnation. Though cities like Benares, Patna, Hyderabad were doing well, recording visible growth, most of the other cities and large towns maintained a stiffed existence.

The entire country groaning under the strain of internecine warfare, paying way for British domination in India, could not keep its urban prosperity unmolested where the entire economy was greatly shaken to its very foundation. To this was added an unsympathetic, almost hostile, attitude of the new rulers to the Indian industries which gradually languished under the pressure of unequal competition and forcible closure of foreign markets. At the time when Hamilton wrote his 'Description of Hindostan', the slump in industry had just begun. In all probability this could not have been so disastrous as to halt the progress of the cities immediately. The roots had started drying up long before that time. The installation of British Power in India, beginning as early as 1765, had a negative effect on the urban development in the country. The towns and cities hitherto acting as centres of political and economic activities of independent kingdoms lost their freedom of action. Their functions being restricted in many fields, the very purpose for which the cities existed became largely superfluous. The entire economy of the country was going through a devastating change necessary to serve the needs of the ruling power. The towns and cities had to fit in into this changing pattern. Their obligations and responsibilities were not the same as before. Their economic or political role was replaced by a role in general administration where most of the important towns and cities were converted into some time administrative headquarters of the British India. This meant a great curtailment of activities in a much wider field which quite naturally could not be conducive to keep on the normal growth unhampered. Decadence slowly crept into the urban life, making its toll high or low depending on circumstances.

The physical conditions of the important cities of this time give a strong impression about the general poverty of the urban scene. Even prosperous cities like Benares and Patna were no exception to this rule. In Benares, over twelve thousand houses were built of stone or brick, from one to six stories high[251], but still a greater number were mud houses and the streets every where were extremely narrow.

REFERENCES

1. Gardner, Brian, *The East India Company,* Rupert Hart-Davis, London, 1971, p. 18.
2. Danvers, Frederick Charles, *The Portuguese in India,* Frank Cass & Co. Ltd., London, 1966 (2nd Ed.) in 2 Vols. p. 27 (I).
3. Napier, William, *Lands of Spice & Treasure, Encyclopedia of Discovery and Exploration,* Vol. 5. Aldus Books Ltd., London 1971, p. 34.
4. *Ibid.*, p. 34.
5. Whiteway, R.S., *The Rse of Portuguese Power in India 1497-1550,* published by Susil Gupta, 2nd Ed., 1967, p. 78.
6. Danvers, *op. cit.*, p. 48(I).
7. *Ibid.*, p. 63 (I).
8. *Ibid.*, p. 64 (I).
9. Hunter, William Wilson, *A History of British India,* in two Vols., Indian Reprints Publishing Co., Delhi, First Indian Edition, 1972, p. 104 (I).
10. Gibb, *op. cit.*, p. 364.
11. Danvers, *op. cit.*, 65.
12. Hunter, *op. cit.*, p. 108 (I).
13. *Ibid.*
14. Danvers, *op. cit.* p. 69 (I).
15. *Ibid.*, p. 71 (I).
16. *Ibid.*, p. 81 (I).
17. Hunter, *op. cit.*, p. 109 (I).
18. *Ibid.*, p. 110 (I).
19. Danvers, *op. cit.*, p. 210 (I).
20. *Ibid.*, p. 353 (I).
21. *Ibid.*, p. 375 (I).
22. *Ibid.*, p. 388 (I).
23. *Ibid.*, p. 400 (I).
24. *Ibid.*, p. 402 (I).
25. *Ibid.*, p. 404 (I).
26. *Ibid.*, p. 406 (I).
27. *Ibid.*, p. 418 (I).
28. Whiteway, *op. cit.*, p. 250.
29. Danvers, *op. cit.*, p. 423 (I).
30. Napier, *op. cit.*, p. 154.
31. Smith, Vincent, *Oxford History of India,* p. 379.

32. Smith, V., *op. cit.*, p. 331.
33. Dodwell, H.H., *The Cambridge History of India,* Vol. V, British India, Second Indian Reprint, S. Chand & Co., Delhi, 1963, p. 33.
34. *Ibid.*
35. Hunter, *op. cit.*, p. 70 (II).
36. *Ibid.*, p. 55.
37. Dodwell, *op. cit.*, p. 40.
38. *Ibid.*
39. *Ibid.*
40. *Ibid.*
41. *Ibid.*
42. Napier, *op. cit.*, p. 154.
43. Majumdar, Ray Chaudhuri and Datta, *op. cit.*, p. 626.
44. *Ibid.*
45. Dodwell, *op. cit.*, p. 41.
46. Roberts, P.E., *History of British India,* 3rd Ed., Oxford Univrsity Press, 1958, p. 38.
47. *Ibid.*
48. Danvers, *op. cit.*, p. 321 (II).
49. Majumdar, Ray Chaudhuri and Datta, *op. cit.*, p. 626.
50. *Ibid.*
51. *Ibid.*
52. Danvers, *op. cit.*, p. 321 (II).
53. Dodwell, *op. cit.*, p. 37.
54. Danvers, *op. cit.*, p. 325 (II).
55. *Ibid.*
56. *Ibid.*, p. 328 (II).
57. Dodwell, *op. cit.*, p. 37.
58. Napier, *op. cit.*, p. 154.
59. *Ibid.*
60. Hunter, *op. cit.*, p. 54 (II).
61. Majumdar, Ray Chaudhuri and Datta, *op. cit.*, p. 629.
62. *Ibid.*
63. *Ibid.*
64. Hunter *op. cit.*, p. 71 (II).
65. *Ibid.*, p. 76 (II).
66. *Ibid.*, p. 79 (II).
67. *Ibid.*, p. 92 (II).
68. *Ibid.*, p. 93 (II).
69. *Ibid.*
70. *Ibid.*
71. *Ibid.*, p. 65 (II).
72. *Ibid.*, p. 66 (II).
73. *Ibid.*
74. *Ibid.*, p. 78 (II).
75. *Ibid.*
76. *Ibid.*
77. *Ibid.*, p. 95 (II).

78. Danvers, *op. cit.*, p. 343 (II).
79. Napier, *op. cit.*, p. 154.
80. Powell-Price, J.C., *A History of India,* Thomas Nelson & Sons Ltd., Edinburgh, 1958, p. 412.
81. *Ibid.*
82. *Ibid.*
83. Hunter, *op. cit.*, p. 194 (II).
84. Napier, *op. cit.*, 154.
85. Hunter, *op. cit.*, pp. 266-267 (II).
86. Smith, V. *op. cit.*, 332.
87. Sen, S.P., *The French in India (1763-1816),* Munshiram Manoharlal, New Delhi, 1971, p. 110.
88. Dodwell, *op. cit.*, p. 69.
89. *Ibid.*, p. 71.
90. *Ibid.*, p. 73.
91. Sen, S.P., *op. cit.*, p. 93.
92. *Ibid.*, p. 109.
93. Dodwell, *op. cit.*, p. 74.
94. Sen, S.P., *op. cit.*, p. 107.
95. Smith, V., *op. cit.*, p. 335.
96. *Ibid.*, p. 331.
97. *Ibid.*, p. 335.
98. Roberts, P.E., *op. cit.*, p. 75.
99. *Ibid.*, p. 76.
100. Ball, *op. cit.*, p. 186 (I).
101. Roberts, *op. cit.*, p. 154.
102. *Ibid.*, p. 92.
103. Sen, S.P., *op. cit.*, p. 55.
104. *Ibid.*, p. 58.
105. Danvers, *op. cit.*, p. 331 (II).
106. Hunter, *op. cit.*, p. 214 (II).
107. *Ibid.*, p. 217 (II).
108. *Ibid.*, p. 218 (II).
109. Spear, Percival, *The Nabobs, A Study of the Social Life of the English in Eighteenth Century India,* p. 66.
110. *Ibid.*, p. 69.
111. *Ibid.*, p. 75.
112. *Ibid.*, p. 76.
113. *Ibid.*, p. 71.
114. Hunter, *op. cit.*, p. 80 (II).
115. *Imperial Gazetteer,* Vol. XVI, p. 368.
116. Hunter, *op. cit.*, p. 80 (II).
117. *Ibid.*, p. 81 (II).
118. Gardner, Brian, *The East India Company,* Rupert Hart-Davis, London, 1971, p. 56.
119. *Ibid.*
120. Hunter, *op. cit.*, p. 84 (II).
121. *Imperial Gazetteer,* Vol. IX, p. 260.

122. Hunter, *op. cit.*, p. 254 (II).
123. *Ibid.*, p. 256 (II).
124. Majumdar, Ray Chaudhuri and Datta, *op. cit.*, p. 636.
125. *Ibid.*, p. 631.
126. Roberts, *op. cit.*, p. 70.
127. Hunter, *op. cit.*, p. 254 (II).
128. *Ibid.*
129. *Ibid.*, p. 257 (II).
130. *Ibid.*, p. 262 (II).
131. *Ibid.*
132. *Ibid.*, p. 267 (II).
133. *Ibid.*, p. 268 (II).
134. Busteed, H.E., *Echoes from Old Calcutta*, 3rd Edition, Calcutta, 1897, p. 3.
135. Majumdar, Ray Chauduri and Datta, *op. cit.*, p. 632.
136. *Ibid.*, p. 634.
137. Martin, James Ranald, *Notes on the Medical Topography of Calcutta*, 1737, p. 6.
138. Hamilton, Alexander, *A New Account of the East Indies*, Vol. II, 1727, p. 12.
139. Steward, Charles, *The History of Bengal*, p. 402.
140. Gardner, *op. cit.*, p. 67.
141. Roberts, *op. cit.*, p. 70.
142. *Imperial Gazetteer*, Vol. IX, p. 26.
143. Busteed, *op. cit.*, p. 5.
144. *Ibid.*
145. Smith, V., *op. cit.*, p. 466.
146. Martin, James R., *op. cit.*, p. 9.
147. *Ibid.*
148. Rennell, James, *Memoir of a Map of Hindustan or the Moghul Empire*, 2nd Ed., London, 1792, pp. 58, 59.
149. *Ibid.*
150. Majumdar, Ray Chaudhuri and Datta, *op. cit.*, pp. 633-634.
151. Smith, V., *op. cit.*, p. 472.
152. *Ibid.*
153. *Ibid.*, p. 476.
154. *Ibid.*
155. Majumdar, Ray Chaudhuri and Datta, *op. cit.*, pp. 658-660.
156. *Ibid.*, p. 675.
157. *Ibid.*, p. 680.
158. Marshall, P.J., *Problems of Empire, Britain and India, 1757-1813*, George Allen and Unwin Ltd., London, 1968, p. 17.
159. *Ibid.*, p. 163.
160. *Ibid.*, p. 167.
161. Bearce, George D., *British Atitude towards India 1784-1858*, Oxford University Press, London, 1961, p. 51.
162. Smith, V. *op. cit.*, pp. 449-450.
163. Spear, *op. cit.*, p. 34.
164. *Ibid.*, p. 49.
165. *Ibid.*, p. 72.

166. Majumdar, Ray Chaudhuri and Datta, *op. cit.*, p. 569.
167. Datta, Kalikinkar, *Survey of India's Social Life and Economic Condition in the Eighteenth Century (1707-1813)*, Firma K.L. Mukhopadhaya, Calcutta, 1961, p. 81.
168. Orme, Robert, *Of the Government and People of Hindostan*, Pustak Kendra, Lucknow, 1971 (Reprint), p. 8.
169. *Ibid.*, p. 12.
170. Sinha, N.K., *Ibid.*, p. 110 (I).
171. Dutt, Romesh, *The Economic Life History of India under Early British Rule 1757-1837*, Vol. I, Publications Division, Ministry of Information and Broadcasting, Government of India, 2nd Ed., 1963, p. 161.
172. Ghosal, H.R., *Economic Transition in the Bengal Presidency (1793-1833)*, Firma K.L. Mukhopadhyay, Calcutta, 2nd Ed., 1966, p. 15.
173. Orme, *op. cit.*, p. 10.
174. *Ibid.*
175. Dutta, Romesh, *op. cit.*, p. 170.
176. *Ibid.*
177. Ghosal, *op. cit.*, p. 15.
178. *Ibid.*, p. 13.
179. *Ibid.*, p. 10.
180. Tripathi, A., *Trade and Commerce in the Bengal Presidency, 1793-1833*, Orient Longmans, Calcutta, 1956, p. 267.
181. Dutta, R., *op. cit.*, p. 161.
182. *Ibid.*, p. 163.
183. *Ibid.*, p. 165.
184. *Ibid.*, p. 173.
185. Datta, Kalikinkar, *op. cit.*, p. 83.
186. Sinha, N.K., *op. cit.*, p. 112 (I).
187. Sinha, N.C., *Studies in Indo-British Economy Hundred Years Ago*, A. Mukherjee & Co., Calcutta, 1946, p. 13.
188. *Ibid.*, p. 18.
189. Ghosal, *op. cit*, p. 55.
190. Hamilton, Walter, A., *Geographical, Statistical and Historical Description of Hindostan and the Adjacent Countries*, Oriental Publishers, Delhi, First Indian Ed., (1820).
191. Spear, *op. cit.*, p. 91.
192. Dutt, R., *op. cit.*, 192.
193. Ghosal, *op. cit.*, 86.
194. *Ibid.*, p. 77.
195. Dutt, R., *op. cit.*, 192.
196. Ghosal, *op. cit.*, p. 131.
197. Datta, Kalikinkar, *op. cit.*, p. 93.
198. *Ibid.*
199. *Ibid.*, p. 94.
200. *Ibid.*, p. 101.
201. Ghosal *op. cit.*, p. 116.
202. *Ibid.*, p. 117.
203. *Ibid.*, p. 120.

204. Dutt, R., *op. cit.*, p. 176.
205. Tripathi, A., *op. cit.*, p. 24.
206. Majumdar, Ray Chaudhuri and Datta, *op. cit.*, p. 802.
207. Sinha, N.C., *op. cit.*, p. 9.
208. *Ibid.*
209. Tripathi, A., *op. cit.*, p. 165.
210. Sinha, N.C., *op. cit.*, p. 10.
211. Dutt, R., *op. cit.*, p. 176.
212. Majumdar, Ray Chaudhuri and Datta, *op. cit.*, p. 803.
213. Dutt, R., *op. cit.*, p. 202.
214. *Ibid.*, p. 212.
215. Hamilton, Walter, *op. cit.*, p. XXXVIII, Vol. I.
216. *Ibid.*, p. 55 (I).
217. *Ibid.*, p. 722 (I).
218. *Ibid.*, p. 421 (I).
219. *Ibid.*, p. 136 (II).
220. *Ibid.*, p. 348 (I).
221. *Ibid.*, p. 411 (I).
222. *Ibid.*, p. 159. (II).
223. *Ibid.*, p. 8 (II).
224. *Ibid.*, p. 699 (I).
225. *Ibid.*, p. 572 (I).
226. *Ibid.*, p. 262 (I).
227. *Ibid.*, p. 164 (I).
228. *Ibid.*, p. 309 (II).
229. *Ibid.*
230. Spear, *op. cit.*, p. 66.
231. Hamilton, Walter, *Ibid.*, p. 348 (II).
232. *Ibid.*
233. *Ibid.*
234. *Ibid.*, p. 185 (I).
235. *Ibid.*, p. 184 (I).
236. *Ibid.*, p. 185 (I).
237. *Ibid.*, p. 163 (I).
238. *Ibid.*
239. *Ibid.*, p. 696 (I).
240. *Ibid.*, p. 476 (I).
241. *Ibid.*, p. 235 (II).
242. *Ibid.*, p. 687 (I).
243. *Ibid.*, p. 745 (I).
244. *Ibid.*, p. 207 (II).
245. *Ibid.*, p. 557 (I).
246. *Ibid.*, p. 708 (I).
247. *Ibid.*, p. 100 (II).
248. *Ibid.*, p. 112 (II).
249. *Ibid.*, p. 387 (II).
250. *Ibid.*, p. 471 (II).
251. *Ibid.*, p. 305 (I).

5

The State of Urbanisation on the Eve of the Twentieth Century

The consolidation of British power in India, guaranteeing peace and security of life, naturally created a better atmosphere for urban functions, though not necessarily for a greater urban development. This does not, however, mean that the towns and cities remained static, registering no progress in their individual cases. As a matter of fact, cities for which earlier estimates are available, provide instances of both development and degradation. Taking Hamilton's figures for the sixteen largest cities of India existing in the first quarter of the nineteenth century, one may conclude that the overall situation did not improve much in regard to a general increase of the urban population in the country. This is very much conveyed by what we get from the early census reports at all-India level beginning at ten years interval from 1872 onwards.

According to the first census, conducted in 1872, there were only sixteen urban centres in undivided India, containing more that one hundred thousand people each, and another twenty seven, each having over fifty thousand heads (Table 5.1).

Table 5.1 shows that, altogether, there were only forty-three urban centres in India at the beginning of the last quarter of the nineteenth century considered to be the largest, with a minimum population of fifty thousand. The picture does not seem to be at all encouraging in view of stability of the society, enjoyed over decades of British rule in the country.

Table 5.1 : Towns and Cities in 1872

	Towns	*Population*
1.	Calcutta	794,645
2.	Bombay	644,405
3.	Madras	397,522
4.	Lucknow	284,779
5.	Benares	175,188
6.	Patna	158,900
7.	Delhi	154,417
8.	Agra	149,008
9.	Allahabad	143,693
10.	Banglore	142,513
11.	Amritsar	135,813
12.	Cawnpore	122,770
13.	Poona	118,886
14.	Ahmedabad	116,873
15.	Surat	107,149
16.	Bareilly	102,982
17.	Lahore	98,924
18.	Howrah	97,784
19.	Nagpur	97,784
20.	Meerut	81,386
21.	Farukkabad	79,204
22.	Trichinopoly	76,530
23.	Shahjahanpur	72,136
24.	Bhagalpur	69,678
25.	Dacca	69,212
26.	Mirzapur	67,274
27.	Gaya	66,843
28.	Moradabad	62,417
29.	Monghyr	59,698
30.	Muttra	59,281
31.	Peshawar	58,555
32.	Aligarh	58,539
33.	Mysore	57,815
34.	Mooltan	56,826
35.	Jubbulpore	56,188
36.	Kurrachee	53,526
37.	Sholapur	53,403
38.	Tanjore	52,175
39.	Madura	51,987
40.	Bellary	51,766
41.	Gorakhpur	51,177
42.	Cuttack	50,878
43.	Salem	50,012

A comparative analysis of the estimates given by Hamilton and the First Census of India reveal some interesting facts. It may be noted that the total number of cities, crossing the mark of one hundred thousand inhabitants, remained, surprisingly, the same between the space of about five decades. The similarity in number is nothing more than co-incidental, but what strikes our notice is that, it gives a real insight into the prevailing condition of urban development. This is very forcibly brought out by the changes that occurred in the position of individual cities during this period. In Hamilton's day, Benares occupied the most exalted position amount the sixteen great cities of India. Hamilton's estimate about Benares, whether exaggerated or not, does not conceal the truth that no other city matched it in his days. According to his calculations, Calcutta, the nearest rival, was much below in rank which Hamilton had no special reason to hide. But the passage of five decades brought Benares down to the fifth position in the scale (Table 5.1), with its population reduced nearly to one-fourth of its previous figure. Calcutta, Bombay and Madras, all of English origin, had emerged by this time as the three largest cities of India and this position they maintained between them for nearly another century, till 1961. The population in each recorded a high increase between 1820 and 1872, being almost four times in Bombay. In contrast to the greatly improved position of these three cities, deterioration is amply manifest especially in the case of Surat, Patna, Hyderabad, Dacca and Murshidabad where the population decreased by more than three to two times, thereby bringing, Hyderabad and Murshidabad below the level of the 'Largest Towns' of that time while Dacca, largely depopulated, maintained a shrunken existence. Degradation in size also took place in the case of Nagpur, Baroda and Srinagar (Kashmir of Hamilton) which no longer enjoyed the prestigious position of the great sixteen. In fact, apart from Nagpur, the other two lost their position out of the forty-three largest towns of the time. In their place new towns emerged—six in all—to occupy places in the list of sixteen first-grade towns. Regarding the geographical distribution of these forty-three centres, it is highly interesting to note that ten out of the first sixteen and altogether twenty-seven were situated in North India, and remaining sixteen, belonging to both first and second order, were widely strewn over central to south India.

A decade later, in 1881, the number of 'great cities', as called by the Census Commissioner—having more than one hundred thousand residents stood at twenty-one, and those belonging to the second grade, with a population between the range of 59,000-99,999, were thirty-four in all. Besides, there were 109 towns where the number of inhabitants ranged between 20,000 and 49,999. As it appears, the number of towns has not changed much during the space of a decade. There has been an addition of only five new 'great cities' to the list, while the total number of the second grade towns has increased by seven. The rate of increase in equally insignificant for the succeeding two decades. Between 1881 and 1891, the number of the first grade towns, or the great cities, rose by the five, thus maintaining a strange similarity and the increase in the second grade towns was 13, while it was still larger in the third grade towns, with an addition of 37. The rate, however, slowed down in the next decade with one more addition to the list of both the first and second grade towns and with a reduction of five from the list of third grade towns.

The overall picture does not appear to be very much encouraging. It may be said that the addition of five great cities in each of the first two decades indicates a substantial gain in the way of urban development made within a period of only two decades. A scrutiny of the two lists (Table 5.2) showing the names of the great cities of 1772 and 1881 presents some interesting facts. As for example. Hyderabad, shown as the fourth largest city of India in 1891 does not find a place among the great cities of 1881 which seems to be rather incongruous in view of the fact that since inception in the sixteenth century, it has been one of the leading cities of the country and it is not probable that maintaining a population of about 200,000 in Hamilton's time it could have degraded to a position even not to appear in the list of the forty-three great towns in 1872 for which the minimum population was taken as 50,000. On the other hand, the population figures for Calcutta give an erroneous picture. Although Calcutta emerged as the largest city in 1872 with 794,645 heads, the latter actually included the population of the suburbs lying beyond its municipal boundary[3]. Eleswhere the population of the city is shown as 447,601 for 1972[4], which seems to be the population of its municipal area. The Census Commissioner of India for 1881 also reports that the population of Calcutta (766,298), in fact, includes also the residents of the tree sub-urban municipalities since they, along with the city municipality, actually represent the four blocks of Calcutta really composing one great city[5]. Besides, Howrah, shown as a city, had no separate identity which grew as an integral part of Calcutta separated only by a river, and in the opinion of the Census Commissioner, it was "as much a portion of that town (Calcutta) as Southwark of Lambeth is of London"[6]. In fact, the origin and development of Howrah depended largely on its acting as the principal railway head for Calcutta. The most important conclusion one can draw from all these facts is that—the urban growth did not remain confined within municipal boundaries of the city any more and already, by 1881, it spilled over, giving rise to three separate municipalities and one city beyond the river barrier, all of them representing the actual extension cf the city area, although under different names for administrative reasons. The inclusion of Howrah gives a population of 871,504 for Calcutta.

But dismaying features are difficult to be ignored when the total urban development a whole is considered. As has already been pointed out, the increase in the number of both the second and third grade towns has been far from satisfactory; by 1901, it almost came to a halt, giving rather retrogressing signs when not only the third grade towns decreased in number, but even the number in the immediate two higher grades did not increase appreciably. Had the rate of urban growth been strong, at least the number of towns belonging to the first and second grade would have increased simultaneously through the expansion of the second and third grade towns. This did not happen. Moreover, the size of the great cities did not improve much over the space of three decades, majority of them remaining below the mark of 200,000. Cities crossing this mark while four in 1872, five in 1881, six in 1891 and seven in 1901, while none of them had yet attained the million-mark. The rate of growth of the individual cities had also not been very spectacular during this period, of the sixteen cities existing during all this period fourteen recorded increase varying widely from 6.69 per cent, being the lowest for Calcutta, to 60.00 per cent, being the highest for Kanpur. On the whole, however, the cities having gained in size by1901, did not have a steady increase in many cases. In all, there were ten cities, *e.g.*, Bombay, Varanasi, Allahabad, Banglore, Amritsar, Poona, Surat, Baroda, Meerut and Gwalior—which declined in one decade or another. Besides, two more

Table 5.22 : Cities having a popultion of above 100,000 between 1872 and 1901

Sr. No.	*City*	*1872*	*City*	*1881*	*City*	*1891*	*City*	*1901*
1.	Calcutta	794,645	Bombay	773,196	Bombay	821,764	Calcutta	933,754
2.	Bombay	644,405	Calcutta	684,658	Calcutta	741,144	Bombay	812.912
3.	Madras	397,552	Madras	405,848	Madras	452,518	Madras	541.167
4.	Lucknow	284,779	Hyderabad	354,962	Hyderabad	415,039	Hyderbad	448.466
5.	Benares	175,188	Lucknow	261,303	Lucknow	273,028	Lucknow	264.049
6.	Patna	158,900	Benares	199,700	Benares	219,467	Benares	209.331
7.	Delhi	154,417	Delhi	173,393	Delhi	192,579	Delhi	214.115
8.	Agra	149,008	Patna	170,654	Cawnpore	188,712	Cawnpore	202,797
9.	Allahabad	143,693	Agra	160,203	Bangalore	180,336	Ahmedabad	185.889
10.	Bangalore	142,513	Bangalore	155,857	Lahore	176,854	Agra	180.022
11.	Amritsar	135,813	Amritsar	151,896	Allahabad	175,246	Allahabad	172,032
12.	Cawnpore	122,770	Cawnpore	151,444	Agra	168,662	Amritsar	162.429
13.	Poona	118,886	Lahore	149,369	Patna	165,192	Jaipur	160.167
14.	Ahmedabad	116,873	Allahabad	148,547	Poona	161,390	Bangalore	159.046
15.	Surat	107,149	Jeypore	142,578	Jaipore	158,905	Howrah	157.594

Sr. No.	*City*	*1872*	*City*	*1881*	*City*	*1891*	*City*	*1901*
16.	Bareilly	102,982	Poona	129,751	Ahmedabad	148,412	Poona	153,320
17.			Ahmedabad	127,621	Amritsar	136,766	Patna	134,785
18.			Bareilly	113,417	Bareilly	121,039	Barilley	131,208
19.			Surat	109,844	Meerut	119,390	Nagpur	127,734
20.			Howrah	105,206	Srinagar	118,960	Srinagar	122,618
21.			Baroda	101,818	Nagpur	117,014	Meerut	118,129
22.					Howrah	116,606	Madurai	105,984
23.					Baroda	116,420	Baroda	103,790
24.					Surat	109,229	Surat	129,500
25.					Karachi	105,199	Gwalior	138,612
26.					Gwalior	104,083		

cities—Patna and Lucknow—recorded decrease, 15.17 and 7.27 per cent respectively during this period. The most redeeming feature about the great cities of the time is that none of them degraded from the first to the second grade; but what the majority lacked is the steadiness.

Another very important fact also does not escape our notice. That is about the names of the cities appearing on the list for all the four census years which are too familiar to be mistaken. None of them is a new centre; each has maintained a long history, going in some instances back to a hoary past. This is almost equally applicable to the second and third grade towns existing in 1901. It rather appears as highly strange to know that the peace offered by the British administration in India did not help much in the real proliferation of urban activities in the country. Towns and cities which made a beginning long before British rule came to be established were still functioning with their previous role curtailed to suit the existing situation. The positive contribution of the changed, undisturbed situation was a degree of stability introduced into urban life which no longer was threatened with immediate disaster in the face of catastrophic political changes. This element of permanency is the most valuable achievement accomplished by the British rule in India. From this time towns and cities stayed on though the rate of progress was not steady in all cases.

To understand this, one may again have to turn back to the economic condition of the country discussed in the previous chapter. The complete breakdown of the industrial structure and the resulting dryingup of the channels of commerce, the latter keeping a constant flow of wealth, both in gold and material, into the country, made a permanent damage to the material status of the urban centres, especially since they were more directly involved that the others. The collapse of the industry and commerce, providing the driving, force for the many of these urban centres, greatly limited their functional scopes, thereby throwing a large section of the people out of occupation. No statistics is available to support this assumption, but this is precisely what happened when the principal vocations of the people found no way of expression. There is no way of assessing the stupendous national loss thus incurred, except that the contemporary urban centres bore this mark in many ways from which they could not revive for a long time.

Nevertheless, the urban system, long developed on the basis of political and economic functions, interlaced by a wide network of road and river-ways, did not undergo any drastic change. The revised economic policy of the British Government needed the services of the existing towns cities for keeping the administration in India in an effective form on the one hand, and for running the industries in full swing at home country on the other. The vast resources of the varied types of raw materials were needed to be collected from the remote corners of the country for which the towns and cities were required as collecting and distributing centres for channelising the goods through the principal ports. The finished products of the home industries needed the service of the same channels for their distribution in the country-wide market of India. The quick rise of Calcutta, Bombay and Madras as the three largest cities of India surpassing all others make it abundantly clear that their role as the three principal ports had significant part to play in their development.

It has to be remembered that, since this time a major change took place in the character of the urban centres. The gradual imposition of British rule slowly deprived them of their original importance. It is not to be forgotten that the urban centres existing at the time when foreign power was making slow ingress into their spheres of activities were born as seats of political or economic functions. In fact, no centre exised without some of these two important functions. Capital centres turned into great seats of commerce and industry, sometimes cultural activities added to them under the direct partonage of the ruling King or Emperor. They offered the markets for all the products, whether material or cultural, origination from the country-side. They were the repositories for talents of all descriptions to assemble and make profitable living. The urban centres, offering easy access to people from all walks of life and all countries of the world, turned into great places of activities and exchange of commodities. But, as such they were never places of attraction for the village folk who remained content in the rural surroundings. There is a fundamental difference between urban and rural life in India with that of the West. One is apt to ignore this and make rush judgement about the urbanmindedness of the Indian villagers. In the West mainly in Europe, the village had little to offer in its harsh, natural surroundings. The people living under great stress had always been attracted to urban life offering better comforts. Besides the limited resources from the very beginning kept the people on the move, making them more curious, adventurous and uncompromising with fate. This out-ward pressure from the homeland remained highly powerful, giving rise to centuries of colonisation. The pressure also acted in another way. It gave rise to greater urban activities where people could find a way of living. In contrast to this, India offers a different picture. Here nature has been more helpful in supporting a rich agrarian life over a very long period. Villages nestled everywhere, making an easy life. The Indian village offered everything on a modest scale to its inhabitants. As described eleswhere, every village was a self-sufficient unit having servicemen for its essential needs, ranging from the political (administrative) to religious matters. The caste-system made a permanent foundation for providing them. This has remained unaltered even today, though village have largely fallen from that status due to various reasons. But it was never a closed society, insulated from other influences. The very attitude to life made such influences largely ineffective so far as the greater masses were concerned. The villagers learnt through centuries of experience to be satisfied with their little wants met. There was no larger degree of necessity for the villagers to go to the urban areas for a living. This does not mean that the villagers had been characteristically apathetic to urban life. Had it been so, the towns and cities could not get so many talents needed for building up its economic and cultural edifice. A close, intimate relationship had always remained between the rural and urban sectors, people having special needs to be fulfilled had love over to urban places; but that movement had never taken a massive character to be termed as migration. Even those casual goers kept the permanent homes in the villages. This is very much true even today; an Indian has always a village address, though the tie is fast breaking up.

This particular trait of Indian character is high significance for understanding the course and nature of urban development in the country. The urban life made no heavy demands on Indian rural life as it had done in the West through its greater drainage of man and material. The Indian rural scene, remaining largely undisturbed that way, continued to make an essential link between urban needs and their supplies. They had always maintained a direct commercial relationship with the towns and cities, supplying their wants. In turn, they received what little they needed without adopting urban way of life. The time-old customs and habits, derived from strong religious training, made the life of the villager different, growing with belief that the values get destroyed in an urban atmosphere. Judged from that angle, it may appear as an aversion to urban life. But it is more aloofness than mere aversion that had long kept the villager tied to his rural surroundings. The ease, peace and comfort of village kept him village-bound. As long as the villages were not ravaged by natural or artificial calamities, people loved to stay back in the quietude of the villages. Besides, in village every individual was somebody, taking an important role in the daily life, having special place in the little society of his own. In the urban place the identity is lost in the mainstream of life encumbered by many problems like, congestion, social crimes and a degraded social status. To the experienced eye of the villager the shortcomings of urban life were not unknown. Thus, urban life had nothing special to offer him. What he needed was the market for his products and this he got without sacrificing his much cherished independence. It is, therefore, not surprising to see that the most famous industries of the past originated in the villages and thrived well down to the period when the British power was already firmly established in the country. This was the reason why the traditional art did not get entirely lost when the industries were gradually destroyed by the foreign rulers. The time-old unexcelled skill and ingenuity in spinning, weaving, ivory and wood carving, gold, silver and precious stone ornamental work, leather work, etc., earned as a family-trade hibernated in the rural recluses to reappear in almost full form when time was propitious at a much later period.

It is generally admitted that, in general, urban development in any country reflect its material progress. From that point of view, material progress of India with 9.1 per cent of the total population residing in urban centres in 1881[7] was far behind England and Wales where the percentage of urban population was 63.04[8]. Taking the current picture of India's 27.78 per cent against Great Britain's 89 per cent of the total population living in urban areas, it would appear that the former is four times backward in material progress than that to the latter. The argument is not tenable when Great Britain is pitted against the U.S.A., or Sweden is compared with the U.S.S.R. Both Great Britian and Sweden maintain a higher proportion of urban dwellers as compared with the U.S.A. and the U.S.S.R. respectively. But one should hesitate before comparing the material as well as cultural achievements between these two groups. The higher proportion of urban population in Great Britain and Sweden is directly the result of the scarcity of agricultural land, giving rise to greater concentrations in urban areas. Just opposite is the case with the U.S.A. and the U.S.S.R. where till able land makes a much higher proportion of the total area than in either of the former countries, thereby keeping more people tied to rural areas. True, more and more mechanisation of agriculture will release more people in future from rural areas who will naturally flock into urban areas. But such a condition is indirectly a pressure ejecting people out of their village surroundings. This obviously means an increase of the proportion of urban population at the cost of rural depopulation. The question is whether this town-ward movement goes on unchecked until the rural areas cannot yield any more surplus population. There is, however, an answer to this question. Successful agriculture is not possible without minimum human labour, and mechanisation being not equally successful in all types of agricultural activities, will, together, determine the proportion of total population of a country required to stay back in the countryside. Already a reverse movement from the urban to the rural areas have started, especially in the developed countries. People, no longer satisfied with the artificial atmosphere created by the steel and concrete within the city, are moving away from the city centre. The extreme congestion in the city, the noise, the traffic-jams, the increasing degree of social crimes are driving people fast out of the city to its surroundings countryside providing more elbow-space and a peaceful atmosphere. This advantage of going back to the countryside however is enjoyed by a minute section of the society who can afford to spend on daily transport to the city. But this cannot be considered as a village-ward movement since people migrating from the city still cling to the city as their work-place. This gives rise to the suburban growth which, taking the courses of main roads, continues unabated into the countryside. There is a present tendency with the large cities of the world of building housing estates in the suburban areas for accommodating the growing population of the cities. This amorphous urban sprawl, sending huge tentacles into the rural areas, very forcefully expressed by Toyenbee as march of city into the country[9], is greatly eroding the rich agricultural land, converting it into a vast jungle of buildings with slow, but steady, encroachment of industries. Suburban development of similar type is already changing the rural landscape of the large cities of India, like Delhi, Bombay and Calcutta. Urban exodus of this nature may be a partial solution to relieve the extreme congestion in the cities, but it, in no way, brings people back to rural life. Again, the question may be raised as to the necessity of keeping rural life alive or not. In the modern context or urban development in the Western countries the distinction between urban and rural life is gradually becoming narrow. With the creation of urban amenities the rural areas are taking on an urban look; the distinction lies chiefly in the functions which still keep them rural. It can thus be concluded that rural life cannot be fully replaced by urban life however a country is materially advanced. The prime necessity of keeping the people fed makes the service of the rural areas absolutely unavoidable. The increasing need for food, not to say of raw materials for the growing industries, in tune not only with the growth of population, but also the rising standard of living, is hastening the time when imports of food will be further curtailed, compelling every country to depend more on its own resources. Such a situation will require more people on the rural front engaged in primary activities, than many of the advanced countries realise today.

To turn to the slow progress of urban development India in the closing decades of the nineteenth century, it can now be concluded that two sets of factors were mainly responsible for this : (*a*) first, the erosion of economic independence took the edge out of the vitality of the existing urban centres which no longer attracted people for commercial and industrial purposes. The rulers did no take much interest in their growth by revitalising their economy except using them as points of transaction and administrative functions; (*b*) second, the general disinterest for urban life on the part of ruralities was born of agricultural affluence and different social attitudes. Many take this reluctance as lack of urban-mindedness. Impoverishment of the agricultural scene, mounting pressure of population and change in social values with spread of education may, in future, accelerate the town-ward movement, no doubt, but the basic fact remains unaltered that the situation will never be like that of the West where the rural and the urban life make two contrasting themes whereas in India the village still is another meaning of 'home' for its tradition-bound masses. Besides, improvement of agriculture, distribution of land among the landless farmers, extensions of the agricultural frontier into hitherto drier zones or reclaimed lands, greater utilisation of the inland water and forest resources will undoubtedly improve the position of rural life, drawing the jobless, floating masses away from the urban places. In this way, the towns and villages remain as complementary units, having precisely defined roles in the society. The separate entity of each has no conflict because each of them serves a different purpose of the society.

Urban Progress in Twentieth Century

At the opening of the twentieth century only 10.84 per cent of the total population of the country were living in the urban areas of the country. Apparently, this is not much of an improvement of the situation since 1881 when 9.1 per cent were already urban. The imposition of British rule did not accelerate the pace of urbanisation in a very great way. The appearance of the urban scene also showed no signs of any marked improvement. In the opinion of the Census Commissioner of 1871, the metropolitan division of Calcutta did not possess a large number of towns. The town even in the neighbourhood of Calcutta were nothing but villages, "closely studded and densely populated"[10]. In 1872, the entire stretch of the Hooghly banks, right up to Nabadwip in the north, became thickly populated. The villages here grouped for municipal purpose and shown as towns in the census lists actually contained rice fields in the very heart of them. [11]"Even the Suburban town, making a part of the city of Calcutta, comprised fifty one villages, with large tracts of cultivated lands[12].

In 1881, the Census Commissioner finds the societal condition adverse to the rapid increase of urbanisation and the basis of social organisation "essentially anti-urban"[13]. The encouragement to industry, according to him, being of weak character mainly handicapped urban growth. In his opinion, this was largely the result of the self-sufficient condition of the rural communities which cared little for urban life. According to him, the practice of giving same social status to the village weaver and the dealer in goods of non-local origin, bringing money into the society, carried an impression of anti-commercial attitude of the rural communities. The Census Commissioner further points out that the chief trade being in raw materials helped little in the increase of urban population. The domestic manufactures, still extant, were hand-made, and large-scale industries could not grow up in the absence of mineral fuel or water power. The pace of urbanisation remained at a low key due, primarily, to the lack of industrial development and was equally hard hit by the unyielding attitude of the rural buyers which gave rise to a calculating price-level[14].

The observations made by the Census Commissioner of India, 1881, is neither surprising, nor very unlikely under the prevailing situation. The Indian village society was not really 'anti-urban', but rather, less enthusiastic in adopting urban-life, reason for which have been given in the preceding paragraphs. But this had never been a main obstacle to urban development during the earlier centuries when living in the villages, the rural population had taken full share in economic activities of the country, and exchange in services in equal measure from both directions gave rise to flourishing urban centres. This was not the case as witnessed by the Census Commissioner; the situation had obviously changed, deteriorating so much so as to leave the villages isolated in their own surroundings, severed from urban connections. The reasons provided by the Census Commissioner like, the disinterested outlook for industrial development or the anti-commercial attitude making urban development slow in the country appear to be far from convincing. The fact that the merchants were not given a higher status in the society could not have any plausible impact on the growth of urban centres, since their role and position had long been defined and accepted in the caste-bound society. On the other hand, cottage-based industries could not be a great handicap for urban development, since they provided the principal basis for the rise of innumerable towns and cities through centuries. The defect lay not in the nature of industrial function but in their virtual collapse under the British rule, plus, the atmosphere which was not at all conducive to the development of large-scale industries for a long time. As a matter of fact, mineral rule, like, coal, available in plenty was already known to the rulers, but their utilisation was not given a free hand till few more decades elapsed. The situation, in summary, was uninviting for any Indian enterprise whether in industrial or commercial ventures which could infuse new blood into the veins of the urban-body for its regeneration.

A decade later, in 1891, the urban population of India stood at 9.48 per cent of the total for the country. In the territory directly under British rule it was, however, lower (9.22 per cent) than in the Feudatory States (10.38 per cent)[15]. The urban centres were represented by the seaports, the presidency towns, and the few trading and manufacturing centres and, according to the Census Commissioner for 1891, the main factors in the development of such centres were the investment of foreign capital and scope given to the Indian trading classes."To a minor degree, too, the artisan and professional has contributed to the growth of such towns"[16]. By that time, many of the former capitals, had greatly deteriorated. The Census Commissioner found highly flourishing cities, like, Vijayanagar in complete ruin, Bijapur a skeleton of its former self, Surat greatly degraded from its old position, Murshidabad reduced to a large village, Patna deprived of its previous glory, Agra and Dacca somehow maintaining their status[17]. Like his predecessor, Baines, the Census Commissioner for 1891, make similar observations about the Indian attitude to urban life. In his opinion, city life and its attractions were no more than a "nebulous hypothesis"[18] for the great majority of the common people, while the upper class had a strong dislike for them. This he takes as the reason for the slow tempo of urbanisation in the country. Elsewhere he maintains that the great trade "in arms, ornaments, fine fabrics, cloth of gold, illuminated manuscripts and other objects"[19], creating an artificial stimulus for urban growth, could not last long "under the plain utilitarianism of the British system of Government"[20] as expenditure on such products were economically unproductive.

The idea one may gather from the statements of Baines is not at all confusing, such as, the majority of the Indians still lived in the villages, and urban activities during the early decades of British rule in India has been reduced to administrative functions supplemented by commerce, mainly in foreign goods. This was followed by a planned systematic demolition of the old local industries which provided the basic, sustaining force for urban growth. The change thus introduced in the urban functions had a great effect on the urban life in general and a number of great cities gradually decayed. Those which could survive the shock had to lean on other means, such as enlarged administrative and military importance, and managed to make an existence out of them. It may be highly increasing to know that in

1891, 21 out of the 26 first grade towns, and another 20 out of the total 47 second grade towns of the country had either forts or military cantonments in them. It is further interesting to note that, barring a few, almost all these towns were administrative headquarters, representing either a State, whether British or Feudatory, or a district. Prior to this, for administrative convenience, British India had been divided into districts, the latter corresponding roughly with the 'Sarkars' of the Mughal India. Thus, in 1787, Bengal and Bihar were composed of 23 districts, Madras 26 and Bombay 13, etc.[21] each of which had its administrative seat located at the most important urban centre existing at that time. Thus, in course of time administrative headquarters emerged as the most prominent towns and cities of the country while others, not so fortunate in that way, made slow progress. The leading role of the urban centres selected as seats of administration added also another feature of their urbanscape. This was the 'Civil Lines' or the European section of the city with its well-laid streets, widely spaced buildings introducing English architectural styles into Indian cities and with enough of green and open space breathing an air of ease and comfort in sharp contrast to the crowded atmosphere of the old city. The social significance of this new element cannot be ignored. The 'Civil Lines', appearing as an appendage of the main city, kept the Europeans separate from the main life-stream of the country. They lived ruled without taking any part in the city life; the 'Civil Lines', almost a self-contained unit, created a city within a city, but forbidden for the natives. The most disheartening feature of these appendages is that they looked alike everywhere in form and architecture, in the general layout of the streets and housing arrangements, without revealing the slightest difference as a response to contrasting environments. Monotony being the prevailing character, they, judged in isolation, do not yield any information about the conditions of cities of which they formed an integral part. This detachment had a deep impact on the urban life in general. The plans and their achievements systematically carried out in them life no imprint on the main city-body where crowdedness and squalor went hand in hand unchecked due to the absence of proper planning. The cities grew more and more unlivable while the civil lines lay placid in a tranquil atmosphere. A similar, if not more important, development had taken place by this time in a completely different direction. A number of Hill Stations were established at selected spots on the hills and mountains of the north, central and south India. Developed at high altitudes they gave rise to a new set of urban centres for the specific use of the British administrators for temporary shifting of their capital to these places during the hot summer period. Growing as specially favoured spots, their plan and architecture following English style, the summer resorts introduced a new element into the India urban scene, but being mostly out of bounds for the common Indians they remained alienated from the general life of the country. In this connection one cannot ignore the fact that, except in making the Hill Stations the direct initiative of the ruling English is not found to have been more vigorous in the urban development of the country. All through their administration they lived apart, making a separate pocket for themselves adorned with all comfort and beauty and leaving the main city to go its own way. Even the small district towns exhibit this form. This attitude of distinct aloofness became very strongly manifest in the development of the town and cities in general which made no visible headway either in their activities or in their appearance. Left to themselves they could prosper much, no doubt. But there also the prohibiting hands of the rulers were active. They were to serve the purpose of British administration and for this development and improvement were kept limited to that bare necessity. The tailoring of urban functions to the absolute minimum of administrative, commercial or educational services may be gauged from the fact that industry could not have any foothold in them for a long time. This restraining hand did not allow the urban sector to have a free atmosphere of growth, and the restricted flow of money into the urban centres did not give an opportunity of an overall improvement of the situation.

Apart from the cantonments, the civil lines and the Hill Stations, positive steps to improve the scene were taken in the form of constructing roads, sewerage, pipelines for supplying drinking water, road lights, shopping centres, public cemeteries, etc. Municipalities were established in most of the important urban centres as early as 1881, invested with a large amount of power for civic administration. But all these failed to have any great impact on the city life in general in the absence of proper planning and revival of the economy.

Urban Trend in Recent Times

The total urban population of India has grown from 25,851,873 in 1901 (the adjusted figure of population for the area under Indian Union) to 285,354,954[22] when the total population increased from 238,396,327 in 1901 (adjusted figure) to 1,027,015,247[23]. Thus, the urban population has increased more than 1003.80 per cent over the period of the last hundred years (1901-2001) when increase in the total population of the country is about 330.80 per cent. But this apparently phenomenal increase of population in the urban sector is not equally reflected in the decennial increase where urban population is considered as the proportion of the total population (Table 5.3), which indication the actual level of urbanisation in the country.

Table 5.3 : Urban Population of India shown as Percentage of Total Population

Year	*Urban Population* as % of *Total Population (TP)*
1901	10.84
1911	10.94
1921	11.18
1931	11.99
1941	13.86
1951	17.29
1961	17.97
1971	19.91
1981	23.34
1991	25.72
2001	27.77

Sources : Census of India 1971, Series 1, Part II-A (i).
Census of India 1991, Series 1, Paper 2 of 1991.
Census of India 2001, Provisional, Paper 2.

It is discouraging to note that figures for respective decades indicating the proportion of urban population in India has increased only a little over two-and-a-half-times during the last one hundred years which is quite small as compared with many other countries of the world (Table 5.4). In India, the progress has, indeed, been very slow, increasing from 10.89 per cent in 1901 to 27.78 per cent in 2001 when the level of urbanisation across the world, as estimated by some authors, is above 50 per cent at the close of the twentieth century which is expected to rise to about two-thirds by 2050 when 69 per cent of the world population will become urban dwellers. In other words, while in India a component of about 28 per cent of the total population of the country are urban residents at the present moment, in the world as whole more that 50 per cent of the total population have taken residence in the urban areas. India's performance in this regard has been far from satisfactory, taking a back seat, falling behind in the race when even Africa, East and South Asia made spectacular progress in the recent decades.

Table 5.4 : Urbanisation in the World by Regions (% of Total Population)

Regions	*1920*	*1950*	*1980*	*1990*	*2000*
World	19.4	28.4	41.3	45.9	51.3
More Developed Regions (MDCs)	38.7	51.8	70.7	75.9	80.3
Europe	46.2	55.2	75.9	82.4	88.4
North Amercia	51.9	63.8	73.7	77.2	80.8
Australia and New Zealand	60.6	74.3	81.5	82.8	83.7
Soviet Union	16.0	39.3	64.8	71.3	76.1
Latin Amercia	22.4	40.6	64.8	70.7	75.2
Less Developed Countries (LDCs)	8.4	16.6	30.5	36.3	42.5
Africa	7.0	14.4	28.9	35.7	42.5
Asia	8.8	15.7	27.4	32.3	38.9
East Asia	9.0	16.0	33.1	38.6	45.4
South Asia	8.5	15.5	23.1	28.1	34.9
India*	11.8 (1921)	17.2 (1931)	23.3 (1981)	25.7 (1991)	27.7 (2001)

Sources : 1. Palen John J., *The Urban Wrold*, 1987.
* 2. Census of India 1971-2001.

On the other hand, low increase in the proportion of people living in urban areas appears as a sharp contrast to the overall difference in increase in the absolute number of population in India between 1901 and 2001—330.80 per cent of the total against 1003.80 per cent of the urban population. This contradictory situation can be explained by the fact that in spite of significant increase in the volume of urban population, which is over three times more than of the total population, the apparent gain has eaten up by a much larger increase in the absolute number of the total population in the country.

The increase of urban population by more than ten times between 1901 and 2001, has been result of increase in the number of urban places as well as the growth of individual centres during this period, of which the second factors has played a very important role, acquiring more importance through the later decades. As a matter of fact, the total number of urban places has risen from 1917 in 1901 to 5161 in 2001, which means on overall increase of 3244 urban centres between 1901 and 2001 (Table 5.5). The addition of 3244 towns cities

Table 5.5: Number of Towns and Cities (including all Size-Classes) in India, 1901-2001

Year	*All Classes*	*Class I*	*Class II*	*Class III*	*Class IV*	*Class V*	*Class VI*
1901	1811	24	43	130	391	744	479
1911	1754	23	40	135	364	707	485
1921	1894	29	45	145	370	734	571
1931	2017	35	56	183	434	800	509
1941	2190	49	74	242	498	920	407
1951	2795	76	91	327	608	1124	569
1961	2270	102	129	437	719	711	172
1971	2476	148	173	558	827	623	147
1981	3245	216	270	738	1053	739	229
1991	3609	296	341	927	1135	725	185
2001	5161	417	NA	NA	NA	NA	NA

Source : Census of India 1991, Series-1, Paper 2 of 1991 (excludes Jammu & Kashmir and Assam).
Census of India 2001, Provisional, Paper 2.

The Census of India has adopted this size-class introduced first in 1961.
Class I with a population of 100,000 and above.
Class II with a population of 50,000-99,999.
Class III with a population of 20,000-49,999.
Class IV with a population of 10,000-19,999.
Class V with a population of 5,000-9,999.
Class VI with a population of not less than 5000.
Besides, in the Census of India, 991 all places with a municipality, corporation, cantonment board of notified town area commitee were included.

over the space of a century may not appear to make an impressive picture for a vast country as India is. Besides, the decennial increase in the total number of urban places has been far from steady, presenting cases of declines in two decades – 1901-1911 and 1951-1961 the last one happening in 1951-1961 when the total number fell by 525. Looking at the actual number of towns in their respective size-classes, it becomes quite evident that these belonging to the higher classes have maintained a more steady progress in their number than those in the lower size-classes. Barring at one instance, in each case of Class I, II and IV urban places, their number has never decreased between 1901 and 1991 (data in this respect not available for 2001), but the Table does not convey the actual picture as counts for two states—Assam and Jammu & Kashmir—are not included. However, in every decade the total number of towns/cities in these three size-classes has gone increasing while the record of increase for Class III towns has remained uninterrupted. In contrast, the number of the Class VI, the smallest in size, having fallen sharply in the last four decades, 1961 and 1991. De-classification, which means losing urban status altogether, or merger with the larger towns has been a common incidence in the case of many of these lower order towns.

From a general point of view, the larger centres have proved to be more viable than the smaller ones. Some interesting facts emerge from a comparative analysis of the number of towns/cities belonging to the higher order (I-IV) and those in the lower order (V-VI). Such as, (*a*) till 1951, the lower class towns were much larger in number that those of the higher class, the former comprising nearly two-and-a-half times of their number in 1901 (Table 5.6). (*b*) This sharp difference with declining intensity through the decades reversed in 1951 and since then the number of higher order towns/cities came to be larger than the lower order ones, the latter recording a steady fall with ever-widening gap between the two. (*c*) Viewed from another angle, the viability as well as the popularity (in the sense of usefulness to the incoming population or the migrants) or attraction of the larger towns/cities having gone through a severe test of time seems to have attained and unassailable position in the later decades, making the larger towns/cities as the primary choice of the migrants, whether urban or rural, the city-ward migration being one of the major factors for the subsequent growth of the larger centres. This is somewhat reflected

Table 5.6: Comparative Status of different Size-Classes 1901-1991

Year	*Number of Towns/Cities in Class I-IV*	*Number of Towns in Class V-VI*
1901	588	1223
1911	562	1192
1921	589	1305
1931	708	1309
1941	863	1327
1951	1102	1693
1961	1387	883
1971	1706	770
1981	2277	968
1991	2699	910

Source : Census of India, Series 1, Paper 2 of 1991.

in the increase in the number of higher order centres. For instances, for the first three decades, 1891-1901, 1901-1911 and 1911-1921, the total number of such centres remained more or less the same. The first spurt came in 1931, and for the next two decades, 1921-1931 and 1931-1941, the number recorded an appreciable increase. If the first phase is called the phase of stagnation, the second phase may be called the phase of rejuvenation, because of the fact that the existing towns and cities got a new lease of life, many of them scaling over from a lower to higher position through the added vigour in their activities, offering a greater attraction to migrants. The third and the current phase started in 1951 and from then onwards the number of larger urban centres started increasing at a faster rate, strengthening the view that they have become the dominating and the most characteristic feature of the Indian urban scene today. The reality of the situation may be properly gauged, as discussed later, from a consideration of the actual number (population) involved in even a slight increase in the largest cities.

While all these trends definitely indicate the instability of the small towns, the stability of the larger centres as well as the growth of individual centres are equally substantiated. As mentioned earlier, many of the small towns degraded from their position in the face of competition with the larger urban centres and thus lost their urban status altogether at most point of time. The Registrar General of the Indian Census 1961, records that, in all, 803 urban centres, including

1 from Class III, 42 from Class IV, 407 from Class V and 353 from Class VI, have been eliminated from the list of towns[24] for 1961 as they held no longer that position. On the other hand, 461 settlements were declared as towns in the same year of which 107 were placed in Class IV, 243 in Class V, and 111 in Class VI, thus reducing the total number of towns by 341 belonging to these three Classes between 1961 and 1971. One of the reasons cited by the Registrar General of Census 1971, for the decrease in total number of towns by 360 in 1961 is the "application of uniform and rigid definition of urban area adopted for the first time in 1961 census"[25] before which the recognition of towns used to be made on a more flexible manner. On this basis the case of 360 towns losing urban status "particularly visible in Class V and Class VI towns"[26] may be accounted for, but this is not a satisfactory explanation for the exclusion of a still larger number of towns, amounting to a total of 803 from the list of towns in 1961. The loss of urban status by such a large number of towns, ranging from Class III to Class VI, positively indicates the cases of actual decline where the respective centres might have suffered a considerable reduction in population so as to be declassified. Similar cases of decline resulting in the loss of urban status or derecognition are available for 1971, when altogether 122 towns, comprising 3 from Class III, 32 from Class IV, 69 from Class V and 21 from Class VI ceased to be recognised as towns[27]. This has happened in the case of many other towns, gradually becoming mostly confined to the lower two classes of towns—Class V and Class VI—through the later decades, having a serious impact on urban development and the economy of the country.

It may, rather, be different for one not associated with the conditions of life in India, to realise that, settlements, once declared as urban places, may loss the distinction next time when a fresh census is made. It has to be borne in mind that the distinctive feature of an urban settlement at the lower levels are not far removed from that of a rural settlement. For instance the towns having a population of less than 5,000 to 19,999, belonging to Class IV to Class V, merely maintain an urban way of life in either of their physical or their social behaviour. The typical corporate life, making a strong basis for urban functions as manifest in the small towns of the Western World, is greatly missing in the small Indian towns which, most of the cases evolve from an originally rural base. The village, under favourable circumstances may gradually give rise to certain non-agricultural functions which slowly may turn the place into an urban centre, offering services to the surrounding areas. The process of such development does not take the form of transformation from rural to urban in the true sense of the term as the change that taken place—from rural to urban—is mostly confined to its functional or economic character without having any measurable social (and cultural) impact on the society as a whole. What really happens in such situation is — a greater section of the working population becomes engaged in non-agricultural activities, a string of shops appear along the principal thoroughfare, movement of the vehicular traffic becomes more conspicuous, ill-built, mean structures of all shapes/sizes and descriptions spring up in the most unassorted assembly, jostling, with each for frontal space, and public and private houses further add to the melee, intensifying the crowded atmosphere of the roadside areas. The land use along the two fronts of the one or two main, quite often crooked road—even not properly paved or maintained at any instances—is of an extremely mixed character, creating confusion, and utter disorder. Beyond this thin belt of congestion, the high pitch of activity at once melts down to a languid placidity of virtual rural life, demonstrated by widely-spaced houses, occasionally intervened by agricultural patches or small water bodies. Usually the towns of this non-descript type are invariably small in size with a very limited service facility, and the shocking state of infrastructural development in them make them least attractive for supporting any major activities. They make a superficial existence, failing to take any deep root in the area of their origin.

The emergence of such urban centres is a very common feature in India where the economic conditions have been far from stable over a long period or decades, if not for the last few centuries, worsening further from the inception of colonial rule in the country in mid-eighteenth century. However, the construction of irrigation works during the colonial rule contributing in some measure to the revitalisation of agriculture in many areas gradually providing a larger surplus for transport, the newly laid roads and the railway lines coupled with the improvement of the existing roads and thus increasing the accessibility of particular settlements along the principal routes, infused changes into the functional character of many of them, adding to the vitality of much centres. Taking such opportunities some of them, by way of multiplying their activities, emerged as towns, though without undergoing any characteristic change of a lasting nature whether in their physical or cultural contexts. They represent nothing more than larger villages, containing a conglomeration of poor structures thickly huddled together in the heart of the centre while the remaining area of the same centre went on keeping the unvariegated landscape of a rural settlement.

One needs to be cautioned at this stage from taking a notion that settlements of this nature are boom towns: they are far from that. There is no trigger action to make an hitherto obsolete settlement burst into vigorous activity. All that happens is a new lease of life obtained from the newly created advantages through years of painstaking efforts. On the contrary, any slight change in the situation may tip the balance unfavourably, and dislodge the settlement from its achieved position. This, in fact, has been the case with many of the small towns where a mere diversion in the flow of traffic made them badly hit, eroding the very base of their economic sustenance. There cannot be any doubt about the fact that most of these towns of lower order rarely have any basic foundation for keeping the urban status undisturbed, that is, once gained it could be of a permanent nature, absorbing even major socio-economic shocks. Apart from taking mainly the role of transactors of goods collected from the nearby areas and forwarding them to their ultimate destinations lying at some distance of the production zone, these towns have scarcely taken up the producer's or the manufacturer's rôle. They are usually not the selector's choice for turning out finished products. Apart from the lack of infrastructure, the absence of market for such products in the face of very poor buying capacity in and around these small towns has been the primary obstacle to attract capital enterprise and efficient work-force. Besides a few schools and may be a college, a few medicine stores, a moderate shopping area, and suck like, these towns have nothing much to offer in the form of a special service to the people living in and around them. At the same time the prospect of earning opportunities offered by them is too limited to keep the working people fully engaged whenever the flow or trade dries up. This has quite often led to the migration of the working population and thereby shrinking the size of the settlement (in terms of total population in it) under such extraneous circumstances. Not that all the towns of this category have suffered in this way. Many of them, on the other hand, have been able to stabilise their position through functional efficiency. The most notable among them happen to be the administrative centres which, by way of offering facilities, could attract new functions to be added to their usual chores. Further, according to the policy adopted by the Census of India 1961, the recognition of a place as a town or withdrawal of the name recognition henceforward depended largely on the fulfilment of conditions laid down by it.

The loss of urban status by a large number of towns in the lower size classes strongly signifies an insecure position where settlements, once declared as towns, are denied that status in the subsequent census. It presents the most overriding problem regarding urban development in the country where, as observed above as a specific instance, as many as 803 towns reverted to their rural position within the space of a decade. The trait of impermanence appears as the fundamental weakness of the Indian urban scene at its lower level. Till 1961, impermanence has been a characteristic feature of the small towns. To cite figures, it may be of interest to note that a total of 279 towns, classified as Class IV (numbering 10), Class V (128), and Class VI (241) in 1911 were removed from the list of towns in 1961, while only 38 centres enjoying Class IV (5), Class V (27) and Class VI (6) status in 1911, had no place in the list of towns for 1971.[28]

The comparative figures for 1981 and 1991 indicate an improvement in the situation, with lesser number of towns losing urban status in the lower category, like Class V and VI, and the larger towns showing a greater degree of stability as evidenced by them moving higher up in the scale in many cases. For Class V the total number has changed from 739 in 1981 to 725 in 1991 and for Class VI, it has been from 229 in 1981 to 185 in 1991. De-classification and the movement from lower to higher order are attributed to be the major reasons for this change. In contrast, the number of towns in size Class IV increased from 1053 in 1981 to 1135 in 1991 (Table 5.5) and for size Class III, it was from 738 in 1981 to 927 in 1991. In both cases this is partly due do the "upward movement of urban agglomerations/towns from lower size class and partly due to formation of new urban agglomerations"[29] The same reasons apply to the next higher class (Class II), the total number having increased from 270 (1981) to 341 (1991), and the Class I towns (called cities by Census of India) registered an increase from 216 (1981) to 296 (1991).

What is more striking about the picture conveyed by Table 5.5 is that during the last two decades (1971-1981 and 1981-1991), there is a particular pattern in the descrease and increase in the number of towns/cities of different size-classes. Such as, the decrease in the number of towns belonging to the lower classes (V and VI) is much smaller—14 and 44 respectively—than increase in number of the higher classes : it has been 80 for Class I; 71 for Class II; 189 for Class III and 82 for Class IV. Second, the population under each category, from 1901 to 1991, further makes the point very clear in regard to the stability of the towns/cities of different size-classes. From 1961 onwards, the role of the lower tow classes of town—Class V and Class VI—has weakened remarkably effected by a sharp drop in their share of urban population in the country (Table 5.7). For Class V, its share in the proportion of the total urban population of India records a steady decline from 1911 onwards, while it is a faltering decline for Class VI till 1951, after which, from 1961 onwards the decline becomes quite abrupt as well as very steep, the latter holding barely one-fourth per cent of the total urban population of the country when it is 0.60 per cent for Class V towns in 1991.

In the backdrop of this the position of the higher class towns—Class I to Class IV—is different though here as well the record of growth is not steady for three of the four higher class urban centres : It has been of a faltering nature all through—from 1911 to 1991. Here, too, the performance has been different among the higher class towns/cities. For instance, the share of the Class IV towns has dwindled heavily, decreasing from 20.83 per cent in 1901 the highest for it—to a mere 7.77 per cent in 1991. The reasons for this decline, however, are different. The upward movement, caused by increase in population has pushed many of them into the next higher class—generally into Class III—as is reflected in the highest number of increase (189) in the decade for Class III towns in 1991. But at the same time the fact cannot be ignored that in spite of a significant increase in the number of Class IV towns between 1981 and 1991, their share in the total urban population of the country has fallen to the lowest (7.77%) for the entire period (1901-1991), indicating that as urban centres they are losing on the whole their attraction for migrants. On the other hand, two other higher class towns—Class II and Class III—have more or less retained their position almost unchanged over this time

Table : 5.7: Urban Population by Size-Class, 1901-1991 (in % of Total Urban Population)

Year	*Class I*	*Class II*	*Class III*	*Class IV*	*Class V*	*Class VI*
1901	26.00	11.29	15.64	20.83	20.14	6.10
1911	27.48	10.51	16.40	19.73	19.31	6.57
1921	29.70	10.39	15.92	18.29	18.67	7.03
1931	31.20	11.65	16.80	18.00	17.14	5.21
1941	38.23	11.42	16.35	15.78	15.08	3.14
1951	44.63	9.96	15.72	13.63	12.97	3.09
1961	51.42	11.23	16.94	12.77	6.87	0.77
1971	57.24	10.92	16.01	10.94	4.45	0.44
1981	60.42	11.63	14.33	9.54	3.58	0.50
1991	65.20	10.95	13.19	7.77	0.60	0.29
2001	59.82	–	–	–	–	–

Source : Census : Census of India 1991 and Census of India 2001.

in their share of the total urban population the proportion, though slightly faltering, has not altered much in spite of notable changes in the actual volume of population increasing in every succeeding decade except in 1901-1911 for Class II towns. Between them, the proportion for Class III towns has always been higher in accordance with their number being larger than Class II towns. But what is really puzzling is their respective shares which may be a definite indication that as towns, they are more sought after although that does not mean that their attraction as urban places has improved much through this period of economic revival. In comparison, the role of Class I towns (Cities) appears to be remarkable in view of their (*a*) unfaltering increase in number (from 24 in 1901 to 417 in 2001)—nearly 18 times, the highest for any class between 1901 and 2001; (*b*) a steady increase in the share of total urban population in the country which has always been higher than for any other class of town in each of the preceding ten decades. In 1991, these towns together held 65.20 per cent of the total urban population of India and 59.82 per cent in 2001, which has been more half of the total since 1961 (51.42%), establishing beyond doubt the growing popularity of them giving this unchallenged position amount the urban centre of the country.

On the whole, as it appears, urbanisation in India coming in grip with prevailing situation in the country, came to be stable for the first time in 1921, registering an overall increase in the total number of towns (Table 5.5), where continued undisturbed through the succeeding decades even though many of the small towns have dropped out of the list in each decade. The cessation of the First World War (1914-19) might have helped in settling down to a more peaceful life, and subsequent improvement of the economy from which the larger centres profited more than the smaller ones, the former performing a larger range basic functions based on better infrastructure for a steady growth. The trend that set in has continued uninterrupted till now, gathering further momentum with time inviting greater attention power, politic and money contributing to their progress.

The Role of Larger Urban Centres : Underscoring the Current Trend

The most characteristic element of urban trend in India today is the overwhelmingly domination role of the larger cities, specifically the largest ones, their sustained growths further encouraged by the current politico-economic forces. This preferred-child treatment of them by those in authority, sometimes dwarfing the interest of many other highly deserving centres, may not be as large in size, has a twisting effect on urban development in the country which is amply manifest in the overburdening of the giant cities subject to limitless sprawl as a consequence with their attenuated life-comforting services. In other words, the largest urban centres receive greater attention of the planner and deriving greater benefit in infrastructural development, they have a greater attraction for the investors.

In order to perceive the role of the large urban centres in the context of Indian urban situation a distinction needs to be made between the Million-Plus cities and cities having population less than a million, all of which are placed under Class I towns by the Census of India. Till 1991, the total number of Class I towns has increased from 24 in 1901 to 300 (including Assam and Jammu & Kashmir) and later on to 417 in 2001, the rate of increases per decade—as mentioned earlier—having been the highest for any class. The Census of India 1991 makes a further classification of them on the basis of their population size. Such as

M1	Less than 200,000
M2	200,000-299,999
M3	300,000-499,999
M4	500,000-999,999
M5	1,000,000 and above
(i)	1,000,000-1,999,999
(ii)	2,000,000-4,999,999
(iii)	5,000,000 and above

Applying the same formula for 2001, a comparative picture may be obtained about the pattern of distribution of these higher order Urban centres—known as cities—in India for the last two decades (Table 5.8). It provides an interesting insight into the prevalent characteristics of Indian urbanisation. First, increase in the total number of cities—from 300 to 417—over the space of a decade in quite impressive, with an addition of 177 cities, most of them if not all, having gone up the scale from their original Class II or even lower position due to increase in population as a result more of migration than natural increase.

Together, the 417 Class I urban centres, or cities of different grades as defined by the Census of India, contain 59.82 per cent of the total urban population (TUP) of the country, slightly less than the proportion held in 1991 (65.20%) when the Million-Plus cities alone on their part, numbering 27, in all in 2001, have 42.78 per cent of the TUP (Total Urban Population). In 1991, it was however 32.07 per cent. Viewed from another angle, the role of cities in sharing the total urban population (TUP) under them differ widely with their size, the largest ones, though smaller in number, holding the highest proportion, 42.78 per cent in 27 M5 or Million-Plus cities (Table 5.8) and 58.22 per cent are distributed among the remaining 390 Class I cities. Again, 41 M4 cities have the third largest proportion (17.77%) which is a little less than contained by the M1 cities (18.31%) the latter representing the largest number (228) in the size-classes of Class I cities.

Table 5.8: Cities by Different Size-Classes in India, 1991-2001

Cities by Population Size	*Number of Cities*		*Population*		*Population as % of total Population TCP*	
	1991	2001	1991	2001	1991	2001
Class I (Cities)	300	417	139,730,050	170,707,575	100	100
M1 (Less than 200,000)	167	228	22,939,086	31,265,034	16.31	18.31
M2 (200,000-299,999)	40	75	9,606,814	18,213,052	6.88	10.67
M3 (300,000-499,999)	40	46	15,586,157	17,871,961	11.15	10.47
M4 (500,000-999,999)	30	41	20,936,734	30,336,282	14.98	17.77
M5 (1,000,000 & above)	23	27	70,661,259	73,021,246	50.57	42.78

417 Class I cities in 2001 represent 59.82 per cent of the Total Urban Population in India.

Source : (*a*) Census of India 1991 Series 1 Paper 2 of 1991.
(*b*) Census of India 2001 (complied from original data for all classes of towns and cities).

The pattern in the distribution of urban population among the Class I cities of different size categories compared with that in the previous decade appears to have stayed almost unaltered. Then as well the M5 cities, the smallest in number (23) of the total number of Class I cities (300), maintained the largest proportion, 50.57 per cent of the total while the remaining 277 and 49.43 per cent, the second largest proportion confined to M1 cities being largest in number in Class I, followed by M4 cities numbering 41, with the third largest concentration (Table 5.8).

The Role of Larger Versus Smaller Centres in Determining Urban Trend

The overall dominance of the Class I urban centres as the major area of concentration of urban population in India is beyond dispute. The moot question is whether the pattern they indicate is going to be the determining trend of urban development in near as well as distant future in this country. Before seeking an answer to these apparently two basic questions having serious implications on the development policy in the year to come, one feels tempted to have an analytical approach to the situation as revealed by facts available.

The data provided by the Census of India gives a clear idea in this respect. A careful analysis of the decadal variation, or the rate of growth and decline of urban centres for the period of the last four decades (1971-2001) brings out the prevailing pattern of urban development in the country in perspective of the respective roles adopted by individual classes of urban centres, ranging in size from the largest to the medium ones. An shown in Table 5.9, for each of the classes of urban centres—M5 to Class IV—ten centres have been selected for the purpose, taking mostly the largest of each category considering the fact that the largest ones usually have greater growth-potential than the others. These centres, representing different states and thus having a wider spatial coverage in various contrasting situations, exhibit their growth-pattern over a period of four succeeding decades which is further summarised in Table 5.10.

As presented by Table 5.10, in the case of Class I urban centres, ranging from M1 to M5, (*a*) there are instances of negative growth or decline on altogether six occasions, (that is decades) over the period of four decades (1971-2001) in 6 out of a total of 50 cities considered. (*b*) Besides that, each of the cities irrespective of their class position, have maintained growth rates widely variable, ranging from a mere 0.22 per cent (1991-2001), being the lowest in New Delhi, to the highest of 395.58 per cent (1971-81) in Durgapur (West Bengal). (*c*) On the whole, growth rate of 20-30 per cent and 30-39 per cent emerge as the move common feature in the largest number of decades — 39 in each case with the growth rate of 40-49 per cent and 10-19 per cent respectively in the second and third places (Table 5.10). In other words, in majority of the decades, the rate of growth for Class I cities has ranged between 20 and 39 per cent though high rates of 100 or above per cent have been registered in 8 decades with an absolute high of 395.58 per cent in one decade, as mentioned above. (*d*) The tendency towards a high rate of growth in the Class I cities becomes obvious from the fact that decades witnessing high rates of growth is much larger in number than otherwise, with 75 decades recording growth over 40 per cent in comparison to 34 decades having less than 20 per cent.

Table 5.9: Decadal Variation of Population in Selected Cities and Towns 1971-2001

Size-Class M5 (1,000,000 and above)			
Serial No.	*City*	*Year*	*Decadal Variation (in %)*
1.	Greater Mumbai (Maharashtra)	1971	+ 43.80
		1981	+ 38.01
		1991	+ 20.21
		2001	+ 20.23
2.	Delhi M.C.	1971	+ 54.57
		1981	+ 48.55
		1991	+ 42.59
		2001	+ 36.83
3.	Bangalore (Karnataka)	1971	+ 35.02
		1981	+ 60.72
		1991	+ 7.04
		2001	+ 61.93
4.	Chennai (Tamil Nadu)	1971	+ 42.81
		1981	+ 27.35
		1991	+ 15.82
		2001	+ 11.10
5.	Ahmedabad (Gujarat)	1971	+ 37.88
		1981	+ 45.05
		1991	+ 23.31
		2001	+ 22.36
6.	Hyderabad M. Corp (Andhra Pradesh)	1971	+ 43.70
		1981	+ 32.85
		1991	+ 39.42
		2001	+ 18.37
7.	Pune (Maharashtra)	1971	+ 41.09
		1981	+ 48.55
		1991	+ 47.38
		2001	+ 62.87
8.	Kanpur (Uttar Pradesh)	1971	+ 31.06
		1981	+ 28.39
		1991	+ 31.49
		2001	+ 29.30

9.	Surat (Gujarat)	1971	+ 53.85
		1981	+ 92.63
		1991	+ 62.03
		2001	+ 62.58
10.	Jaipur (Rajasthan)	1971	+ 52.50
		1981	+ 58.82
		1991	+ 48.87
		2001	+ 59.78

Size-Class M4 (500,000-999,999)

1.	Allahabad (U.P.)	1971	+ 19.10
		1981	+ 25.57
		1991	+ 30.91
		2001	+ 22.80
2.	Amritsar (Punjab)	1971	+ 8.33
		1981	+ 30.79
		1991	+ 19.27
		2001	+ 37.51
3.	Visakhapatnam (A.P.)	1971	+ 68.12
		1981	+ 60.37
		1991	+ 32.67
		2001	+ 29.20
4.	Ghaziabad (Uttar Pradesh)	1971	+ 88.06
		1981	+ 112.01
		1991	+ 69.63
		2001	+ 110.11
5.	Rajkot (Gujarat)	1971	+ 54.84
		1981	+ 48.06
		1991	+ 24.96
		2001	+ 73.81
6.	Jabalpur (MP)	1971	+ 44.30
		1981	+ 44.09
		1991	+ 20.48
		2001	+ 28.58
7.	Coimbatore (Tamil Nadu)	1971	+ 24.47
		1981	+ 24.63
		1991	+ 21.13
		2001	+ 8.16
8.	Madurai (TN)	1971	+ 29.26

		1981	+ 29.48
		1991	+ 15.93
		2001	+ 3.02
9.	Srinagar Jammu & Kashmir	1971	+ 41.42
		1981	NA
		1991	NA
		2001	NA
10.	Solapur (Maharashtra)	1971	+ 18.00
		1981	+ 28.30
		1991	+ 18.15
		2001	+ 44.57
	Size-Class M3 (300,000-499,999)		
1.	Durgapur (West Bengal)	1971	+ 395.58
		1981	+ 50.89
		1991	+ 33.42
		2001	+ 18.51
2.	Asansol (W.B.)	1971	+ 50.83
		1981	+ 17.57
		1991	+ 42.79
		2001	+ 85.73
3.	Ajmer (Rajasthan)	1971	+ 13.67
		1981	+ 42.11
		1991	+ 7.01
		2001	+ 20.71
4.	Kolhapur (Maharashtra)	1971	+ 38.20
		1981	+ 31.49
		1991	+ 18.93
		2001	+ 19.76
5.	Ulhasanagar (Maharashtra)	1971	+ 56.33
		1981	+ 62.45
		1991	+ 34.77
		2001	+ 28.23
6.	Siliguri (W.B.)	1971	+ 48.90
		1981	+ 58.36
		1991	+ 46.83
		2001	+ 107.46
7.	Saharanpur (U.P.)	1971	+ 21.70

		1981	+ 31.04
		1991	+ 26.59
		2001	+ 21.13
8.	Dehra Dun (Uttaranchal)	1971	+ 30.85
		1981	+ 27.30
		1991	+ 27.72
		2001	+ 65.84
9.	Jamnagar (Gujarat)	1971	+ 42.96
		1981	+ 39.01
		1991	+ 17.24
		2001	+ 37.56
10.	Bhatpara (W.B.)	1971	+ 38.69
		1981	+ 27.63
		1991	+ 16.70
		2001	+ 45.25
	Size-Class M2 (200,000-299,999)		
1.	Latur (Maharashtra)	1971	+ 71.48
		1981	+ 59.62
		1991	+ 76.06
		2001	+ 52.07
2.	Mathura (U.P.)	1971	+ 12.88
		1981	+ 11.71
		1991	+ 53.80
		2001	+ 32.73
3.	Shajahanpur (U.P.)	1971	+ 22.79
		1981	+ 36.72
		1991	+ 28.19
		2001	+ 25.36
4.	Chandrapur (Maharashtra)	1971	+ 45.94
		1981	+ 54.09
		1991	+ 95.07
		2001	+ 31.78
5.	New Delhi	1971	+ 15.39
		1981	– 19.53
		1991	+ 7.73
		2001	+ 0.22

6.	Noida (U.P.)	1971	NA
		1981	NA
		1991	NA
		2001	+ 75.53
7.	Kakatpalle (A.P.)	1971	NA
		1981	+ 116.53
		1991	+ 227.18
		2001	+ 56.76
2.	Kulti (W.B.)	1971	– 13.46
		1981	+ 69.41
		1991	+ 45.18
		2001	+ 166.28
9.	Kakinada (A.P.)	1971	+ 33.64
		1981	+ 37.89
		1991	+ 23.61
		2001	+ 3.59
10.	Brahmapur (Orissa)	1971	NA
		1981	+ 28.15
		1991	+ 29.55
		2001	+ 37.58
	Size-Class M1 (Less than 200,000)		
1.	Dhanbad (Jharkhand)	1971	+ 39.21
		1981	+ 50.58
		1991	+ 25.88
		2001	+ 31.47
2.	Serampore (W.B.)	1971	+ 51.92
		1981	+ 24.78
		1991	+ 7.68
		2001	+ 44.40
3.	Dindigul (T.N.)	1971	+ 38.17
		1981	+ 27.78
		1991	+ 11.08
		2001	+ 7.86
4.	Gandhinagar	1971	+ 47.34
		1981	+ 159.58
		1991	+ 94.97
		2001	+ 60.90

5.	Burhanpur (M.P.)	1971	+ 28.21
		1981	+ 33.85
		1991	+ 22.57
		2001	+ 12.47
6.	Nadiad (Gujarat)	1971	+ 37.13
		1981	+ 31.79
		1991	+ 16.93
		2001	+ 15.55
7.	Eluru (A.P.)	1971	+ 17.27
		1981	+ 32.38
		1991	+ 26.62
		2001	– 10.87
8.	Yamunanagar (Haryana)	1971	+ 40.41
		1981	+ 50.57
		1991	+ 31.97
		2001	+ 31.43
9.	Agartala (Tripura)	1971	+ 8.65
		1981	+ 31.84
		1991	+ 19.25
		2001	+ 20.10
10.	Pali (Rajasthan)	1971	+46.64
		1981	+83.75
		1991	+49.39
		2001	+36.12
	Size-Class Class II (50,000-99,999)		
1.	Ambur (T.N.)	1971	+ 36.89
		1981	+ 22.28
		1991	+ 14.67
		2001	+ 31.86
2.	Bally (W.B.)	1971	+ 30.79
		1981	+ 41.06
		1991	+ 33.55
		2001	+ 26.81
3.	Baripada (Orissa)	1971	+ 41.50
		1981	+ 40.34
		1991	+ 22.96
		2001	+ 91.55

4.	Giridih (Jharkhand)	1971	+ 9.29
		1981	+ 62.36
		1991	+ 19.05
		2001	+ 26.51
5.	Barnala (Punjab)	1971	+ 46.99
		1981	+ 37.16
		1991	+ 72.59
		2001	+ 27.87
6.	Chhatarpur (M.P.)	1971	+ 45.72
		1981	+ 61.01
		1991	+ 40.00
		2001	+ 36.81
7.	Churu (Rajasthan)	1971	+ 25.82
		1981	+ 17.73
		1991	+ 33.36
		2001	+ 18.44
8.	Khurja (U.P.)	1971	+ 21.10
		1981	+ 33.58
		1991	+ 19.76
		2001	+ 22.42
9.	Mahasena (Gujarat)	1971	+ 58.39
		1981	+ 41.23
		1991	+ 20.61
		2001	+ 12.63
10.	Roorkee (U.P.)	1971	+ 41.34
		1981	+ 30.05
		1991	+ 29.72
		2001	+ 20.97
	Size-Class Class III (20,000-49,999)		
1.	Ayodhya (U.P.)	1971	NA
		1981	NA
		1991	+ 33.72
		2001	+ 21.59
2.	Bankura (W.B.)	1971	NA
		1981	+ 75.26
		1991	+ 69.45
		2001	+ 51.18
3.	Barh (Bihar)	1971	+ 25.47
		1981	+ 35.04
		1991	+ 42.47
		2001	+6.61

4.	Challakere (Kerala)	1971	+ 62.50
		1981	+ 43.07
		1991	+ 53.44
		2001	+ 27.68
5.	Dhuri (Punjab)	1971	+ 17.97
		1981	+ 40.41
		1991	+ 38.04
		2001	+ 31.76
6.	Macherla (A.P.)	1971	+ 42.02
		1981	+ 46.18
		1991	+ 43.31
		2001	+ 11.56
7.	Nasirabad (Rajasthan)	1971	+ 6.56
		1981	+ 34.53
		1991	+ 20.86
		2001	+ 17.38
8.	Ottapalam (Kerala)	1971	+ 130.23
		1981	– 6.72
		1991	+ 90.81
		2001	+ 11.42
9.	Pammal (T.N.)	1971	NA
		1981	+ 207.56
		1991	+ 30.59
		2001	+ 36.91
10.	Sahade (Maharashtra)	1971	NA
		1981	+ 35.94
		1991	+ 27.77
		2001	+ 55.86
	Size-Class Class IV (10,000-19,000)		
1.	Alibag (Maharashtra)	1971	+ 20.22
		1981	+ 17.95
		1991	+ 15.94
		2001	+ 19.64
2.	Chamoli Gopeswar (Uttaranchal)	1971	NA
		1981	+ 52.80
		1991	+ 58.01
		2001	+ 29.42
3.	Dharampur (Gujarat)	1971	+ 22.27
		1981	+ 18.05
		1991	+ 17.48
		2001	+ 20.19

4.	Doom Dooma (Assam)	1971	+ 28.30
		1981	NA
		1991	+ 43.08
		2001	+ 31.81
5.	Kanyakumari (T.N.)	1971	NA
		1981	+ 22.14
		1991	+ 3.89
		2001	+ 14.90
6.	Maheshwar (M.P.)	1971	+ 20.88
		1981	+ 17.65
		1991	+ 32.64
		2001	+ 28.06
7.	Mahwa (Rajasthan)	1971	NA
		1981	NA
		1991	NA
		2001	+ 49.40
8.	Munderi (Kerala)	1971	NA
		1981	NA
		1991	NA
		2001	+ 12.23
9.	Ondal (W.B.)	1971	+ 16.98
		1981	– 31.59
		1991	+ 26.73
		2001	+ 3.15
10.	Teliamura (Tripura)	1971	NA
		1981	NA
		1991	NA
		2001	– 29.13

Sources : 1. Cencus of India 1971, Series 1, Part II-A (i).
2. Census of India 1981, Series 1, Part II-B (i).
3. Census of India 1991, Series 1, Paper 2
4. Census of India 2001, Provisional, Paper 2..

Note : Following abbreviation have been used : Maha (Maharashtra), Kar (Karnataka); Guj (Gujarat); AP (Andhra Pradesh); UP (Uttar Pradesh); Raj (Rajasthan); Pun (Punjab); MP (Madhya Pradesh); WB (West Bengal); Utta (Uttaranchal); Ori (Orissa); Tri (Tripura); Jhar (Jharkhand); Bi (Bihar); Ker (Kerala); Asm (Assam).

Table 5.10: Number of Decades with Rates of Growth for Towns and Cities in India 1971-2001

Size Class	*Rate of Growth (in %)*								
	Rate Below 10	*10-19*	*20-29*	*30-39*	*40-49*	*50-59*	*60-69*	*70-79*	*100 & above*
Class I/M5 (1,000,000 & above)	1	3	7	8	10	5	5	1	Nil
Class I/M4 (500, 000-999,999)	2	5	12	4	5	1	3	2	2
Class I/M3 (300,000-499,999)	1	7	8	9	6	4	2	1	2
Class I/M2 (200,000-299,999)	3	3	5	7	2	5	1	4	3
Class I/M1 (Less than 200,000)	3	6	7	11	5	3	1	2	1
Total of decades under each % group for Class I.	10	24	39	39	28	18	12	10	8
Class II (50,000-99,999)	1	6	11	9	8	1	2	2	Nil
Class III (20,000-49,999)	2	4	5	8	6	3	2	2	2
Class IV (10,000-19,999)	2	9	9	2	2	2	Nil	Nil	Nil
Total of decades under each % group for Class II-IV towns	5	20	25	19	16	5	4	4	2

Source : Based on Table 5.9.

Class I/M5 : Taken class-wise, the picture becomes more convincing in this respect. For instance, going downward in scale, these is no instance of negative growth or decline among the 10 M5 or Million-Plus cities for this entire period which seems to be the strongest point for these giant cities, maintaining quite a high profile of growth where, in 21 out of 40 decades, the rate of growth is above 40 per cent. However, the rate of growth varies widely over this period, ranging from 7.4 per cent (1981-1991) in Bangalore (Karnataka) to 92.63 per cent (1971-1981) in Surat (Gujarat). Between 1991 and 2001, three cities, namely Pune (62.87%), Surat (62.58%) Bangalore (61.93%) recorded a growth of over 60 per cent each, while consistently high rate of growth has been maintained by a number of cities, like Surat, Jaipur, Pune, Delhi M.C. etc.

Class I/M4 : There has been one instance of negative growth, the population of Madurai (Tamil Nadu) having declined by 3.02 per cent in the last decade (1991-2001) besides which the record of growth appears unblemished for the 10 of the largest cities of this group. In majority of the cases, 21 out of a total 37 decades for which record is available, a growth rate of 20 to 39 per cent per decade was maintained, and though there are two instances of growth-rate exceeding 100 per cent in a decade, the overall performance of the cities belonging to this class looks less encouraging as compared with Class M/5 cities since 13 decades in this class against 21 in Class M/5 witnessed a rate of growth above 40 per cent. However the rate of growth similarly varies widely, from 8.33 per cent (1961-1971) in Amritsar (Punjab) to 112.01 per cent (1971-1981) in Ghaziabad (Uttar Pradesh), while in the last decade (1991-2001), it has varied between 8.16 per cent (Coimbatore, Tamil Nadu) to 110.11 per cent (Ghaziabad).

Class I/M3 : There is no record of decline in any decade for the 10 cities under this class, a large number of decades experiencing a growth rate of 20-30 per cent and in 15 out of a total of 40 decades, the growth rate exceeded 40 per cent decade including two cases having over 100 per cent growth. In fact, in one of them, Durgapur (West Bengal) 395.58 per cent (1961-1971), the highest for all the Class I cities was achieved which is indeed phenomenal in terms of increase in population in a single decade in a hitherto obscure place. It was the result of setting up of the giant steel plant along with other ancillary industries in due course. But the tempo could not be sustained later on and the city has a record of steadily declining growth in the subsequent decades. There is also another case needing an explanation for the abrupt jump in its rate of growth as presented by Siliguri with 107.46 per cent in 1991-2001. The annexation of a large adjoining area, comprising 17 new wards in the newly formed municipal corporation added to its original 30 wards in 1993 — the added portion forming a separate town till then — is the reason for this high inflation. Besides Siliguri (and Durgapur), there are however four cases having experienced high rates of growth, exceeding 60 per cent, and in 1991-2001, it varied from 18.51 per cent to 107.46 per cent, including two places, Asansol (West Bengal) with 85.73 per cent and Dehra Dun (Uttaranchal) having 65.84 per cent increase in population in a single decade.

Class I/M2 : Records are not available for five decades for this group of selected cities but had been two cases of decline in population, one in Kulti (-3.46% in 1961-1971) in West Bengal and the other in New Delhi (-9.53 per cent in 1961-1971). Again, though on three occasions the rate of growth exceeded 100 per cent per decade, the overall performance of the cities under this class looks less impressive than the three other previous groups of cities. As evidenced in 12 out of 33 decades the rate of growth is 20-39 per cent per decade and only in 15 decades it is above 40 per cent.

At the same time it shows a wider variation, ranging from a paltry 0.22 per cent (1991-2001) in New Delhi to 227.18 per cent (1981-1991) in Kukaktpalle (Andhra Pradesh), the latter gaining urban status only in 1971 for the first time. In 1991-2001, the growth rate for all the centres varied from 0.22 per cent (New Delhi) to 166.28 per cent (Kulti, West Bengal) with centres like Noida in Uttar Pradesh (with 75.03%), Kukatpalle (56.76%) and Latur in Maharashtra (with 52.07%) experiencing a growth rate of over 50 per cent.

Class I/M1 : Eluru (Andhra Pradesh) presents the only case of decline in 1991-2001 (-10.87%) for the ten selected cities of this category besides which each decade has a record of growth for all the cities during the period 1971-2001, maintaining a farely wide range, varying from the lowest of 7.86 per cent (1991-2001) in Dindigul (Tamil Nadu) to the highest of 159.58 per cent (1971-1981) in Gandhinagar (Gujarat), the latter obtaining urban status only in 1961.

In majority of the cases, 18 out of 39 decades of recorded growth, the rate has been 20-39 per cent, and it exceeds 40 per cent per decade for 12 occasions, including one with more than 100 per cent. Further, there are some cities, like Gandhinagar (Gujarat), Yamunanagar (Haryana), Pali (Rajasthan) and Dhanbad (Jharkhand) which maintain a consistently high record of growth, and barring one case of decline (Eluru), the record of growth for 1991-2001, ranging from 7.86 per cent to 60.90 per cent seems to be quite convincing in terms of their role in urban development.

Class II Towns : Set against this domination of Class I cities of different sizes, the Class II towns make competitive existence, with a crucial role to play as transit places between them and the cities of higher order for people moving away from the towns of lower order or elsewhere.

Interestingly enough, no negative growth or decline is observed for any of the selected ten of the largest towns of this category, and growth-rate ranging between 9.29 per cent (1961-1971) in Giridih in Jharkhand, as the lowest, to the highest of 91.55 per cent (1991-2001) at Baripada in Orissa, appears to be less varied than in the cities of different size-classes. Exactly, in half of the total number of decades the growth-rate is 20-39 per cent, and it is above 40 per cent in 12 decades. The range of growth for respective centres during the last four decades is not very high either, and in the last decade, between 1991 and 2001, besides in Baripada, it is lower than about 37 per cent in all other centres.

Class III Towns : In spite of the absence of any data for five decades for the ten of the largest towns of this category selected of this purpose, when, presumably they did not enjoy urban status, the record of growth for these towns looks impressive. Apart from one case of decline, as presented by Ottapalam in Kerala with –6.72 per cent (1971-1981), the growth rate ranging between 5.36 per cent (1961-1971) in Nasirabad (Rajasthan) and 207.56 per cent (1971-1981) in Pammal (Tamil Nadu) includes encouraging instances of higher rates when at 9 instances, it exceeded 50 per cent per decade. In fact apparently Class III towns show better performances, with growth-rate exceeding 40 per cent at 15 instances, including two cases recording over 100 per cent increase. The growth-rate of the last decade, ranging between 6.61 per cent and 55.86 per cent is encouraging in view of the size of these towns.

Class IV Towns : This is not however the situation with the Class IV towns. leaving aside 12 decades without data, there are two cases of decline, Ondal in West Bengal with –31.59 per cent (1971-1981) and Teliamura in Tripura with –29.13 per cent (1991-2001). The rate of growth remaining confined to the range of 20-39 per cent per decade in 18 out of a total of 26 decades, and which does not exceed 59 per cent at any instance, makes a rather dismal picture.

All these observations naturally lead to one of the obvious conclusions that contrary to general belief, there is no basic difference between the urban centres of higher or lower orders—from Class I/M5 to Class IV—so far as the rate of growth (decadal, including the annual), or even decline is concerned. It is not that higher order centres are growing at a faster rate than the lower order centres, or *vice versa*. No general rule applies here, or no pattern is visible. First, growth seem to be the most common feature with very few cases of decline, the latter as well being a far from common feature, or is particularly identifiable with any class-size. Second, the rate of growth is irrespective of the size of urban centres, that is it is not size-specific, and very low or very high rate of growth, again is not a distinctive characteristic of any particular set (size) of urban centres. Among the top most Million-Plus cities, perhaps, Kolkata, not listed here, is the lone case showing signs of slackening growth within its municipal limits though (but is not the case of Metropolitan Kolkata maintaining unabated growth). Third, the growth pattern does not follow any standard rule in regard to its preference for particular decade or decades. That is to say that no decade or decades may be identified as more productive in enhancing the rate of growth or decelerating the same, or has always been different for different sets of urban centres.

What is however of great significance is that the Million-Plus cities have sustained a high rate of growth through the decades and thus having a great impact on urban development in the country, exercising much greater influence (weight as well) on the whole process than cities or towns of lesser size. It needs to be remembered in this connection that a 20 per cent increase in a Million-Plus city is much more effective in increasing the urban component than a similar increase in a city or town of lesser size. For instance, in a case like that, a Million-Plus city with a population of, say, 2 million experiencing 20 per cent growth is a decade adds 400,000 heads while a city with 200,000 population will make an addition of 40,000 heads at this rate of growth, decreasing further with the lower order urban centres, falling to as low as 2,000 heads in the case of a town with a population of 10,000 which means a difference of 100 to 5 times respectively between the Million-Plus and a Class IV town.

Hence, in the prevailing situation the urban growth in the country is largely determined by the growth of larger than the smaller urban centres, the impact of the former, because of sheer volume, having overwhelmingly the most dominant role in shaping urban trend. Even if the total number of Class I cities is only 417 as against 4,744 in 2001, a mere 10 per cent increase in the former will make an addition of 17,070,754 heads (taking the actual total urban population for the 417 cities in 2001) against 11,464,737 heads added by the remaining 4,744 towns of all classes in 2001 (based on similar calculation).

Perhaps, no further evidence is necessary in justifying the present situation where the larger urban centres will continue to be the major contributor to urban growth in the country as long as the rate of growth in them does not decline drastically, a highly unlikely situation yet for a long time to come where the engine of economic growth, a factor governing urban development in any country, is rather slow in its operation.

The larger urban centres having the major concentration of the urban component of the total population is not a unique urban feature of India alone. Corroborative evidence may be traced in many other developing countries of the world where it happens to be the characteristic feature of urban development, having a higher growth rate which, in Asia, was 3.5 per cent per annum in 1990-95 and is only expected to dip below 2 per cent after 2015-2020[30]. Eventually, more and more urban population continue to concentrate in the larger cities of the developing countries and the "number of mega cities that are defined by the United Nations as cities with 10 million or more inhabitants is increasing rapidly, particularly in the less developed regions ... In mid-1995, 10 out of 14 cities with a population of 10 million or more were located in the less developed regtions. Asia had 7 mega-cities... By 2015, Asia will be home to 18 mega-cities"[31] (including Mumbai, Kolkata, Delhi and Hyderabad)[32]. In the world as a whole, "urban dwellers living in the largest cities of 10 million or more increased from 1.7 to 7.1 per cent between 1950 and 1995, and it is expected to reach 10.6 per cent by 2015"[33]. In India, it is already 25.29 per cent of the total urban population of the country in 2001, making a very strong reminder about their overpowering role and extreme lopsidedness in urban distribution.

India Versus the Rest of the World

The level of urbanisation in the world is changing fast but the commensurate progress in India has so far been slow and even compared with the achievements of many of the developing countries of the world, India is lagging far behind in this respect. Nevertheless India's problem in managing the staggering volume of her urban population poses a grave concern for the country, portending a far worse situation without right planning. It goes without saying that economic development in a country acts as a booster for urbanisation, and both going on in tandem can bring about sweeping changes in the country's life in general. What is happening elsewhere in the world, at least in some of the developing countries having faced a similar situation as India faces today, may act as a kind of model in reshaping the urban future in India.

The actual gravity of the situation cannot be properly visualised unless one can assume the expected volume of urban population in India in the future years to come. In this connection it becomes imperative to find out India's position on the basis of a comparative assessment of it with that of the other countries of the world in regard to both, the total population and the total urban population of each country. Table 5.11 shows this where the actual position in both is presented for 25 topmost (referring to the total population) countries of the world. What is highly interesting and significant here is not the level of urbanisation as expressed by the urban component of the total population of each country, but the actual size or volume of the urban population, the absolute number held by each which is directly involved with the economy, development, and planning in any country at any point of time since both the absolute numbers are not static. They change with time, bringing fresh problems to be faced by the society involving changes in economic, development and planning policies. For instance, at present China leads the world with the largest volume of urban population, amounting to over 382 million heads followed by India with over 285 million, and the U.S.A. with more than 205 million in the third place, each keeping its corresponding place in total population in tact. But after that, the corresponding position in these two regards — TP and TUP — goes away. Such as,

Table 5.11: Total Population and Total Urban Population of 25 Selected Countries of the World

S. No.	Country	Year	Total Population (TP)	Total Urban Population (TUP)	TUP as % of PP
1.	Egypt	1997	62,011,000	27,264,000	44.0
2.	South Africa	1997	8,802,304	3,618,255	41.1
3.	Cuba	1996	11,018,567	8,226,065	74.7
4.	Canada	1996	28,846,760	22,461,210	77.9
5.	Brazil*	1996	161,087,000	127,285,000	79.0
6.	Peru	1998	24,800,768	17,838,479	71.9
7.	India**	2001	1,027,015,247	285,354,954	27.8
8.	Indonesia	1998	202,906,850	78,594,650	38.7
9.	Japan	1995	125,570,246	98,009,107	78.1
10.	Malayasia	1995	21,665,500	11,317,218	52.2
11.	Pakistan	1998	130,579,571	42,458,339	32.5
12.	Turkey	1998	63,451,000	41,566,223	65.5
13.	China (excl. Hong Kong annexed* on 1 July 1997)	1996	1,232,084,000	382,447,000	31.0
14.	Bangladesh*	1996	120,073,000	22,640,000	19.0
15.	Sri Lanka*	1996	139,973,000	48,742,000	35.0
16.	Republic of Korea*	1996	45,314,000	37,363,000	83.0
17.	Philippines*	1996	69,282,000	38,115,000	55.0
18.	Nigeria*	1996	115,020,000	46,525,000	40.0
19.	Mexico*	1996	92,717,000	68,243,000	74.0
20.	Russian Federation*	1996	148,126,000	113,001,000	76.0
21.	France	1993	57,654,379	42,553,509	73.8
22.	United Kingdom*	1996	58,144,000	51,903,000	89.0
23.	Italy*	1996	57,226,000	38,145,000	67.0
24.	Germany*	1996	81,922,000	71,039,000	87.0
25.	United States of America*	1996	269,444,000	205,719,000	76.0

Source :

a) *Demographic Yearbook 1998,* United Nations, 15th Issue, New York, 2000.

b) World Urbanization Prospects: The 1996 Revision, United Nations, New York, 1998.

c) Census of India 2001.

Brazil enjoying the fourth global position in urban population stands fifth in total population; while Indonesia having that position, ranks seventh in world-order in terms of its total population. Similarly, Germany, coming twelfth in total population occupies eighth rank in urban population.

The primary objective of these observations is to emphasise the point of the pressure created by the increasing volume of urban population in different countries and the rate at which they increase. Presumably, the higher rate of urban growth still extant in developing countries increasing urban population at a greater pace will make the situation more critical in the coming decades without relenting pressure as long as there is no dip in the rate. In contrast, whatever position is enjoyed today by the developed countries like Germany, the U.S.A. the U.K., Japan and such like, it is likely to change the least because of the low rate of urban growth.

The annual rate of change in urban population is remarkable in all the developed countries, giving rise even to sharp declines, indicating the phenomenon of deconcentration when people getting tired of fast urban life migrate from the city to the placidity of rural surroundings. This appears to be the case in Japan as well. On the other hand, in 12 (Egypt, South Africa, India, Indonesia, Malayasia, Pakistan, Turkey, China, Bangladesh, Sri Lanka, Nigeria and Philippines) out of the 25 countries with the largest population in the world the annual rate remains higher than the world's average of 2.21 per cent even as late as in 2000-2005. Even in 2025-30, besides Turkey and China, more of these countries are likely to improve their position enough to fall below world's average. This slow change, or reduction in the rate of growth of urban population in these countries instead of slowing down the pace of urbanisation will have a serious impact on the countries involved in shouldering an ever-increasing volume of urban population.

A look at Table 5.12 makes the idea more convincing. The list includes the five most populous countries in the world with projected total urban population of the world and the individual share of each country in it for the period, 2005-2030. It appears that except in the U.S.A., the urban population maintains a steady growth through the decades in India, China, Indonesia and Brazil while in the U.S.A., the growth slackens in 2010, and never recovers again, making a steady

Table 5.12 : Urban Population of the Five Most Populous Countries of the World and It is shown as Percentage of the World's Total (TUP)

Country	*Year 2005*	*Year 2010*	*Year 2015*	*Year 2020*	*Year 2025*	*Year 2030*
World	3,227,055,000	3,586,415,000	3,962,150,000	4,346,879,000	4,736,200,000	5,117,038,000
As % of World's TUP	—	—	—	—	—	—
India	330,119,000	380,208,000	435,112,000	498,777,000	565,799,000	634,054,000
As % of World's TUP	10.23	10.61	10.98	11.47	11.95	12.39
China	507,725,000	577,683,000	647,121,000	711,698,000	773,155,000	828,037,000
As % of World's TUP	15.73	14.16	16.33	16.37	16.32	16.18
U.S.A.	225,651,000	238,092,000	251,751,000	265,021,000	277,245,000	284,863,000
As % of World's TUP	6.99	6.64	6.35	6.10	5.85	5.57
Indonesia	101,521,000	116,941,000	132,027,000	146,176,000	160,345,000	174,608,000
As % of World's TUP	3.15	3.26	3.33	3.36	3.38	3.41
Brazil	149,895,000	161,760,000	172,621,000	182,139,000	190,907,000	198,926,000
As % of World's TUP	4.64	4.51	4.36	4.35	4.03	3.89

Note : TUP = Total Urban Population.

Source : World Urbanisation Prospects : The 1996 Revision, Table A.3.

decline afterwards. The rate of growth is much higher in India and China than in any other country so that these two countries carry the largest load of the world's urban population which increases consistently in India. While, together these two countries hold more than one-fourth of the world's total urban population (TUP), the brute fact that India will have to feed, clothe, house and care for over 330 million urban residents in around 2005, and over 634 million in about 2030 — just less than thirty years from now — seems to be the most unnerving prospect for any planner.

REFERENCES

1. Miscellaneous Statistics Relating to British India Calcutta, Office of the Superintendent of Government Printing, 1876, No. 7, p. 7.
2. Census of 1881, Indian Empire, Statistics of Population Vol. II, Form XVI, Calcutta, 1883, by Plowden, W.C., Census Commissioner for India: Census of India, 1891, General Tables for British Provinces and Feudatory States, Vol. I, London, 1892; Census of India, 1901, Vol. IA, Part II (Tables), Table IV, Calcutta, 1903, by Risely, H.H. and Gait, E.A.
3. Miscellaneous Statistics Relating to British India etc. *op. cit.*
4. Report of the Census of Madras Presidency, 1871, Vol. I & II, p. 96.
5. Census of 1881, Plowden W.C., p. 276.
6. *Ibid.*
7. Plowden, *op. cit.*, p. 272.
8. *Ibid.*, p. 276.
9. *Ibid.*, p. 99.
10. Report of the Census of Madras Presidency, 1871, p. 99.
11. *Ibid.*
12. *Ibid.*
13. Plowden, *op. cit.*, p. 274.
14. *Ibid.*, pp. 274-275.
15. Census of India, 1891, p. 2.
16. *Ibid.*, p. 45.
17. *Ibid.*, p. 46.
18. *Ibid.*, p. 45.
19. *Ibid.*, p. 46.
20. *Ibid.*
21. Smith, V.A. and Spear, P., *Oxford History of India*, p. 628.
22. Census of India 2001, Provisional, Paper 2 (Rural-Urban Distribution).
23. *Ibid.*
24. Census of India 1961, *General Population Tables*, Part II-A (ii).
25. Census of India 1971, *General Population Tables*, Series 1, Part II-A (i).
26. *Ibid.*

27. *Ibid.*, Statement 7, pp. 190-191.
28. *Ibid.*, Statement 11, p. 195.
29. Census of India 1991, Paper 2 of 1991, *Provisional Population Totals : Rural-Urban Distributions.*
30. United Nations, *Urbanization Prospects : The 1996 Revision*, New York, 1998, pp. 12-13.
31. *Ibid.*, p. 23.
32. *Ibid.*, p. 24.

BIBLIOGRAPHY

Agarwala, V.S., 1963, *India as Known to Panini*, Second Edition, Varanasi.

Agrawal, D.P. and Ghosh, A., 1973, (Ed.) *Radio Carbon and Indian Archaeology,* Tata Institute of Fundamental Research, Bombay.

Auboyar, Jeannine, 1965, *Daily Life in Ancient India – From Approximately 200 B.C. to A.D. 700*, Asia Publishing House, Great Britain.

Ball, V., 1889, *Travels in India by Jean Baptiste Tavernier*, Macmillan and Co., London.

Basham, A.L., 1953, *The Wonder that was India,* Orient Longmans.

Beal, Samuel, 1969, *Si-Yu-Ki : Buddhist Records of the Western World*, Oriental Books Reprint Corporation.

Bearce, George D., 1961, *British Attitude Towards India 1784-1858*, Oxford University Press, London.

Bernier, Francois, 1972, *Travels in the Mogul Empire*, S. Chand and Co., New Delhi, Third Edition.

Beveridge, A.S., 1970, *Babur-Nama (Memoris of Babur),* Translated from Original Turki Text, Oriental Books Reprint Corporation, Delhi.

Beveridge, H., 1972, *The Akbar-Nama of Abu-I-Fazl*, Asiatic Society of Bengal.

Bhan, Suraj, 1973, *The Sequence and Spread of Prehistoric Cultures in the Upper Saraswati Basin, in Radio Carbon and Indian Archaeology*, Ed. Agrawal and Ghosh.

Bhargava, Monohar Lal, 1964, *The Geography of Rigvedic India – A Physical Geography of Sapta Saindhava*, The Upper India Publishing House Ltd., Lucknow.

Blockman, H., 1927, *The Ain-i-Akbari*, Asiatic Society of Bengal, Calcutta.

Bridget and Allchin, Reymond, 1968, *The Birth of Indian Civilization: India and Pakistan before 500 B.C.*, Penguin Books.

Briggs, John, 1965, *History of the Rise of the Mahomedan Power in India,* Translated from the original Persian of Mahomed Kasim Ferishta, Editions India, Calcutta.

Busteed, H.E., 1972 *Echoes from Old Calcutta*, Irish University Press, Shannor, Ireland.

Cambridge History of India, Cambridge University Press, Vol. I.

Census of Madras Presidency 1871, Vols. I and II.

Census of 1881, Indian Empire, Statistics of Population, Vol. II, From XVI, Calcutta, Plowden W.C.

Census of India 1891, General Tables for British Provinces and Feudatory States, Vol.I, 1892, London.

Census of India 1901, Vol. IA, Part II.

Census of India 2001, Paper 2 (Rural-Urban Distribution).

Chandra Sekhar, *Census of India 1971*, General Population Tables, Part II-A.

Childe, Gordon, 1965, *What Happend in History*, Penguin Books.

Christaller, Walter, 1966, *Central Places in Southern Germany*, Translated by C.W. Baskin, Englewood Cliffs, Prentice Hall.

Clarke, Grahame, 1969, *World Pre-History : A New Outline*, Cambridge University Press.

Danver, Frederick Charles, 1966, *The Portuguese in India*, Frank Cass and Co. Lt., London, Second Edition, Vols. 1 and 2.

Dates, G.F., 1973, *Pre- and Protohistoric Researches in Pakistan and Afghanistan, in Radio Carbon and Indian Archaeology*, Ed. Agrawal and Ghosh.

Datta, Kalikinkar, 1961, *Survey of India's Social Life and Economic Condition in the Eighteenth Century (1701-1813)*, Firma K.L. Mukhopadhyay, Calcutta.

Dodwell, H.H., 1963, *The Cambridge History of India*, Vol. V, British India, Second Indian Reprint, S. Chand and Co., Delhi.

Dutt, Romesh, 1963, *The Economic Life History of India under Early British Rule 1757-1837*, Publications Division, Ministry of Information and Broadcasting, Government of India, Second Edition.

Elliot, H.M., and Dowson, J., *The History of India as Told by Its Own Historians*, Kitab Mahal, Allahabad (First Indian Edition) Vols. III, IV and V.

Fick, Richard, 1972, *The Social Organisation in North-East India in Buddha's Time,* Translated by S.K. Maitra, Indological Book House, Delhi.

Gardner, Brian, 1971, The East India Company, Rupert Hart-Davis, London.

General Tables for British Provinces and Feudatory States, 1892, Vol. I, London.

Ghosal, H.R., 1966, *Economic Transition in the Bengal Presidency (1793-1833),* Firma K.L. Mukhopadhyaya, Calcutta, Second Edition.

Gibb, H.A.R., 1969, *Ibn Battuta, Travels in Asia and Africa,* Routledge and Keagan Paul, London.

Gordon, D.H., 1960, *The Pre-Historic Background of Indian Culture,* Bhulabhai Memorial Institute, Bombay.

Hambly, Gavin, 1968, *Cities in Mughul India*, UBS Publishers' Distributors, Delhi.

Hamilton, Alexander, 1927, *A New Account of the East Indies,* Vol. II.

Hamilton, Walter, 1820, *A Geographical, Statistical and Historical Description of Hindostan and the Adjacent Countries*, Orient Publishers, Delhi, First Indian Edition, Vols. 1 and 2.

Havell, E.B., *The History of Aryan Rule in India*, K.M.N. Publishers, New Delhi.

Hawkes, Jacquetta and Woolley, Leonard, 1963, *History of Mankind, Cultural and Scientific Development*, Vol. 1, George Allen and Unwin, London.

Hunter, W.W., 1972, *A History of British India*, Vols. 1 and 2, Indian Reprints Publishing Co., Delhi, First Indian Edition.

Imperial Gazetteer, 1908, Clarendon Press, Oxford, Vols. V, IX and XI.

Jain, Ramchandra, 1972, (Ed.) *McCrindle's Ancient India as Described by Megasthenes and Arrian*, Today and Tomorrow's Printers and Publishers, New Delhi.

Jain, Ramchandra, Ed. *McCrindle's Ancient India as Described by Ptolemy*, Today and Tomorrow's Printers and Publishers, New Delhi.

Jarrett, H.S. and Sarkar, Jadunath, Ed., 1949, *Ain-i-Akbari of Abul Fazl-I-Allami,* Vol. II, Royal Asiatic Society, Calcutta, Second Edition.

Jayaswal, K.P., 1967, *Hindu Polity : A Constitutional History of India in Hindu Times*, The Bangalore Printing Publishing Co., Bangalore, Fourth Edition.

Kangle, R.P., 1972, *The Kautiliya Arthasastra*, University of Bombay, Third Edition.

Kosambi, D.D., 1965, *The Culture and Civilisation of Ancient India in Historical Outline,* Routledge and Kegan Paul, London.

Lane-Poole, Stanley, 1963, *Medieval India under Mohammedan Rule,* A Universal Publication, Delhi.

Mackay, Ernest, 1971, *Early Indus Civilisation* (Revised and Enlarged by Dorothy Mackay), Indological Book Corporation, Delhi.

Majumdar, R.C., 1960, *The Classical Accounts of india*, Firma K.L. Mukhopadhyay, Calcutta.

Majumdar, R.C., Ray Chaudhuri, H.C., Dutta, K., 1970, *An Advanced History of India*, Macmillan, St. Martin's Press, London, Third Edition.

Munucci, Niccolao, 1965, *Storia do Mogor or Mogul India*, Translated by William Irvine, Editions Indian, Calcutta.

Marshall, P.J., 1968, *Problems of Empire, Britain and India, 1757-1813*, George Allen and Unwin Ltd., London.

Martin, James Ronald, 1737, *Notes on the Medical Geography of Calcutta.*

Masson-Oursel, Paul, William-Grasbowska, Helena and Stern Philippe, 1967, *Ancient India and Indian Civilization*, Routledge and Kegan Paul Ltd., London.

McCrindle, J.W., *The Invasion of India by Alexander the Great etc.*, Today and Tomorrow's Printers and Publishers, New Delhi, New Edition.

McCrindle, J.W., 1971, *Ancient India as Described in Classical Literature,* Philo Press, Amsterdam.

McCrindle, J.W., 1973, *The Commerce and Navigation of the Erythraean Sea and Ancient I dia*, Philo Press, Amsterdam.

Mishra, D.P., 1971, *Studies in he Proto-History of India*, Orient Longmans.

Miscellaneous Statistics Relating to British India, Calcutta, 1876 Office of the Superintendent of Government Printing, No. 7.

Misra, Sudama, 1973, *Janapada State in India*, Bharatiya Vidya Prakasana, Varanasi.

Mitra, A., *Census of India 1961*, General Population Tables, Part II Vol. I.

Mitra, Asok, 1970, *Delhi Capital City,* Thomson Press (India) Ltd., New Delhi.

Mookerjee, Radhakumud, 1962, *A History of Indian Shipping*, Kitab Mahal, Second Edition.

Mookerjee, Radhakumud, 1961, *Glimpses of Ancient India*, Bharatiya Vidya Bhavan, Bombay.

Morelenad, W.H., Geyl, P., 1925, *Jahangir's India, The 'Remonstrantie' of Francisco Pelsaert,* Cambridge, W. Heffer and Sons Ltd.

Nanda, A.R., *Census of India 1991,* Paper 2 of 1991.

Napier, William, 1971, *Lands of Spices and Treasure, Encyclopeadia of Discovery and Exploration,* Aldus Books Ltd., London, Vol. 5.

Nazim, Muhammad, 1971, *The Life and Times of Sultan Mahamud of Ghazni*, Munshiram Manoharlal, New Delhi, Second Edition.

Orme, Robert, 1971, *Of the Government and People of Hindostan*, Pustak Kendra, Lucknow, Reprint.

Piggott, Stuart, 1961, *Prehistoric India to 1000 B.C.,* Penguin Press.

Powell-Price, J.C., 1958, *A History of India*, Thomas Nelson and Sons Ltd., Edinburgh.

Puri, B.N., 1968, *India in the Time of Patanjali,* Bharatiya Vidya Bhavan, Bombay.

Puri, B.N., 1966, Cities of Ancient India, Meenakshi Prakasan, Meerut.

Raj, Jaimal, 1974, *The Rural-Urban Economy and Social Changes in Ancient India*, Bharatiya Vidya Prakasan, Varanasi.

Rao, S.R., 1972, *Lothal and the Indus Civilization*, Asia Publishing House, London.

Rapsom, E.J., 1962, *Cambridge History of India*, S. Chand and Co., Delhi, Second Indian Reprint.

Ray Chaudhuri, Hem Chandra, 1972, *Political History of Ancient India*, University of Calcutta, Seventh Edition.

Rennell, James, 1792. *Mamoir of a Map of Hindustan of the Mogul Empire*, London, Second Edition.

Rhys Davids, T.W., 1971, *Buddhist India*, Motilal Banarasidass, Delhi.

Risely, H.H. and Gait, E.A., 1903., *Census of India*, Calcutta.

Roberts, P.E., 1958, *History of British India*, Oxford University Press, Third Edition.

Rogers, Alexander and Beveridge, Henry, 1968, *The Tuzuk-i-Jahangiri or Memoirs of Jahangir*, Munshiram Manoharlal, Delhi.

Sachau, Edward, C., 1964, *Alberuni's India*, S. Chand and Co., New Delhi.

Sankalia, H.D., 1962, *Prehistory and Protohistory in India and Pakistan*, University of Bombay.

Sastri, K.A. Nilkanta, 1967, *Cultural Contacts between Aryans and Dravidians*, Manaktalas, Bombay.

Sen, Surendranath, 1949, *Indian Travels of Thevenot and Carreri*, National Archives of India, New Delhi.

Sen, S.P., 1971, *The French in India (1763-1816)*, Munshiram Manoharlal, New Delhi.

Shamasastry, R., 1960, *Kautilya's Arthasastra*, Mysore Printing and Publishing House, Sixth Edition.

Sinha, K.K., 1973, *Stratigraphy and Chronology of Early Kausambi, in Radio Carbon and Indian Archaeology*, Ed. Agrawal and Ghosh.

Sinha, N.C., 1946, *Studies in Indo-British Economy Hundred Years Ago*, A. Mukherjee and Co., Calcutta.

Sinha, N.K., 1961, *The Economic History of Bengal*, Firma K.L. Mukhopadhyaya, Vols. 1 and 2, Second Edition.

Sircar, D.C., 1971, *Studies in the Geography of Ancient and Medieval India*, Motilal Banarasidass, Delhi, Second Edition.

Smith, Vincent A., 1962, *The Early History India from 600 B.C. to the Mohammedan Conquest*, Revised by Edwards, S.M., Clarendon Press, Oxford, Fourth Edition.

Smith, Vincent A., 1962, *Akbar, The Great Mogul 1542-1605*, S. Chand and Co., Delhi.

Smith, Vincent A., 1970, The Oxford History of India, 1970, Edited by Percival Spear, Clarendon Press, Oxford, Third Edition.

Spate, O.H.K. and Learmonth, A.T.A., 1957, *India and Pakistan*, Methuen and Co. Ltd., Second Edition Reprinted in 1963.

Spear, Percival, 1963, *The Nabobs, A Study of the Social Life of the English in Eighteenth Century India*, Oxford University Press, London.

The Statesman, Calcutta Edition. August 10 and October 9, 1976.

Stewart, Charles, *The History of Bengal. 1971*, Oriental Publishers, Delhi.

Thaper, B.K., 1973, *Synthesis of the Multiple Data as Obtained from Kalibangan, in Radio Carbon and Indian Archaeology*, (Ed.) Agrawal and Ghosh.

Thomas, Walters, 1961, *On Yuan Chawng's Travels in India (A.D. 629-645),* Edited by Rhys Davids T.W. and Bushell J.W., Royal Asiatic Society, London, First Edition.

Toynbee, Arnold, 1970, *Cities on the Move*, Oxford University Press, London.

Tripathi, A., 1956, *Trade and Commerce in the Bengal Presidency. 1793-1853*, Oriental Longmans, Calcutta.

Tripathi, Vibha, 1973, *Introduction of Iron in India – A Chronological Perspective. in Radio Carbon and Indian Archaeology*, (Ed.) Agrawal and Ghosh.

United Nations, 1972, *Statistical Year Book,* New York 1973, 24th Issue.

United Nations, 1998, *World Urbanisation Prospects,* New York

Wheeler, Mortimer, 1966, *Civilizations of the Indus Valley and Beyond,* Thames and Hudson, London.

Wheeler, Mortimer, 1966, *Early India and Pakistan to Asoka*, Thames and Hudson, London, Revised Edition.

Wheeler, Mortimer, 1968, *The Indus Civilizations – Supplementary Volume to the Cambridge History of India*, Cambridge University Press, Third Edition.

Whiteway, R.S., 1967, *The Rise of Portuguese Power in India 1497-1550,* Published by Sushil Gupta, Second Edition.

Yule, Henry, 1971, *The Book Ser Marco Polo*, The Venetian, Concerning the Kigndoms and Marvels of the East, John Murray, London.

Index